CARAVAN AND MOTORHOME ATLAS BRITAIN

Scale 1:160,000
or 2.52 miles to 1 inch

1st edition June 2024 © AA Media Limited 2024

All cartography in this atlas edited, designed and produced by the Mapping Services Department of AA Media Limited (A05781).

This atlas contains Ordnance Survey data © Crown copyright and database right 2024. Contains public sector information licensed under the Open Government Licence v3.0. Mapping contains some caravan site locations available from openstreetmap.org © under the Open Database License found at opendatacommons.org

Published by AA Media Limited, whose registered office is Grove House, Lutyens Close, Basingstoke, Hampshire RG24 8AG, UK. Registered number 06112600

ISBN: 978 0 7495 8416 0

A CIP catalogue record for this book is available from The British Library.

Acknowledgements: AA Media Limited would like to thank the following for information used in the creation of this atlas:
Cadw, English Heritage, Forestry Commission, Historic Scotland, National Trust and National Trust for Scotland, RSPB, The Wildlife Trust, Scottish Natural Heritage, Natural England, The Countryside Council for Wales. Award winning beaches from 'Blue Flag' and 'Keep Scotland Beautiful' (summer 2023 data): for latest information visit www.blueflag.org and www.keepscotlandbeautiful.org. Road signs are © Crown Copyright 2024. Reproduced under the terms of the Open Government Licence. Network Rail (information, photographs and images), National Highways, Transport Scotland, Welsh Government, Isle of Man (Dept. of Infrastructure), local highway authorities (various). Traffic signs © Crown copyright 2024. Reproduced under the terms of the Open Government Licence. Boundary data from Transport for London Transport Data Service powered by TfL Open Data. Nexus (Newcastle district map).
Image credits: Nerthuz / Alamy Stock Photo (front cover); Porth Beach Holiday Park, Newquay (page XIV). Tour images sourced from www.unsplash.com (Lands End – Benjamin Elliott (pXV); Doone Valley – Ben Way (pXVI); Stonehenge – Jack B (pXVII); Blaenau Ffestiniog – v2osk (pXVIII); Bridge of Sighs – Jean-Luc Benazet (pXX); Gloucester – Shane Young (pXXII); Rievaulx Abbey – Mike Cassidy (pXXIII); Aysgarth – Nathan Langer (pXXIV); Harrop Tarn – Jonny Gios (pXXV); Glencoe – Matthew Feeney (pXXVI)
Printed by 1010 Printing International Ltd, China

* Nielsen BookScan Total Consumer Market (UK Standard scale atlases) 1–39 weeks to 2 October 2023.

Contents

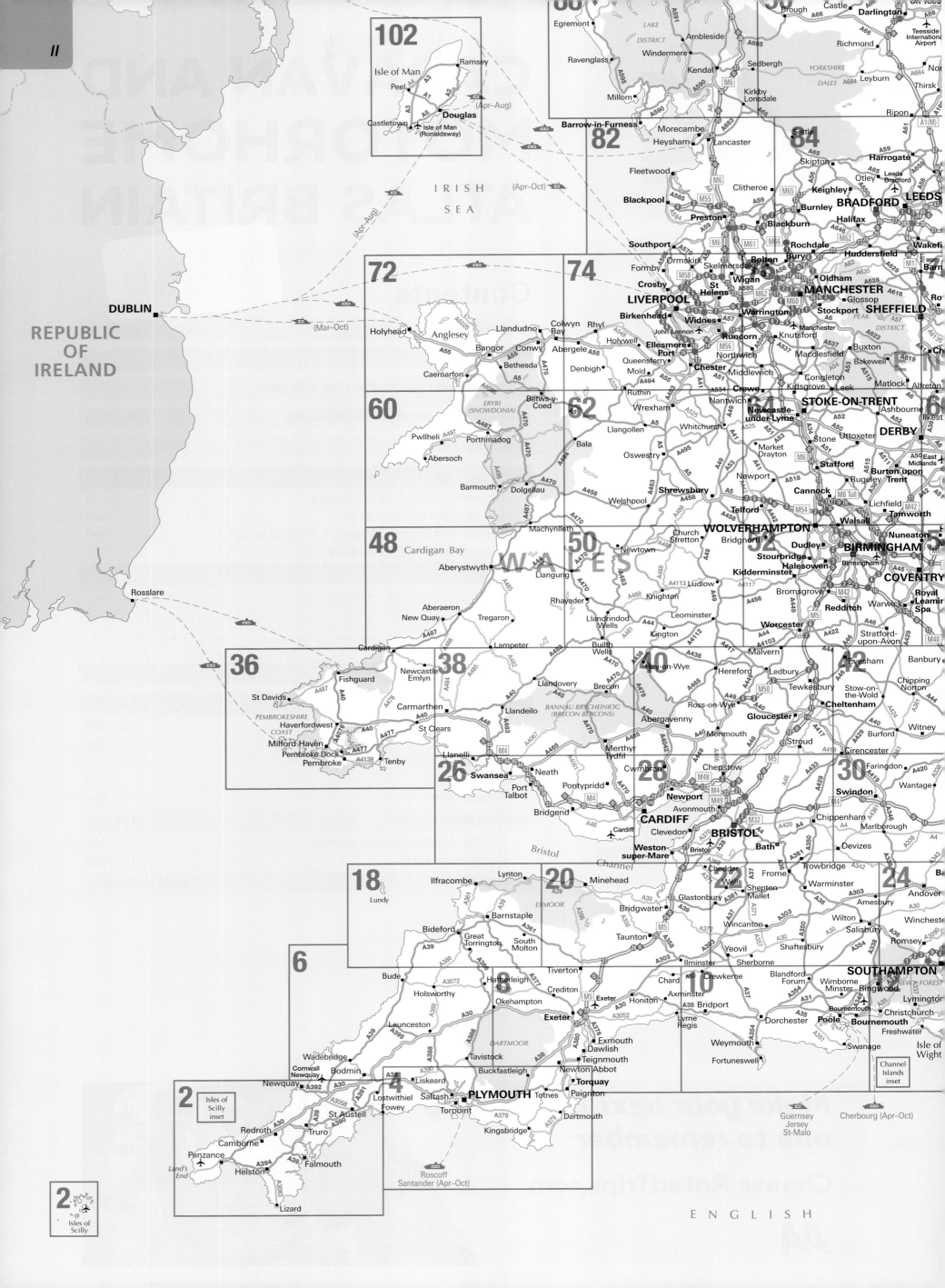

II

102

Isle of Man

Ramsey
Peel
Douglas
Castletown
Isle of Man (Ronaldsway)

(Apr–Aug)

IRISH
SEA

(Apr–Oct)

DUBLIN

REPUBLIC
OF
IRELAND

(Mar–Oct)

Rosslare

72

Holyhead
Anglesey
Bangor
Conwy
Bethesda
Caernarfon

Llandudno
Colwyn Bay
Rhyl
Abergele
Holywell
Queensferry
Denbigh
Mold

60

ERYRI
(SNOWDONIA)
Pwllheli
Porthmadog
Abersoch
Barmouth
Dolgellau

Betws-y-Coed
Bala

62

Wrexham
Llangollen
Oswestry
Whitchurch

48

Cardigan Bay
Aberystwyth
Llangurig
Aberaeron
New Quay
Tregaron
Lampeter
Cardigan

WALES

Newtown
Rhayader
Llandrindod Wells
Builth Wells
Knighton
Leominster
Kington

50

36

St Davids
Fishguard
Newcastle Emlyn
Haverfordwest
Carmarthen
St Clears
Milford Haven
Pembroke Dock
Pembroke
Tenby
Llanelli

PEMBROKESHIRE
COAST

38

Llandovery
Brecon
Llandeilo

BANNAU BRYCHEINIOG
(BRECON BEACONS)

Hay-on-Wye
Abergavenny
Monmouth

40

Hereford
Ledbury
Ross-on-Wye

26

Swansea
Neath
Port Talbot
Bridgend
Pontypridd

Merthyr Tydfil
Cwmbran

28

Newport
Avonmouth
Chepstow
Stroud

CARDIFF

Cardiff
Clevedon
Weston-super-Mare

BRISTOL
Bath

Bristol Channel

18

Ilfracombe
Lynton

EXMOOR
Barnstaple
Bideford
Great Torrington
South Molton

20

Minehead

6

Bude
Holsworthy
Launceston
Wadebridge
Bodmin
Newquay
St Austell
Lostwithiel
Fowey
Liskeard
Saltash
Torpoint

Hatherleigh
Okehampton
Crediton

DARTMOOR
Tavistock
Buckfastleigh
Newton Abbot

Tiverton
Exeter
Exmouth
Dawlish
Teignmouth

4

PLYMOUTH
Totnes
Dartmouth
Kingsbridge
Paignton
Torquay

2

Isles of Scilly inset

Redruth
Truro
Camborne
Penzance
Helston
Falmouth
Lizard
Land's End

Cornwall
Newquay

2

Isles of Scilly

Roscoff
Santander (Apr–Oct)

Channel Islands inset

Guernsey
Jersey
St-Malo

Cherbourg (Apr–Oct)

ENGLISH

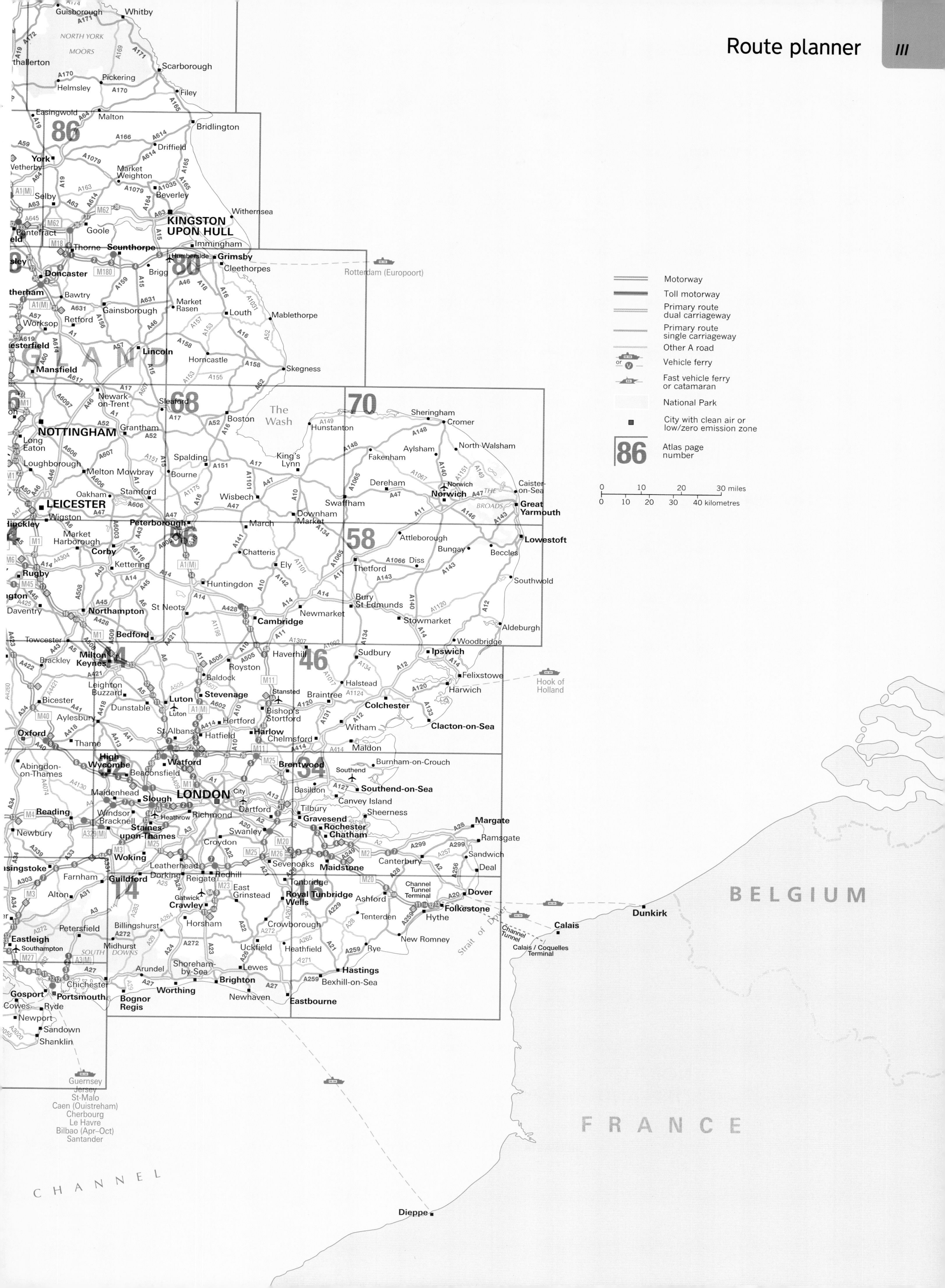

Map legend

Motorway

Toll motorway

Primary route
dual carriageway

Primary route
single carriageway

Other A road

Vehicle ferry

Fast vehicle ferry
or catamaran

National Park

City with clean air or
low/zero emission zone

86   Atlas page
number

0   10   20   30 miles
0 10 20 30 40 kilometres

Map area (labels)

NORTH YORK MOORS

Guisborough Whitby
thalterton Scarborough
Helmsley Pickering Filey
Easingwold Malton Bridlington
York Driffield
Wetherby Market Weighton Beverley
Selby KINGSTON UPON HULL Withernsea
Goole Thorne Scunthorpe Immingham
Doncaster Humberside Grimsby
Bawtry Brigg Cleethorpes
Gainsborough Market Rasen Louth Mablethorpe
Worksop Retford
Lincoln Horncastle Skegness
Mansfield
Newark-on-Trent Sleaford Boston The Wash Sheringham Cromer
NOTTINGHAM Grantham Hunstanton North Walsham
Long Eaton Spalding King's Lynn Fakenham Aylsham
Loughborough Bourne Wisbech Dereham Norwich Caister-on-Sea
Melton Mowbray Stamford Swaffham THE BROADS Great Yarmouth
Oakham March Downham Market
LEICESTER Peterborough Attleborough Lowestoft
Wigston Chatteris Ely Diss Bungay Beccles
Market Harborough Corby Kettering Thetford Southwold
Hinckley Huntingdon Bury St Edmunds Stowmarket Aldeburgh
Rugby St Neots Newmarket Woodbridge
Daventry Northampton Cambridge Ipswich
Towcester Bedford Haverhill Sudbury Felixstowe
Brackley Milton Keynes Royston Baldock Halstead Harwich Hook of Holland
Bicester Leighton Buzzard Stevenage Stansted Braintree Colchester
Aylesbury Dunstable Luton Bishop's Stortford Clacton-on-Sea
Oxford Hertford Witham Maldon
Thame St Albans Hatfield Harlow Chelmsford
Abingdon-on-Thames High Wycombe Watford Brentwood Burnham-on-Crouch
Beaconsfield Southend Southend-on-Sea
Maidenhead Slough LONDON City Basildon Canvey Island
Reading Windsor Bracknell Richmond Dartford Tilbury Sheerness Margate
Newbury Heathrow Swanley Gravesend Rochester Chatham Ramsgate
Staines-upon-Thames Croydon Sandwich Deal
Woking Leatherhead Sevenoaks Maidstone Canterbury
Basingstoke Farnham Guildford Dorking Reigate Redhill Tonbridge Channel Tunnel Terminal Dover
Alton Crawley East Grinstead Royal Tunbridge Wells Ashford Folkestone
Petersfield Billingshurst Horsham Crowborough Hythe
Eastleigh Midhurst SOUTH DOWNS Uckfield Heathfield New Romney Calais
Southampton Arundel Lewes Rye Calais / Coquelles Terminal
Gosport Chichester Shoreham-by-Sea Brighton Hastings Bexhill-on-Sea Dunkirk
Portsmouth Bognor Regis Worthing Newhaven Eastbourne
Cowes Ryde
Newport Sandown
Shanklin

Guernsey
Jersey
St-Malo
Caen (Ouistreham)
Cherbourg
Le Havre
Bilbao (Apr–Oct)
Santander

Rotterdam (Europoort)

BELGIUM

FRANCE

CHANNEL

Strait of Dover

Channel Tunnel

Dieppe

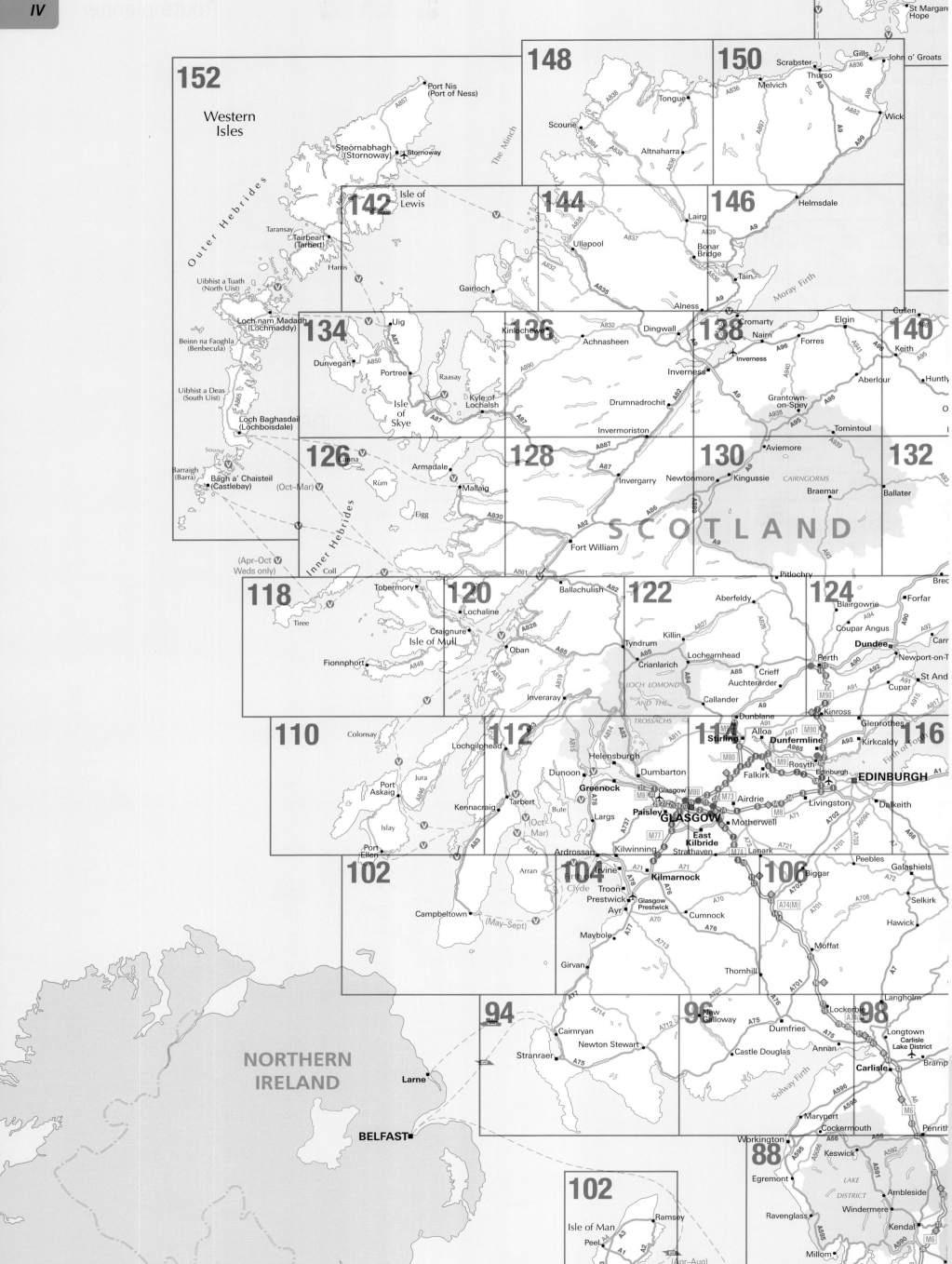

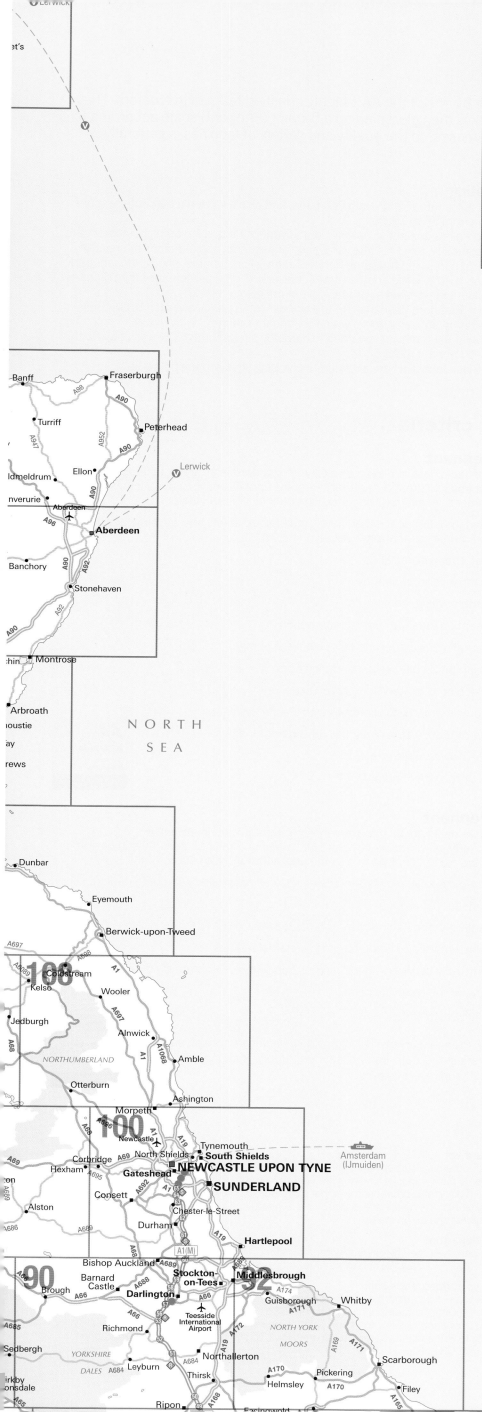

147
Orkney Islands

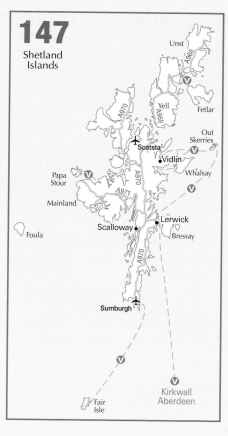

147
Shetland Islands

EMERGENCY DIVERSION ROUTES

In an emergency it may be necessary to close a section of motorway or other main road to traffic, so a temporary sign may advise drivers to follow a diversion route. To help drivers navigate the route, black symbols on yellow patches may be permanently displayed on existing direction signs, including motorway signs. Symbols may also be used on separate signs with yellow backgrounds.

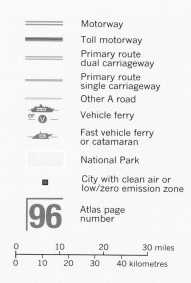

═══	Motorway
━━━	Toll motorway
═══	Primary route dual carriageway
───	Primary route single carriageway
───	Other A road
or Ⓥ	Vehicle ferry
	Fast vehicle ferry or catamaran
	National Park
■	City with clean air or low/zero emission zone
96	Atlas page number

0   10   20   30 miles
0 10 20 30 40 kilometres

The AA classification scheme
Parks that sign up to the AA Caravan & Camping scheme are visited each year by one of the AA's highly qualified team of inspectors. They thoroughly check the site's touring pitches, facilities and hospitality. Each park is then classified on a 5-point (Pennant) scale according to their style and the range of facilities they offer. As the number of Pennants increases, so the quality and variety of facilities is generally greater.

What can you expect at an AA-rated park?
All AA parks must meet a minimum standard: they should be clean, well maintained and welcoming. In addition they must have a local authority site licence (unless specially exempt), and satisfy local authority fire regulations.

The AA inspection
Each park pays an annual fee for the inspection, recognition and rating, and receive a text entry in the *AA Caravan & Camping Guide* and an entry on the website *RatedTrips.com*.

The annual inspection of each campsite is unannounced and the rating represents an entirely independent view.
When assessing a campsite, AA inspectors use common quality standards, agreed with the UK tourist authorities, and summarised below.

AA rating
Each park is rated from 1 to 5 Pennants, and also awarded a percentage score ranging from 50 to 100%.
This score is a qualitative assessment of various factors including customer care and hospitality, toilet facilities and park landscaping and indicates the relative quality of parks with the same Pennant rating. For example, one 3-Pennant park may score 70%, while another may achieve 90%. The percentage score dictates the colour of Pennants awarded – platinum, gold or black.
►►►►► Platinum Pennants are the highest-rated parks, awarded to camping sites scoring 95% and above with a 5-Pennant rating
►►► Gold Pennants are awarded to camping sites scoring 90% and above within the 1–5 Pennant ratings
►►► Black Pennants are awarded to camping sites scoring below 90%

The AA Pennant criteria

1-Pennant
These parks offer a fairly simple standard of facilities including:

- No more than 30 pitches per acre
- At least 5% of the total pitches allocated to touring caravans
- An adequate drinking water supply and reasonable drainage
- Washroom with flush toilets
- Chemical disposal arrangements and adequate refuse disposal
- Well-drained grounds and some level pitches
- Adequate entrance and access roads

2-Pennant
Parks in this category should meet all of the above requirements, but offer an increased level of facilities, services, customer care, security and ground maintenance. They should include the following:

- Separate washrooms (at required number/pitch ratio) with hot and cold water direct to each basin
- Externally lit toilet blocks
- Warden available at indicated times
- Dish-washing facilities, covered and lit
- Basic security and a reception area

3-Pennant
Many parks come within this rating and the range of facilities is wide. All parks will be of a very good standard and will meet the following minimum criteria:

- Facilities and park grounds are well maintained, and attention to customer care and security
- Clean modern toilet blocks with all-night lighting
- Modern shower cubicles with hot water (at required number/pitch ratio)
- Electric hook-ups
- Some hardstanding/wheel runs/firm, level ground
- Laundry with automatic washing and drying facilities
- Warden availability and 24-hour contact number clearly signed

4-Pennant
These parks have achieved an excellent standard in all areas, including landscaping of grounds, natural screening and attractive park buildings, and customer care and park security. Expected facilities include:

- Smart, modern and immaculately maintained toilets and washing facilities (at required number/pitch ratio)
- Baby changing facilities
- A shop on site, or near by
- Warden available 24 hours
- Reception area with tourist information
- Internal roads, paths and toilet blocks lit at night
- Maximum 25 pitches per camping acre
- Toilet blocks heated October to Easter
- Approximately 50% of pitches with electric hook-ups
- Approximately 10% of pitches have hardstandings
- Late arrivals enclosure
- Security barrier and/or CCTV

5-Pennant
Premier parks are of an extremely high standard, set in attractive surroundings with superb mature landscaping. Facilities, security and customer care are exceptional. As well as the above they will also offer:

- First-class toilet facilities including several designated self-contained cubicles
- Heated toilet block(s)
- Ideally electric hook-ups to 75% of pitches
- Approximately 20% of pitches have hardstandings
- Some fully-serviced 'super' pitches (larger size, with water and electricity)
- A motorhome service point
- Excellent security

Many Premier Parks will also provide a heated swimming pool, well-equipped shop, café/ restaurant and bar and dog walking area (if dogs are accepted)

Useful tips

Booking information
It is advisable to book in advance during peak holiday times such as school or public holidays. It is also wise to check whether or not a reservation entitles you to a particular pitch. It does not necessarily follow that an early booking will secure the best pitch; you may simply have the choice of what is available at the time you check in.

Some parks will not accept overnight bookings unless payment for the full minimum period (e.g. two or three days) is made.
Not all parks are open all year so check ahead before setting off on your travels.

Motorhomes
At some parks motorhomes are only accepted if they remain static throughout the stay. Also check that there are suitable and level pitches at the parks where you plan to stay.

Last arrival
Unless otherwise stated, parks will usually accept arrivals at any time of the day or night, but some have a special 'late arrivals' enclosure where you have to make temporary camp to avoid disturbing other people on the park. Please note that on some parks, access to the toilet block is by key or pass card only, so if you know you will be late, do check what arrangements can be made.

Last departure
Most parks will specify their latest departure time. Do check with the park if this is not given. If you overstay the departure time you could be charged for an extra day.

Join us at *RatedTrips.com*
To discover more about the sites listed on these pages, and further information on all AA-rated establishments, including hotels, B&Bs and glamping sites, visit *RatedTrips.com*. All sites and parks listed there link to local pubs, restaurants, local walks, places to visit and things to do in the area. Plus, you'll find plenty of travel inspiration for your next UK holiday.

Listing of AA-rated sites

The listing below shows caravan and camping sites in the AA-Pennant rated scheme as of September 2023. Aimed primarily for caravan and motorhome owners, it excludes those parks with tent-only pitches, sites offering glamping accommodation only and holiday home parks.

The parks are listed alphabetically by name within each country, and each entry shows the Pennant rating. This is followed by the address, telephone number, website and total number of pitches. Each site also has a map reference shown in bold, consisting of the atlas page number and grid reference to the square in which it can be found in the atlas.

The abbreviation C & C is used to denote Caravan & Camping or Camping & Caravanning.

AA-Pennant rating

Sites are rated between 1-5 Pennants, which can be black, gold or platinum depending on the quality percentage score achieved at the annual inspection (see page opposite).

Platinum Pennants ▶▶▶▶▶
Awarded to sites scoring 95% and above with a 5-Pennant rating. These entries are highlighted grey in the listings.

Gold Pennants ▶▶▶
Awarded to sites scoring 90% and above within the 1−5 Pennant ratings.

Premier Parks
Accolade awarded to sites with a 5-Pennant rating and scoring less than 95%. These entries are highlighted yellow in the listings.

Black Pennants ▶▶▶
Awarded to all sites scoring less than 90% within the 1−5 Pennant ratings

---

ENGLAND

Acton Field Camping Site ▶▶
Langton Matravers, Swanage
BH19 3HS
Tel: 01929 424184
actonfieldcampsite.co.uk
Total pitches: 80
11 N9

Alders Caravan Park ▶▶▶▶▶
Home Farm, Alne, York
YO61 1RY
Tel: 01347 838722
alderscaravanpark.co.uk
Total pitches: 87
85 Q2

Andrewshayes Holiday Park ▶▶▶▶
Dalwood, Axminster
EX13 7DY
Tel: 01404 831225
andrewshayes.co.uk
Total pitches: 150
9 N5

Ashe Farm C & C Site ▶▶▶▶
Thornfalcon, Taunton
TA3 5NW
Tel: 01823 443764
ashefarm.co.uk
Total pitches: 30
21 L9

Atlantic Bays Holiday Park ▶▶▶▶▶
Padstow, Cornwall
PL28 8PY
Tel: 01841 520855
atlanticbaysholidaypark.co.uk
Total pitches: 70
6 C10

Atlantic Coast Holiday Park ▶▶▶▶
Gwithian, Hayle
TR27 5BL
Tel: 01736 752071
atlanticcoastpark.co.uk
Total pitches: 15
2 F6

Ayr Holiday Park ▶▶▶▶▶
St Ives, Cornwall
TR26 1EJ
Tel: 01736 795855
ayrholidaypark.co.uk
Total pitches: 100
2 E6

Back of Beyond Touring Park ▶▶▶▶▶
234 Ringwood Road, St Leonards, Dorset
BH24 2SB
Tel: 01202 876968
backofbeyondtouringpark.co.uk
Total pitches: 80
11 Q4

Bagwell Farm Touring Park ▶▶▶▶
Knights in the Bottom, Chickerell, Weymouth
DT3 4EA
Tel: 01305 782575
bagwellfarm.co.uk
Total pitches: 320
10 G8

Bank House Farm ▶▶▶▶
Mill Lane, Hulme End, Hartington
SK17 0EX
Tel: 01298 687333
bankhousefarmcamping.co.uk
Total pitches: 100
77 L11

Bardsea Leisure Park ▶▶▶▶▶
Priory Road, Ulverston
LA12 9QE
Tel: 01229 584712
bardsealeisure.co.uk
Total pitches: 83
89 J11

Barlings Country Holiday Park ▶▶▶▶
Barlings Lane, Langworth
LN3 5DF
Tel: 01522 753200
barlingscountrypark.co.uk
Total pitches: 84
79 Q8

Barnstones C & C Site ▶▶▶▶
Great Bourton, Banbury
OX17 1QU
Tel: 01295 750289
barnstonescaravanpark.co.uk
Total pitches: 49
43 K3

Bath Chew Valley Caravan Park ▶▶▶▶▶
Ham Lane, Bishop Sutton
BS39 5TZ
Tel: 01275 332127
bathchewvalley.co.uk
Total pitches: 45
29 J10

Bay View Farm C & C Park ▶▶▶▶
Croyde, Devon
EX33 1PN
Tel: 01271 890501
bayviewfarm.co.uk
Total pitches: 70
18 H6

Bay View Holiday Park ▶▶▶▶▶
Bolton-le-Sands, Carnforth
LA5 9TN
Tel: 01524 732854
holgates.co.uk
Total pitches: 100
83 L1

Beacon Cottage Farm Touring Park ▶▶▶▶▶
Beacon Drive, St Agnes
TR5 0NU
Tel: 01872 552347
beaconcottagefarmholidays.co.uk
Total pitches: 60
2 H4

Beaconsfield Holiday Park ▶▶▶▶▶
Battlefield, Shrewsbury
SY4 4AA
Tel: 01939 210370
beaconsfieldholidaypark.co.uk
Total pitches: 60
63 N8

Beara Farm C & C Site ▶
Colston Road, Buckfastleigh
TQ11 0LW
Tel: 01364 642234
Total pitches: 30
5 M4

Beech Croft Farm C & C Park ▶▶▶▶
Beech Croft, Blackwell in the Peak, Buxton
SK17 9TQ
Tel: 01298 85330
beechcroftfarm.co.uk
Total pitches: 30
77 L9

Beehive Woodland Lakes ▶▶▶▶
Rosliston, Swadlincote
DE12 8HZ
Tel: 01283 763981
beehivefarm-woodlandlakes.co.uk
Total pitches: 46
65 N9

Bellingham C & C Club Site ▶▶▶▶▶
Brown Rigg, Bellingham
NE48 2JY
Tel: 01434 220175
campingandcaravanningclub.co.uk/bellingham
Total pitches: 64
99 M2

Belmont Camping ▶▶▶
Belmont Hall, Great Budworth, Northwich
CW9 6HN
Tel: 01606 891235
belmontcamping.co.uk
Total pitches: 10
76 C8

Beverley Park C & C Park ▶▶▶▶▶
Goodrington Road, Paignton
TQ4 7JE
Tel: 01803 843887
beverley-holidays.co.uk
Total pitches: 125
5 Q5

Birchwood Tourist Park ▶▶▶▶
Bere Road, Coldharbour, Wareham
BH20 7PA
Tel: 01929 554763
birchwoodtouristpark.co.uk
Total pitches: 175
11 L6

Bissoe Valley Touring Park ▶▶▶
Bissoe, Truro
TR4 8RJ
Tel: 07904 540709
bissouvalleytouringpark.co.uk
Total pitches: 16
3 J6

Blue Dolphin Holiday Park ▶▶▶▶
Gristhorpe Bay, Filey
YO14 9PU
Tel: 01723 515155
haven.com/bluedolphin
Total pitches: 210
93 M10

Blue Rose Caravan & Country Park ▶▶▶▶
Star Carr Lane, Brandesburton
YO25 8RU
Tel: 01964 543366
bluerosepark.com
Total pitches: 58
87 L6

Bolberry House Farm C & C Park ▶▶▶▶
Bolberry, Salcombe
TQ7 3DY
Tel: 01548 561251
bolberryhousefarm.com
Total pitches: 70
5 L9

Boscrege C & C Park ▶
Ashton, Helston
TR13 9TG
Tel: 01736 762231
caravanparkcornwall.com
Total pitches: 50
2 F8

Briarfields Motel & Touring Park ▶▶▶▶
Gloucester Road, Cheltenham
GL51 0SX
Tel: 01242 235324
briarfields.net
Total pitches: 72
41 P7

Bridestowe Caravan Park ▶▶▶
Bridestowe, Okehampton
EX20 4ER
Tel: 01837 861261
glebe-park.co.uk
Total pitches: 13
7 P7

Bridge House Marina & Caravan Park ▶▶▶▶▶
Nateby Crossing Lane, Nateby, Garstang
PR3 0JJ
Tel: 01995 603207
bridgehousemarina.co.uk
Total pitches: 50
83 L6

Broadhembury C & C Park ▶▶▶▶▶
Steeds Lane, Kingsnorth, Ashford
TN26 1NQ
Tel: 01233 620859
broadhembury.co.uk
Total pitches: 100
16 H3

Brook Lodge Farm C & C Park ▶▶▶▶
Cowslip Green, Redhill, Bristol, Somerset
BS40 5RB
Tel: 01934 862311
brooklodgefarm.com
Total pitches: 29
28 G10

Burns Farm Caravan, Camping & Glamping ▶▶▶▶▶
St Johns in the Vale, Keswick
CA12 4RR
Tel: 017687 79225
burns-farm.co.uk
Total pitches: 32
89 J2

Burrowhayes Farm C & C Site & Riding Stables ▶▶▶▶
West Luccombe, Porlock, Minehead
TA24 8HT
Tel: 01643 862463
burrowhayes.co.uk
Total pitches: 120
20 D4

Burton Constable Holiday Park & Arboretum ▶▶▶▶▶
Old Lodges, Sproatley, Kingston upon Hull
HU11 4LJ
Tel: 01964 562508
burtonconstableholidaypark.co.uk
Total pitches: 105
87 M8

Cairndale Caravan Park ▶▶▶
Cumwhitton, Brampton (Nr Carlisle)
CA8 9BZ
Tel: 01768 896280
Total pitches: 5
98 G8

Caistor Lakes ▶▶▶▶▶
99a Brigg Road, Caistor
LN7 6RX
Tel: 01472 859626
caistorlakes.co.uk
Total pitches: 28
80 B3

Cakes & Ale ▶▶▶▶
Abbey Lane, Theberton, Leiston
IP16 4TE
Tel: 01728 831655
cakesandale.co.uk
Total pitches: 55
59 N8

California Chalet & Touring Park ▶▶▶
Nine Mile Ride, Finchampstead, Wokingham
RG40 4HU
Tel: 0118 973 3928
californiaholidaypark.co.uk
Total pitches: 44
31 R9

Cambrose Touring Park ▶▶▶
Portreath Road, Redruth
TR16 4HT
Tel: 01209 890747
cambrosetouringpark.co.uk
Total pitches: 60
2 H5

Camping Caradon Touring Park ▶▶▶▶▶
Trelawne, Looe
PL13 2NA
Tel: 01503 272388
campingcaradon.co.uk
Total pitches: 75
4 C6

Capesthorne Hall ▶▶▶▶
Congleton Road, Siddington, Macclesfield
SK11 9JY
Tel: 01625 861221
capesthorne.com/caravan-park
Total pitches: 50
76 F9

Cardinney C & C Park ▶▶▶▶
Crows-an-Wra, Penzance
TR19 6HX
Tel: 01736 810880
cardinney-camping-park.co.uk
Total pitches: 60
2 C9

Carlyon Bay C & C Park ▶▶▶▶▶
Bethesda, Cypress Avenue, Carlyon Bay
PL25 3RE
Tel: 01726 812735
carlyonbay.net
Total pitches: 180
3 P4

Carnevas Holiday Park ▶▶▶▶
Carnevas Farm, St Merryn, Cornwall
PL28 8PN
Tel: 01841 520230
carnevasholidaypark.com
Total pitches: 195
6 B10

Cartref C & C ▶▶▶▶
Cartref, Ford Heath, Shrewsbury, Shropshire
SY5 9GD
Tel: 01743 821688
cartrefcaravansite.co.uk
Total pitches: 44
63 L10

Carvynick Holiday Park ▶▶▶▶
Summercourt, Newquay
TR8 5AF
Tel: 01872 510716
carvynick.co.uk
Total pitches: 47
3 L3

Castlerigg Hall C & C Park ▶▶▶▶▶
Castlerigg Hall, Keswick
CA12 4TE
Tel: 017687 74499
castlerigg.co.uk
Total pitches: 68
89 J2

Chacewater Park ▶▶▶▶
Coxhill, Chacewater
TR4 8LY
Tel: 01209 820762
chacewaterpark.co.uk
Total pitches: 100
3 J6

Chapel Fields Holiday Park ▶▶▶▶
Trunch Lane, Chapel St Leonards, Skegness
PE24 5UA
Tel: 01754 879600
chapel-fields.com
Total pitches: 60
81 K9

Charoland Farm Caravan Site ▶▶▶▶
Greenhalgh Lane, Greenhalgh, Preston
PR4 3HL
Tel: 07876 196434
charolandfarm.co.uk
Total pitches: 10
83 J8

Cheddar Mendip Heights C & C Club Site ▶▶▶▶
Townsend, Priddy, Wells
BA5 3BP
Tel: 01749 870241
campingandcaravanningclub.co.uk/cheddar
Total pitches: 90
22 C3

Church Farm C & C Park ▶▶▶▶
High Street, Sixpenny Handley, Salisbury
SP5 5ND
Tel: 01725 552563
churchfarmcandcpark.com
Total pitches: 35
23 M10

Church Stile Farm & Holiday Park ▶▶▶▶
Church Stile, Nether Wasdale
CA20 1ET
Tel: 01946 726252
churchstile.com
Total pitches: 50
88 F6

Clippesby Hall ▶▶▶▶▶
Hall Lane, Clippesby, Great Yarmouth
NR29 3BL
Tel: 01493 367800
clippesbyhall.com
Total pitches: 120
71 N9

Cofton Holidays ▶▶▶▶▶
Starcross,
Dawlish
EX6 8RP
Tel: 01626 890111 **8 H8**
coftonholidays.co.uk
Total pitches: 450

Concierge Camping ▶▶▶▶▶
Ratham Estate, Ratham Lane,
West Ashling, Chichester
PO18 8DL
Tel: 01243 573118 **13 P3**
conciergecamping.co.uk
Total pitches: 27

Constable Burton Hall Caravan Park ▶▶▶▶
Constable Burton
DL8 5LJ
Tel: 01677 450428 **91 K8**
cbcaravanpark.co.uk
Total pitches: 120

Coombe Touring Park ▶▶▶▶▶
Race Plain, Netherhampton,
Salisbury
SP2 8PN
Tel: 01722 328451 **23 N7**
coombecaravanpark.co.uk
Total pitches: 50

Cornish Farm Touring Park ▶▶▶▶▶
Shoreditch, Taunton
TA3 7BS
Tel: 01823 327746 **21 K9**
cornishfarm.com
Total pitches: 48

Cosawes Park ▶▶▶▶▶
Perranarworthal, Truro
TR3 7QS
Tel: 01872 863724 **3 J7**
cosawes.co.uk
Total pitches: 59

Cote Ghyll C & C Park ▶▶▶▶▶
Osmotherley,
Northallerton
DL6 3AH
Tel: 01609 883425 **91 Q7**
coteghyll.com
Total pitches: 77

Country View Holiday Park ▶▶▶▶▶
Sand Road, Sand Bay,
Weston-super-Mare
BS22 9UJ
Tel: 01934 627595 **28 D9**
cvhp.co.uk
Total pitches: 190

Court Farm Campsite ▶▶▶
St Stephen,
St Austell
PL26 7LE
Tel: 01726 823684 **3 M4**
courtfarmcornwall.co.uk
Total pitches: 30

Crealy Theme Park & Resort ▶▶▶▶▶
Sidmouth Road,
Clyst St Mary, Exeter
EX5 1DR
Tel: 01395 234888 **9 J7**
crealy.co.uk
Total pitches: 120

Crows Nest Caravan Park ▶▶▶▶
Gristhorpe,
Filey
YO14 9PS
Tel: 01723 582206 **93 M10**
crowsnestcaravanpark.com
Total pitches: 43

Dacre Lakeside Park ▶▶▶
Brandesburton, Driffield
YO25 8RT
Tel: 0800 180 4556 **87 L6**
dacrepark.co.uk
Total pitches: 8

Deepdale Camping & Rooms ▶▶▶▶
Deepdale Farm,
Burnham Deepdale
PE31 8DD
Tel: 01485 210256 **69 Q3**
deepdalecamping.co.uk
Total pitches: 80

Dibles Park ▶▶▶▶▶
Dibles Road, Warsash,
Southampton, Hampshire
SO31 9SA
Tel: 01489 575232 **12 H4**
diblespark.co.uk
Total pitches: 11

Doubletrees Farm ▶▶▶▶
Luxulyan Road, St Blazey Gate,
Par
PL24 2EH
Tel: 01726 812266 **3 P4**
doubletreesfarm.co.uk
Total pitches: 32

Easewell Farm Holiday Village ▶▶▶▶
Mortehoe Station Road, Mortehoe,
Woolacombe
EX34 7EH
Tel: 01271 872302 **19 J4**
woolacombe.co.uk
Total pitches: 328

East Creech Farm Campsite ▶▶▶
East Creech, Wareham
BH20 5AP
Tel: 01929 480519 **11 M8**
eastcreechfarm.co.uk
Total pitches: 80

East Fleet Farm Touring Park ▶▶▶▶▶
Chickerell, Weymouth
DT3 4DW
Tel: 01305 785768 **10 G9**
eastfleet.co.uk
Total pitches: 400

Eastham Hall Holiday Park ▶▶▶▶
Saltcotes Road,
Lytham St Annes, Lancashire
FY8 4LS
Tel: 01253 737907 **83 J9**
easthamhall.co.uk
Total pitches: 113

Eastview Caravan Park ▶▶▶▶
Trunch Lane, Chapel St Leonards,
Skegness
PE24 5UA
Tel: 01754 875324 **81 K9**
eastviewcaravans.co.uk
Total pitches: 53

Eden Valley Holiday Park ▶▶▶▶▶
Lanlivery,
Nr Lostwithiel
PL30 5BU
Tel: 01208 872277 **3 Q3**
edenvalleyholidaypark.co.uk
Total pitches: 56

Exe Valley Caravan Site ▶▶▶▶▶
Mill House, Bridgetown,
Dulverton
TA22 9JR
Tel: 01643 851432 **20 E6**
exevalleycamping.co.uk
Total pitches: 48

Eye Kettleby Lakes ▶▶▶▶▶
Eye Kettleby, Melton Mowbray
LE14 2TN
Tel: 01664 565900 **67 J9**
eyekettlebylakes.com
Total pitches: 130

Fen Farm Caravan Site ▶▶▶▶
East Mersea, Mersea Island,
Colchester
CO5 8FE
Tel: 01206 383275 **47 J9**
fenfarm.co.uk
Total pitches: 90

Fernwood Caravan Park ▶▶▶▶
Lyneal, Ellesmere, Shropshire
SY12 0QF
Tel: 01948 710221 **63 M5**
fernwoodpark.co.uk
Total pitches: 60

Fields End Water Caravan Park & Fishery ▶▶▶▶▶
Benwick Road, Doddington, March
PE15 0TY
Tel: 01354 740199 **56 G2**
fieldsendwater.co.uk
Total pitches: 80

Filey Brigg Touring Caravan & Country Park ▶▶▶
North Cliff, Filey
YO14 9ET
Tel: 01723 513852 **93 M10**
fileybriggcaravanpark.co.uk
Total pitches: 158

Fir Tree Caravan Park ▶▶▶▶
Jewison Lane, Sewerby,
Bridlington
YO16 6YG
Tel: 01262 676442 **87 M1**
flowerofmay.com
Total pitches: 45

Fishpool Farm Caravan Park ▶▶▶▶
Fishpool Road, Delamere,
Northwich
CW8 2HP
Tel: 01606 883970 **75 P10**
fishpoolfarmcaravanpark.co.uk
Total pitches: 50

Flaxton Meadows ▶▶▶▶▶
York Lane, Flaxton, York
YO60 7QZ
Tel: 01904 393943 **86 C3**
flaxtonmeadows.co.uk
Total pitches: 35

Flower of May Holiday Park ▶▶▶▶▶
Lebberston Cliff, Filey,
Scarborough
YO11 3NU
Tel: 01723 584311 **93 M10**
flowerofmay.com
Total pitches: 300

Forest Glade Holiday Park ▶▶▶▶
Near Kentisbeare,
Cullompton, Devon
EX15 2DT
Tel: 01404 841381 **9 L3**
forest-glade.co.uk
Total pitches: 80

Forest Park ▶▶▶▶
Northrepps Road, Cromer
NR27 0JR
Tel: 01263 513290 **71 J4**
forest-park.co.uk
Total pitches: 262

Foxholme Springs Touring Park ▶▶▶▶
Gale Lane, Nawton,
Helmsley
YO62 7SD
Tel: 01439 772336 **92 D10**
foxholmecaravanpark.co.uk
Total pitches: 60

Freshwater Beach Holiday Park ▶▶▶▶▶
Burton Bradstock,
Bridport
DT6 4PT
Tel: 01308 897317 **10 D7**
freshwaterbeach.co.uk
Total pitches: 500

Giants Head C & C Park ▶▶▶
Old Sherborne Road,
Cerne Abbas,
Dorchester
DT2 7TR
Tel: 01300 341242 **10 G4**
giantshead.co.uk
Total pitches: 50

Glebe Leisure ▶▶▶
Stratton Lane, Fringford
OX27 8RJ
Tel: 01869 277800 **43 M6**
glebeleisure.co.uk
Total pitches: 39

Glen Wyllin Campsite ▶▶▶
Kirk Michael,
Isle of Man
IM6 1AL
Tel: 01624 878231 **102 d4**
glenwyllincampsite.co.uk
Total pitches: 90

Globe Vale Holiday Park ▶▶▶▶▶
Radnor, Redruth
TR16 4BH
Tel: 01209 891183 **2 H5**
globevale.co.uk
Total pitches: 138

Glororum Caravan Park ▶▶▶▶
Glororum Farm, Bamburgh
NE69 7AW
Tel: 01670 860256 **109 K3**
northumbrianleisure.co.uk
Total pitches: 43

Golden Cap Holiday Park ▶▶▶▶
Seatown, Chideock, Bridport
DT6 6JX
Tel: 01308 422139 **10 C6**
wdlh.co.uk
Total pitches: 108

Golden Coast Holiday Park ▶▶▶▶
Station Road, Woolacombe
EX34 7HW
Tel: 01271 872302 **19 J5**
woolacombe.com
Total pitches: 89

Golden Sands Holiday Park ▶▶▶▶▶
Quebec Road, Mablethorpe
LN12 1QJ
Tel: 01507 477871 **81 J6**
haven.com/goldensands
Total pitches: 45

Golden Square C & C Park ▶▶▶▶▶
Oswaldkirk, Helmsley
YO62 5YQ
Tel: 01439 788269 **92 C10**
goldensquarecaravanpark.com
Total pitches: 129

Golden Valley C & C Park ▶▶▶▶
Coach Road, Ripley,
Derbyshire
DE55 4ES
Tel: 01773 513881 **66 C2**
goldenvalleycaravanpark.co.uk
Total pitches: 45

Goosewood Holiday Park ▶▶▶▶▶
Sutton-on-the-Forest, York
YO61 1ET
Tel: 01347 810829 **86 B3**
flowerofmay.com
Total pitches: 100

Grange Farm ▶▶▶▶
Grange Chine, Brighstone,
Isle of Wight
PO30 4DA
Tel: 01983 740296 **12 G8**
grangefarmholidays.com
Total pitches: 60

Grange Farm Campsite ▶▶▶
Station Road, Thorpe-le-Soken,
Clacton-on-Sea
CO16 0HG
Tel: 01255 862006 **47 L7**
grangefarmcampsite.co.uk
Total pitches: 50

Great Kellow Farm ▶▶▶
Polperro, Looe
PL13 2QL
Tel: 01503 272387 **4 B6**
greatkellowfarm.co.uk
Total pitches: 30

Greaves Farm Caravan Park ▶▶▶
Field Broughton,
Grange-over-Sands
LA11 6HR
Tel: 015395 36587 **89 K10**
greavesfarmcaravanpark.co.uk
Total pitches: 20

Greenacre Place Touring Caravan Park ▶▶▶▶
Bristol Road, Edithmead, Highbridge
TA9 4HA
Tel: 01278 785227 **21 M4**
greenacreplace.com
Total pitches: 10

Greenacres Camping ▶▶▶
Barrow Lane, North Wootton,
Glastonbury
BA4 4HL
Tel: 01749 890497 **22 D5**
greenacres-camping.co.uk
Total pitches: 40

Green Acres Caravan Park ▶▶▶▶▶
High Knells, Houghton, Carlisle
CA6 4JW
Tel: 01228 675418 **98 E6**
caravanpark-cumbria.com
Total pitches: 35

Greenhill Farm C & C Park ▶▶▶▶▶
Greenhill Farm, New Road,
Landford, Salisbury
SP5 2AZ
Tel: 01794 324117 **24 D9**
greenhillfarm.co.uk
Total pitches: 160

Greenhills Holiday Park ▶▶▶▶
Crowhill Lane, Bakewell,
Derbyshire
DE45 1PX
Tel: 01629 813052 **77 M10**
greenhillsholidaypark.co.uk
Total pitches: 172

Greensprings Touring Park ▶▶▶▶
Rockley Lane, Worsbrough
S75 3DS
Tel: 01226 288298 **77 Q3**
greensprings-park.edan.io
Total pitches: 65

Grouse Hill Caravan Park ▶▶▶▶
Flask Bungalow Farm,
Fylingdales,
Robin Hood's Bay
YO22 4QH
Tel: 01947 880543 **93 J7**
grousehill.co.uk
Total pitches: 175

Gunvenna Holiday Park ▶▶▶▶▶
St Minver, Wadebridge
PL27 6QN
Tel: 01208 862405 **6 D9**
gunvenna.com
Total pitches: 75

Haggerston Castle Holiday Park ▶▶▶▶▶
Beal, Berwick-upon-Tweed
TD15 2PA
Tel: 01289 381333 **108 G1**
haven.com/haggerstoncastle
Total pitches: 140

Hallsdown Farm Touring Park ▶▶▶▶
Arlington, Barnstaple
EX31 4SW
Tel: 01271 850847 **19 M5**
hallsdownfarm.co.uk
Total pitches: 30

Halse Farm C & C Park ▶▶▶▶
Winsford, Somerset
TA24 7JL
Tel: 01643 851259 **20 D6**
halsefarm.co.uk
Total pitches: 44

Harbury Fields ▶▶▶▶▶
Harbury Fields Farm, Harbury,
Nr Leamington Spa
CV33 9JN
Tel: 01926 612457 **54 B8**
harburyfields.co.uk
Total pitches: 59

Harford Bridge Holiday Park ▶▶▶▶▶
Peter Tavy, Tavistock
PL19 9LS
Tel: 01822 810349 **7 P9**
harfordbridge.co.uk
Total pitches: 125

Harrogate Caravan Park ▶▶▶▶
Great Yorkshire Showground,
Harrogate
HG2 8NZ
Tel: 01423 546145 **85 L4**
harrogatecaravanpark.co.uk
Total pitches: 67

Harrow Wood Farm Caravan Park ▶▶▶
Poplar Lane, Bransgore
BH23 8JE
Tel: 01425 672487 **12 C5**
caravan-sites.co.uk
Total pitches: 60

Hawkshead Hall Farm ▶▶▶
Hawkshead,
Ambleside
LA22 0NN
Tel: 015394 36221 **89 K7**
hawksheadhall-campsite.co.uk
Total pitches: 55

Haw Wood Farm Caravan Park ▶▶▶▶▶
Hinton, Saxmundham
IP17 3QT
Tel: 01502 359550 **59 N6**
hawwoodfarm.co.uk
Total pitches: 72

Headon Farm Caravan Site & Storage ▶▶▶
Hollacombe, Holsworthy
EX22 6NN
Tel: 01409 254477 **7 L4**
headonfarm.co.uk
Total pitches: 20

Heathfield Farm Camping ▶▶▶▶
Heathfield Road, Freshwater,
Isle of Wight
PO40 9SH
Tel: 01983 407822 **12 E7**
heathfieldcamping.co.uk
Total pitches: 81

Heathland Beach Holiday Park ▶▶▶▶
London Road, Kessingland
NR33 7PJ
Tel: 01502 740337 **59 Q3**
heathlandbeach.co.uk
Total pitches: 63

Heligan C & C Park ▶▶▶▶
Pentewan, St Austell
PL26 6BT
Tel: 01726 842714 **3 N5**
heligancampsite.com
Total pitches: 89

Hendra Holiday Park ▶▶▶▶▶
Newquay
TR8 4NY
Tel: 01637 875778 **3 K3**
hendra-holidays.com
Total pitches: 548

Herding Hill Farm Touring & Camping Site ▶▶▶▶▶
Shield Hill, Haltwhistle,
Northumberland
NE49 9NW
Tel: 01434 320175 **99 K5**
herdinghillfarm.co.uk
Total pitches: 22

Hexham Racecourse Caravan Site ▶▶▶
Hexham Racecourse, Hexham
NE46 2JP
Tel: 01434 606847 **99 P6**
hexham-racecourse.co.uk/page/
accommodation/caravan-camping-site
Total pitches: 50

Hidden Valley Park ▶▶▶▶▶
West Down, Braunton,
Ilfracombe, Devon
EX34 8NU
Tel: 01271 813837 **19 K5**
hiddenvalleypark.com
Total pitches: 114

Higher Hendra Park ►►►
Higher Hendra, Treamble,
Rose, Truro
TR4 9PS
Tel: 01872 571496
higherhendraholidays.co.uk
Total pitches: 10
3 K3

Higher Penderleath C & C Park ►►►►
Towednack, St Ives, Cornwall
TR26 3AF
Tel: 01736 798403
penderleath.co.uk
Total pitches: 75
2 D7

Higher Rew C & C Park ►►►
Higher Rew, Malborough, Salcombe
TQ7 3BW
Tel: 01548 842681
higherrew.co.uk
Total pitches: 90
5 M9

Higher Well Farm Holiday Park ►►►
Waddeton Road, Stoke Gabriel
TQ9 6RN
Tel: 01803 782289
higherwellfarmholidaypark.co.uk
Total pitches: 90
5 P5

Highfield Farm Touring Park ►►►►
Long Road, Comberton,
Cambridge
CB23 7DG
Tel: 01223 262308
highfieldfarmtouringpark.co.uk
Total pitches: 120
56 H9

Highlands End Holiday Park ►►►►►
Eype, Bridport, Dorset
DT6 6AR
Tel: 01308 422139
wdlh.co.uk
Total pitches: 195
10 C6

High Moor Farm Park ►►►►
Skipton Road, Harrogate
HG3 2LT
Tel: 01423 563637
highmoorfarmpark.co.uk
Total pitches: 320
85 K4

Hillside Caravan Park ►►►►►
Canvas Farm, Moor Road,
Knayton, Thirsk
YO7 4BR
Tel: 01845 537349
hillsidecaravanpark.co.uk
Total pitches: 60
91 Q9

Hogsdown Farm C & C Park ►►►
Lower Wick, Dursley
GL11 6DD
Tel: 01453 810224
hogsdownfarm.co.uk
Total pitches: 45
29 L3

Holiday Resort Unity ►►►►►
Coast Road, Brean Sands,
Brean
TA8 2RB
Tel: 01278 751235
hru.co.uk
Total pitches: 453
21 L3

Hollingworth Lake Caravan Park ►►►
Rakewood Road, Rakewood,
Littleborough
OL15 0AT
Tel: 01706 378661
hollingworthlakecaravanpark.com
Total pitches: 50
84 E12

Hollins Farm Holiday Park ►►►►►
Far Arnside, Carnforth
LA5 0SL
Tel: 01524 701767
holgates.co.uk
Total pitches: 12
89 M11

Home Farm Caravan and Campsite ►►►
Rectory Lane, Puncknowle,
Dorchester
DT2 9BW
Tel: 01308 897258
caravanandcampingwestdorset.co.uk
Total pitches: 47
10 E7

Homing Park ►►►►
Church Lane, Seasalter,
Whitstable
CT5 4BU
Tel: 01227 771777
homingpark.co.uk
Total pitches: 43
35 K9

Huntingdon Boathaven & Caravan Park ►►►
The Avenue, Godmanchester,
Huntingdon
PE29 2AF
Tel: 01480 411977
huntingdonboathaven.co.uk
Total pitches: 24
56 E6

Hutton-le-Hole Caravan Park ►►►►
Westfield Lodge, Hutton-le-Hole
YO62 6UG
Tel: 01751 417261
huttonleholecaravanpark.co.uk
Total pitches: 42
92 E9

Hylton Caravan Park ►►►►
Eden Street, Silloth
CA7 4AY
Tel: 016973 32666
stanwix.com
Total pitches: 90
97 M7

Island Lodge C & C Site ►►►►►
Stumpy Post Cross, Kingsbridge
TQ7 4BL
Tel: 01548 852956
islandlodgesite.co.uk
Total pitches: 30
5 M7

Isle of Avalon Touring Caravan Park ►►►►
Godney Road, Glastonbury
BA6 9AF
Tel: 01458 833618
avaloncaravanpark.co.uk
Total pitches: 120
22 C5

Jasmine Caravan Park ►►►►►
Cross Lane, Snainton,
Scarborough
YO13 9BE
Tel: 01723 859240
jasminepark.co.uk
Total pitches: 68
93 J10

Karrageen C & C Park ►►►►
Bolberry, Malborough,
Kingsbridge
TQ7 3EN
Tel: 01548 561230
karrageen.co.uk
Total pitches: 70
5 L9

Kennford International Holiday Park ►►►►►
Kennford, Exeter
EX6 7YN
Tel: 01392 833046
kennfordinternational.co.uk
Total pitches: 22
8 G7

Killerby Old Hall Cottages & Caravan Site ►►►►
Killerby Lane, Killerby, Cayton,
Scarborough
YO11 3TW
Tel: 01723 583799
killerbyoldhall.co.uk
Total pitches: 31
93 L10

Killiwerris Touring Park ►►►►►
Penstraze, Chacewater, Truro,
Cornwall
TR4 8PF
Tel: 01872 561356
killiwerris.co.uk
Total pitches: 17
3 J5

Kingfisher Caravan Park ►►►►
Low Moor Lane, Farnham,
Knaresborough
HG5 9JB
Tel: 01423 869411
kingfisher-caravanpark.co.uk
Total pitches: 35
85 M3

King's Lynn C & C Park ►►►►►
New Road, North Runcton,
King's Lynn
PE33 0RA
Tel: 01553 840004
kl-cc.co.uk
Total pitches: 150
69 M9

Kingsmead Centre Camping ►►►►
Clayhidon, Devon
EX15 3TR
Tel: 01823 421630
kingsmeadcentre.com
Total pitches: 41
21 J10

Kirkstead Holiday Park ►►►►
North Road, Trusthorpe,
Mablethorpe
LN12 2QD
Tel: 01507 441483
kirkstead.co.uk
Total pitches: 60
81 K7

Kite Hill Farm C & C Park ►►►
Firestone Copse Road,
Wootton Bridge, Isle of Wight
PO33 4LE
Tel: 01983 883261
kitehillfarm.co.uk
Total pitches: 50
13 J6

Knight Stainforth Hall Caravan & Campsite ►►►►►
Stainforth, Settle
BD24 0DP
Tel: 01729 822200
knightstainforth.co.uk
Total pitches: 100
84 B2

Ladycross Plantation Caravan Park ►►►►
Egton, Whitby
YO21 1UA
Tel: 01947 895502
ladycrossplantation.co.uk
Total pitches: 130
92 G5

Lady Heyes Holiday Park ►►►►►
Kingsley Road, Frodsham
WA6 6SU
Tel: 01928 788557
ladyheyespark.com
Total pitches: 65
75 P8

Lady's Mile Holiday Park ►►►►►
Dawlish, Devon
EX7 0LX
Tel: 01626 863411
ladysmile.co.uk
Total pitches: 570
8 H9

Lakefield Caravan Park ►►►
Camelford, Devon
PL32 9TX
Tel: 01840 213279
lakefieldcornwall.com/camping-touring
Total pitches: 40
6 G8

Lakeland Leisure Park ►►►►►
Moor Lane, Flookburgh
LA11 7LT
Tel: 01539 558556
haven.com/lakeland
Total pitches: 177
89 K12

Lakeside Caravan Park & Fisheries ►►►►
Sluice Road, Denver, Downham Market
PE38 0EG
Tel: 01366 383491
lakesidedenver.co.uk
Total pitches: 100
69 L11

Lamb Cottage Caravan Park ►►►►►
Dalefords Lane, Whitegate,
Northwich
CW8 2BN
Tel: 01606 882302
lambcottage.co.uk
Total pitches: 45
75 Q10

Langstone Manor C & C Park ►►►►►
Moortown, Tavistock
PL19 9JZ
Tel: 01822 613371
langstonemanor.co.uk
Total pitches: 40
7 P10

Lanyon Holiday Park ►►►►
Loscombe Lane, Four Lanes,
Redruth
TR16 6LP
Tel: 01209 313474
lanyonholidaypark.co.uk
Total pitches: 25
2 H7

Larches Caravan Park ►►►►
Mealsgate, Wigton
CA7 1LQ
Tel: 016973 71379
facebook.com/TheLarchesCaravanPark
Total pitches: 35
97 P10

Lee Valley C & C Park, Edmonton ►►►►
Meridian Way, Edmonton
N9 0AR
Tel: 03000 030 625
visitleevalley.org.uk/wheretostay
Total pitches: 144
33 L3

Lee Valley Campsite, Sewardstone ►►►►
Sewardstone Road, Chingford
E4 7RA
Tel: 03000 030 623
visitleevalley.org.uk/wheretostay
Total pitches: 99
33 M3

Lee Valley Caravan Park, Dobbs Weir ►►►►
Charlton Meadows,
Essex Road, Hoddesdon
EN11 0AS
Tel: 03000 030 619
leevalleypark.org.uk/en/content/cms/
where-to-stay-and-short-breaks/dobbs-
weir-caravan-park
Total pitches: 70
45 M10

Lickpenny Caravan Site ►►►►
Lickpenny Lane,
Tansley, Matlock
DE4 5GF
Tel: 01629 583040
lickpennycaravanpark.co.uk
Total pitches: 80
77 Q11

Lime Tree Park ►►►►
Dukes Drive,
Buxton
SK17 9RP
Tel: 01298 22988
limetreeparkbuxton.com
Total pitches: 106
77 K9

Lincoln Farm Park Oxfordshire ►►►►►
High Street, Standlake
OX29 7RH
Tel: 01865 300239
lincolnfarmpark.co.uk
Total pitches: 90
43 J11

Little Bodieve Holiday Park ►►►
Bodieve Road,
Wadebridge
PL27 6EG
Tel: 01208 812323
littlebodieve.co.uk
Total pitches: 195
6 E10

Little Ranch Leisure ►►►
Begdale, Elm, Wisbech
PE14 0AZ
Tel: 01945 860066
littleranchleisure.co.uk
Total pitches: 40
69 J11

Littlesea Holiday Park ►►►►►
Lynch Lane,
Weymouth
DT4 9DT
Tel: 01305 774414
haven.com/littlesea
Total pitches: 141
10 G9

Little Trevothan C & C Park ►►►►
Trevothan, Coverack, Helston,
Cornwall
TR12 6SD
Tel: 01326 280260
littletrevothan.co.uk
Total pitches: 80
3 J11

Lobb Fields C & C Park ►►►
Saunton Road,
Braunton
EX33 1HG
Tel: 01271 812090
lobbfields.com
Total pitches: 180
19 J6

Long Acres Touring Park ►►►►
Station Road, Old Leake,
Boston
PE22 9RF
Tel: 01205 871555
long-acres.co.uk
Total pitches: 40
68 G2

Long Hazel Park ►►►►
High Street, Sparkford, Yeovil,
Somerset
BA22 7JH
Tel: 01963 440002
longhazelpark.co.uk
Total pitches: 47
22 D8

Longnor Wood Holiday Park ►►►►►
Newtown, Longnor, Nr Buxton
SK17 0NG
Tel: 01298 83648
longnorwood.co.uk
Total pitches: 47
77 K11

Lynmouth Holiday Retreat ►►►►
Lynton, Devon
EX35 6LD
Tel: 01598 753349
channel-view.co.uk
Total pitches: 76
19 P4

Manor Farm C & C Site ►►►►
East Runton,
Cromer
NR27 9PR
Tel: 01263 512858
manorfarmcaravansite.co.uk
Total pitches: 250
71 J4

Manor Farm Holiday Centre ►►►►
Charmouth,
Bridport
DT6 6QL
Tel: 01297 560226
manorfarmholidaycentre.co.uk
Total pitches: 400
10 B6

Manor Wood Country Caravan Park ►►►►►
Manor Wood, Coddington,
Chester
CH3 9EN
Tel: 01829 782990
cheshire-caravan-sites.co.uk
Total pitches: 45
63 M1

Marsh Farm Caravan Site ►►
Sternfield, Saxmundham
IP17 1HW
Tel: 01728 602168
marshfarm-caravansite.co.uk
Total pitches: 45
59 M8

Marsh House Holiday Park ►►►►
Marsh House Farm, Carnforth,
Lancashire
LA5 9JA
Tel: 01524 732854
holgates.co.uk/our-parks/marsh-house
Total pitches: 74
83 L1

Marton Mere Holiday Village ►►►►►
Mythop Road, Blackpool
FY4 4XN
Tel: 01253 767544
haven.com/martonmere
Total pitches: 82
82 H8

Mayfield Park ►►►►►
Cheltenham Road,
Cirencester
GL7 7BH
Tel: 01285 831301
mayfieldpark.co.uk
Total pitches: 105
42 B10

Meadowbank Holidays ►►►►►
Stour Way, Christchurch
BH23 2PQ
Tel: 01202 483597
meadowbank-holidays.co.uk
Total pitches: 41
12 B6

Mena Farm: Touring, Camping, Glamping ►►►►
Bodmin, Lanivet
PL30 5HW
Tel: 01208 831845
menafarm.co.uk
Total pitches: 25
3 P2

Mill Farm C & C Park ►►►►
Fiddington, Bridgwater,
Somerset
TA5 1JQ
Tel: 01278 732286
millfarm.biz
Total pitches: 275
21 K5

Mill Park Touring C & C Park ►►►►►
Mill Lane, Berrynarbor,
Ilfracombe, Devon
EX34 9SH
Tel: 01271 882647
millpark.com
Total pitches: 125
19 L4

Minnows Touring Park ►►►►►
Holbrook Lane,
Sampford Peverell
EX16 7EN
Tel: 01884 821770
minnowstouringpark.co.uk
Total pitches: 59
20 G10

Monkey Tree Holiday Park ►►►►►
Hendra Croft, Scotland Road,
Newquay
TR8 5QR
Tel: 01872 572032
monkeytreeholidaypark.co.uk
Total pitches: 511
3 K3

Monkton Wyld Holiday Park ►►►►►
Scott's Lane, Charmouth,
Dorset
DT6 6DB
Tel: 01297 631131
monktonwyld.co.uk
Total pitches: 155
9 Q5

Moon & Sixpence ►►►►►
Newbourn Road, Waldringfield,
Woodbridge
IP12 4PP
Tel: 01473 736650
moonandsixpence.co.uk
Total pitches: 50
47 N3

Moor End Farm ►►
Acaster Malbis, York
YO23 2UQ
Tel: 01904 706727
moor-end-farm.co.uk
Total pitches: 12
86 B6

Moor View Touring Park ►►►►
California Cross,
Modbury, Devon
PL21 0SG
Tel: 01548 821485
moorviewtouringpark.co.uk
Total pitches: 68
5 L6

Moss Wood Caravan Park ►►►►
Crimbles Lane, Cockerham
LA2 0ES
Tel: 01524 791041
mosswood.co.uk
Total pitches: 25
83 L5

Naburn Lock Caravan Park ►►►►
Naburn, York
YO19 4RU
Tel: 01904 728697
naburnlock.co.uk
Total pitches: 115
86 B6

Newberry Valley Park ►►►►►
Woodlands,
Combe Martin
EX34 0AT
Tel: 01271 882334
newberryvalleypark.co.uk
Total pitches: 110
19 L4

New Hall Farm Touring Park ▶▶▶
New Hall Lane, Edingley,
Newark-on-Trent
NG22 8BS
Tel: 01623 883041
newhallfarm.co.uk
Total pitches: 25
66 H1

New House Caravan Park ▶▶▶▶
Kirkby Lonsdale
LA6 2HR
Tel: 015242 71590
newhousecaravanpark.co.uk
Total pitches: 50
89 Q11

Newlands Holidays ▶▶▶▶▶
Charmouth, Bridport
DT6 6RB
Tel: 01297 560259
newlandsholidays.co.uk
Total pitches: 240
10 B6

New Lodge Farm C & C Site ▶▶▶▶
New Lodge Farm, Bulwick, Corby
NN17 3DU
Tel: 01780 450493
newlodgefarm.com
Total pitches: 72
55 N2

New Parkside Farm Caravan Park ▶▶▶
Denny Beck, Caton Road, Lancaster
LA2 9HH
Tel: 015247 70723
newparksidefarm.co.uk
Total pitches: 40
83 L2

Ninham Country Holidays ▶▶▶▶
Ninham, Shanklin,
Isle of Wight
PO37 7PL
Tel: 01983 864243
ninham-holidays.co.uk
Total pitches: 140
13 J8

Norden Farm Touring C & C Site ▶▶▶▶
Corfe Castle, Dorset
BH20 5DS
Tel: 01929 480098
nordenfarm.com
Total pitches: 140
11 M8

Norfolk Coast C & C at Fakenham Racecourse ▶▶▶
Fakenham Racecourse, Fakenham
NR21 7NY
Tel: 01328 862388
norfolkcoast-caravancampingholidays.co.uk
Total pitches: 120
70 D6

Northam Farm Caravan & Touring Park ▶▶▶▶▶
Brean, Burnham-on-Sea
TA8 2SE
Tel: 01278 751244
northamfarm.co.uk
Total pitches: 350
21 M2

North Morte Farm C & C Park ▶▶▶▶
North Morte Road, Mortehoe,
Woolacombe
EX34 7EG
Tel: 01271 870381
northmortefarm.co.uk
Total pitches: 180
19 J4

Noteworthy Farm C & C ▶▶▶
Bude Road, Holsworthy
EX22 7JB
Tel: 01409 253731
noteworthy-devon.co.uk
Total pitches: 5
7 K4

Oakdown Holiday Park ▶▶▶▶▶
Gatedown Lane, Weston,
Sidmouth
EX10 0PT
Tel: 01297 680387
oakdown.co.uk
Total pitches: 150
9 M7

Old Hall Caravan Park ▶▶▶▶▶
Capernwray, Carnforth
LA6 1AD
Tel: 01524 733276
oldhallcaravanpark.co.uk
Total pitches: 38
83 M1

Old Oaks Touring & Glamping ▶▶▶▶▶
Wick Farm, Wick, Glastonbury
BA6 8JS
Tel: 01458 831437
theoldoaks.co.uk
Total pitches: 88
22 C5

Orchard Farm Holiday Village ▶▶▶▶
Stonegate, Hunmanby, Filey,
North Yorkshire
YO14 0PU
Tel: 01723 891582
orchardfarmholidayvillage.co.uk
Total pitches: 91
93 M11

Orchard Park ▶▶▶▶
Frampton Lane, Hubbert's Bridge,
Boston
PE20 3QU
Tel: 01205 290328
orchardpark.co.uk
Total pitches: 87
68 E3

Ord House Country Park ▶▶▶▶▶
East Ord,
Berwick-upon-Tweed
TD15 2NS
Tel: 01289 305288
maguirescountryparks.co.uk
Total pitches: 79
117 L11

Otterington Park ▶▶▶▶
Station Farm, South Otterington,
Northallerton, North Yorkshire
DL7 9JB
Tel: 01609 780656
otteringtonpark.com
Total pitches: 62
91 P9

Outney Meadow Caravan Park ▶▶▶
Outney Meadow, Bungay, Suffolk
NR35 1HG
Tel: 01986 892338
outneymeadow.co.uk
Total pitches: 65
59 L3

Oxon Hall Touring Park ▶▶▶▶▶
Welshpool Road,
Shrewsbury
SY3 5FB
Tel: 01743 340868
morris-leisure.co.uk
Total pitches: 105
63 M9

Park Cliffe C & C Estate ▶▶▶▶▶
Birks Road, Tower Wood,
Windermere
LA23 3PG
Tel: 015395 31344
parkcliffe.co.uk
Total pitches: 60
89 L8

Park Foot Holiday Park ▶▶▶▶▶
Howtown Road,
Pooley Bridge
CA10 2NA
Tel: 017684 86309
parkfootullswater.co.uk
Total pitches: 323
89 M2

Parkers Farm Holiday Park ▶▶▶▶
Higher Mead Farm,
Ashburton,
Devon
TQ13 7LJ
Tel: 01364 654869
parkersfarmholidays.co.uk
Total pitches: 100
8 E10

Parkland C & C Site ▶▶▶▶▶
Sorley Green Cross,
Kingsbridge
TQ7 4AF
Tel: 01548 852723
parklandsite.co.uk
Total pitches: 50
5 M7

Pebble Bank Caravan Park ▶▶▶▶
Camp Road, Wyke Regis,
Weymouth
DT4 9HF
Tel: 01305 774844
pebblebank.co.uk
Total pitches: 40
10 G9

Pecknell Farm Caravan Park ▶▶▶
Barnard Castle
DL12 9DF
Tel: 01833 638357
pecknell.co.uk
Total pitches: 20
90 G3

Peewit Caravan Park ▶▶▶
Walton Avenue,
Felixstowe
IP11 2HB
Tel: 01394 284511
peewitcaravanpark.co.uk
Total pitches: 45
47 N5

Penhalt Farm Holiday Park ▶▶▶
Widemouth Bay, Bude
EX23 0DG
Tel: 01288 361210
penhaltfarm.co.uk
Total pitches: 100
6 H5

Pennymoor C & C Park ▶▶▶
Modbury,
Nr Salcombe, Devon
PL21 0SB
Tel: 01548 830542
pennymoor-camping.co.uk
Total pitches: 119
5 L6

Perran Sands Holiday Park ▶▶▶▶
Perranporth, Truro
TR6 0AQ
Tel: 01872 573551
haven.com/perransands
Total pitches: 341
3 J3

Petwood Caravan Park ▶▶▶▶
Stixwould Road, Woodhall Spa
LN10 6QH
Tel: 01526 354799
petwoodcaravanpark.com
Total pitches: 98
80 D11

Piccadilly Caravan Park ▶▶▶▶
Folly Lane West, Lacock
SN15 2LP
Tel: 01249 263164
piccadillylacock.co.uk
Total pitches: 41
29 P8

Pinecones C & C ▶▶▶▶▶
A149 Bypass, Dersingham,
Norfolk
PE31 6WL
Tel: 01485 544224
Total pitches: 70
69 N6

Plough Lane Touring Caravan Site ▶▶▶▶▶
Plough Lane, Chippenham,
Wiltshire
SN15 5PS
Tel: 01249 750146
ploughlane.co.uk
Total pitches: 52
29 Q7

Polladras Holiday Park ▶▶▶▶
Carleen, Breage, Helston
TR13 9NX
Tel: 01736 762220
polladrasholidaypark.co.uk
Total pitches: 39
2 F8

Polmanter Touring Park ▶▶▶▶▶
Halsetown, St Ives
TR26 3LX
Tel: 01736 795640
polmanter.com
Total pitches: 294
2 E7

Portesham Dairy Farm Campsite ▶▶▶▶
Portesham, Dorset
DT3 4HG
Tel: 01305 871297
porteshamdairyfarm.co.uk
Total pitches: 90
10 F7

Porth Beach Holiday Park ▶▶▶▶
Porth, Newquay
TR7 3NH
Tel: 01637 876531
porthbeach.co.uk
Total pitches: 185
3 K2

Porthtowan Tourist Park ▶▶▶▶▶
Mile Hill, Porthtowan, Truro
TR4 8TY
Tel: 01209 890256
porthtowantouristpark.co.uk
Total pitches: 80
2 H5

Presingoll Farm C & C Park ▶▶▶▶
St Agnes
TR5 0PB
Tel: 01872 552333
presingollfarm.co.uk
Total pitches: 90
2 H5

Primrose Valley Holiday Park ▶▶▶▶
Filey
YO14 9RF
Tel: 01723 513771
haven.com/primrosevalley
Total pitches: 35
93 M11

Priory Hill ▶▶▶
Wing Road, Leysdown-on-Sea,
Sheerness
ME12 4QT
Tel: 01795 510267
prioryhill.co.uk
Total pitches: 34
35 J8

Quarryfield Holiday Park ▶▶▶
Crantock, Newquay
TR8 5RJ
Tel: 01637 830338
quarryfield.co.uk
Total pitches: 145
3 K2

Quiet Waters Caravan Park ▶▶▶
Hemingford Abbots
PE28 9AJ
Tel: 01480 463405
quietwaterscaravanpark.co.uk
Total pitches: 20
56 F6

Ranch Caravan Park ▶▶▶▶▶
Station Road,
Honeybourne, Evesham
WR11 7PR
Tel: 01386 830744
ranch.co.uk
Total pitches: 120
42 C3

Rawcliffe Manor Caravan Park ▶▶▶▶
Manor Lane, Shipton Road, York
YO30 5TZ
Tel: 01904 640845
lysanderarms.co.uk
Total pitches: 13
86 A4

Red Bank Farm ▶▶▶
Bolton-le-Sands
LA5 8JR
Tel: 01524 823196
redbankfarm.co.uk
Total pitches: 60
83 L2

Red Shoot Camping Park ▶▶▶▶
Linwood, Ringwood
BH24 3QT
Tel: 01425 473789
redshoot-campingpark.com
Total pitches: 94
12 C3

Reighton Sands Holiday Park ▶▶▶▶
Reighton Gap, Filey
YO14 9SH
Tel: 01723 890476
haven.com/reightonsands
Total pitches: 147
93 N11

Riddings Wood Holiday Park ▶▶▶▶
Bullock Lane,
Riddings, Alfreton
DE55 4BP
Tel: 01773 605160
riddingswoodholidaypark.co.uk
Total pitches: 75
66 C2

Ridge Farm C & C Park ▶▶▶
Barnhill Road, Ridge,
Wareham
BH20 5BG
Tel: 01929 556444
ridgefarm.co.uk
Total pitches: 60
11 M7

Ripley Caravan Park ▶▶▶▶▶
Knaresborough Road,
Ripley, Harrogate
HG3 3AU
Tel: 01423 770050
ripleycaravanpark.com
Total pitches: 60
85 L3

River Dart Country Park ▶▶▶▶
Holne Park,
Ashburton
TQ13 7NP
Tel: 01364 652511
riverdart.co.uk
Total pitches: 170
5 M3

Riverside C & C Park ▶▶▶▶▶
Marsh Lane, North Molton
Road,
South Molton
EX36 3HQ
Tel: 01769 579269
exmoorriverside.co.uk
Total pitches: 58
19 P8

Riverside Caravan Park ▶▶▶▶
Leigham Manor Drive,
Plymouth
PL6 8LL
Tel: 01752 344122
riversidecaravanpark.com
Total pitches: 259
4 H5

Riverside Caravan Park ▶▶▶▶
High Bentham, Lancaster
LA2 7FJ
Tel: 015242 61272
riversidecaravanpark.co.uk
Total pitches: 61
83 P1

Riverside Holiday Park ▶▶▶
Gwills Lane, Newquay
TR8 4PE
Tel: 01637 873617
riversideholidaypark.co.uk
Total pitches: 65
3 K3

River Valley Holiday Park ▶▶▶▶▶
London Apprentice,
St Austell
PL26 7AP
Tel: 01726 73533
rivervalleyholidaypark.co.uk
Total pitches: 45
3 P4

Roadford Lake ▶▶▶
Roadford Lake, Lower Goodacre,
Broadwoodwidger, Lifton
PL16 0JL
Tel: 01409 211507
southwestlakes.co.uk
Total pitches: 49
7 M6

Robin Hood C & C Park ▶▶▶▶▶
Green Dyke Lane,
Slingsby
YO62 4AP
Tel: 01653 628391
robinhoodcaravanpark.co.uk
Total pitches: 46
92 E11

Rosedale Abbey Caravan Park ▶▶▶▶▶
Rosedale Abbey,
Pickering
YO18 8SA
Tel: 01751 417272
rosedaleabbeycaravanpark.co.uk
Total pitches: 100
92 E7

Roselands C & C Park ▶▶▶
St Just, Penzance
TR19 7RS
Tel: 01736 788571
roselands.co.uk
Total pitches: 25
2 B8

Rose Farm Touring & Camping Park ▶▶▶▶▶▶
Stepshort, Belton,
Nr Great Yarmouth
NR31 9JS
Tel: 01493 738292
rosefarmtouringpark.com
Total pitches: 145
71 P11

Rosewall Camping ▶▶▶
Osmington Mills,
Weymouth
DT3 6HA
Tel: 01305 832248
weymouthcamping.com
Total pitches: 225
10 H8

Rudding Holiday Park ▶▶▶▶▶
Follifoot, Harrogate
HG3 1JH
Tel: 01423 870439
ruddingholidaypark.co.uk
Total pitches: 86
85 L4

Run Cottage Touring Park ▶▶▶▶
Alderton Road, Hollesley,
Woodbridge
IP12 3RQ
Tel: 01394 411309
runcottage.co.uk
Total pitches: 45
47 P3

Ruthern Valley Holidays ▶▶▶
Ruthernbridge,
Nr Bodmin
PL30 5LU
Tel: 01208 831395
ruthernvalley.com
Total pitches: 26
6 E11

Rutland C & C ▶▶▶▶▶
Park Lane, Greetham,
Oakham
LE15 7FN
Tel: 01572 813520
rutlandcaravanandcamping.co.uk
Total pitches: 130
67 M9

St Helens in the Park ▶▶▶▶▶
Wykeham, Scarborough
YO13 9QD
Tel: 01723 862771
sthelenscaravanpark.co.uk
Total pitches: 250
93 K10

St Ives Bay Beach Resort ▶▶▶▶▶
73 Loggans Road,
Upton Towans,
Hayle
TR27 5BH
Tel: 01736 752274
stivesbay.co.uk
Total pitches: 240
2 F6

St Leonards Farm C & C Park ▶▶▶▶
Ringwood Road, West Moors, Ferndown,
Bournemouth
BH22 0AQ
Tel: 01202 872637
stleonardsfarmpark.com
Total pitches: 151
11 Q4

Salcombe Regis C & C Park ▶▶▶▶▶
Salcombe Regis, Sidmouth
EX10 0JH
Tel: 01395 514303
salcombe-regis.co.uk
Total pitches: 100
9 M7

Sand le Mere Holiday Village ▶▶▶▶▶
Southfield Lane, Tunstall
HU12 0JF
Tel: 01964 670403
sand-le-mere.co.uk
Total pitches: 72
87 P9

Scratby Hall Caravan Park ▶▶▶▶
Scratby,
Great Yarmouth
NR29 3SR
Tel: 01493 730283
scratbyhall.co.uk
Total pitches: 85
71 P9

Sea Barn Farm Camping Park ▶▶▶
Fleet Road, Fleet,
Weymouth
DT3 4ED
Tel: 01305 782218
seabarnfarm.co.uk
Total pitches: 199
10 F8

Searles Leisure Resort ▶▶▶▶▶
South Beach Road, Hunstanton
PE36 5BB
Tel: 01485 534211
searles.co.uk
Total pitches: 255
69 M4

Seaview Holiday Park ►►►►►
Preston, Weymouth
DT3 6DZ
Tel: 01305 832271 **10 H8**
haven.com/parks/dorset/seaview
Total pitches: 82

Senlac Wood ►►►
Catsfield Road, Catsfield, Battle
TN33 9LN
Tel: 01424 773969 **16 C8**
senlacwood.co.uk
Total pitches: 35

Seven Acres C & C Site ►►►
Seven Acres, West Woodlands, Frome
BA11 5EQ
Tel: 01373 464222 **22 H4**
Total pitches: 16

Seven Acres Caravan Park ►►►
Holmrook, Cumbria
CA19 1YD
Tel: 01946 822777 **88 E6**
sevenacrespark.co.uk
Total pitches: 37

Severn Gorge Park ►►►►►
Bridgnorth Road, Tweedale, Telford
TF7 4JB
Tel: 01952 684789 **64 C11**
severngorgepark.co.uk
Total pitches: 12

Shaws Trailer Park ►►
5 Main Street, Harrogate
HG2 7NE
Tel: 01423 884432 **85 L4**
shaws-trailer-park.edan.io
Total pitches: 60

Ship & Anchor Marina ►►
Station Road, Ford, Arundel
BN18 0BJ
Tel: 01243 551262 **14 E10**
Total pitches: 120

Shrubbery Touring Park ►►►►
Rousdon, Lyme Regis
DT7 3XW
Tel: 01297 442227 **9 P6**
shrubberypark.co.uk
Total pitches: 120

Silverdale Caravan Park ►►►►►
Middlebarrow Plain, Cove Road, Silverdale,
Nr Carnforth
LA5 0SH
Tel: 01524 701508 **89 M11**
holgates.co.uk
Total pitches: 80

Silver Sands Holiday Park ►►►►
Gwendreath, Kennack Sands, Helston
TR12 7LZ
Tel: 01326 290631 **3 J11**
silversandsholidaypark.co.uk
Total pitches: 35

Skegness Holiday Park ►►►►►
Richmond Drive, Skegness
PE25 3TQ
Tel: 01754 762097 **81 K11**
haven.com/parks/lincolnshire/skegness-holiday-park
Total pitches: 49

Skelwith Fold Caravan Park ►►►►►
Ambleside, Cumbria
LA22 0HX
Tel: 015394 32277 **89 K6**
skelwith.com
Total pitches: 150

Skirlington Leisure Park ►►►►►
Driffield, Skipsea
YO25 8SY
Tel: 01262 468213 **87 M5**
skirlington.com
Total pitches: 280

Skyburriowe Farm ►►►
Garras, Helston
TR12 6LR
Tel: 01326 221646 **2 H10**
skyburriowefarm.co.uk
Total pitches: 30

Sleningford Watermill Caravan Camping Park ►►►►
North Stainley, Ripon
HG4 3HQ
Tel: 01765 635201 **91 M11**
sleningfordwatermill.co.uk
Total pitches: 150

Solway Holiday Village ►►►►
Skinburness Drive, Silloth, Cumbria
CA7 4QQ
Tel: 016973 31236 **97 M7**
cove.co.uk/solway
Total pitches: 130

South End Caravan Park ►►►►
Walney Island, Barrow-in-Furness
LA14 3YQ
Tel: 01229 472823 **82 F3**
southendcaravanpark.co.uk
Total pitches: 50

Southfork Caravan Park ►►►►
Parrett Works, Martock, Somerset
TA12 6AE
Tel: 01935 825661 **21 P9**
southforkcaravans.co.uk
Total pitches: 27

South Lytchett Manor C & C Park ►►►►►
Dorchester Road, Lytchett Minster, Poole
BH16 6JB
Tel: 01202 622577 **11 M6**
southlytchettmanor.co.uk
Total pitches: 150

South Meadows Caravan Park ►►►►►
South Road, Belford
NE70 7DP
Tel: 01668 213326 **109 J3**
southmeadows.co.uk
Total pitches: 169

South Penquite Farm ►►►
South Penquite, Blisland, Bodmin
PL30 4LH
Tel: 01208 850491 **6 G10**
southpenquite.co.uk
Total pitches: 40

Southwinds C & C Park ►►►
Polzeath Road, Polzeath
PL27 6QU
Tel: 01208 863267 **6 D9**
polzeathcamping.co.uk
Total pitches: 165

Stanmore Hall Touring Park ►►►►►
Stourbridge Road, Bridgnorth
WV15 6DT
Tel: 01746 761761 **52 D2**
morris-leisure.co.uk
Total pitches: 129

Stanwix Park Holiday Centre ►►►►►
Greenrow, Silloth
CA7 4HH
Tel: 016973 32666 **97 M8**
stanwix.com
Total pitches: 121

Stithians Lake Country Park ►►►
Stithians Lake, Menherion, Redruth
TR16 6NW
Tel: 01209 860301 **2 H7**
southwestlakes.co.uk
Total pitches: 40

Stonehenge Campsite & Glamping Pods ►►►►
Berwick St James, Salisbury
SP3 4TQ
Tel: 07786 734732 **23 N5**
stonehengecampsite.co.uk
Total pitches: 35

Summerlands Caravan Park ►►►
College Farm, Rockbourne Road, Coombe Bissett
SP5 4LP
Tel: 01722 718259 **23 P8**
summerlandscaravanpark.co.uk
Total pitches: 26

Summer Valley Touring Park ►►►►
Shortlanesend, Truro, Cornwall
TR4 9DW
Tel: 07933 212643 **3 K5**
summervalley.co.uk
Total pitches: 55

Sumners Ponds Fishery & Campsite ►►►►
Chapel Road, Barns Green, Horsham
RH13 0PR
Tel: 01403 732539 **14 G5**
sumnersponds.co.uk
Total pitches: 86

Sunnymead Farm Camping & Touring Site ►►►►
Ilfracombe, Devon
EX34 8NZ
Tel: 01271 879845 **19 K4**
sunnymead-farm.co.uk
Total pitches: 30

Swiss Farm Touring & Camping ►►►►
Marlow Road, Henley-on-Thames
RG9 2HY
Tel: 01491 573419 **31 Q5**
swissfarmhenley.co.uk
Total pitches: 140

Sykeside C & C Park ►►►
Brotherswater, Hartsop, Patterdale, Penrith
CA11 0NZ
Tel: 017684 82239 **89 L4**
sykeside.co.uk
Total pitches: 86

Tall Trees Touring Park ►►►
Old Mill Lane, Forest Town, Mansfield
NG19 0JP
Tel: 01623 626503 **78 F11**
talltreestouringpark.co.uk
Total pitches: 37

Tanner Farm Touring C & C Park ►►►►
Tanner Farm, Goudhurst Road, Marden
TN12 9ND
Tel: 01622 832399 **16 C3**
tannerfarmpark.co.uk
Total pitches: 120

Tehidy Holiday Park ►►►►
Harris Mill, Illogan, Portreath
TR16 4JQ
Tel: 01209 216489 **2 H6**
tehidy.co.uk
Total pitches: 18

Tencreek Holiday Park ►►►►►
Polperro Road, Looe
PL13 2JR
Tel: 01503 262447 **4 C6**
dolphinholidays.co.uk
Total pitches: 254

The Grange Touring Park ►►►►
Yarmouth Road, Ormesby St Margaret, Great Yarmouth
NR29 3QG
Tel: 01493 730306 **71 P9**
grangetouring.co.uk
Total pitches: 70

The Green Caravan Park ►►►
Wentnor, Bishop's Castle
SY9 5EF
Tel: 01588 650605 **51 L2**
greencaravanpark.co.uk
Total pitches: 140

The Inside Park ►►►►
Down House Estate, Blandford Forum, Dorset
DT11 9AD
Tel: 01258 453719 **11 L4**
theinsidepark.co.uk
Total pitches: 125

The Laurels Holiday Park ►►►►
Padstow Road, Whitecross, Wadebridge
PL27 7JQ
Tel: 01208 813341 **6 D10**
thelaurelsholidaypark.co.uk
Total pitches: 30

The Old Brick Kilns ►►►►►
Little Barney Lane, Barney, Fakenham
NR21 0NL
Tel: 01328 878305 **70 E5**
old-brick-kilns.co.uk
Total pitches: 65

The Orchards Holiday Caravan Park ►►►►►
Main Road, Newbridge, Yarmouth, Isle of Wight
PO41 0TS
Tel: 01983 531331 **12 G7**
orchards-holiday-park.co.uk
Total pitches: 120

The Quiet Site ►►►►►
Ullswater, Watermillock
CA11 0LS
Tel: 07768 727016 **89 L2**
thequietsite.co.uk
Total pitches: 100

The Rickels C & C Park Ltd ►►►
Bircham Road, Stanhoe, King's Lynn
PE31 8PU
Tel: 01485 518671 **69 Q5**
therickels.co.uk
Total pitches: 40

Thornwick Bay Holiday Village ►►►►►
North Marine Road, Flamborough
YO15 1AU
Tel: 01262 850569 **93 P12**
haven.com/parks/yorkshire/thornwick-bay
Total pitches: 67

Thorpe Hall C & C Site ►►►►
Rudston
YO25 4JE
Tel: 01262 420393 **87 L2**
thorpehall.co.uk
Total pitches: 78

Thorpe Park Holiday Centre ►►►►►
Cleethorpes
DN35 0PW
Tel: 01472 813395 **80 F2**
haven.com/thorpepark
Total pitches: 134

Tollgate Farm C & C Park ►►►►
Budnick Hill, Perranporth
TR6 0AD
Tel: 01872 572130 **3 J3**
tollgatefarm.co.uk
Total pitches: 102

Treago Farm Caravan Site ►►►
Crantock, Newquay
TR8 5QS
Tel: 01637 830277 **3 J2**
treagofarm.co.uk
Total pitches: 90

Trebellan Park ►►►
Newquay
TR8 5QS
Tel: 01637 830277 **3 K3**
treagofarm.co.uk
Total pitches: 150

Tregavone Touring Park ►►►
St Merryn, Cornwall
PL28 8JZ
Tel: 01841 520148 **6 C10**
tregavonefarm.co.uk
Total pitches: 40

Tregedna Farm Touring C & C Park ►►►
Maenporth, Falmouth
TR11 5HL
Tel: 01326 250529 **3 J8**
tregednafarmholidays.co.uk
Total pitches: 40

Treglisson Touring Park ►►►
Wheal Alfred Road, Hayle
TR27 5JT
Tel: 01736 753141 **2 F7**
treglisson.co.uk
Total pitches: 26

Treloy Touring Park ►►►►►
Newquay
TR8 4JN
Tel: 01637 872063 **3 L2**
treloy.co.uk
Total pitches: 223

Trenance Holiday Park ►►►►
Edgcumbe Avenue, Newquay
TR7 2JY
Tel: 01637 873447 **3 K2**
trenanceholidaypark.co.uk
Total pitches: 50

Trencreek Holiday Park ►►►►
Hillcrest, Higher Trencreek, Newquay
TR8 4NS
Tel: 01637 874210 **3 K2**
trencreekholidaypark.co.uk
Total pitches: 194

Trentfield Farm ►►►
Church Laneham, Retford
DN22 0NJ
Tel: 01777 228651 **79 K8**
trentfield.co.uk
Total pitches: 45

Trethem Mill Touring Park ►►►►►
St Just-in-Roseland, Nr St Mawes, Truro
TR2 5JF
Tel: 01872 580504 **3 L7**
trethem.com
Total pitches: 84

Trevalgan Touring Park ►►►►►
Trevalgan, St Ives
TR26 3BJ
Tel: 01736 791892 **2 D6**
trevalgantouringpark.co.uk
Total pitches: 135

Trevarrian Holiday Park ►►►►
Mawgan Porth, Newquay, Cornwall
TR8 4AQ
Tel: 01637 860381 **6 B11**
trevarrian.co.uk
Total pitches: 185

Trevarth Holiday Park ►►►►
Blackwater, Truro
TR4 8HR
Tel: 01872 560266 **3 J5**
trevarth.co.uk
Total pitches: 30

Trevaylor C & C Park ►►►►
Botallack, St Just
TR19 7PU
Tel: 01736 787016 **2 B8**
cornishcamping.co.uk
Total pitches: 50

Trevedra Farm C & C Site ►►►►►
Sennen, Penzance
TR19 7BE
Tel: 01736 871818 **2 B9**
trevedrafarm.co.uk
Total pitches: 100

Trevornick ►►►►►
Holywell Bay, Newquay
TR8 5PW
Tel: 01637 830531 **3 J3**
trevornick.co.uk
Total pitches: 575

Trewan Hall ►►►►
St Columb Major, Cornwall
TR9 6DB
Tel: 01637 880261 **3 M2**
trewan-hall.co.uk
Total pitches: 200

Trewince Farm Touring Park ►►►
Portscatho, Truro
TR2 5ET
Tel: 01872 580430 **3 L8**
trewincefarm.co.uk
Total pitches: 25

Tristram C & C Park ►►►
Polzeath, Wadebridge
PL27 6TP
Tel: 01208 862215 **6 D9**
polzeathcamping.co.uk
Total pitches: 100

Tudor C & C ►►►►
Shepherds Patch, Slimbridge, Gloucester
GL2 7BP
Tel: 01453 890483 **41 L11**
tudorcaravanpark.com
Total pitches: 75

Twitchen House Holiday Village ►►►►►
Mortehoe Station Road, Mortehoe, Woolacombe
EX34 7ES
Tel: 01271 872302 **19 J4**
woolacombe.co.uk
Total pitches: 252

Two Mills Touring Park ►►►►►
Yarmouth Road, North Walsham
NR28 9NA
Tel: 01692 405829 **71 K6**
twomills.co.uk
Total pitches: 81

Ullswater Holiday Park ►►►►
High Longthwaite, Watermillock, Penrith
CA11 0LR
Tel: 017684 86666 **89 L2**
ullswaterholidaypark.co.uk
Total pitches: 160

Ulwell Cottage Caravan Park ►►►►►
Ulwell Cottage, Ulwell, Swanage
BH19 3DG
Tel: 01929 422823 **11 N8**
ulwellcottagepark.co.uk
Total pitches: 77

Upper Lynstone Caravan Park ►►►►
Lynstone, Bude
EX23 0LP
Tel: 01288 352017 **6 H4**
upperlynstone.co.uk
Total pitches: 65

Upper Tamar Lake ►►
Kilkhampton, Bude
EX23 9SB
Tel: 01288 321712 **7 K2**
southwestlakes.co.uk
Total pitches: 28

Vale of Pickering Caravan Park ►►►►►
Carr House Farm, Allerston, Pickering
YO18 7PQ
Tel: 01723 859280 **92 H10**
valeofpickering.co.uk
Total pitches: 120

Waldegraves Holiday Park ►►►►►
Mersea Island, Colchester
CO5 8SE
Tel: 01206 382898 **47 J9**
waldegraves.co.uk
Total pitches: 126

Waleswood C & C Park ►►►►►
Delves Lane, Waleswood, Wales Bar, Wales, South Yorkshire
S26 5RN
Tel: 07825 125328 **78 D7**
waleswood.co.uk
Total pitches: 163

Walnut Cottage Holiday Park ►►►►
Milward Rise, Kenley,
Shrewsbury
SY5 6NS
Tel: 07812 606787 **51 P1**
camping-much-wenlock.co.uk/home
Total pitches: 16

Wareham Forest Tourist Park ►►►►►
North Trigon, Wareham
BH20 7NZ
Tel: 01929 551393 **11 L6**
warehamforest.co.uk
Total pitches: 200

Waren C & C Park ►►►►►
Waren Mill, Bamburgh
NE70 7EE
Tel: 01668 214366 **109 J3**
meadowhead.co.uk/parks/waren
Total pitches: 150

Warner Farm ►►►►
Warner Lane, Selsey,
Chichester
PO20 9EL
Tel: 01243 604499 **13 P6**
cove.co.uk/sealbayresort/camping-
touring
Total pitches: 250

Warren Farm Holiday Centre ►►►►►
Brean Sands, Brean,
Burnham-on-Sea
TA8 2RP
Tel: 01278 751227 **28 D11**
warrenfarm.co.uk
Total pitches: 575

Waterfoot Caravan Park ►►►►
Pooley Bridge, Penrith,
Cumbria
CA11 0JF
Tel: 017684 86302 **89 M2**
waterfootpark.co.uk
Total pitches: 34

Watergate Bay Touring Park ►►►►►
Watergate Bay,
Tregurrian
TR8 4AD
Tel: 01637 860387 **6 B11**
watergatebaytouringpark.co.uk
Total pitches: 171

Waterrow Touring Park ►►►►►
Wiveliscombe, Taunton
TA4 2AZ
Tel: 01984 623464 **20 G8**
waterrowpark.co.uk
Total pitches: 42

Waters Edge Caravan Park ►►►►
Crooklands,
Nr Kendal
LA7 7NN
Tel: 015395 67708 **89 N10**
watersedgecaravanpark.co.uk
Total pitches: 26

Waters Edge Country Park ►►►►►►
River Road, Stanah,
Thornton-Cleveleys,
Blackpool
FY5 5LR
Tel: 01253 823632 **83 J6**
knepsfarm.co.uk
Total pitches: 40

Wayfarers C & C Park ►►►►►
Relubbus Lane, St Hilary,
Penzance
TR20 9EF
Tel: 01736 763326 **2 E8**
wayfarerspark.co.uk
Total pitches: 32

Wells Touring Park ►►►►►►
Haybridge, Wells
BA5 1AJ
Tel: 01749 676869 **22 C4**
wellstouringpark.co.uk
Total pitches: 56

Westbrook Park ►►►►►
Little Hereford, Herefordshire
SY8 4AU
Tel: 01584 711280 **51 P7**
westbrookpark.co.uk
Total pitches: 53

West Fleet Holiday Farm ►►►
Fleet, Weymouth
DT3 4EF
Tel: 01305 782218 **10 F8**
westfleetholidays.co.uk
Total pitches: 200

Westgate Carr Farm ►►►
Westgate Carr Road, Pickering
YO18 8LX
Tel: 01751 471417 **92 F10**
Total pitches: 25

Whitefield Forest Touring Park ►►►►►
Brading Road, Ryde,
Isle of Wight
PO33 1QL
Tel: 01983 617069 **13 K7**
whitefieldforest.co.uk
Total pitches: 90

Whitehill Country Park ►►►►
Stoke Road, Paignton,
Devon
TQ4 7PF
Tel: 01803 782338 **5 P5**
whitehill-park.co.uk
Total pitches: 260

Whitemead Caravan Park ►►►►
East Burton Road,
Wool
BH20 6HG
Tel: 01929 462241 **11 K7**
whitemeadcaravanpark.co.uk
Total pitches: 105

Widdicombe Farm Touring Park ►►►►
Marldon, Paignton, Devon
TQ3 1ST
Tel: 01803 558325 **5 P4**
widdicombefarm.co.uk
Total pitches: 180

Willowbank Holiday Home & Touring Park ►►►►
Coastal Road, Ainsdale,
Southport
PR8 3ST
Tel: 01704 571566 **75 J2**
willowbankcp.co.uk
Total pitches: 87

Willow Holt Caravan Park ►►►►
Lodge Road, Tattershall
LN4 4JS
Tel: 07919 003254 **80 D11**
willowholt.co.uk
Total pitches: 63

Willow Valley Holiday Park ►►►►
Bush, Bude, Cornwall
EX23 9LB
Tel: 01288 353104 **7 J3**
willowvalley.co.uk
Total pitches: 41

Wimbleball Lake ►►►
Brompton Regis,
Dulverton
TA22 9NU
Tel: 01398 371460 **20 F7**
swlakestrust.org.uk
Total pitches: 30

Wolds View Country Park ►►►►
115 Brigg Road, Caistor
LN7 6RX
Tel: 01472 851099 **80 B3**
woldsviewtouringpark.co.uk
Total pitches: 60

Wolds Way C & C ►►►►
West Knapton, Malton
YO17 8JE
Tel: 01944 728463 **92 H11**
ryedalesbest.co.uk
Total pitches: 70

Wolvey Villa Farm C & C Park ►►►
Wolvey,
Hinckley
LE10 3HF
Tel: 01455 220493 **54 C3**
wolveycaravanpark.itgo.com
Total pitches: 110

Wooda Farm Holiday Park ►►►►►
Poughill, Bude
EX23 9HJ
Tel: 01288 352069 **7 J3**
wooda.co.uk
Total pitches: 200

Woodclose Caravan Park ►►►►►
High Casterton,
Kirkby Lonsdale
LA6 2SE
Tel: 01524 271597 **89 Q11**
woodclosepark.com
Total pitches: 22

Woodhall Country Park ►►►►►
Stixwold Road,
Woodhall Spa
LN10 6UJ
Tel: 01526 353710 **80 D11**
woodhallcountrypark.co.uk
Total pitches: 141

Woodlands Grove C & C Park ►►►►►
Blackawton,
Dartmouth
TQ9 7DQ
Tel: 01803 712598 **5 N6**
woodlandsgrove.com
Total pitches: 350

Woodland Springs Adult Touring Park ►►►►►
Venton, Drewsteignton
EX6 6PG
Tel: 01647 231648 **8 D6**
woodlandsprings.co.uk
Total pitches: 93

Woodland Waters ►►►►
Ancaster, Grantham
NG32 3RT
Tel: 01400 230888 **67 N3**
woodlandwaters.co.uk
Total pitches: 128

Woodovis Park ►►►►►
Gulworthy, Tavistock
PL19 8NY
Tel: 01822 832968 **7 N10**
woodovis.com
Total pitches: 50

Woodyhyde Camp Site ►►►
Valley Road,
Corfe Castle
BH20 5HT
Tel: 01929 480274 **11 N8**
woodyhyde.co.uk
Total pitches: 150

Woolsbridge Manor Farm Caravan Park ►►►►
Three Legged Cross,
Wimborne
BH21 6RA
Tel: 01202 826369 **11 Q4**
woolsbridgemanorcaravanpark.co.uk
Total pitches: 60

Yeatheridge Farm Caravan Park ►►►►
East Worlington,
Crediton, Devon
EX17 4TN
Tel: 01884 860330 **8 E3**
yeatheridge.co.uk
Total pitches: 103

York Caravan Park ►►►►►
Stockton Lane, York,
North Yorkshire
YO32 9UB
Tel: 01904 424222 **86 B4**
yorkcaravanpark.com
Total pitches: 55

York Meadows Caravan Park ►►►►
York Road, Sheriff Hutton, York,
North Yorkshire
YO60 6QP
Tel: 01347 878508 **86 B2**
yorkmeadowscaravanpark.com
Total pitches: 45

SCOTLAND

Achindarroch Touring Park ►►►
Duror
PA38 4BS
Tel: 01631 740329 **121 J2**
achindarrochtp.co.uk
Total pitches: 37

Aden C & C ►►►
Station Road, Mintlaw
AB42 5FQ
Tel: 077886 885435 **141 N6**
adencaravanandcamping.co.uk
Total pitches: 21

Aird Donald Caravan Park ►►►►
London Road, Stranraer
DG9 8RN
Tel: 01776 702025 **94 F6**
aird-donald.co.uk
Total pitches: 50

Anwoth Caravan Site ►►►►
Gatehouse of Fleet,
Castle Douglas
DG7 2JU
Tel: 01557 814333 **96 C7**
swalwellholidaygroup.co.uk/anwoth
Total pitches: 28

Auchenlarie Holiday Park ►►►►►
Gatehouse of Fleet
DG7 2EX
Tel: 01556 506200 **95 P8**
swalwellholidaygroup.co.uk
Total pitches: 49

Barrhill Holiday Park ►►►►
Barrhill, Girvan
KA26 0PZ
Tel: 01465 821355 **95 J2**
barrhillholidaypark.com
Total pitches: 20

Beecraigs C & C Site ►►►►
Beecraigs Country Park,
The Visitor Centre, Linlithgow
EH49 6PL
Tel: 01506 284516 **115 J6**
westlothian.gov.uk/stay-at-beecraigs
Total pitches: 36

Belhaven Bay C & C Park ►►►►
Belhaven Bay, Dunbar,
East Lothian
EH42 1TS
Tel: 01368 865956 **116 F5**
meadowhead.co.uk
Total pitches: 52

Black Rock Park ►►►►
Balconie Street,
Evanton
IV16 9UN
Tel: 07706346563 **137 Q3**
wyldecrestholidayparks.co.uk/property_
location/black-rock-caravan-holiday-park
Total pitches: 33

Blair Castle Caravan Park ►►►►►
Blair Atholl, Pitlochry
PH18 5SR
Tel: 01796 481263 **130 F11**
blaircastlecaravanpark.co.uk
Total pitches: 184

Brighouse Bay Holiday Park ►►►►►
Brighouse Bay, Borgue,
Kirkcudbright
DG6 4TS
Tel: 01557 870267 **96 D9**
gillespie-leisure.co.uk
Total pitches: 190

Broomfield Holiday Park ►►►
West Lane,
Ullapool
IV26 2UT
Tel: 01854 612020 **144 E6**
broomfieldhp.com
Total pitches: 140

Cairnsmill Holiday Park ►►►►►
Largo Road, St Andrews
KY16 8NN
Tel: 01334 473604 **125 K10**
cairnsmill.co.uk
Total pitches: 62

Carradale Bay Caravan Park ►►►
Carradale, Kintyre,
Argyll & Bute
PA28 6QG
Tel: 01583 431665 **103 L2**
carradalebay.com
Total pitches: 74

Craigtoun Meadows Holiday Park ►►►►►
Mount Melville,
St Andrews
KY16 8PQ
Tel: 01334 475959 **125 J9**
craigtounmeadows.co.uk
Total pitches: 56

Dovecot Caravan Park ►►►
North Water Bridge, Inglismaldie,
Laurencekirk
AB30 1QL
Tel: 01674 840630 **132 G11**
dovecotcaravanpark.co.uk
Total pitches: 25

Drumroamin Farm Camping & Touring Site ►►►
Kirkinner, Newton Stewart,
Wigtown
DG8 9DB
Tel: 01988 840613 **95 N8**
drumroamin.co.uk
Total pitches: 48

Faskally Caravan Park ►►►►
Pitlochry
PH16 5LA
Tel: 01796 472007 **130 G12**
faskally.co.uk
Total pitches: 300

Feughside Caravan Park ►►►►
Strachan, Banchory
AB31 6NT
Tel: 01330 850669 **132 G6**
feughsidecaravanpark.co.uk
Total pitches: 27

Galabank C & C Group ►►
North Street, Annan
DG12 5DQ
Tel: 01461 203539 **97 P5**
annan.org.uk/accommodation/
caravan-parks.html
Total pitches: 30

Glendaruel Caravan Park ►►►
Glendaruel,
Argyll & Bute
PA22 3AB
Tel: 01369 820267 **112 E4**
glendaruelcaravanpark.co.uk
Total pitches: 27

Glen Dochart Holiday Park ►►►►
Luib, Crianlarich, Stirling
FK20 8QT
Tel: 01567 820637 **122 E7**
glendochart-caravanpark.co.uk
Total pitches: 35

Glenearly Caravan Park ►►►►
Dalbeattie,
Dumfries & Galloway
DG5 4NE
Tel: 01556 611393 **96 G6**
glenearlycaravanpark.co.uk
Total pitches: 39

Glen Nevis C & C Park ►►►►
Glen Nevis,
Fort William
PH33 6SX
Tel: 01397 702191 **128 F10**
glen-nevis.co.uk
Total pitches: 380

Hillhead Caravan Park ►►►►
Kintore, Inverurie
AB51 0YX
Tel: 01467 632809 **133 J1**
hillheadcaravan.com
Total pitches: 17

Hoddom Castle Caravan Park ►►►►►
Hoddom, Lockerbie
DG11 1AS
Tel: 01576 300251 **97 N4**
hoddomcastle.co.uk
Total pitches: 200

Huntly Castle Caravan Park ►►►►►
The Meadow, Huntly
AB54 4UJ
Tel: 01466 794999 **140 E8**
huntlycastle.co.uk
Total pitches: 90

Invercoe C & C Park ►►►►
Ballachulish, Glencoe
PH49 4HP
Tel: 01855 811210 **121 L1**
invercoe.co.uk
Total pitches: 60

Inver Mill Farm Caravan Park ►►►►
Inver, Dunkeld
PH8 0JR
Tel: 01350 727477 **123 P4**
invermillfarm.com
Total pitches: 65

King Robert the Bruce's Cave C & C Park ►►►►
Kirkpatrick Fleming,
Gretna
DG11 3AT
Tel: 01461 800285 **98 B4**
brucescave.co.uk
Total pitches: 75

Kings Green Caravan Site ►►►
South Street, Port William,
Newton Stewart
DG8 9SG
Tel: 01988 700489 **95 L9**
kingsgreencaravanpark.com
Total pitches: 30

Kippford View Holiday Park ►►►►
Palnackie, Castle Douglas
DG7 1PF
Tel: 01557 870267 **96 G6**
gillespie-leisure.co.uk
Total pitches: 20

Linwater Caravan Park ►►►►
West Clifton,
East Calder
EH53 0HT
Tel: 0131 333 3326 **115 K7**
linwater.co.uk
Total pitches: 60

Milton of Fonab Caravan Park ►►►►
Bridge Road, Pitlochry
PH16 5NA
Tel: 01796 472882 **123 N2**
fonab.co.uk
Total pitches: 154

Mount View Caravan Park ►►►
Abington,
South Lanarkshire
ML12 6RW
Tel: 01864 502808 **106 B5**
borderleisureparks.co.uk/mount-view
Total pitches: 42

Ryan Bay Caravan Park ►►►
Innermessan,
Stranraer
DG9 8QP
Tel: 01776 889458 **94 F6**
hagansleisure.co.uk/holidays/ryan-bay-
holiday-residential-park-sw-scotland
Total pitches: 30

Sands of Luce Holiday Park ►►►►►
Sands of Luce, Sandhead,
Stranraer
DG9 9JN
Tel: 01776 830456 **94 G8**
sandsofluce.com
Total pitches: 80

Sandyhills Bay Holiday Park ►►►►
Sandyhills, Dalbeattie
DG5 4NY
Tel: 01557 870267 **96 H7**
gillespie-leisure.co.uk
Total pitches: 24

Seal Shore Camping and Touring Site ►►►►
Kildonan,
Isle of Arran,
North Ayrshire
KA27 8SE
Tel: 01770 820320 **103 Q5**
campingarran.com
Total pitches: 43

Seaward Holiday Park ►►►►►
Dhoon Bay,
Kirkudbright
DG6 4TJ
Tel: 01557 870267 **96 D8**
gillespie-leisure.co.uk
Total pitches: 25

Seton Sands Holiday Village ►►►►►
Longniddry
EH32 0QF
Tel: 01875 813333 **116 A6**
haven.com/setonsands
Total pitches: 40

Shieling Holidays Mull ►►►►
Craignure, Isle of Mull,
Argyll & Bute
PA65 6AY
Tel: 01680 812496 **120 D5**
shielingholidays.co.uk
Total pitches: 90

Staffin C & C ►►►
Staffin,
Isle of Skye
IV51 9JX
Tel: 01470 562213 **135 J2**
staffincampsite.co.uk
Total pitches: 50

The Paddocks Motorhome Site ►►►►►
Old Greenock Road, Bishopton
PA7 5PA
Tel: 01505 864 333 **113 N7**
ingliston.com
Total pitches: 30

Thirlestane Castle C & C Site ►►►
Thirlestane Castle, Lauder
TD2 6RU
Tel: 01578 718884 **116 C11**
thirlestanecastlepark.co.uk
Total pitches: 60

Thurston Manor Leisure Park ►►►►►
Innerwick, Dunbar
EH42 1SA
Tel: 01368 840643 **116 G6**
thurstonmanor.co.uk
Total pitches: 120

Turriff Caravan Park ►►►►
Station Road, Turriff
AB53 4ER
Tel: 01888 562205 **140 H6**
turriffcaravanpark.com
Total pitches: 70

Twenty Shilling Wood Caravan Park ►►►
Comrie, Perth & Kinross
PH6 2JY
Tel: 01764 670411 **123 J8**
twentyshillingwoodcaravanpark.co.uk
Total pitches: 14

Witches Craig C & C Park ►►►►
Blairlogie, Stirling
FK9 5PX
Tel: 01786 474947 **114 E2**
witchescraig.co.uk
Total pitches: 60

WALES

Abererch Sands Holiday Centre ►►►
Pwllheli
LL53 6PJ
Tel: 01758 612327 **60 F5**
abererch-sands.co.uk
Total pitches: 70

Aeron Coast Caravan Park ►►►►
North Road, Aberaeron
SA46 0JF
Tel: 01545 570349 **48 H8**
aeroncoast.co.uk
Total pitches: 100

Afon Teifi C & C Park ►►►►
Pentrecagal, Newcastle Emlyn
SA38 9HT
Tel: 01559 370532 **37 Q2**
afonteifi.co.uk
Total pitches: 110

Anchorage Caravan Park ►►►►
Bronllys, Brecon
LD3 0LD
Tel: 01874 711246 **39 Q5**
anchoragecp.co.uk
Total pitches: 110

Bank Farm Caravan Park ►►►►
Middletown,
Welshpool
SY21 8EJ
Tel: 01938 570526 **63 J9**
bankfarmcaravans.co.uk
Total pitches: 40

Beach View Caravan Park ►►►►
Bwlchtocyn, Abersoch
LL53 7BT
Tel: 01758 712956 **60 E7**
beachviewabersoch.co.uk
Total pitches: 47

Bodnant Caravan Park ►►►►
Nebo Road, Llanrwst,
Conwy Valley
LL26 0SD
Tel: 01492 640248 **73 P11**
bodnant-caravan-park.co.uk
Total pitches: 54

Bridge Caravan Park & Camping Site ►►►►
Dingestow
NP25 4DY
Tel: 01600 740241 **40 F9**
bridgecaravanpark.co.uk/site/
getting-here.html
Total pitches: 94

Bron Derw Touring Caravan Park ►►►►►
Llanrwst
LL26 0YT
Tel: 01492 640494 **73 N11**
bronderw-wales.co.uk
Total pitches: 48

Bryn Bach C & C Site ►►►►
Bwlchtocyn,
Abersoch
LL53 7BT
Tel: 07391 561160 **60 E7**
abersochcamping.co.uk
Total pitches: 47

Caerfai Bay Caravan & Tent Park ►►►►►
Caerfai Bay, St Davids, Haverfordwest
SA62 6QT
Tel: 01437 720274 **36 E6**
caerfaibay.co.uk
Total pitches: 106

Cenarth Falls Resort Limited ►►►►►
Cenarth,
Newcastle Emlyn
SA38 9JS
Tel: 01239 710345 **37 P2**
cenarth-holipark.co.uk
Total pitches: 30

Commonwood Leisure ►►►►
Buck Road, Holt,
Wrexham
LL13 9TF
Tel: 01978 664547 **63 L2**
commonwoodleisure.com/cabins-tents
Total pitches: 5

Daisy Bank Caravan Park ►►►►►
Snead, Montgomery
SY15 6EB
Tel: 01588 620471 **51 J2**
daisy-bank.co.uk
Total pitches: 64

Deucoch Touring & Camping Park ►►►►
Sarn Bach, Abersoch
LL53 7LD
Tel: 01758 713293 **60 E7**
deucoch.com
Total pitches: 70

Dinlle Caravan Park ►►►►►
Dinas Dinlle,
Caernarfon
LL54 5TW
Tel: 01286 830324 **72 G12**
thornleyleisure.co.uk
Total pitches: 175

Disserth C & C Park ►►►►
Disserth, Howey,
Llandrindod Wells
LD16NL
Tel: 01597 860277 **50 E9**
disserth.biz
Total pitches: 25

Eisteddfa ►►►►
Eisteddfa Lodge, Pentrefelin,
Criccieth
LL52 0PT
Tel: 01766 522696 **60 H4**
eisteddfapark.co.uk
Total pitches: 100

Fforest Fields C & C Park ►►►►►
Hundred House,
Builth Wells
LD1 5RT
Tel: 01982 570406 **50 F10**
fforestfields.co.uk
Total pitches: 120

Fishguard Bay Resort ►►►►
Garn Gelli, Fishguard
SA65 9ET
Tel: 01348 811415 **37 J3**
fishguardbay.com
Total pitches: 50

Greenacres Holiday Park ►►►►►
Black Rock Sands,
Morfa Bychan,
Porthmadog
LL49 9YF
Tel: 01766 512781 **61 J5**
haven.com/greenacres
Total pitches: 39

Hafan y Môr Holiday Park ►►►►►
Pwllheli
LL53 6HJ
Tel: 01758 612112 **60 G5**
haven.com/hafanymor
Total pitches: 75

Haulfryn Caravan Park ►►►►
Babell Road, Babell,
Holywell
CH8 8PW
Tel: 07986 435564 **74 G8**
haulfryncaravanpark.co.uk
Total pitches: 29

Hendre Mynach Touring C & C Park ►►►►►
Llanaber Road,
Barmouth
LL42 1YR
Tel: 01341 280262 **61 K9**
hendremynach.co.uk
Total pitches: 240

Home Farm Caravan Park ►►►►►
Marian-glas,
Isle of Anglesey
LL73 8PH
Tel: 01248 410614 **72 H7**
homefarm-anglesey.co.uk
Total pitches: 102

Hunters Hamlet Caravan Park ►►►►
Betws-yn-Rhos,
Abergele
LL22 8PL
Tel: 01745 832237 **74 C9**
huntershamlet.co.uk
Total pitches: 30

Islawrffordd Caravan Park ►►►►►
Talybont,
Barmouth
LL43 2AQ
Tel: 01341 247269 **61 K8**
islawrffordd.co.uk
Total pitches: 105

Kiln Park Holiday Centre ►►►►►
Marsh Road, Tenby
SA70 8RB
Tel: 01834 844121 **37 M10**
haven.com/kilnpark
Total pitches: 146

Lakeside Caravan Park ►►►►
LLangorse, Brecon
LD3 7TR
Tel: 01874 658226 **39 Q6**
llangorselake.co.uk
Total pitches: 40

Llandovery Caravan Park ►►►
Church Bank,
Llandovery
SA20 0DT
Tel: 01550 721065 **38 H5**
llandovery-caravan-camping-park.co.uk
Total pitches: 20

Llwyn-Bugeilydd C & C Site ►►►
Criccieth
LL52 0PN
Tel: 01766 522235 **60 H4**
snowdoniacaravanpark.co.uk
Total pitches: 40

Llys Derwen C & C Site ►►►►
Ffordd Bryngwyn, Llanrug,
Caernarfon
LL55 4RD
Tel: 01286 673322 **73 J11**
llysderwen.co.uk
Total pitches: 20

Nolton Cross Caravan Park ►►►
Nolton,
Haverfordwest
SA62 3NP
Tel: 01437 710701 **36 G7**
noltoncross-holidays.co.uk
Total pitches: 15

Pencelli Castle C & C Park ►►►►►
Pencelli, Brecon
LD3 7LX
Tel: 01874 665451 **39 Q7**
pencelli-castle.com
Total pitches: 80

Penisar Mynydd Caravan Park ►►►►
Caerwys Road, Rhuallt, St Asaph
LL17 0TY
Tel: 01745 582227 **74 F8**
penisarmynydd.co.uk
Total pitches: 71

Pitton Cross C & C Park ►►►
Pitton, Rhossili, Swansea
SA3 1PT
Tel: 01792 390593 **26 C5**
pittoncross.co.uk
Total pitches: 50

Plas Gwyn C & C Park ►►►►
Llanrug, Caernarfon
LL55 2AQ
Tel: 01286 672619 **73 J11**
plasgwyn.co.uk
Total pitches: 42

Plassey Holiday Park ►►►►►
The Plassey, Eyton,
Wrexham
LL13 0SP
Tel: 01978 780277 **63 K3**
plassey.com
Total pitches: 90

Pont Kemys C & C Park ►►►►►
Chainbridge, Abergavenny
NP7 9DS
Tel: 01873 880688 **40 E10**
pontkemys.com
Total pitches: 65

Presthaven Beach Holiday Park ►►►►►
Gronant, Prestatyn
LL19 9TT
Tel: 01745 856471 **74 F7**
haven.com/presthaven
Total pitches: 50

Red Kite Touring and Lodge Park ►►►►►
Van Road,
Llanidloes
SY18 6NG
Tel: 01686 412122 **50 C4**
redkitetouringpark.co.uk
Total pitches: 66

Rhydolion ►►►
Llangian, Abersoch
LL53 7LR
Tel: 01758 712342 **60 D6**
rhydolion.co.uk/caravan_camping.htm
Total pitches: 28

Riverside Camping ►►►►
Seiont Nurseries, Pont Rug,
Caernarfon
LL55 2BB
Tel: 01286 678781 **72 H11**
riversidecamping.co.uk
Total pitches: 73

Riverside C & C Park ►►►►
New Road, Crickhowell,
Powys
NP8 1AY
Tel: 01873 810397 **40 B8**
riversidecaravanscrickhowell.co.uk
Total pitches: 35

Riverside Caravan Park ►►►►
Ynys Forgan Farm,
Morriston, Swansea
SA6 6QL
Tel: 01792 775587 **26 G2**
riversideswansea.com
Total pitches: 90

Skysea C & C Park ►►►►
Port Eynon, Gower,
Swansea
SA3 1NL
Tel: 01792 390795 **26 C5**
porteynon.com
Total pitches: 150

The Trotting Mare Caravan Park ►►►►►
Overton,
Wrexham
LL13 0LE
Tel: 01978 711963 **63 L4**
thetrottingmare.co.uk
Total pitches: 54

Trawsdir Touring C & C Park ►►►►
Llanaber,
Barmouth
LL42 1RR
Tel: 01341 280999 **61 K8**
barmouthholidays.co.uk
Total pitches: 70

Tretio C & C Park ►►►
St Davids,
Pembrokeshire
SA62 6DE
Tel: 01437 781600 **36 F5**
tretio.com
Total pitches: 40

Tyddyn Isaf Caravan Park ►►►►►
Lligwy Bay, Dulas,
Isle of Anglesey
LL70 9PQ
Tel: 01248 410203 **72 H6**
tyddynisaf.co.uk
Total pitches: 80

Tyn Cornel Camping ►►►
Frongoch, Bala
LL23 7NU
Tel: 07859 431630 **62 B4**
tyncornelcamping.co.uk
Total pitches: 37

Ty'n Rhos Caravan Park ►►►
Lligwy Bay, Moelfre,
Rhos Lligwy,
Isle of Anglesey
LL72 8NL
Tel: 01248 852417 **72 H6**
bodafonpark.co.uk
Total pitches: 30

Well Park C & C Site ►►►►
New Hedges, Tenby
SA70 8TL
Tel: 01834 842179 **37 M10**
wellparkcaravans.co.uk
Total pitches: 100

Wernddu Caravan Park ►►►►
Old Ross Road,
Abergavenny
NP7 8NG
Tel: 01873 856223 **40 D8**
wernddu-golf-club.co.uk
Total pitches: 70

White Tower Holiday Park ►►►►
Llandwrog,
Caernarfon
LL54 5UH
Tel: 01286 830649 **72 G12**
whitetowerpark.co.uk
Total pitches: 52

Ynysymaengwyn Caravan Park ►►►►
Tywyn,
Gwynedd
LL36 9RY
Tel: 01654 710684 **61 K11**
ynysy.co.uk
Total pitches: 80

CHANNEL ISLANDS

La Bailloterie Camping ►►►►
Bailloterie Lane, Vale, Guernsey
GY3 5HA
Tel: 01481 243636 **12 c1**
campinginguernsey.com
Total pitches: 100

Le Vaugrat Camp Site ►►►
Route de Vaugrat, St Sampson,
Guernsey
GY2 4TA
Tel: 01481 257468 **12 c1**
vaugratcampsite.com
Total pitches: 150

CARAVAN AND MOTORHOME TOURING ROUTES

ON THE ROAD: EXPLORE THE UK WITH YOUR CARAVAN OR MOTORHOME

On the following pages you will find 10 suggested tours ranging from 100 to 485 miles. Each tour takes a fascinating journey through the countryside, towns and villages of Britain.

For each tour, you will find a helpful map that summarises the route, together with directions that are broken up into handy chunks that will take you from town to town. Alongside these you will find a brief look at a town on the way, giving you ideas of what you might stop to look at.

Each tour includes a selection of AA-rated caravan parks so you can take as long as you like to make your way along the route. Every tour follows a circular route so you will return to the place you started, but you can easily end the tour at any point if you need to get home sooner.

THINGS TO NOTE

Tours can be started at any point along the route, although a suggested location has been indicated at point **1**, selected as a suitable centre for exploration. It may also be a convenient place to purchase any last-minute supplies or forgotten essentials before setting off on the tour.

Each tour has details of the most interesting places to visit en route, but there will be much more besides, depending on your interests and how much time you have. Always check opening times of any places you intend visiting to avoid disappointment and it is a good idea to check any parking restrictions if you will be towing your caravan or driving a large vehicle.

The summarised route directions are accompanied by a simple map for each tour. For easy reference, each point numbered on the map relates to the numbered stage in the directions. Highlighted places to visit are shown on the map together with any suggested caravan parks – which are listed in the highlighted panel.

It is recommended that you plan ahead, especially in peak season, and book a place to stay in advance. The full contact details of all the parks included here can be found in the AA-listings on pages VII-XIII.

Driving is one of the best ways to explore Britain. The routes in this section have been designed to maximise the enjoyment of discovering some of the country's prettiest scenery and famous sights. Roads are generally good but can be busy.
For a more pleasurable and relaxing trip, aim to travel outside peak times and avoid rush hours if possible.

	CAR TOUR	ROUTE START	DISTANCE (MILES)	PAGE NUMBER
1	West Cornwall	Penzance	150	XV
2	Exmoor and North Devon	Lynton	100	XVI
3	West Wessex	Salisbury	134	XVII
4	Wales	Tenby	485	XVIII–XIX
5	East Anglia circuit	Cambridge	288	XX–XXI
6	The Cotswolds	Chipping Norton	236	XXII
7	North York Moors	York	105	XXIII
8	The Yorkshire Dales	Ripon	152	XXIV
9	The Heart of Lakeland	Carlisle	176	XXV
10	The Western Highlands	Dumbarton	240	XXVI

WEST CORNWALL

An inspiration to writers, poets and artists for centuries, west Cornwall is a land of dramatic coasts, sandy beaches, ancient communities and romantic windswept moors. This route starts within sight of St Michael's Mount and will take you to England's most westerly point, a home for rescued seals, and past many relics of the region's historic mining industry.

START / END Penzance
VIA St Ives, Falmouth, Lizard and Marazion
DISTANCE 150 miles (241 km)
SUGGESTED TIME 3 days

1 PENZANCE - A popular holiday spot since the 19th century, Penzance is all sunshine and stunning sunrises over Mount's Bay and St Michael's Mount.

> Head west out of town to Newlyn, continue south on the B3315 towards Porthcurno. In 6 miles (10km) turn left to continue with B3315 to Land's End

POINT OF INTEREST

LAND'S END
TR19 7AA
England's most westerly point, Land's End is 873 miles (1,405km) from John o'Groats. On a fine day, see the Isles of Scilly, Wolf Rock Lighthouse and the Longships Lighthouse.

> From here, head along the A30 to Sennen, and in a few miles turn left on B3306 to St Just. Continue along the coastal road B3306 to Zennor

2 ZENNOR - This grey stone village huddles around its 12th-century church in a wild, dramatic landscape, and you should be able to see seals along the coast. D H Lawrence and Virginia Woolf both lived here in the 1920s.

> Continue along B3306 to reach St Ives

3 ST IVES - Prosperous as a 19th-century pilchard port, St Ives has two sandy beaches and many excellent museums and galleries. Quaint houses and narrow streets cluster round the 15th-century church.

POINT OF INTEREST

TATE ST IVES
PORTHMEOR BEACH, ST IVES, TR26 1TG
Is an art gallery exhibiting work by modern British artists and is among the most visited attraction in the UK.

> Head out of town on the A3074 to Hayle. From Hayle, take the B3301 to Portreath and in 2 miles (3.2km) turn left to take the unclassified road to Porthtowan. Continue east to the B3277 to turn right onto the A30 then head for Truro on the A390

4 TRURO - A town dominated by a cathedral with three spires and was built on the site of a 16th-century church. The Royal Cornwall Museum in River Street is considered the finest in the county.

> In 5 miles (8km) turn right on A3078 to St Mawes

5 ST MAWES - Home to St Mawes Castle, built by Henry VIII in the 1540s to guard the mouth of the estuary. Trelissick Garden, north of town, has a collection of exotic plants from all over the world.

> Head back out of St Mawes, then turn left on the B3289 to King Harry Ferry. In 1 mile (1.6km) turn right to continue with B3289. At the junction with the A39 turn left, then shortly take another left onto the B3292 into Penryn. Continue to follow signs into Falmouth towards Falmouth Harbour

6 FALMOUTH - One of the finest natural harbours in the world, with beaches to the south of the town, docks and 18th- and 19th-century buildings. Pendennis Castle guards the harbour entrance.

> Continue westwards along the coast on unclassified roads through villages Mawnan Smith and Constantine to reach Gweek

7 GWEEK - This lovely little stone village is better known for its seal sanctuary. Meet resident grey seals and see where other rescued seals are cared for and rehabilitated. The underwater viewing areas provide an incredible close-up experience.

> Head south along unclassified roads. In 2 miles (3.2km) turn left on the B3293 onto Goonhilly Downs. In 3 miles (4.8km) turn right onto the unclassified road to Ruan Minor and Cadgwith. Follow signs down to The Lizard

8 LIZARD POINT is the southernmost point in England with dramatic 180-foot (55m) cliffs and a lighthouse.

> Return on the A3083 for 3.7 miles (6km) to Mullion. Head to Poldhu Cove, then back to the A3083. From Helston visit Porthleven along the B3304 then carry onto the A394. Head west to Marazion

9 MARAZION - Famous for St Michael's Mount, the granite island located offshore, but also a fascinating place in its own right, with its bustling village and sandy beach. There are opportunities for great surfing and a variety of other water sports.

> Continue west back to Penzance

CAMPSITES EN ROUTE

▶▶▶▶▶ **AYR HOLIDAY PARK**
ST IVES, CORNWALL
A well-established park on a cliff side overlooking St Ives Bay. There are stunning views from most pitches, and the town centre, harbour and beach are only half a mile away.

▶▶▶▶▶ **PORTHTOWAN TOURIST PARK**
TRURO, CORNWALL
A neat, level grassy site on high ground above Porthtowan. The site has a well-stocked shop and there is a purpose-built games and meeting room.

▶▶▶ **SILVER SANDS HOLIDAY PARK**
KENNACK SANDS, HELSTON, CORNWALL
A small, family-owned park in a remote location. A footpath through the woods leads to the beach and the local pub, less than a mile away.

▶▶▶▶▶ **TRETHEM MILL TOURING PARK**
TRURO, CORNWALL
This top-notch, adults-only park is a tranquil haven tucked away in a lovely rural setting. Immaculately maintained park with good amenities. A pizza van visits once a week.

▶▶▶▶▶ **TREVALGAN TOURING PARK**
ST IVES, CORNWALL
A luxury, family camping and touring park with stunning coastal and countryside views. The park is surrounded by open farmland, with gorse and heather-covered hills behind.

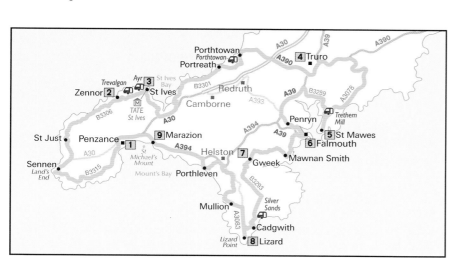

02

EXMOOR AND NORTH DEVON

Bright bays, steep coasts, low coastlines, lonely moorland and charming stone villages combine to make this a memorable tour. Starting out from Devon's northern coast, you'll pass by one of England's smallest churches, through villages full of fascinating historic buildings, and across the splendid expanse of Exmoor, once an ancient royal hunting forest.

START / END Lynton
VIA Porlock, Barnstaple and Mortehoe
DISTANCE 100 miles (161 km)
SUGGESTED TIME 3 days

1 LYNTON - Paired with Lynmouth, Lynton is 500ft (150m) above it, joined by a zig-zag path and a cliff railway of 1890. Lynton was just a hamlet which became a Victorian resort, and features many Victorian and Edwardian buildings as well as a very fanciful town hall that dates to 1900. The Lynton and Exmouth Museum is here, and the Valley of the Rocks, to the west, has very romantic scenery.

POINT OF INTEREST

THE VALLEY OF ROCKS
EX35 6JH
To the west of Lynton is the Valley of Rocks, a dry river valley that is thought to be the remains of part of the East Lyn river. The area is well known for its goats, geology and incredible views of the Bristol Channel from some of the highest sea cliffs in England. Wonderful for some breath-taking walks, in both sense of the term.

> From Lynton take the B3234, dropping very steeply down into Lynmouth

2 LYNMOUTH - Set at the confluence of the East and West Lyn rivers. The River Lyn is very strongly embanked now and on leaving the town you will see the gorge down which the flood water came with such devastation in 1952. The poet Shelley lived in Lynmouth for a time.

> Take the A39 to Porlock

3 PORLOCK - Once down the notorious steep hill, and a descent of 1,350 feet (411m), pause to admire Porlock Weir, a small village of thatched cottages fringing a tiny harbour. Culbone Church is possibly the smallest surviving medieval church in England, and can only be reached on foot. Just off the A39 is Selworthy. Much of this pretty village is owned by the National Trust.

> Continue past Minehead, then turn right into Dunster village (care required) onto the A396, then on to Wheddon Cross. Turn right onto B3224 and continue to Simonsbath

4 SIMONSBATH - Situated 1,100 feet (335m) above sea-level, Simonsbath is one of the highest villages in Exmoor, in the centre of what used to be the Royal Exmoor Forest. Climb steeply out of the small village and on to the moors.

> Turn left onto unclassified roads towards South Molton. In 8 miles (13km) turn left onto A399, then at the roundabout turn right onto A361 to Barnstaple

5 BARNSTAPLE - One of North Devon's major market towns, this was once a busy ship-building town, but the River Taw became too silted in the 19th century. There are many fine examples of Georgian architecture. Queen Anne's Walk is a pleasant colonnade, and you can still see the Tome Stone, where merchants used to set their money to make their contracts binding. The Museum of Barnstaple and North Devon is here, at The Square. The fine long bridge over the River Taw has 16 arches and dates from the 13th century.

> Continue on the A361 towards Ilfracombe. At Braunton, take the B3231 to Croyde. Follow unclassified roads through Georgeham to Woolacombe. Turn left to Mortehoe

6 MORTEHOE - With a long history of farming, as well as some time as a base for smugglers and wreckers, this charming small town has a little Norman church, with a tower dating from around 1270. In a sheltered position just inland from Morte Point, it was probably founded in 1170 by Sir William de Tracey, and it may be his tomb that lies in the south transept. The church is dark, pretty and simple. There is some glorious stained glass, and a superb mosaic chancel arch, completed in 1905.

> Head east to pick up the B3343. Carry on ahead at roundabout to join A3123. Turn left onto B3230 into Ilfracombe. Head east along A399 towards Kentisbury, then turn left onto unclassified roads to pass Hunter's Inn. Continue to reach A39, then turn left back to Lynton

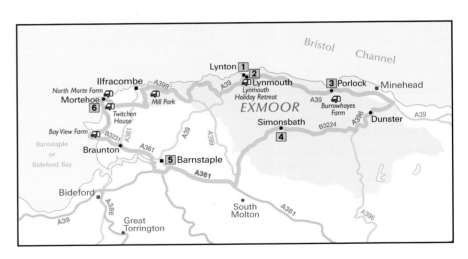

CAMPSITES EN ROUTE

▶▶▶▶ **BAY VIEW FARM CARAVAN & CAMPING PARK**
CROYDE, DEVON
A popular park close to surfing beaches and rock pools, with a public footpath leading directly to the sea. Set in a stunning location with views out over the Atlantic to Lundy Island.

▶▶▶▶ **BURROWHAYES FARM CARAVAN & CAMPING SITE & RIDING STABLES**
PORLOCK, SOMERSET
A delightful site on the edge of Exmoor that slopes gently down to Horner Water. From the riding stables escorted rides can be taken onto the moors.

▶▶▶▶ **LYNMOUTH HOLIDAY RETREAT**
LYNTON, DEVON
Set on the clifftop, this is a well-maintained park on the edge of Exmoor. Pitches can be selected from those in a hidden hedged area or those with panoramic views over the coast.

▶▶▶▶▶ **MILL PARK TOURING CARAVAN & CAMPING PARK**
BERRYNARBOR, DEVON
Attractive park set in a wooded valley with a stream that runs into a lake where coarse fishing is available. Family room, camping meadow, and excellent children's play area.

▶▶▶▶▶ **NORTH MORTE FARM CARAVAN & CAMPING PARK**
MORTEHOE, DEVON
Set in spectacular coastal countryside close to National Trust land and 500 yards from Rockham Beach. This attractive park is very well run by friendly family owners.

▶▶▶▶▶ **TWITCHEN HOUSE HOLIDAY VILLAGE**
WOOLACOMBE, DEVON
An attractive park with excellent leisure facilities, all-weather activities and entertainment. The touring area pitches have either sea views or a woodland countryside outlook.

WEST WESSEX

Starting from an ancient cathedral city on the banks of the Avon, you'll cross a region steeped in history and mystery, as well as stunning natural architecture. Stonehenge may be the best known of England's man-made landmarks, but it's overshadowed by the majesty of the mighty Cheddar Gorge. Other major sights include mystical Glastonbury Tor, and Wells, England's smallest city.

START / END Salisbury
VIA Wells, Glastonbury and Shaftesbury
DISTANCE 134 miles (216 km)
SUGGESTED TIME 2–3 days

1 SALISBURY - Built beside the River Avon, with an ornate 13th-century cathedral, Salisbury has many streets named after the goods once sold here — Fish Row, Butchers Row, and so on. Highlights include the 16th-century façade of Joiner's Hall on St Ann Street and the 18th-century Guildhall.

> Head north on the A345, then take the first left onto unclassified roads for the Woodfords. In 5 miles (8km) reach Amesbury. Head west signed Honiton, then right onto the A360 to Stonehenge

POINT OF INTEREST
STONEHENGE
At Stonehenge huge stones 15 to 20 feet (4.5 to 6m) high have been the subject of enormous speculation. Was it a temple for Romans or Druids? How were 26-ton stones brought here? One thing is certain — the axis is aligned with the mid-winter and midsummer sun; perhaps this revered monument is a giant calendar.

> Continue on the A360 north and turn left onto the B390 just past Shrewton. On reaching the A36 turn right, then right again after 1 mile (1.6km) onto the B3414 to Warminster. Take the A350 to Westbury and then the A3098 for 7 miles (11km) to Frome

2 FROME - This attractive old market town has steep narrow streets scattered with medieval and Tudor buildings. Look for Cheap Street with its ancient shops, the 1726 Blue House, St John's Church, and the bridge over the Frome, one of only three English bridges to have buildings on it.

> From Frome, pick-up the A361 to Shepton Mallet and then take the A371 to Wells

3 WELLS - England's smallest city, Wells gets its name from the springs that bubble into a pool in the bishop's garden. The cathedral was begun in the 12th century and finished in the 15th, and its astronomical clock in the north transept is one of the oldest in Britain.

> Leave Wells on the A371 to Cheddar

4 CHEDDAR - The cliffs of Cheddar Gorge tower to a height of 450 feet (137m) above the village. Near the bottom, climb Jacob's Ladder for the best views and visit caves where you can search for the River Yeo. If it's cheese you're after, there's a replica 1920s factory that shows how it was made.

> Leave Cheddar on the B3151 to Glastonbury

5 GLASTONBURY - The abbey was sacked in the 16th century. Joseph of Arimathea is said to have come here in AD 63, and legend has it that the wooden staff he pushed into the ground turned into a thorn bush. The town also has connections to King Arthur and the Holy Grail.

> Leave Glastonbury on the A361 and in 7 miles (12km) turn left onto the A37, then right onto the A371 signposted Castle Cary. Shortly, fork left onto the B3081 to Bruton and then on to Redlynch. At the crossroads turn left towards Stourhead. In 3 miles (5km) turn right, and shortly right again to join the B3092, continuing towards Stourhead and then Mere. Pass under the A303 and turn right onto the B3092 to Gillingham, then to Shaftesbury via the B3081

6 SHAFTESBURY - On a hill 700 feet (213m) above sea-level, Shaftesbury commands marvellous views across Dorset's Blackmoor Vale. The town is best known for Gold Hill, a steep, beautifully preserved cobbled street.

> Leave Shaftesbury on the A30, signposted Salisbury. In 14 miles (23km) in Barford St Martin bear right to continue on A30 to Wilton

7 WILTON - Once the capital of Wessex, it's now well known for 16th-century Wilton House, which contains an amazing art collection including Rubens, Van Dyck and Tintoretto.

> Take the A36 for 4 miles (6.5km) to return to Salisbury

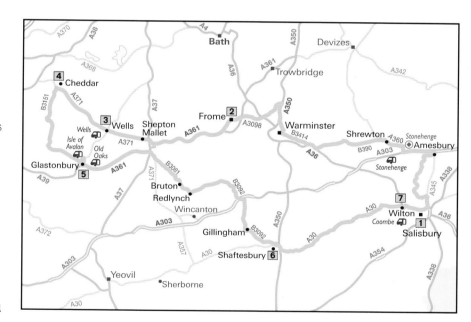

CAMPSITES EN ROUTE

▶▶▶▶▶ **COOMBE TOURING PARK**
SALISBURY, WILTSHIRE

An attractive site adjacent to the racecourse with views over the downs. A lovely park, offering real peace and quiet, with a fully-equipped function room and kitchen.

▶▶▶▶ **ISLE OF AVALON TOURING CARAVAN PARK**
GLASTONBURY, SOMERSET

A popular site, on the south side of this historic town, within easy walking distance of the centre. It is a level park, with a separate tent field, that provides a quiet environment.

▶▶▶▶▶ **OLD OAKS TOURING & GLAMPING**
GLASTONBURY, SOMERSET

An exceptional, adults-only park in well maintained grounds. The perfect 'get away from it all' spot where you can enjoy walking, cycling, fishing or simply relaxing amid the wildlife.

▶▶▶▶ **STONEHENGE CAMPSITE & GLAMPING PODS**
BERWICK ST JAMES, WILTSHIRE

This small site is close to Stonehenge and Longleat; there are plenty of excellent walks from the campsite and two good pubs nearby.

▶▶▶▶▶ **WELLS TOURING PARK**
WELLS, SOMERSET

A well established, adults-only holiday park set in countryside on the outskirts of Wells, within easy walking distance of the city centre. The park has an excellent coffee shop.

WALES

Covering nearly 500 miles, this route has something for everyone. From the western edge of Carmarthen Bay, you'll drive round the dramatic Pembrokeshire coast, through ancient towns with a rich history of shipbuilding, industry and seafaring. Passing north along the edge of Cardigan Bay to the top of Wales, you then head down through lush green rolling hills and glorious countryside.

START / END Tenby
VIA St Davids, Colwyn Bay and Builth Wells
DISTANCE 485 miles (781 km)
SUGGESTED TIME 5–8 days

1 TENBY - Many have fallen in love with this town, with its beautiful old harbour, handsome Regency houses and narrow medieval streets, all hemmed in by the best-preserved town walls in south Wales.

> Leave Tenby on the A4139 and then turn left onto the B4585 to Manorbier

2 MANORBIER - Medieval traveller and scholar, Gerald of Wales (Giraldus Cambrensis), was born here in 1147 and the castle dates from his time. There are impressive sea views from the ramparts.

> Return to the A4139 for 5 miles (8km) to Lamphey. Continue along the A4139 to Pembroke

3 PEMBROKE - This ancient town was built around the great medieval fortress of Pembroke Castle, the birthplace of Henry Tudor. Beneath the castle is a huge natural cavern known as The Wogan. Nearby Pembroke Dock produced nearly 300 ships, including some of the most powerful in Queen Victoria's navy and four famous Royal Yachts. The dockyard closed suddenly in 1926, with disastrous consequences for the local workforce.

> Take the A477, then join the A4076 to Haverfordwest – 11 miles (18km)

4 HAVERFORDWEST - A ruined 12th-century castle is on the hill above town and a museum is next door at Castle House. The town is divided by the River Cleddau.

> Head northwest along the A487 to Solva

5 SOLVA - Solva's old port still has warehouses and a restored lime kiln and is a favourite sailing spot. Visit Solva Woollen Mill, specialising in carpets, tapestry and floor rugs; it's one of only two remaining woollen mills in Pembrokeshire – in 1900 there were 26.

> Keep on along the A487 for 3 miles (5km) to St Davids

6 ST DAVIDS - The smallest city in Britain was founded on the site of an early Christian community, and is dominated by the cathedral and the graceful, medieval Bishop's Palace. Sea-based activities include whale and dolphin watching.

> Turn northeastwards, still on the A487 to Mathry

7 MATHRY - This little village overlooks the Western Cleddau source stream. 33 dolerite stones taken from the Preseli Hills were used to build Stonehenge.

> Continue along the A487 to Fishguard

8 FISHGUARD - Upper Fishguard stands back from the sea, and from it the road falls steeply to Lower Fishguard, a quaint and largely unspoiled fishing town. The July Fishguard Music Festival is a major attraction. Tregwynt Woollen Mill, at St Nicholas, is open to the public, and produces traditional Welsh weaves.

> Head east to Newport, still travelling on the A487

9 NEWPORT - Robert Owen, the 18th-century founder of the Cooperative movement and so-called father of socialism, was born here in 1771 and, at the tender age of 10, began work in the town's flourishing textiles industry. He went on to run and own some of the largest textile factories in Britain. His former house is now a museum and there are several statues of him around town. The remains of Newport's 12th-century castle can still be seen at a distance. Just west of town is Cerrig y Gof, a group of burial chambers.

> Continue along the A487 to Cardigan

10 CARDIGAN - One of Cardigan's most striking features is the ancient bridge, which spans the River Teifi, but little now remains of Cardigan Castle, where the first National Eisteddfod took place in 1176. Visit the Welsh Wildlife Centre, and the National Coracle Centre and Mill at Cenarth, a few miles along the A484.

> Continue for 38 miles (61km) to Aberystwyth, along the A487

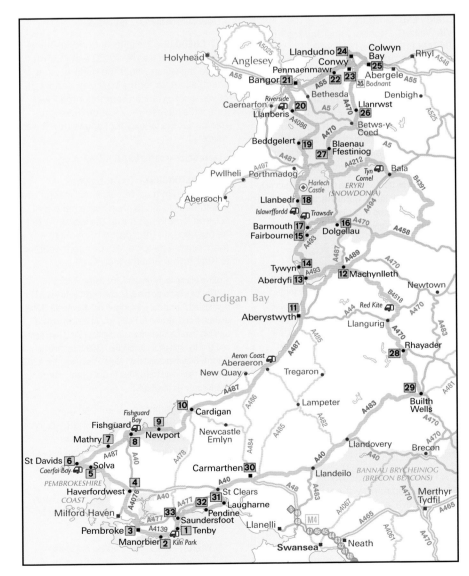

11 ABERYSTWYTH - Once known as the 'Biarritz of Wales', this seaside town is a lively university town. It's also the retail hub for many local villages between the mountains and the sea. Known to locals as 'Aber', it's located near to where the rivers Ystwyth and Rheidol join and has a largely Welsh-speaking population.

> Head inland along the B4353, then turn left onto the A487 at Tre'r-ddol and follow it through to Machynlleth

12 MACHYNLLETH - On the way to Machynlleth, visit the village of Furnace. The large barn-like building beside the A487 is an historic metal smelting site, dating from the 17th century when silver refining took place here. The waterwheel has been restored and you can see the magnificent waterfall that once supplied its power. Machynlleth itself gained fame in the 15th century as the seat of Owain Glyndŵr's short-lived Welsh parliament. The Centre for Alternative Technology, to the north of the town, has working examples of renewable energy, beautiful organic gardens, experimental green buildings and sustainably managed woodland habitats.

> Head west, along the A493 to Aberdyfi

13 ABERDYFI - Sailing boats have replaced the cargo ships that once traded at this harbour on the zDyfi Estuary. There's a fine sandy beach, and you can take a ferry trip across to Ynyslas, with its expansive sand dunes and marshland.

> Drive along the A493 for 5 miles (8km) to Tywyn

14 TYWYN - Popular for surfing and sailing, this resort has miles of golden sandy beaches. St Cadfan's Church dates back to Norman times and houses St Cadfan's Stone, a 7-foot (2m) monument some 1300 years old. The inscriptions on it are thought to be the oldest known writing in Welsh.

> Take the A493 to Fairbourne

15 FAIRBOURNE - Apart from miles of sandy beaches, this town also has the Fairbourne Railway which was built in the 1890s as a horse-drawn tramway. It was later converted to steam and now runs from Fairbourne to the end of the peninsula at Barmouth Ferry. The main line Cambrian coast railway also runs through here.

> Continue along the A493 to Dolgellau

16 DOLGELLAU - Dolgellau has always been a major route centre and is still an important regional capital and market centre. Every July the town hosts a folk festival based around Eldon Square. Walking is popular, and there are strenuous walks up to the summit of Cader Idris, as well as gentle strolls.

> Join the A470 to Llanelltyd, then turn left onto the A496 to Barmouth

17 BARMOUTH - In summer, dodgem cars, funfair rides and chip shops all come alive to cater for visitors — a Welsh Blackpool in miniature, if you like (though without the rollercoasters).

> From Barmouth follow the A496 north to Llanbedr

18 LLANBEDR - At Llanfair, just to the north of Llanbedr, are the slate caverns, where you can walk through the old workings and see the 'Cathedral cavern'.

> Continue along the A496 to Harlech

POINT OF INTEREST
HARLECH CASTLE
LL46 2YH
Harlech Castle is truly a magnificently sited castle, looking out over Cardigan Bay. It was built in the 13th century by Edward I to subdue the Welsh but was captured by Owain Glyndŵr in 1404. Now it's a UNESCO World Heritage Site.

> Head north on the A496 through Talsarnau, then left towards Porthmadog (A487) and across a road bridge to Penrhyndeudraeth. Take the A4085 for 7 miles (11km) to Beddgelert

19 BEDDGELERT - The grave of Gelert is a sad memorial. According to legend, Gelert was a faithful wolfhound killed by Prince Llywelyn, who thought it had killed his son, when in fact the dog had saved him from a wolf. Just outside town is the Sygun Copper Mine, where you can explore the 19th-century mine which was once one of the world's major copper producers.

> Turn right onto the A498, then take the A4086 to Llanberis

20 LLANBERIS - At Llanberis you can take a 60-minute trip in a narrow-gauge train along the shores of Llyn Padarn, in the Padarn Country Park. The famed modern pump storage hydro scheme is close by at Dinorwig, Dolbadarn Castle is in the town, and less than a mile (1.6km) from the High Street is Ceunant Mawr, one of the most impressive waterfalls in Wales. The most popular footpath up Snowdon (Yr Wyddfa) starts here, as does the Snowdon Mountain Railway, the only public rack-and-pinion railway, which climbs 3,000 feet (915m) to the summit in less than 5 miles (8km).

> Take the A4244, then B4547 to follow signs to Bangor

21 BANGOR - One of the smallest cities in Britain. Bangor is known for its university. in term time, its population of 12,000 swells with around 10,000 students. Gwynedd Museum and Art Gallery can be found in town, and contains many culturally important artefacts and modern exhibitions.

> Head east on the A55, towards Llandudno

22 PENMAENMAWR - Llanfairfechan has a sandy beach and beautiful inland scenery, while further along Penmaenmawr has one of the finest beaches in North Wales, stretching between two granite headlands. The village of Aber was once the location of the palace of the Welsh king, Llywelyn the Great.

23 CONWY - Conwy's castle dominates the town, and the ancient city still has its complete medieval walls. There are three remarkable bridges crossing the river, including the Conwy Suspension Bridge, designed and built by Thomas Telford in 1826 and renovated in 1990. The smallest house in Britain, a mere 6 feet (2m) wide and 10 feet (3m) high, stands on the quay.

24 LLANDUDNO - St Tudno gave his name to the town in the 5th century, and a church still stands on the site of his cell. The town is the largest holiday resort in Wales, with two excellent sandy beaches situated between the headlands of Great Orme and Little Orme. The Great Orme Summit Complex can be reached on the Great Orme Tramway, which has been taking passengers up to the top of the 679-foot (207m) summit since 1902. The energetic can enjoy the artificial ski slope and the 2,300-foot (700m) toboggan run. The sights and sounds of civilian life in 1940s Britain are captured in the Home Front Experience.

> Head out on the B5115 to Colwyn Bay

25 COLWYN BAY - This lively seaside town grew in the late 19th century thanks to the railway, and the pier, promenade and many hotels and shops date from this period. The Welsh Mountain Zoo has chimpanzees, birds of prey, a sea lion display and jungle adventure land.

> Follow signs towards Llanrwst to join the A470

POINT OF INTEREST
BODNANT GARDEN
BODNANT RD, TAL-Y-CAFN, COLWYN BAY LL28 5RE
The 80-acre (32-hectare) garden at Bodnant is claimed to be one of the finest gardens in the world. Now owned by the National Trust, it offers visitors much of interest, with native and exotic trees and flowers, and there is a nursery where plants are propagated.

26 LLANRWST - This historic market town is set in a delightful landscape of hills, forests, rivers and lakes. The bridge was designed by Inigo Jones in 1636. At the Trefriw Woollen Mills, you can see bedspreads and tweeds being manufactured, using electricity generated from the River Crafnant.

> Continue heading south on the A470

CAMPSITES EN ROUTE

▶▶▶ **AERON COAST CARAVAN PARK**
ABERAERON, CEREDIGION
A well-managed family park, with direct access to the beach. On-site facilities include an extensive outdoor pool complex and a multi-activity outdoor sports area.

▶▶▶▶▶ **CAERFAI BAY CARAVAN & TENT PARK**
ST DAVIDS, PEMBROKESHIRE
Magnificent coastal scenery and an outlook over St Bride's Bay can be enjoyed from this delightful site, which is located just 300 yards from the bathing beach at Caerfai Bay.

▶▶▶▶ **FISHGUARD BAY RESORT**
FISHGUARD, PEMBROKESHIRE
Set high up on cliffs with outstanding views of the Bay, this site has the Pembrokeshire Coastal Path running right through its centre, so there are some great walking opportunities.

▶▶▶▶▶ **ISLAWRFFORDD CARAVAN PARK**
TALYBONT-ON-USK, POWYS
This site has clear views of Cardigan Bay, the Llŷn Peninsula and the Snowdonia and Cader Idris mountain ranges. This is an excellent, family-run and family-friendly park.

▶▶▶▶▶ **KILN PARK HOLIDAY CENTRE**
TENBY, PEMBROKESHIRE
A large holiday complex complete with leisure and sports facilities and lots of entertainment for all the family. It's a short walk through dunes to the sandy beach.

▶▶▶▶▶ **RED KITE TOURING AND LODGE PARK**
LLANIDLOES, POWYS
This stunningly located park has been created on undulating hills and fields, which include two lakes. This is an adults-only park.

▶▶▶▶ **RIVERSIDE CAMPING**
CAERNARFON, GWYNEDD
Immaculately maintained by the owners, Riverside Camping is set in the grounds of a former garden centre, enjoying a superb location along the bank of the River Seiont.

▶▶▶▶▶ **TRAWSDIR TOURING CARAVANS & CAMPING PARK**
BARMOUTH, GWYNEDD
This quality park enjoys spectacular views toward the sea and hills. There's a children's play area and an illuminated concrete dog walk that leads directly to the nearby pub.

▶▶▶ **TYN CORNEL CAMPING**
BALA, GWYNEDD
A delightful riverside park with mountain views that is a popular base for those who enjoy kayaking and canoeing. Enthusiastic and hands-on managers deliver friendly service.

27 BLAENAU FFESTINIOG - Although demand for slate has fallen away, visitors can get first-hand experience of slate miners' working conditions at the Llechwedd Slate Caverns. The Miners' Tramway is a guided rail tour of an 1846 route, through a chain of enormous caverns first opened to the public in 1972. A modern industry was established at Tan-y-grisiau, where hydroelectricity is produced in a pumped storage scheme. The Ffestiniog Railway runs through 13 1/2 scenic miles (22km) to Porthmadog, and the more energetic can join a mountain bike trail from Trawsfynydd Holiday Village.

> Continue heading south on the A470 to Trawsfynydd, then turn left onto the A4212 to Bala, and finally the B4391, B4393, then B4395 to reach the A458 at Llangadfan. Turn right to follow signs for Machynlleth (A489). After entering Machynlleth take the left turn towards Llyn Clywedog (care required). Pick up the B4518 to Llanidloes, then head south on the A470

28 RHAYADER - An ideal centre for visiting the 'Lakeland of Wales'. The lakes are the reservoirs of the Elan Valley, which provide Birmingham with its water. This peaceful little town has had its share of excitement. The 19th-century Rebecca riots, protesting against toll gate impositions, centred around the town, and the castle was destroyed in the Civil War.

> Follow the A470 to Newbridge-on-Wye. Continue southwards on the A470 to Builth Wells

29 BUILTH WELLS - One of a string of Welsh spa towns that drew crowds of health-seeking Victorians. The castle was built in Norman times by James de San George, who was also responsible for building Harlech, Caernarfon, Beaumaris and Conwy castles.

> Head west on the A483 to LLandovery, then the A40 to Carmarthen

30 CARMARTHEN - Possibly the oldest town in Wales, and the birthplace of Merlin. The Gwili Steam Railway at Bronwydd opened in 1860, but closed in 1973 when milk traffic was transferred to road tankers. It reopened in 1978 and now goes from Bronwydd Arms to Danycoed.

> From the town head along the A40 to St Clears, then south on the A4066 to Pendine

31 LAUGHARNE - A strong influence on Dylan Thomas; the town hall, clock tower and many of the people became part of Under Milk Wood. Thomas moved into the Boathouse with his family in 1949 and along the path to it is 'The Shack', which became his workshop. The Boathouse is now a museum, and the man himself is buried in the local churchyard.

32 PENDINE - Best noted for its golden sand, on which Sir Malcolm Campbell and others made land speed record attempts. Amy Johnson took off from here in 1933 for the start of her epic transatlantic flight.

> Head out of the village on the B4314, then take unclassified roads to Saundersfoot

33 SAUNDERSFOOT - This 19th-century fishing port and coal port has become a family holiday centre with three sandy beaches, rock pools and a sheltered harbour. The village is in a sheltered valley, and there are good walks along the coast.

> Continue back to Tenby

05

EAST ANGLIA CIRCUIT

This longer route covers almost 300 miles (480km) and moves through Suffolk, Norfolk and Cambridgeshire, making the most of these county's coastlines, communities and countryside. As well as historic towns and fascinating locations, it also has its fair share of dramatic geographical features, from coastal marshes and the world-famous Norfolk Broads, to Suffolk's verdant forests.

START / END Cambridge
VIA Lowestoft, Cromer and Hunstanton
DISTANCE 288 miles (463km)
SUGGESTED TIME 3–5 days

1 CAMBRIDGE - Cambridge became famous as a seat of learning when the University was established early in the 13th century, and its elegant colleges and chapels of mellow stone give this beautiful city a stately air. But this is an important market centre and a leader in high technology industries, as well as a university city, and there are many fine buildings and riverside parklands. King's College Chapel and the Bridge of Sighs are musts for all visitors, and in summer you can punt along the River Cam, which flows around the city. No visit would be complete without seeing the Fitzwilliam Museum, with its priceless collections of porcelain, antiquities, paintings and armour.

> Head west on the A603 then take a left turn onto the unclassified road to Grantchester

2 GRANTCHESTER - Grantchester was immortalised in a poem by Rupert Brooke in 1912 about the Old Vicarage, where he lived. The village has a characteristic low church, with a small spire protruding. Since 2014 the town is also well known as the setting of a TV detective series of the same name. Although the show, based on a series of short stories by James Runcie, is set in the 1950s, Grantchester hasn't changed much over the years, so is a major location for filming. Location tours are available.

> Bear left to reach the A1309, then turn right. Shortly turn left onto the A1301 and in 7 miles (12km) reach the A11. (To divert to nearby Duxford turn off the A1301 onto the A505 west towards Royston)

3 DUXFORD - Duxford is a village with a low, squat church and attractive thatched pub, the John Barleycorn. It is famous for the Imperial War Museum at Duxford Airfield, a former Battle of Britain fighter station.

POINT OF INTEREST

IMPERIAL WAR MUSEUM DUXFORD
CB22 4QR

This remarkable museum tells the story of the impact aviation had on the nature of war, on people's lives and on the history of the region. Duxford is Britain's best-preserved World War II fighter station, and has seven impressive hangars – some with listed building status – filled with an extraordinary collection of aircraft and vehicles. Here you can see around 200 aircraft, naval vessels and military vehicles, plus sections dedicated to the Parachute Regiment and the Royal Anglian Regiment. Displays and exhibitions help tell the story of Britain at war. If you're lucky, you may catch an air show, which are a regular feature among the special events.

> Cross under the A11 and continue on the B184 for 4.5 miles (7.2km) to Saffron Walden

4 SAFFRON WALDEN - Saffron Walden's flint church rivals that of Thaxted in magnificence and size; 200 feet (61m) long and nearly as high. Its spire was added in 1831. Wool was a major industry here, but the town also prospered from growing saffron for medicine and dyes. There are delightful old narrow streets to explore, and the museum has exhibitions of furniture, ceramics and toys. Jacobean Audley End House, nearby, is in grounds landscaped by Capability Brown. Elizabeth I stayed here with the poet Sir Philip Sidney, in 1578, and the rooms have been laid out to give a 'lived in' feeling.

> Continue on the B184 for 7 miles (11.2km) to Thaxted

5 THAXTED - Thaxted's 14th-century, cathedral-like flint church is one of the largest in Essex, with a thin, graceful spire rising 181 feet (55m). Another tall building, the tower windmill, was built in 1804, and now houses a small rural museum. The 15th-century Guildhall is built of local wood and plaster, on a foundation of flint.

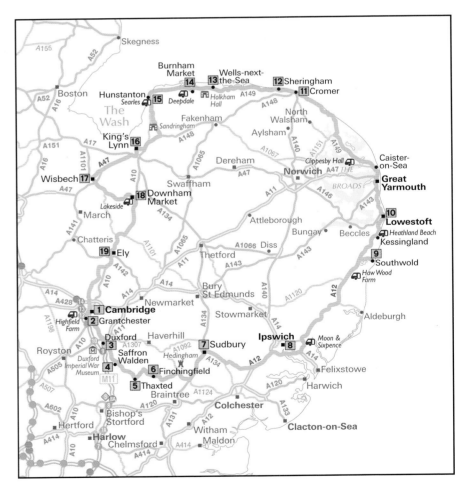

> From Thaxted return north and turn right onto the B1051 to Great Sampford. Bear right on the B1053 into Finchingfield

6 FINCHINGFIELD - Finchingfield's charm has survived in spite of its great popularity. One of its many fine buildings is the gabled and barge-boarded Hill House, set opposite a row of 16th-century cottages and Georgian houses. The Church of St John the Baptist has a Norman tower and Georgian-style bell-cote.

> Continue on the B1053 then in Wethersfield turn left onto the unclassified road to Sible Hedingham

POINT OF INTEREST

HEDINGHAM CASTLE
CO9 3DJ

This impressive Norman castle was built in 1140. It was besieged by King John, visited by Henry VII, Henry VIII and Elizabeth I, and was home to the de Veres, Earls of Oxford, for over 500 years. During the summer months Hedingham's colourful heritage comes to life with a full programme of special events. There are medieval jousts and sieges with authentic living history displays and encampments.

> Turn right on the A1017 then turn left on the A1124 to Halstead. Head north on the A131 to Sudbury

7 SUDBURY - Charles Dickens used this ancient cloth and market town on the River Stour as the model for 'Eatanswill' in The Pickwick Papers. There is a bronze statue of Thomas Gainsborough, the artist, who was born here in 1727, in an elegant Georgian town house now containing many of his paintings. The town was formerly a river port, and one of the old warehouses has been turned into the Quay Theatre. St Peter's Church has fine painted screen panels and a splendid piece of 15th-century embroidery on velvet, the 'Alderman's Pall'.

> Head east on the A134 towards Colchester, then in Leavenheath turn left on the B1068 to Stoke-by-Nayland to eventually reach the A12. Head north towards Ipswich

8 IPSWICH - Suffolk's county town covers a large area and has masses of historic charm in its pedestrianised centre not far from its harbour on the River Orwell. One of England's oldest towns, Ipswich was originally founded as the Anglo-Saxon trading port of Gippeswic in the Kingdom of East Anglia around AD 600 and retains much of its original street plan.

> Head east on the A14, then the A12 towards Lowestoft passing the outskirts of Woodbridge and Saxmundham. Take the A1095, on the right, to visit Southwold

9 SOUTHWOLD - An exhibition on the pier tells the history of the traditional British seaside holiday, complete with saucy postcards, kitsch teapots, palm readers, end-of-the-pier shows, high-diving 'professors' and old-style arcade machines. A separate pavilion contains modern machines by local inventor Tim Hunkin, who also designed the ingenious water clock, with chimes and special effects every half hour. You can eat ice cream or fish and chips, drink a pint of the local beer, play pool in the amusement arcade or watch the fishermen while taking in the sea air. Especially in summer, the pier provides a focus for good old-fashioned fun.

> Return back to the A12 and head north. Just south of Lowestoft, turn right at the roundabout onto the B1437 and divert to Kessingland before continuing to Lowestoft

10 KESSINGLAND & LOWESTOFT - Lowestoft is the most easterly town in England, making it the perfect place from which to see the sun rise. Kessingland Beach is ideal for this purpose, and for general seaside fun. The town also has Africa Alive! a 100-acre safari park, its own charming pier and The Broads right on its doorstep.

POINT OF INTEREST
NORFOLK BROADS / THE BROADS

One of England's most impressive inland water features is this huge patchwork of interlinked streams, lakes and channels that wind sluggishly over the flat land to the east of Norwich. Three major rivers – the Bure, Waveney and Yare – supply most of the water to the meres, ponds and marshes before entering the great tidal basin at Breydon Water and flowing into the sea at Great Yarmouth. Despite the fact that the Broads comprise one of England's best wilderness areas, most natural historians and archaeologists accept that their origin lies in ancient human activity. They were formed when local people mined the extensive peat deposits here, cutting away the fuel to form neat vertical sides. These days the Broads are a place for boat trips and wildlife, formed around small communities that have a unique feel; a mix of seaside, countryside and riverside, that can't be found anywhere else in the UK.

> Head north on the A47 to Great Yarmouth. After crossing the River Yare, at the roundabouts first turn right then left on the A149 towards Caister, then take the unclassified road towards Hemsby. At next roundabout turn left to Ormesby St Margaret, then turn right on the A149. In 11 miles (18km), just past Stalham, turn right on the B1159 to Walcott, then continue to Mundesley. Follow the unclassified coast road to Cromer

11 CROMER - If you're not bored of piers by now, you really should check out Cromer's. Opened in 1901, it has all the hallmarks of the classic English pier, including the only full season end-of-pier show in the world. The town's also rightly famous for its crab, which is still a major source of income for local fishermen.

> Head west on the A149 to Sheringham

12 SHERINGHAM - A charming seaside town with plenty of history, stretching all the way back to the Domesday Book. Along with an impressive 20th-century Catholic church, you can also find the remains of Beeston Hill Y Station on nearby 'Beeston Bump'. This listening station was part of a network that brought captured enemy radio traffic and sent it through to Bletchley Park, the principal centre of Allied code-breaking during the Second World War.

> Continue on the A149 to Wells-next-the-Sea

13 WELLS-NEXT-THE-SEA - The Wells and Walsingham Light Railway runs through 4 miles (6.5km) of countryside to the famous pilgrimage villages of Walsingham and is the longest 10 1/4-inch (26cm) narrow-gauge steam railway in the world. The town of Wells still has many of its 18th- and 19th-century houses, set in a network of alleys and yards near the small quay, which first started trading in wool over 600 years ago.

> Continue west on A149 to Holkham

POINT OF INTEREST
HOLKHAM HALL AND ESTATE
NR23 1AB

In a beautiful deer park with a lake landscaped by Capability Brown, is the 18th-century mansion of Holkham Hall, just south of the village of Holkham. This is one of the finest examples of Palladian revival architecture in England, with room after room of glittering splendour. Its art collection includes work by Rubens, Van Dyck and Gainsborough and there is an amazing marble hall. In the Bygones Collection, over 4,000 items have been assembled from kitchens, dairies and cars. The impressive walled garden alone, covers six acres (2.4ha) and is being lovingly restored to its 18th-century grandeur. You may picnic next to the lake or wander through acres of landscaped gardens and parklands. Today, as you enjoy the lawns and shade of abundant oaks and beeches, it is difficult to imagine that it was once an uncultivated heath. Look out for the flint church of St Withburga standing about half a mile from the Hall.

> Shortly turn left on the B1155 into Burnham Market

14 BURNHAM MARKET - Burnham Market is the main village in a group of seven Burnhams, clustered closely together, and has a handsome, wide village green surrounded by elegant 18th-century houses. The Burnhams were made famous by Horatio Nelson, who probably learned to sail on the muddy creeks of the coast before being sent away to sea at the age of 12. He was born in 1758 at Burnham Thorpe, where his father was the rector, and the lectern in the church is made from timbers from his ship, the Victory.

> Head north out of the town on the B1355 to re-join the A149 and turn left to Hunstanton

CAMPSITES EN ROUTE

►►►►► **CLIPPESBY HALL**
CLIPPESBY, NORFOLK
A lovely country house estate with secluded pitches hidden among the trees. The fabulous 'Basecamp' amenity area comes complete with a reception, a stylish bar and a café area.

►►►► **DEEPDALE CAMPING & ROOMS**
BURNHAM DEEPDALE, NORFOLK
This park is a must for lovers of peace and tranquillity. The touring areas are spread over six distinctive fields, and the site is located just a short stroll from the coastal path.

►►►►► **HAW WOOD FARM CARAVAN PARK**
DUNWICH, SUFFOLK
An unpretentious, family-orientated park set in two large fields surrounded by low hedges. It includes an excellent reception with café, and a play area.

►►►► **HEATHLAND BEACH HOLIDAY PARK**
KESSINGLAND, SUFFOLK
A well-run and maintained park, set in meadowland, with level grass pitches, and mature trees and bushes. There's direct access to Kessingland Beach which is very close by.

►►►► **HIGHFIELD FARM TOURING PARK**
COMBERTON, CAMBRIDGESHIRE
Family run park is on a well-sheltered hilltop with spacious pitches. Around the farm there is a one and a half mile marked walk that has stunning views.

►►►► **LAKESIDE CARAVAN PARK & FISHERIES**
DOWNHAM MARKET, NORFOLK
A peaceful park set around five pretty fishing lakes, with several well maintained grassy touring areas which are sheltered by mature trees and hedging.

►►►►► **MOON & SIXPENCE**
WOODBRIDGE, SUFFOLK
A well-planned site in a parkland setting, occupying a sheltered valley position around an attractive lake with a sandy beach. The park has an adults-only area.

►►►►► **SEARLES LEISURE RESORT**
HUNSTANTON, NORFOLK
A large seaside holiday complex with well managed facilities, adjacent to the beach. There's a wide range of indoor and outdoor activities, including a full entertainment programme.

15 HUNSTANTON - Hunstanton developed as a seaside resort in the 19th-century, and is famous for its red-and-white striped chalk cliffs and excellent beaches. At the Sea Life Sanctuary watch fish, seals and crabs as you walk through varied marine settings. England's only lavender farm, Norfolk Lavender, is just south of town, at Heacham. A national collection of lavender plants is assembled here, and there is a herb garden with over 50 varieties of culinary plants.

> Head south on the A149 towards King's Lynn. In a few miles at the roundabout bear left onto the B1440 to Dersingham. Turn left to continue on the B1440 to Sandringham

POINT OF INTEREST
SANDRINGHAM
PE35 6AB

The royal estate of Sandringham covers 20,000 acres (8,100 hectares) and was bought by Queen Victoria for the Prince of Wales in 1862. The grounds contain the parish Church of St Mary Magdalene, nature trails and a playground. There's a museum as well, based in the former coach houses and stables, and filled with many displays of personal items, such as items given to the monarch on visits abroad, and royal memorabilia.

> Head south on the B1440 to the A148. Turn right then in a few miles enter King's Lynn

16 KING'S LYNN - Known to locals simply as Lynn, its original name, King's Lynn is an architectural dream, with almost every period represented, ranging from St Nicholas' Chapel – built between 1145 and 1420 – to picturesque Burkitt Court almshouses, built in 1909 in memory of a Lynn corn merchant. You can take a stroll to see this living heritage – it makes for a great day out.

> Join the A47 west then in 9 miles (14.5km) turn right on the B198 into Wisbech

17 WISBECH - Wisbech is at the centre of a rich flower- and fruit-growing area. It was once only 4 miles (6km) from the sea, but due to land reclamation is now 11 miles (17km) inland. The Wisbech and Fenland Museum illustrates local history. The Brinks, two rows of houses along the River Nene, are among the finest examples of Georgian architecture in England, and Peckover House contains fine panelling and furniture; in its garden is the ginkgo, or maidenhair tree – the tallest in the land until a storm took away the top.

> Head south on the A1101 to Outwell, then on the A1122 to Downham Market

18 DOWNHAM MARKET - There has been a settlement in this area since Roman times. Denver Sluice, 2 miles (3km) away, is where the River Great Ouse and the Old and New Bedford Rivers are regulated in order to prevent flooding. The most interesting building in the town is the Church of St Edmund, with its Early English tower.

> Head south on the A10 past Littleport into Ely

19 ELY - Ely ('Eel Island') refers to the staple diet of the Saxons who once lived here. The Fens' cathedral city is still a small market centre with ancient buildings and medieval gateways but has a busy quayside. It was founded as a religious community in the 7th century, and during the Norman Invasion was the centre of Anglo-Saxon resistance under Hereward the Wake. Ely also has a parish church, St Mary's, and the vicarage was the home of Oliver Cromwell for 11 years. 900-year-old Ely Cathedral's greatest glory is its unique octagon, designed by Alan de Walsingham after the earlier tower collapsed in 1322.

> Continue to head south on the A10. At Stretham, turn right on the A1123, then in Wilburton turn left on the B1049 through Cottenham and Histon back to Cambridge

06

THE COTSWOLDS

One thing you'll see plenty of on this route is golden Cotswold stone. Whole villages shaped around the wool trade are built of it, and its gentle colour gives the region a warm glow. The Cotswolds is also a protected landscape, so you can expect miles and miles of largely unspoilt countryside, rolling hills and fertile fields, dotted with quintessentially English villages and vibrant market towns.

START / END Chipping Norton
VIA Gloucester and Stratford-upon-Avon
DISTANCE 236 miles (380 km)
SUGGESTED TIME 4 days

1 CHIPPING NORTON - The town's wide main street is a relic of its days as a sheep market. The church that dominates the town was paid for by the proceeds from sheep farming.

> Take the B4026 north and turn left onto the A3400. In 1.5 miles (2.5km) at crossroads turn left onto an unclassified road

POINT OF INTEREST

ROLLRIGHT STONES
OX7 5QB
This Bronze Age circle, which dates from earlier than 1000 BC, was nearly as important as Stonehenge in the Neolithic period. Nicknamed the 'King's Men', it measures a full 100 feet (30m) across. Over the road is the King Stone, a monolith, and nearby, just along the road, is the group of stones called the Whispering Knights, at the site of a prehistoric burial chamber.

> On meeting the A44 turn right to Moreton-in-Marsh. Turn right onto the A429 and in 5 miles (8km) turn left onto the B4035 to Chipping Campden

2 CHIPPING CAMPDEN - Once famous throughout Europe as the centre of the English wool trade. The church is particularly fine, and it's also worth looking for the Ernest Wilson Memorial Garden on the High Street.

> Take the B4081 south, then right onto the A44 past Broadway. Turn left onto the B4632 and head south, all the way to Cheltenham

3 CHELTENHAM - The Promenade, an elegant, wide street lined with Regency houses, has been described as the most beautiful thoroughfare in Britain. The famous Pittville Pump Room is a masterpiece of 19th-century Greek revival.

> Head south, and join the A417 to Birdlip. Here take the B4070, shortly turning right onto an unclassified road. Turn left on the A46 to Painswick, then head north on the B4073 to Gloucester

4 GLOUCESTER - With a magnificent cathedral that's been used as a location in Harry Potter movies, historic docks, remnants of a Roman wall, and some great museums, Gloucester is ideal for a day of wandering.

> Take the A417 for 17 miles (27km) to Ledbury

5 LEDBURY - An unspoiled market town with half-timbered buildings, and many literary links: Robert Browning and William Wordsworth used to visit, and John Masefield was born here. Elizabeth Barrett Browning spent her childhood at Hope End, just out of town.

> Head east on the A449 and then the B4232 through Wynds Gap and into Malvern. Take the B4211 to Upton-upon-Severn, turn left onto the A4104, then in 1 mile (1.6km) right onto the A38 to Tewkesbury

6 TEWKESBURY - Almost all the town's buildings are old timber-framed structures, notably the Bell Inn, and the Royal Hop Pole Inn, which is mentioned in The Pickwick Papers by Charles Dickens. Tewkesbury Abbey is one of the finest Norman abbeys in the country.

> Return on the A38 for a short distance, then take the B4080 to Bredon. Continue along an unclassified road through Kemerton and Beckford, then take the A46 to Evesham. Take the B4088 and an unclassified road to Alcester. Follow the B4089 northeast to Great Alne, then unclassified roads east to Wilmcote. Continue along the unclassified road, then the A3400 for 3 miles (5km) to Stratford-upon-Avon

7 STRATFORD-UPON-AVON - Still a market town despite being one of the world's most famous tourist centres. Shakespeare's Birthplace in Henley Street is now a museum on the Bard. You could also visit the Royal Shakespeare Company Collection, and see a show at the riverside Royal Shakespeare Theatre.

> Take the B4086 to Wellesbourne, then onto Warmington. Turn right onto the B4100 to Banbury. From Banbury head east along the A422. After 2 miles (3km) turn left onto the B4525, then onto the unclassified road to Sulgrave

8 SULGRAVE - The old manor in this attractive stone village was the home of ancestors of George Washington. Not to be missed is the family coat of arms with its stars and stripes carved above the porch.

> Take unclassified road back to the B4525, then turn left, then at crossroads turn right onto minor road to Brackley. Take A43 south and then shortly right onto the B4031 to Aynho and Clifton. Turn left onto A4260 south and then left onto an unclassified road to Steeple Aston. Turn left onto the B4030 to Bicester. Take the A41 and then turn right onto the B4011 towards Thame before turning sharp right to Boarstall. Take minor roads along the edge of Otmoor to Oxford. Leave Oxford on the A44 north and turn left towards Cassington. Turn right to Bladon, then at the A4095 junction turn right, then shortly turn left onto the A44 to Woodstock

PLACE OF INTEREST

BLENHEIM PALACE
OX20 1UL
The birthplace of Winston Churchill, Blenheim Palace was given to the Marlborough family by Queen Anne in 1704, and is still home to the Duke of Marlborough today.

> Continue north on the A44 before turning left onto the B4437 to Charlbury, and finally the B4026 back to Chipping Norton

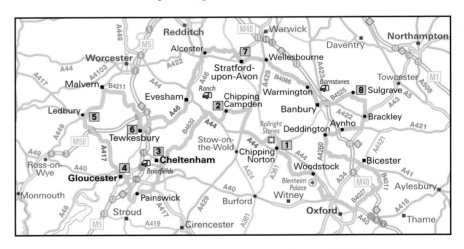

CAMPSITES EN ROUTE

▶▶▶▶ **BARNSTONES CARAVAN & CAMPING SITE**
BANBURY, OXFORDSHIRE

Barnstones is a popular, neatly laid-out site. Well run by a very personable owner, this is an excellent value park. The site is well positioned for stopovers or for visiting nearby Banbury.

▶▶▶▶ **BRIARFIELDS MOTEL & TOURING PARK**
CHELTENHAM, GLOUCESTERSHIRE

A well-designed, level, adults-only park, with a motel. Nicely positioned between Cheltenham and Gloucester, with easy access to the Cotswolds.

▶▶▶▶ **RANCH CARAVAN PARK**
HONEYBOURNE, EVESHAM

An attractive park set amidst farmland in the Vale of Evesham and landscaped with trees and bushes. Tourers have the use of an outdoor heated swimming pool in peak season.

NORTH YORK MOORS

This area of Yorkshire extends from the gentle farmlands of the Vale of York to the wild beauty of the North York Moors, which unfold as a vast, undulating landscape of natural beauty, taking in delightful villages and evocative ruins. Interspersed with winding trails, the terrain is full of hidden dales and valleys, where ancient woodlands shelter elusive wildlife.

START / END York
VIA Pickering, Grosmont and Helmsley
DISTANCE 105 miles (169 km)
SUGGESTED TIME 2 days

1 YORK - This strikingly beautiful walled medieval city is one of Britain's top sights, with a multitude of museums and buildings spanning the centuries. Much of its compact heart is pedestrianised, so it's great to explore on foot. Among the most evocative streets are The Shambles, originally a street of butchers' shops and retaining overhanging, jettied, timber-framed buildings; and Stonegate, where shop signs and frontages span several centuries. A circuit of the medieval walls gives great views over the city and beyond — it's a walk of about two-and-a-half miles.

> From York take the A64, left onto an unclassified road before Whitewell-on-the-Hill, passing Castle Howard, through Coneysthorpe to Malton

2 MALTON - Malton is divided in two by the site of a Roman station. New Malton is the busy market town, and Old Malton, a mile (1.6km) northeast, is a small village. Malton Museum, in the town, contains extensive Romano-British remains from the fort of Derventio and other settlements. Northwards is Eden Camp Modern History Museum, a former prisoner-of-war camp.

POINT OF INTEREST
CASTLE HOWARD
YO60 7DA
Six miles (10km) southwest of Malton, on a signed road, is Castle Howard, a magnificent 18th-century house designed by Sir John Vanbrugh. It has been the home of the Howard family for nearly 300 years and notable features include the central dome, the Temple of the Four Winds and Hawksmoor's mausoleum.

> Follow the road to Old Malton, cross the A64 onto the A169, turning almost immediately left onto an unclassified road through Kirby Misperton, rejoining the A169 north to Pickering

3 PICKERING - This ancient town is the starting point for the North Yorkshire Moors Railway, which runs between Pickering and Grosmont. Parts of the town's Church of St Peter and St Paul date from the 11th century and it contains splendid medieval wall paintings. The ruins of Pickering Castle include a motte-and-bailey, which was founded by William the Conqueror, and is now in the hands of English Heritage.

> Continue along the A169 for about 12 miles (19km), then turn left onto an unclassified road to Goathland

4 GOATHLAND - A picturesque village in an area renowned for spectacular waterfalls, including Nelly Ayre Foss, Mallyan Spout and Thomason Foss.

> Return to the A169 for a short distance, then turn left onto unclassified roads to Grosmont

5 GROSMONT - The northern terminus of the impressive North Yorkshire Moors Railway. A trip on the Moorsrail will take you back to a gentler, slower age, and the locomotive sheds are well worth a visit.

> From Grosmont head north on an unclassified road to reach the A171 then immediately turn left again

to Lealholm, then follow unclassified roads south to Rosedale Abbey

6 ROSEDALE ABBEY - Rosedale's 12th-century Cistercian abbey no longer exists: only a few stones remain in the village. Ruins of railways and kilns at Chimney Bank Top are reminders of the old 19th-century ironstone industry. The famous chimney, once visible for miles, was demolished in 1972 when it was declared unsafe.

> Continue to Hutton-le-Hole

7 HUTTON-LE-HOLE - Hutton-le-Hole's Ryedale Folk Museum, in an ancient cruck-type building, features a marvellous collection of farm equipment, and reconstructed buildings. There are two 4-mile (6km) walks signposted from the centre of the village into the countryside.

> Turn right to Gillamoor crossing the River Dove and through the village to Kirkbymoorside

8 KIRKBYMOORSIDE - Situated at the edge of the moor, this small town is just off the main road, with quiet streets and squares. The church dates from the 12th century and retains some fine Norman masonry and fragments of a Saxon cross.

> Take the A170 for 6 miles (10km) to Helmsley and then B1257 to Rievaulx

9 HELMSLEY - Roads from Cleveland, Thirsk and York converge upon the town square, making Helmsley a busy trade centre. Helmsley Castle dates from 1186 and was once inhabited by the Duke of Buckingham, court favourite of James I and Charles I.

POINT OF INTEREST
RIEVAULX ABBEY
YO62 5LB
Two miles (3km) west of Helmsley is Rievaulx Abbey, one of the largest Cistercian abbeys in England. The 12th-century ruins are surrounded by wooded hills, and above the abbey wall is Rievaulx Terrace, a beautiful landscaped garden with mock-Greek temples completed in 1758.

> Return to the A170 and continue south on the B1257 to Oswaldkirk. Here, turn right onto the B1363 and continue south to Sutton-on-the-Forest

10 SUTTON-ON-THE-FOREST - Set in the undulating Howardian Hills, this is an unusual brick-built village with a stone church. Sutton Park, an early Georgian house, contains antique furniture by Chippendale and Sheraton and a collection of porcelain.

> Return to York on the B1363

CAMPSITES EN ROUTE

▶▶▶▶▶ **GOLDEN SQUARE CARAVAN & CAMPING PARK**
HELMSLEY, NORTH YORKSHIRE
This friendly, immaculately maintained park is set in a quiet rural situation. Terraced on three levels and surrounded by mature trees, it caters particularly for families.

▶▶▶▶ **LADYCROSS PLANTATION CARAVAN PARK**
WHITBY, NORTH YORKSHIRE
The unique forest setting creates an away-from-it-all feeling at this peaceful touring park set in 95 acres of woodland and run by enthusiastic owners.

▶▶▶▶▶ **YORK CARAVAN PARK**
YORK, NORTH YORKSHIRE
This adults-only park, is located close to the inner ring road and ideally placed for touring the coast and York centre. The park has the added attraction of a peaceful fishing lake.

THE YORKSHIRE DALES

Yorkshire's green valleys and wild, often wind-swept moorland provide a rich variety of scenery, with ever-changing views. Curiously weathered rocks add an eerie atmosphere to the landscape of hills and vales, and castles and monastic ruins recall the prosperity of the Middle ages on this tour. The towns and villages are also filled with history as well as that legendary Yorkshire hospitality.

START / END Ripon
VIA Barnard Castle and Hawes
DISTANCE 152 miles (245 km)
SUGGESTED TIME 2–3 days

POINT OF INTEREST

RIPON CATHEDRAL
HG4 1QT
In AD 672 St Wilfrid built a church on this spot. The west front dates from 1220, the east front from 1290, and inside there are 500-year-old woodcarvings, a 16th-century nave and exceptional stained glass.

> From Ripon take the A6108 to Masham

1 MASHAM - The town has a huge market square, dominated by its large Market Cross, and is the home of Theakston's brewery. The bridge over the Ure dates from 1754, and St Mary's has a 15th-century spire on top of a Norman tower.

POINT OF INTEREST

JERVAULX ABBEY
HG4 4PH
By the river, five miles (8km) from town is Jervaulx Abbey, founded in 1156 and destroyed in the 15th century; enough remains to show how impressive it was.

> Follow the A6108 for 8 miles (13km) to Middleham

2 MIDDLEHAM - The massive keep at 12th-century Middleham Castle, the childhood home of Richard III, is one of the largest ever built. From the top you can look out across Wensleydale and the moors.

> Continue north to Leyburn

3 LEYBURN - A prosperous late Georgian market town, and even though most shop fronts have become largely modern, some 18th-century houses survive, notably around Grove Square. There are fine views from The Shawl, a limestone scar not far from the town centre.

> Keep on the A6108 to Richmond

4 RICHMOND - Richmond Castle is a fine Norman fortress, built on to solid rock, started in 1071 but never finished. The Green Howards Museum covers the history of the regiment, including a unique collection of weapons, medals and uniforms. Other sights include Greyfriars Tower, and the Holy Trinity Church.

> Take the B6274 to the junction with the A66 and continue to Greta Bridge. After crossing River Greta turn right onto unclassified roads to Barnard Castle

5 BARNARD CASTLE - The castle, after which the town is named, is now a ruin, but it once stood guard at a crossing point of the River Tees. The Bowes Museum, in a French château-style mansion, contains an outstanding collection of paintings, porcelain, silver, furniture and ceramics.

> Take the A67 to Bowes and follow the A66 west to Brough. Take the A685 to Kirkby Stephen, then the A683 to Sedbergh. From Sedbergh go east along the A684 to Hawes

6 HAWES - Hawes is a centre for sheep-marketing and a focal point of Upper Wensleydale life. The National Park Centre is located at the Dales Countryside Museum, housed in an old engine shed.

POINT OF INTEREST

HARDRAW FORCE
DL8 3LZ
The highest and perhaps most spectacular waterfall in England, is accessible only by foot through the grounds of the Green Dragon Inn. The water drops 90 feet (27m) over the limestone Hardraw Scar, into a narrow valley.

> Take the A684 for a further 4 miles (6.5km) to Bainbridge. Turn left to Askrigg cross over the River Ure and then turn right. From here, continue on unclassified roads, then after Aysgarth take the B6160 to Buckden. Follow the B6160 south and turn left at Threshfield onto the B6265 for 11 miles (18km) to Grassington

7 GRASSINGTON - Wharfedale's principal village and another National Park Centre, for the Yorkshire Dales. Its small passageways, cobbled marketplace, medieval bridge and interesting old buildings all add to the appeal. There are Bronze and Iron Age settlements at Lea Green, north of the village, and further east, along the B6265, are the impressive underground caverns of Stump Cross.

> Continue along the B6265 to Pateley Bridge

8 PATELEY BRIDGE - The ruins of Old St Mary's Church stand on the hillside above the village, and the Nidderdale Museum has fascinating exhibits including a replica cobbler's shop.

> Shortly turn left to continue with B6265 back to Ripon (10 miles/16km)

CAMPSITES EN ROUTE

►►►► CONSTABLE BURTON HALL CARAVAN PARK
CONSTABLE BURTON, NORTH YORKSHIRE
This pretty site in the former deer park of the adjoining Constable Burton Hall, is screened from the road by park walls and surrounded by mature trees in a quiet rural location.

►►► PECKNELL FARM CARAVAN PARK
BARNARD CASTLE, COUNTY DURHAM
A family-run site set on a working farm, in beautiful rural meadowland. There are many walking opportunities that start directly from this friendly site.

►►►► SLENINGFORD WATERMILL CARAVAN CAMPING PARK
NORTH STAINLEY, NORTH YORKSHIRE
The old watermill and River Ure make for an attractive setting for this charming park. Back-to-nature opportunities include a tree trail, bee garden and river walks.

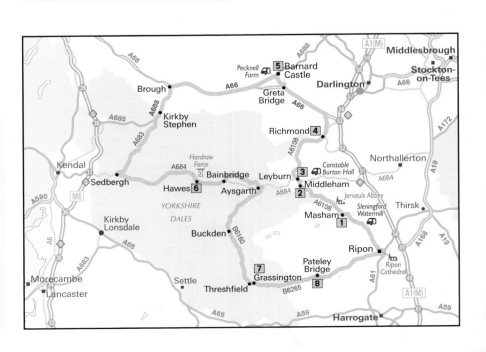

THE HEART OF LAKELAND

Leave the soft red sandstones of Carlisle and the Eden Valley to weave through hills of volcanic rocks and lakes carved out during the last Ice Age, before heading into the Pennines, with their different, gentler beauty. Be sure to leave time aside for a bit of water travel, as you'll enjoy some great opportunities to take a boat trip on some of England's most impressive bodies of water.

START / END Carlisle
VIA Keswick, Ambleside and Haltwhistle
DISTANCE 176 miles (283 km)
SUGGESTED TIME 3–4 days

1 CARLISLE - Cumbria's only city has been important since at least Roman times. You can tell this from the size of the castle, the cathedral and the extensive city walls built around the remains of the Roman town and fort.

> Take the B5299 south from Carlisle to Caldbeck

2 CALDBECK - This traditional, stone-built, fell village is preserved as a conservation area. Many of the mill buildings, dating from the 17th- and 18th-century are still in use.

> Continue on the B5299 before branching left onto unclassified roads through Uldale to Bassenthwaite

3 BASSENTHWAITE - One mile east of the village lies Bassenthwaite Lake, home to an array of wildlife, including ospreys, and where only quiet activities are allowed. On its western shore, Skiddaw rises - one of only three local mountains higher than 3,000 feet (915m).

> Leave Bassenthwaite on the unclassified road towards the B5291 round the northern shores of the lake, then take the A66 south to Braithwaite. Turn right on the B5292 towards Lorton and over Whinlatter Pass. Turn left when reaching the B5289 to Buttermere. Then take the B5289 to Keswick

4 KESWICK - Local graphite used to be used in the manufacture of coloured pencils, so there's a pencil museum which is home to the world's largest pencil.

> From Keswick take the A66 for 4 miles (6.5km), then turn right onto the B5322 through St John's in the Vale and then the A591 south to Grasmere

5 GRASMERE - William Wordsworth wrote here and you can visit Dove Cottage, where he lived with his sister, Dorothy.

> Continue to Ambleside on the A591

6 AMBLESIDE - Set at the northern end of Lake Windermere, Ambleside's many stone houses include Bridge House, a tiny house on a tiny bridge over the Stock Ghyll.

> Leave on the A593 to Coniston, Hawkshead and Near Sawrey

7 CONISTON - Coniston Water is famous as the place where Donald Campbell set a new world speed record and later died in 1967. The Steam Yacht Gondola, a restored 1859 steam launch, takes passengers on regular scheduled trips around the lake.

8 HAWKSHEAD AND NEAR SAWREY - A little further on, at Hawkshead, is the Beatrix Potter Gallery; at Hill Top, in Near Sawrey, Potter wrote some of her world-famous children's stories. The house is open to the public.

> Take the B5285 to the Windermere ferry and cross the Lake to Bowness-on-Windermere

9 BOWNESS-ON-WINDERMERE - This small town with narrow streets and fine 15th-century church is home to the Windermere Jetty Museum, a collection of Victorian and Edwardian boats. Lake Windermere has 14 islands, including one with a round 18th-century mansion house.

> Take the A592 north to Patterdale

CAMPSITES EN ROUTE

▶▶▶▶▶ **CASTLERIGG HALL CARAVAN & CAMPING PARK**
KESWICK, CUMBRIA

Breathtaking views across Derwentwater to Catbells and other well-known Lakeland fells. Castlerigg is notable for the outstanding quality across all aspects of the operation.

▶▶▶▶▶ **HERDING HILL FARM TOURING & CAMPING SITE**
HALTWHISTLE, NORTHUMBERLAND

In an idyllic rural location with gorgeous sunsets, very close to Hadrian's Wall, this beautifully developed campsite is geared to families and offers spacious, serviced hard standings.

▶▶▶▶▶ **SKELWITH FOLD CARAVAN PARK**
AMBLESIDE, CUMBRIA

In the grounds of a former mansion, this park is in a beautiful setting close to Lake Windermere. Touring areas are dotted in paddocks around the extensively wooded grounds.

▶▶▶▶▶ **THE QUIET SITE**
WATERMILLOCK, CUMBRIA

A wonderful sustainable park with breathtaking views across Ullswater. 'The Quiet Bite' offers breakfast crêpes and bacon rolls, as well as an evening pizza takeaway service.

10 PATTERDALE - This attractive village is at the head of Ullswater with scenery dominated by 3,117 foot (950m) Helvellyn mountain.

POINT OF INTEREST
ULLSWATER
Around seven miles (11 km) long, 0.75 miles (1.2km) wide and 207 feet (63m) deep, Ullswater is the second largest lake in the region by both area and volume. Explore it by boat, or on foot along the 20-mile (32km) long Ullswater Way. Ullswater 'Steamers' operate one of the largest heritage boat fleets in the world, offering cruises of the lake most days of the year. Depart from Glenridding in the south and stop on the western shore to walk one mile (1.6km) to Aira Force, a spectacular waterfall.

> Take the A592 alongside Ullswater to Penrith

11 PENRITH - Check out the nearby ruins of Brougham Castle, and the 15th-century Gloucester Arms, one of England's oldest inns; thought to have been a home to the Duke of Gloucester, later Richard III.

> From Penrith follow the A686 through Langwathby towards Alston. Turn left onto the A689 then right, at Knarsdale, onto an unclassified road to Haltwhistle

12 HALTWHISTLE - This small, grey market town is a good starting point for Hadrian's Wall.

POINT OF INTEREST
HADRIAN'S WALL
Britain's most important Roman monument, and part of a UNESCO World Heritage Site, this 73-mile (117km) long wall took around 5 years to build. Close to the small village of Greenhead is The Roman Army Museum and Magna Fort. Both Hadrian's Wall and Pennine Way National Trails are accessible here. Numerous Roman remains can be found along the wall nearby, including the fort at Birdoswald, remains of turrets at Piper Sike, Leahill and Banks East. Near Lanercost, is a section of wall that stands nine feet (2.7m) high.

> Continue on a minor road and B6318 to Greenhead and after Gilshead turn sharp left to take a minor road to Brampton. Pick up the A689 back to Carlisle

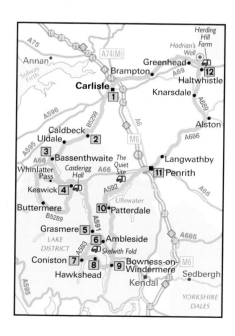

10 THE WESTERN HIGHLANDS

This route will take you through some spectacular and majestic scenery. The Western Highlands have a rugged, untamed beauty made up of awe-inspiring mountain ranges, deep mystical lochs and cascading, melodious waterfalls. The landscape is a patchwork of moors and glens, dotted with charming towns, ancient castles and breath-taking views of distant, romantic isles.

START / END Dumbarton
VIA Lochgilphead, Easdale and Glen Coe
DISTANCE 240 miles (386 km)
SUGGESTED TIME 4 days

1 DUMBARTON - Between the 5th and 9th centuries, Dumbarton was the seat of the Scots kings until 1018, when Dunfermline became capital. In the 19th century, it was a shipbuilding centre, giving birth to the clipper Cutty Sark and the steamer Sir Walter Scott.

> Head north from Dumbarton, to pick up the A82 west and then left onto the A818 to Helensburgh

2 HELENSBURGH - John Logie Baird, the television pioneer, was born here in 1888. Another inventive Helensburgh man was Henry Bell, whose Comet, launched in 1812, was the world's first sea-going steamboat.

POINT OF INTEREST

HILL HOUSE
UPPER COLQUHOUN STREET, HELENSBURGH, G84 9AJ
Charles Rennie Mackintosh, the most famous of Scotland's 20th-century architects, completed Hill House in 1902. The elegant interiors, showing Mackintosh's amazing attention to detail, seem to become more rather than less modern as years go by.

> Turn right onto the A814 past Rhu and Shandon and continue north to Arrochar. Here, turn left on the A83 to Inveraray

3 INVERARAY - Once the county town of Argyll, this gem of 18th-century architecture is reflected in the waters of Loch Fyne near Inveraray Castle. The town's bell tower acts as the Clan Campbell war memorial; and Inveraray Jail is one of the finest museums in Scotland.

> From Inveraray continue on the A83 to Lochgilphead. Turn right on the A816, bear left on the B841 to cross the Crinan Canal

4 CRINAN CANAL - Built to avoid the risky journey round the Mull of Kintyre, this 9-mile (14.5m) waterway is now used mostly by yachts and motor cruisers. From the picnic site at Dunardry a forest walk looks down on the canal.

> Continue on the B841 and turn right at Bellanoch on the B8025. Bear left on the A816 to Kilmartin

5 KILMARTIN - Kilmartin church and churchyard house many medieval grave slabs, and Carnassarie Castle, offers a view into the canyon which swings down from Loch Awe.

> Continue on the A816 past Arduaine and Kilmelford, then finally turn left on the B844 and follow signs to Easdale

6 EASDALE - The steeply arched Clachan Bridge (or 'bridge over the Atlantic') to Seil joins one of Argyll's Slate Islands to the mainland. A quarry at Easdale village, breached by the sea during a storm in November 1881, survives as an open bay.

> Return to the A816 and turn left to Oban

7 OBAN - The 20th-century cathedral of St Columba is the heart of the Roman Catholic diocese of Argyll and the Isles. Elsewhere in the town you can watch glass-blowers and paper-weight makers at work, and visit the 18th-century distillery.

> Leave Oban on the A85. At Connel, turn right on the A828 as it swings over Connel Bridge. Continue on the A828 to Appin village then turn left to Port Appin

8 PORT APPIN - On one of the finest stretches of the coast of Argyll, this village looks out to the island of Lismore and, beyond it, to the hills of Kingairloch.

> Return to the A828 and turn left. Pass Ballachulish Hotel and turn left on the A82

9 BALLACHULISH - This village used to be well known for its ferry across Loch Leven, which has been replaced with a modern bridge. Between 1697 and 1955 Ballachulish was a major centre of the slate industry.

> Take the A82 from Ballachulish, through the valley of Glen Coe

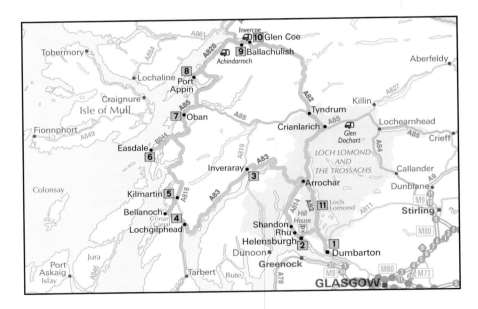

CAMPSITES EN ROUTE

▶▶▶ **ACHINDARROCH TOURING PARK**
DUROR, HIGHLAND
A long-established, well-laid out park which is consistently maintained to a high standard by an enthusiastic and friendly family team.

▶▶▶▶ **GLEN DOCHART HOLIDAY PARK**
LUIB, STIRLING
A small site, with boating and fishing available on Loch Tay. Hill walkers have direct access to numerous walks to suit all levels of ability, including the nearby Munro of Ben More.

▶▶▶▶ **INVERCOE CARAVAN & CAMPING PARK**
GLEN COE, HIGHLAND
A level grass site set on the shore of Loch Leven, with excellent mountain views. The area is ideal for walking and climbing, and also offers a choice of freshwater and saltwater lochs.

10 GLEN COE - From the roof of the National Trust for Scotland Visitor Centre in Glencoe village, there is a fine view of the mountain scenery and glittering waterfalls. You can get details about the many exhilarating walks from the Centre (and climbing, too, for the experienced).

> Continue on the A82 past Tyndrum and Crianlarich, then go south, alongside Loch Lomond

11 LOCH LOMOND - In the north, the loch fills a narrow glacial trough between crammed-in mountains. You can cruise through the islands or cross the loch, walk on the West Highland Way, and sail back to the western shore.

> Continue on the A82 and return to Dumbarton

Motoring information

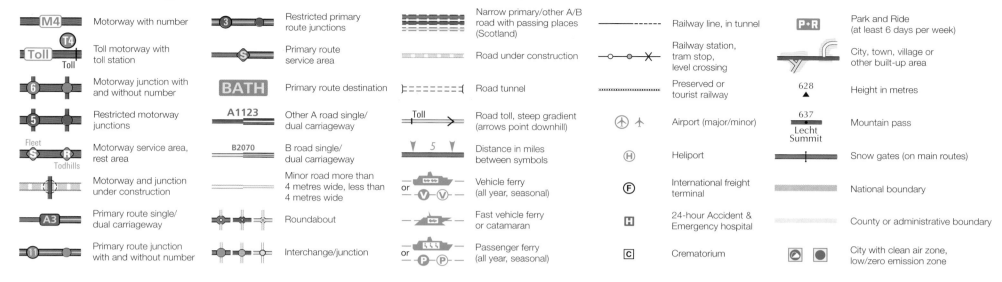

M4 Motorway with number	**3** Restricted primary route junctions	Narrow primary/other A/B road with passing places (Scotland)	- - - - - - Railway line, in tunnel	**P·R** Park and Ride (at least 6 days per week)	
Toll Toll motorway with toll station	**S** Primary route service area	Road under construction	Railway station, tram stop, level crossing	City, town, village or other built-up area	
6 Motorway junction with and without number	**BATH** Primary route destination	Road tunnel	Preserved or tourist railway	628 ▲ Height in metres	
5 Restricted motorway junctions	**A1123** Other A road single/ dual carriageway	**Toll** Road toll, steep gradient (arrows point downhill)	Airport (major/minor)	637 Lecht Summit Mountain pass	
Fleet **S** Todhills Motorway service area, rest area	**B2070** B road single/ dual carriageway	▽ 5 ▽ Distance in miles between symbols	**H** Heliport	Snow gates (on main routes)	
Motorway and junction under construction	Minor road more than 4 metres wide, less than 4 metres wide	or Vehicle ferry (all year, seasonal)	**F** International freight terminal	National boundary	
A3 Primary route single/ dual carriageway	Roundabout	Fast vehicle ferry or catamaran	**H** 24-hour Accident & Emergency hospital	County or administrative boundary	
1 Primary route junction with and without number	Interchange/junction	or Passenger ferry (all year, seasonal)	**C** Crematorium	City with clean air zone, low/zero emission zone	

Caravan & motorhome information

Caravan Site AA-inspected caravan & motorhome site (sites shown include parks with touring pitches and excludes sites that offer pitches only for tents and static-only parks)	Bridge location with height restriction in feet and inches. This atlas primarily shows low bridges and structures signed at 16'6" and under on all roads selected for inclusion on the mapping.
Other caravan & motorhome site	N/b only S/b only E/b only W/b only Bridge height only applies when travelling in direction shown: Northbound, Southbound, Eastbound, Westbound.

Touring information   To avoid disappointment, check opening times before visiting

Scenic route	Viaduct	National Nature Reserve (England, Scotland, Wales)	Windmill	Ski slope (natural, artificial)
i Tourist Information Centre	Vineyard	Local nature reserve	Monument or memorial	National Trust site
i Tourist Information Centre (seasonal)	Brewery or distillery	Wildlife Trust reserve	Beach (award winning)	National Trust for Scotland site
V Visitor or heritage centre	Garden	Forest drive	Lighthouse	English Heritage site
Picnic site	Arboretum	National trail	Golf course	Historic Scotland site
Major shopping centre	Country park	Viewpoint	Football stadium	Cadw (Welsh heritage) site
Abbey, cathedral or priory	Showground	Waterfall	County cricket ground	★ Other place of interest
Ruined abbey, cathedral or priory	Theme park	Hill-fort	Rugby Union national stadium	Boxed symbols indicate attractions within urban area
Castle	Farm or animal centre	Roman antiquity	International athletics stadium	World Heritage Site (UNESCO)
Historic house or building	Zoological or wildlife collection	Prehistoric monument	Horse racing	National Park and National Scenic Area (Scotland)
M Museum or art gallery	Bird collection	1066 Battle site with year	Show jumping	Forest Park
Industrial interest	Aquarium	Preserved or tourist railway	Motor-racing circuit	Sandy beach
Aqueduct	RSPB site	Cave or cavern	Air show venue	Heritage coast

District maps (see pages 154–160)

M60 Motorway and junction	Other road single/ dual carriageway	London Overground station	Clean air zone, low/zero emission zone boundary
M6 Toll M6 Toll motorway (Birmingham District)	Road tunnel	Docklands Light Railway (DLR) station	Central London Congestion Charge Zone
Primary road single/ dual carriageway	Railway line and station	Rail interchange	Ultra Low Emission Zone boundary (London): operates 24 hours a day, every day and covers most of Greater London excluding the M25. Most light vehicles, including cars, vans and minibuses, must meet minimum exhaust emission standards or drivers must pay a daily charge to drive within the zone.
A road single/ dual carriageway	Tramway and tram stop	**M** Metro station (Tyne & Wear)	Motorhomes over 3.5 tonnes (and buses, minibuses and coaches over 5 tonnes) will need to pay the London Low Emission Zone charge instead, if standards are not met.
B road single/ dual carriageway	London Underground station	Subway station (Glasgow)	For further information on all controlled emission zones visit www.gov.uk/clean-air-zones

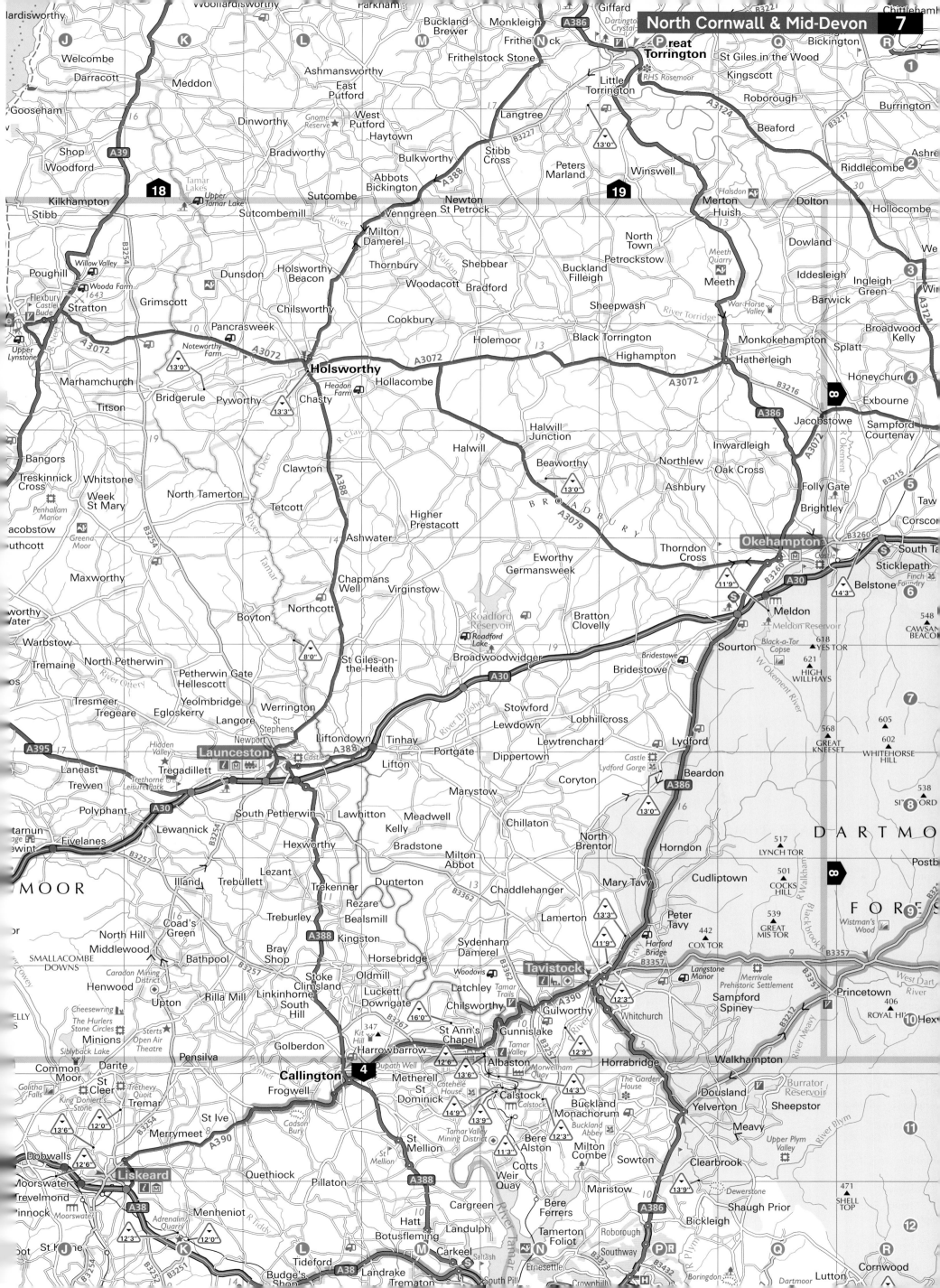

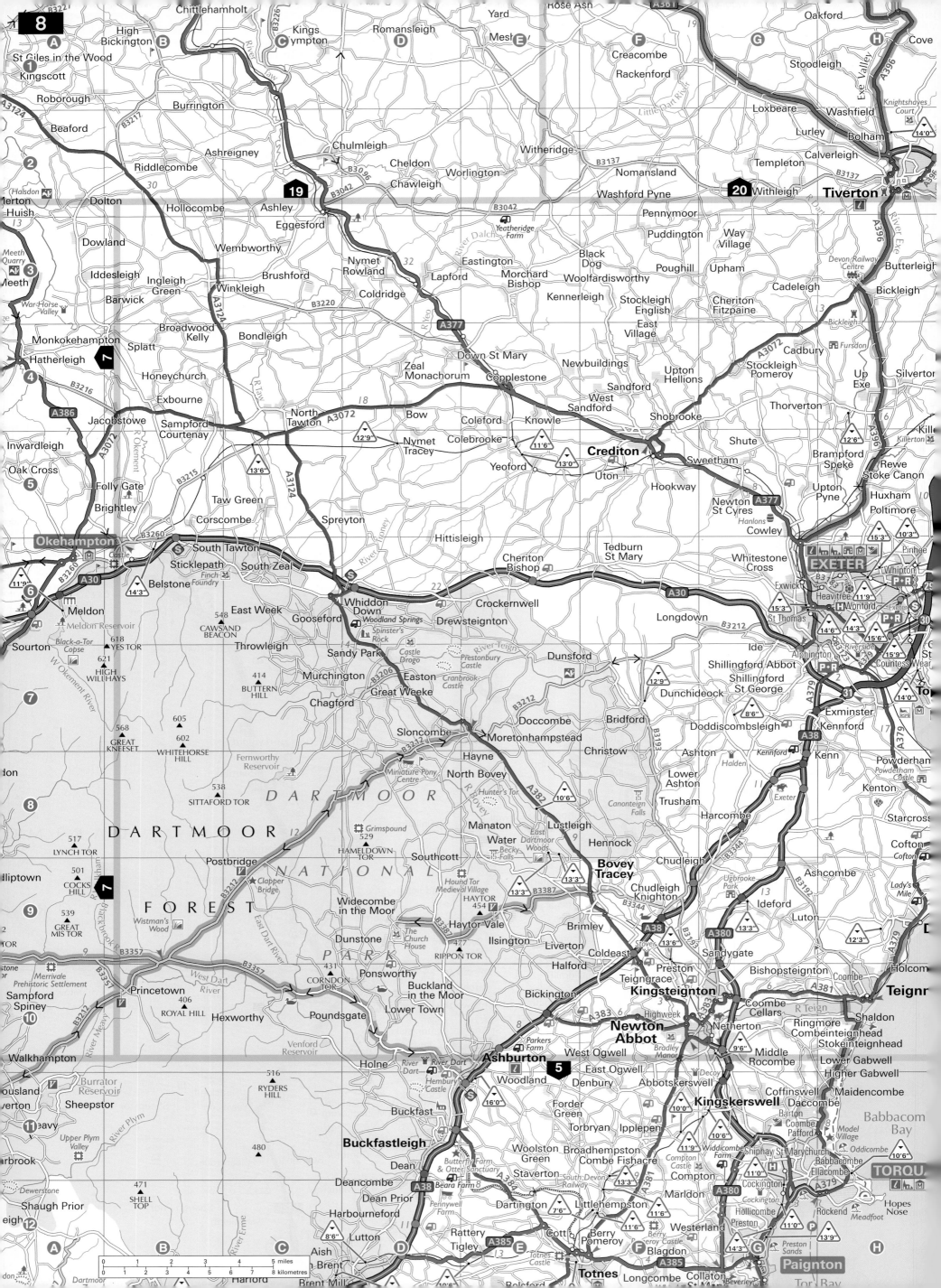

North West Point
Lundy Heritage Coast
LUNDY
142 ▲
Marine Reserve
Shutter Point
Surf Point

(P) (Apr-Oct)

(Apr-Oct) (P)

Baggy Point
Croyde Bay
Bay View Farm
North Devon Heritage Coast

BARNSTAPLE
OR
BIDEFORD BAY

Northam Burrows
Westward Ho!

Shipload Bay
HARTLAND POINT
Titchberry
Damehole Point
Hartland Abbey & Gardens
Stoke
Clovelly
Hartland Heritage Coast
Abbotsham
The Big Sheep
Ford
Bi
Hartland Quay
Speke's Mill Mouth
Hartland
B3248
Buck's Mills
Fairy Cross
Woodtown
Littleh
8'6"
Milford
Docton Mill
Buck's Cross
Horns Cross
A39
Goldworthy
Sa
Philham
Milky Way
10
Hardisworthy
Woolfardisworthy
Parkham
Buckland Brewer
Mo
Frithelstock S

Welcombe
Darracott
Meddon
Ashmansworthy
East Putford
West Putford
Haytown
Gooseham
Dinworthy
Gnome Reserve ★
Stibb Cross
Morwenstow
Higher Sharpnose Point
16
Bradworthy
Bulkworthy
17
La
Shop Woodford
A39
Abbots Bickington
Sutcombe
Newton St Petrock
Lower Sharpnose Point
Tamar Lakes
Upper Tamar Lake
Venngreen
Steeple Point
7
Sutcombemill
River
Milton Damerel
Kilkhampton
Stibb
Holsworthy Beacon
Thornbury
Shebbear
Sandy Mouth
Willow Valley
B3254
Dunsdon
Chilsworthy
Woodacott
Bradford
Northcott Mouth
Poughill
Wooda Farm
1643
Holsworthy
Cookbury
Holemc
Crooklets
Flexbury
Summerleaze
Castle Bude
Stratton
Grimscott
A3072
Pancrasweek
Bude Bay
i Bude
10
Noteworthy Farm
A3072
Headon Farm
A3072
Upper Lynstone
A3072
E
13'0"
F
Holsworthy
G
H
Widemouth Bay
Marhamchurch
Bridgerule
Pyworthy
Chasty
Hollacombe

0 1 2 3 4 5 miles
0 1 2 3 4 5 6 7 8 kilometres

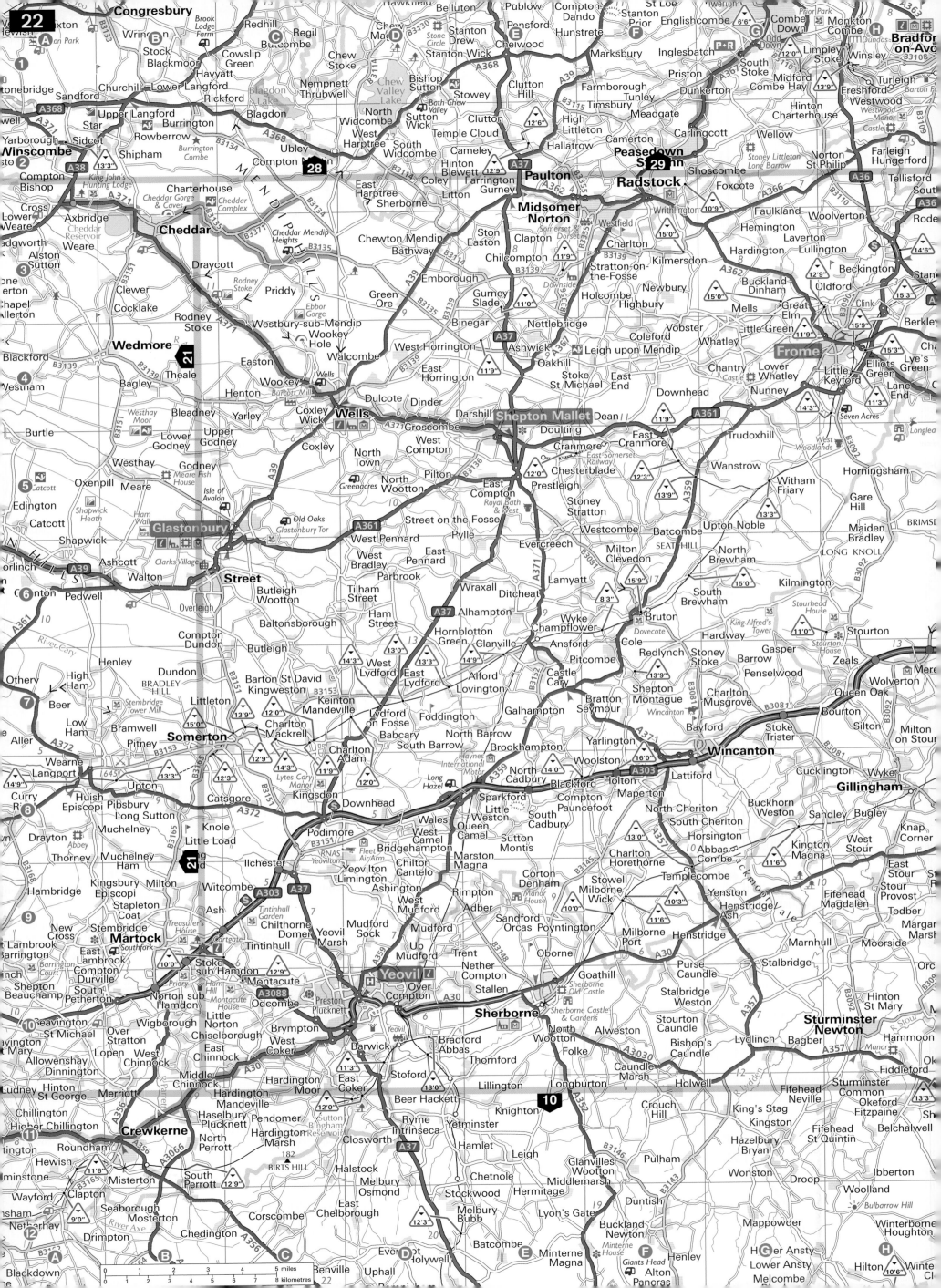

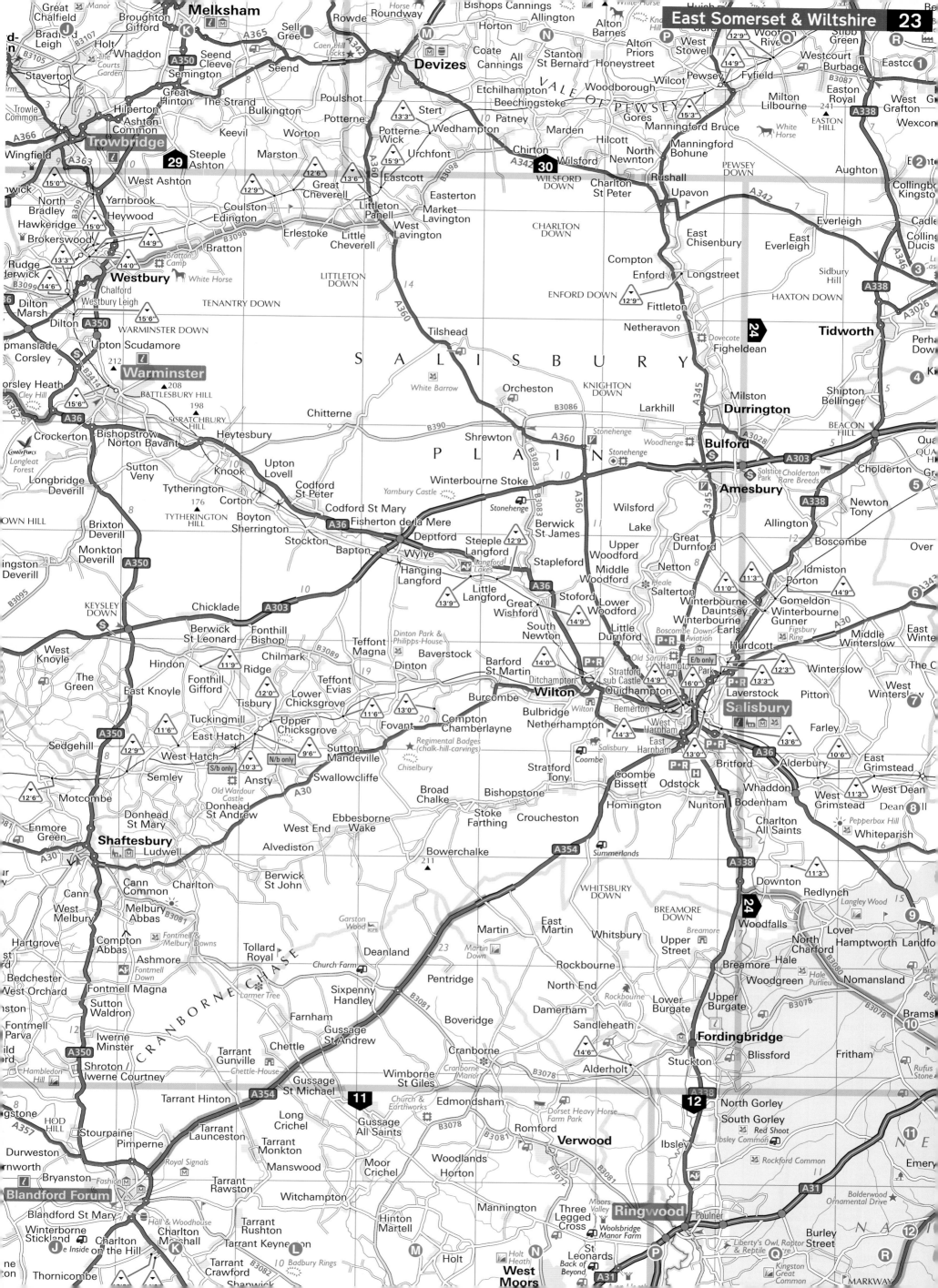

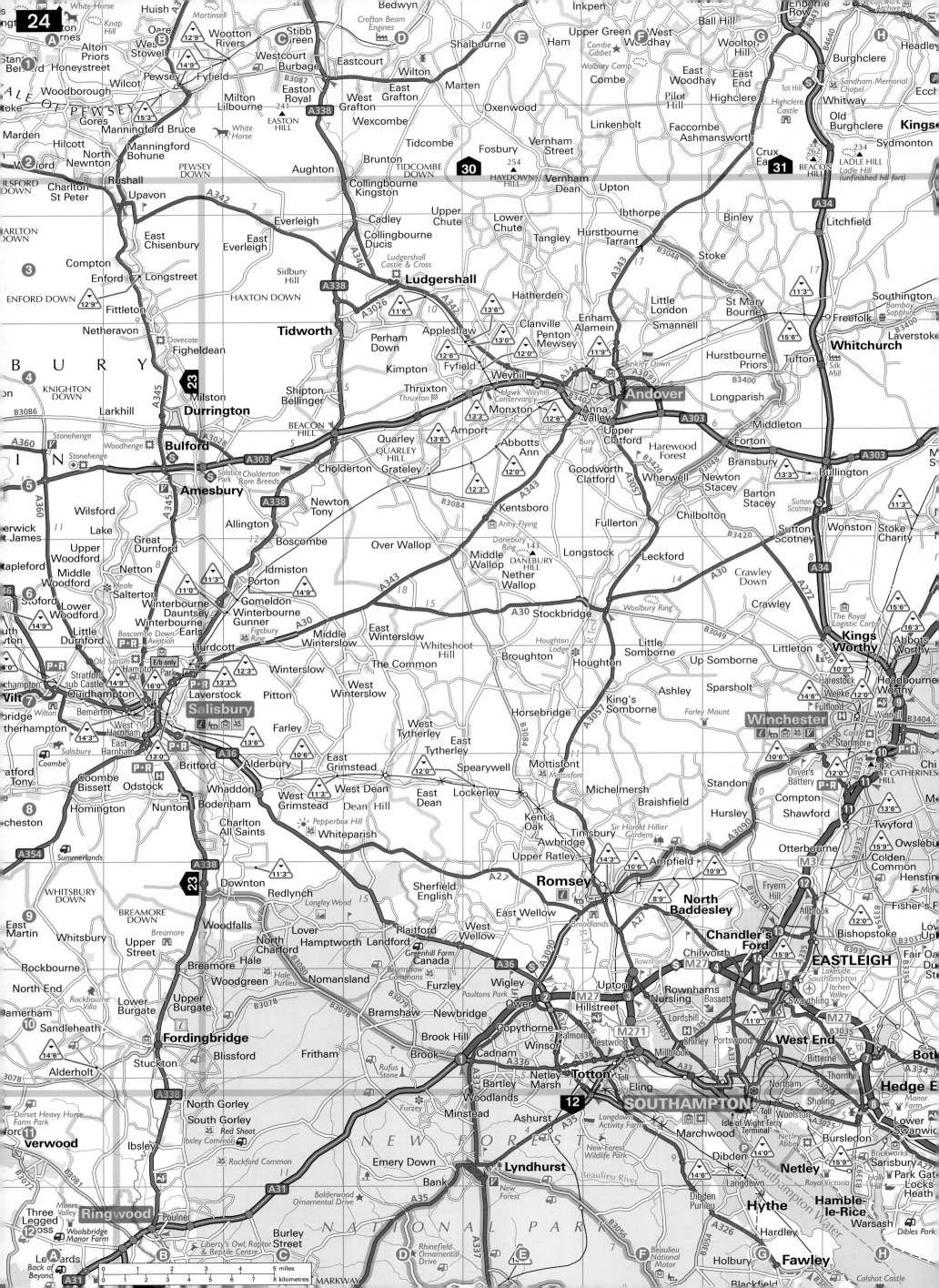

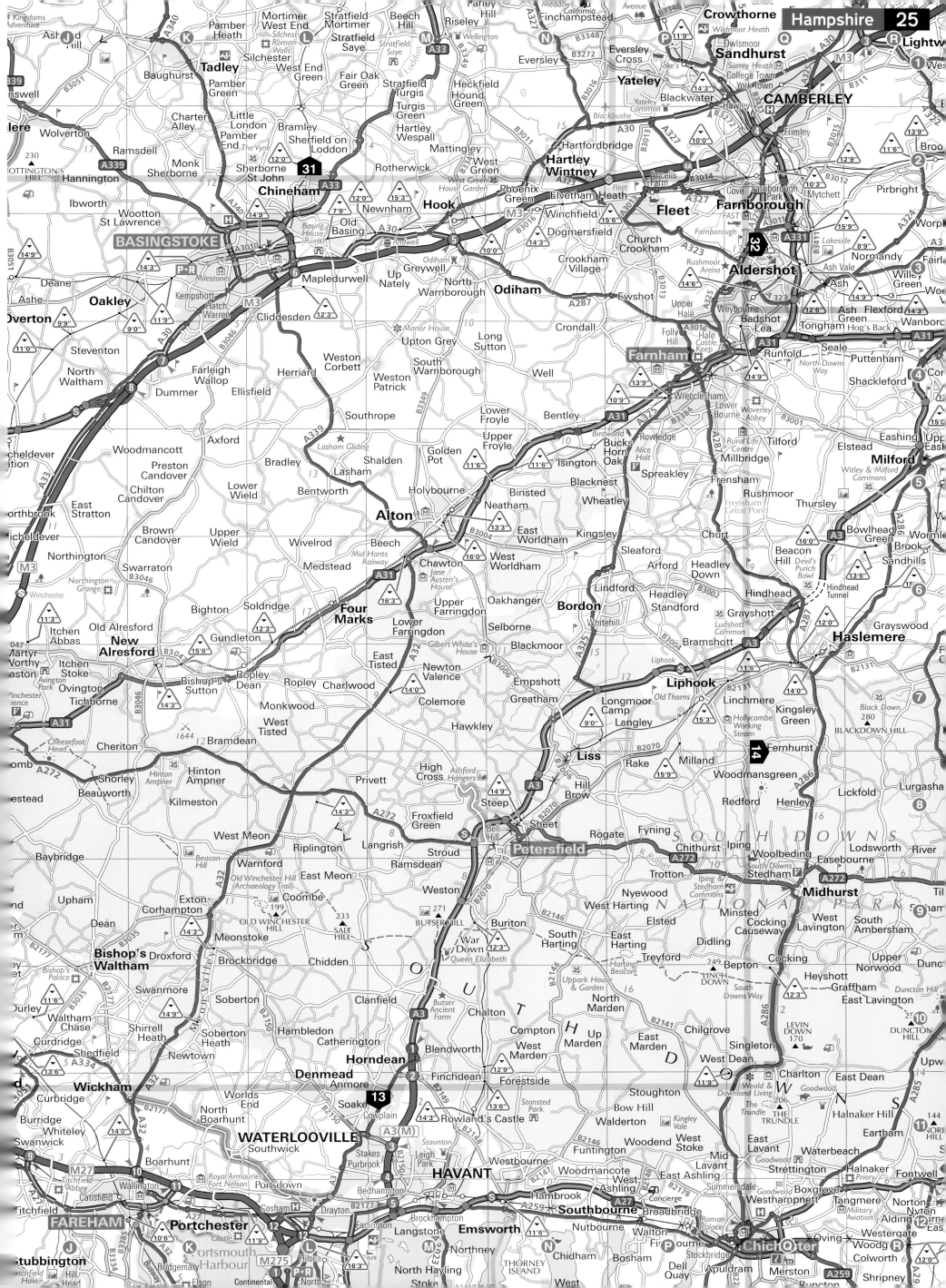

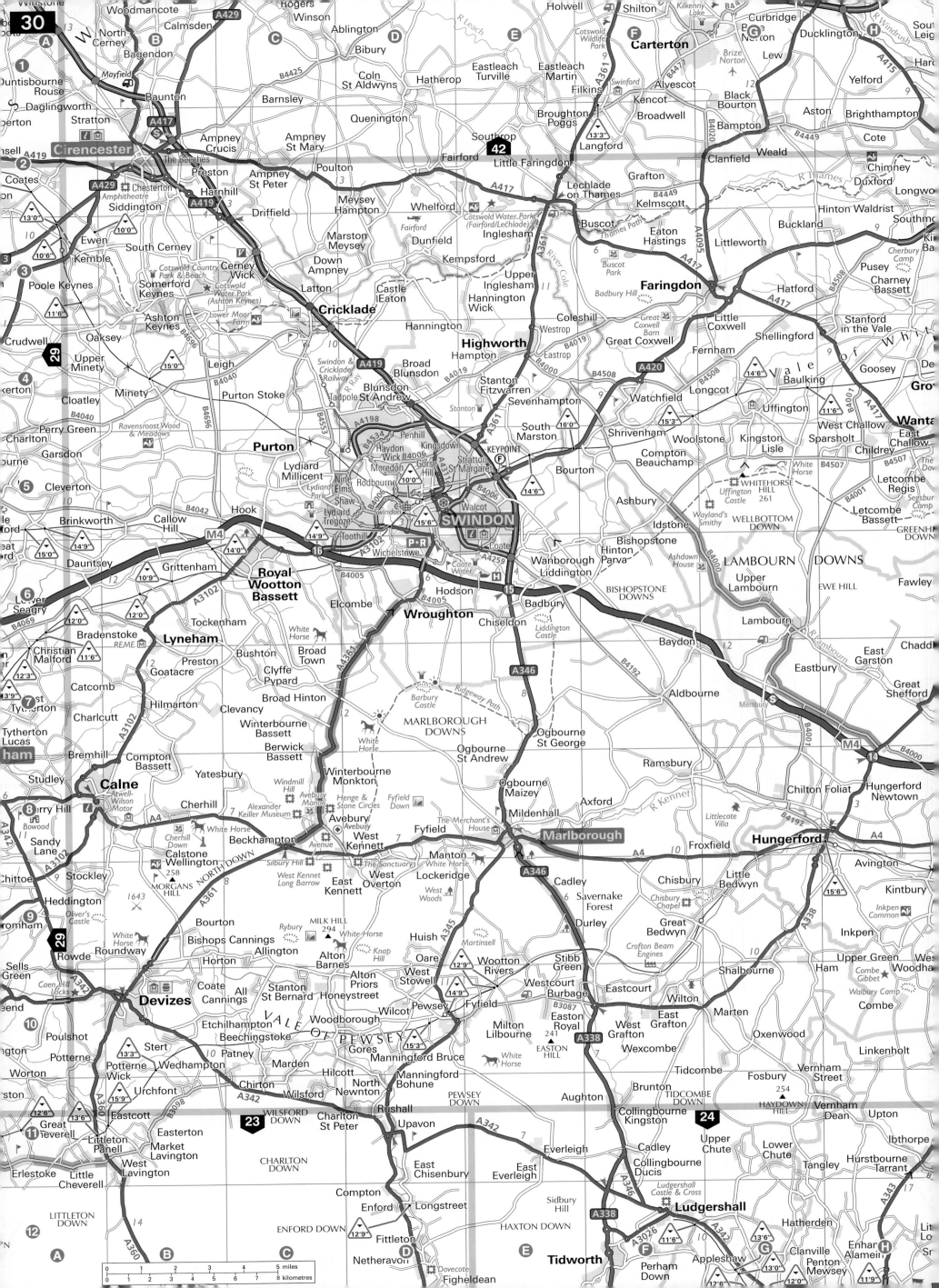

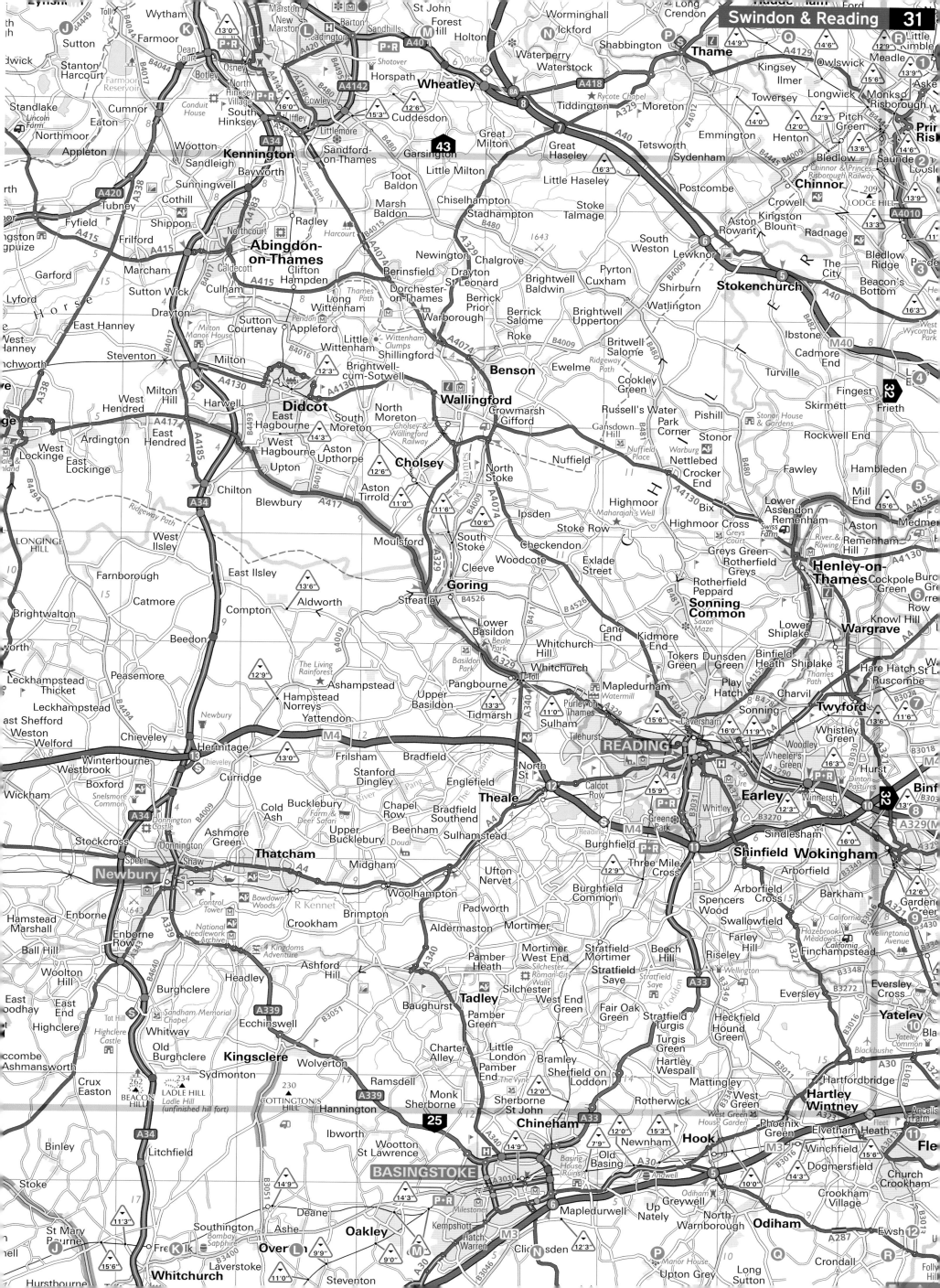

Fishguard Harbour

GOODWICK/ WDIG
FISHGUARD & GOODWICK STATION
FISHGUARD HARBOUR STATION
FOOT PASSENGER TERMINAL
CAR FERRY TERMINAL
Fishguard Bay Hotel
Fishguard Harbour
Penyraber
Lower Town
Tre-Llewelyn Wood
Dyffryn
Manorowen Wood
FISHGUARD/ ABERGWAUN
HIGH STREET
RAFAEL ROUNDABOUT
ST DAVIDS
HAVERFORDWEST
SAC
CARDIGAN
0   500 m

Pembroke Dock (Doc Penfro)

HAVERFORDWEST
Burton
Burton Ferry Terrace
NEYLAND
Cleddau Bridge
Milford Haven Waterway/ Dyfrffordd Aberdaugleddau
FERRY TERMINAL
Travelodge
Llanion
Waterloo
Freight Terminal
PEMBROKE DOCK
PEMBROKE DOCK STATION
London Road
High Street
Military Road
Pennar
SAC
PEMBROKE
CARMARTHEN
0   500 m

Rosslare
STRUMBLE HEAD
Pen Brush
Garn Fawr
Trefasser
Goodwick (Wdig)
Pwll Deri
Pembrokeshire Coast Path
Manorowen
St Nicholas
14'9"
Ynys Daullyn
Granston
Carreg Sampson
Abercastle
Llangloffan
Jordanst
A4219
Porthgain
Trefin
Mathry
Llangloffan Fen
14'6"
B4331
Abereiddy
Llanrhian
16
A487
Berea
Croes-goch
Letterst
14'3"
B4330
St David's Head
Treleddyd-fawr
Tretio
Treglemais
Caer Farchell
River Solva
Llandeloy
Whitesands Bay
Rhodiad y-brenin
Treffgarne Owen
Hayscastle
Hayscast Cross
Bishop's Palace
Whitchurch
St Davids (Tyddewi)
Solva
Penycwn
178
DUDWELL MOUNTAIN
Lewe
Tret
RAMSEY ISLAND
Caerfai Bay
Newgale
Roch
Wolfsdale
Cam
Ramsey Sound
St David's Peninsula Heritage Coast
16
PEMBROKESHIRE COAST NATIONAL PARK
Simpson Cross
Keeston
A487
Rickets Head
Nolton Haven
Nolton
St Brides Bay
St Brides Bay Heritage Coast
Nolton Cross
Druidston
Haroldston West
Portfield Gate
B4341
Broad Haven
Broadway
B4327
Dreen Hill
Little Haven
Walton West
13'6"
Pembrokeshire Coast Path
Talbenny
Tiers Cross
14
Walwyn's Castle
14'6"
(Apr-Sept)
Wooltack Point
Lockley Lodge
SKOMER ISLAND
Marloes
B4327
12'3"
Herbrandston
Steynton
St Ishmael's
Waterston
Broad Sound
Marloes & Dale Heritage Coast
Dale
Hubberston
Hakin
Milford Haven (Aberdaugleddau)
Pem
SKOKHOLM ISLAND
Westdale Bay
Dale Point
Great Castle Head
Milford Haven
(Doc
St Ann's Head
Chapel Bay Fort
Angle
Angle Bay
Rhoscrowther
B4320
Rosslare
Freshwater West
Castlemartin Brook
10
B4319
Castlemartin
Warren
Linney Head
Merri
PEMBROKESHIRE NATIONAL PA
Elegug Stacks
Pembrokes Coast-Pat

0   1   2   3   5 miles
0 1 2 3 4 5 6 7 8 kilometres

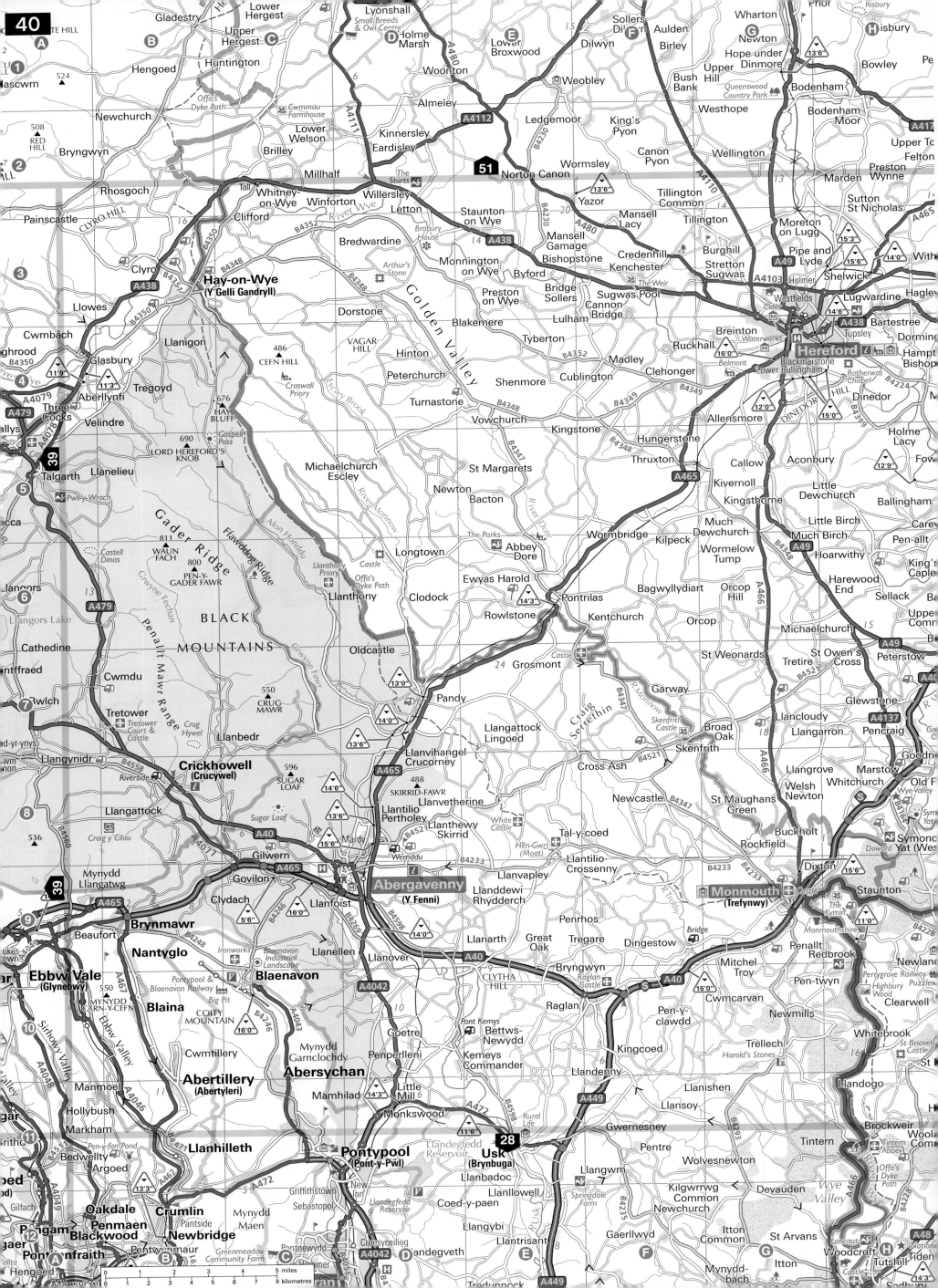

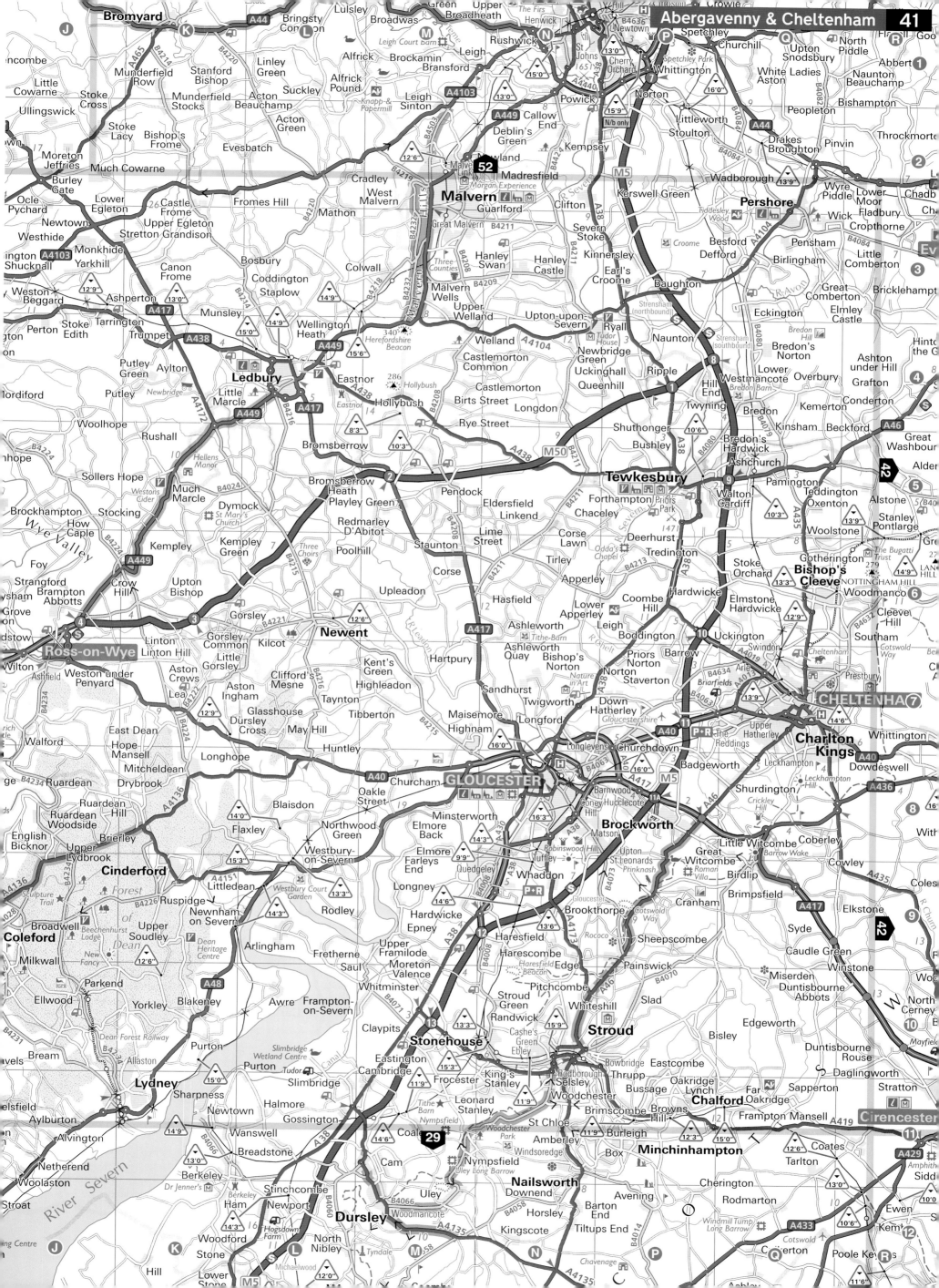

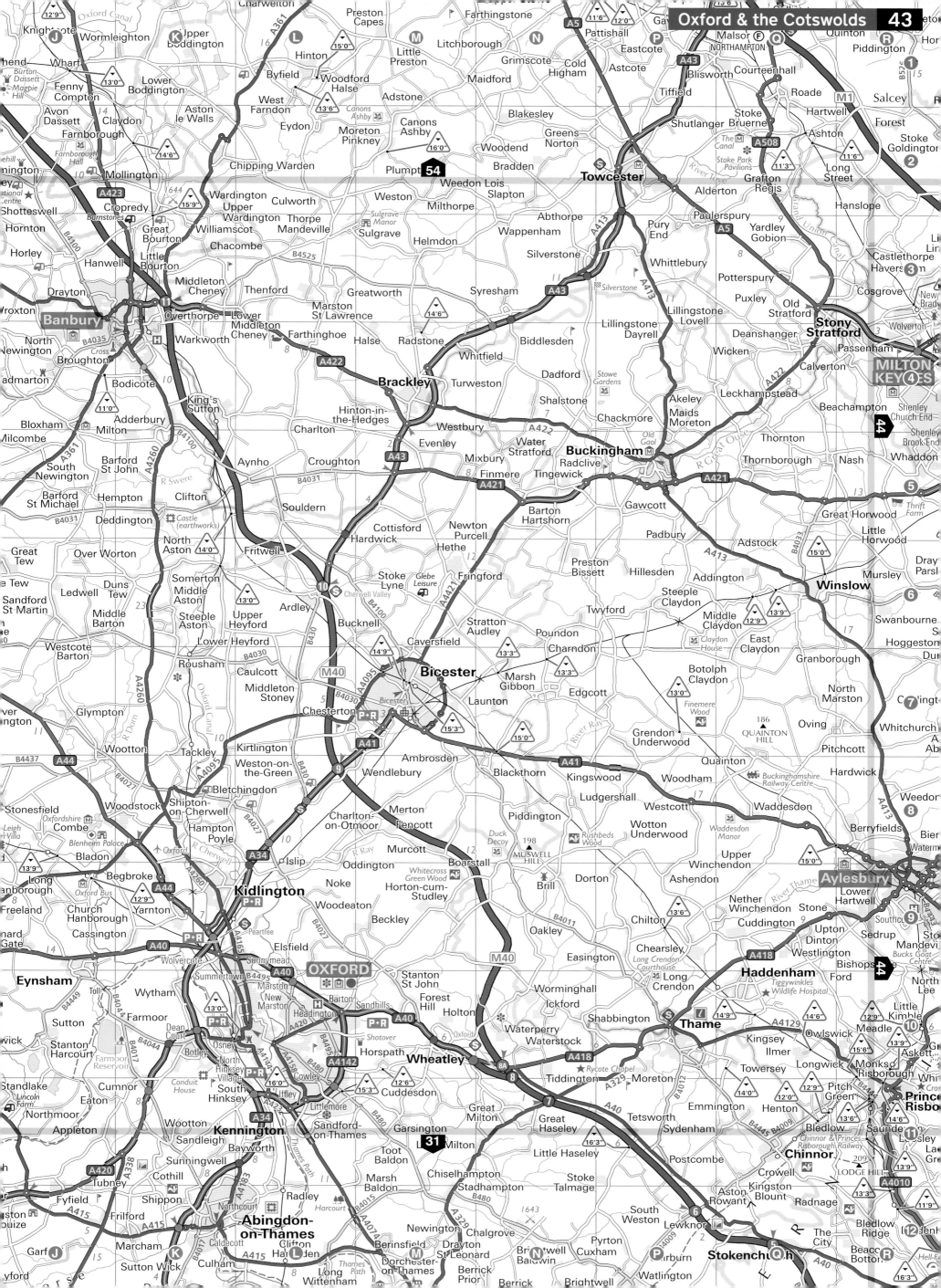

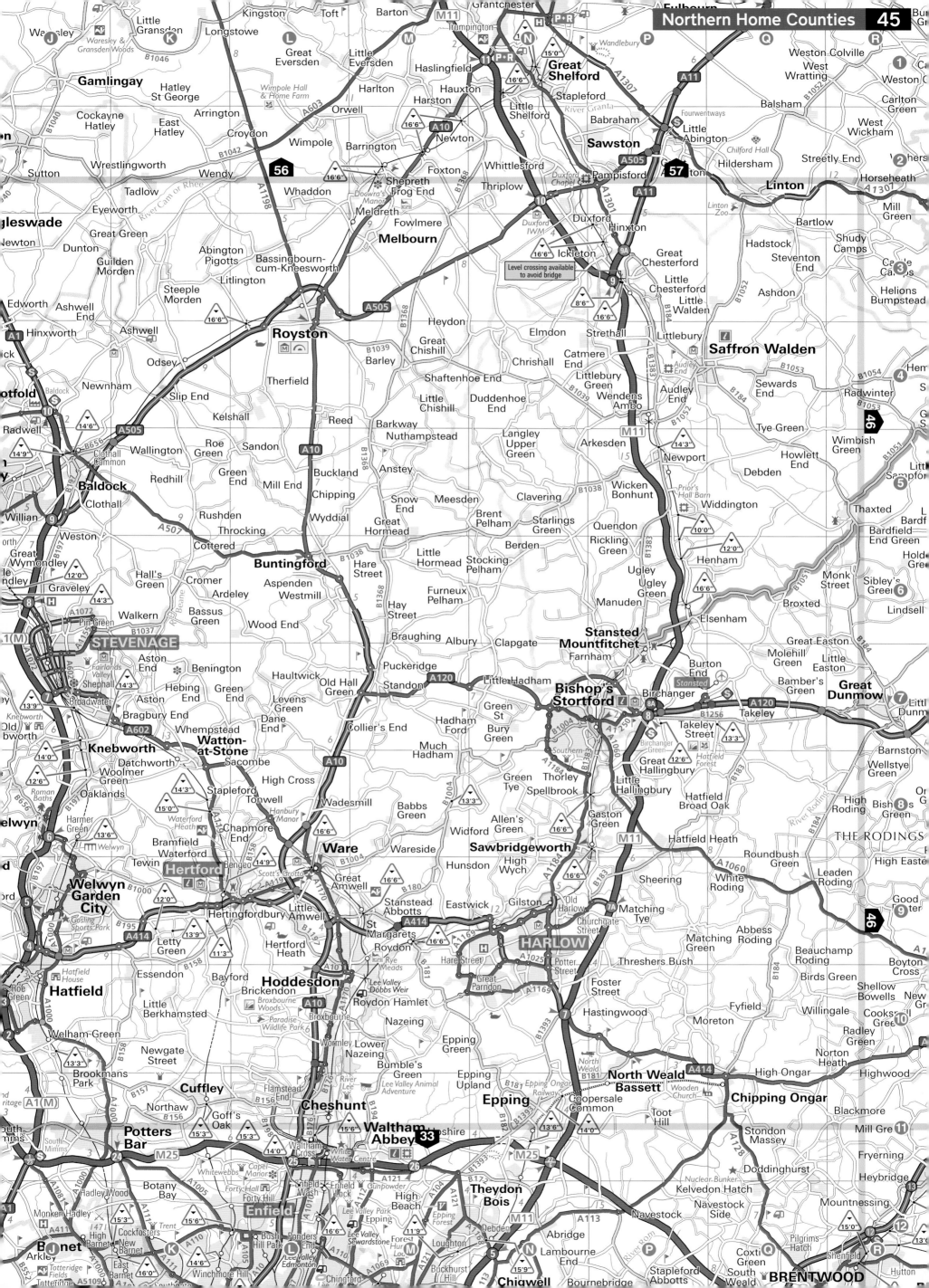

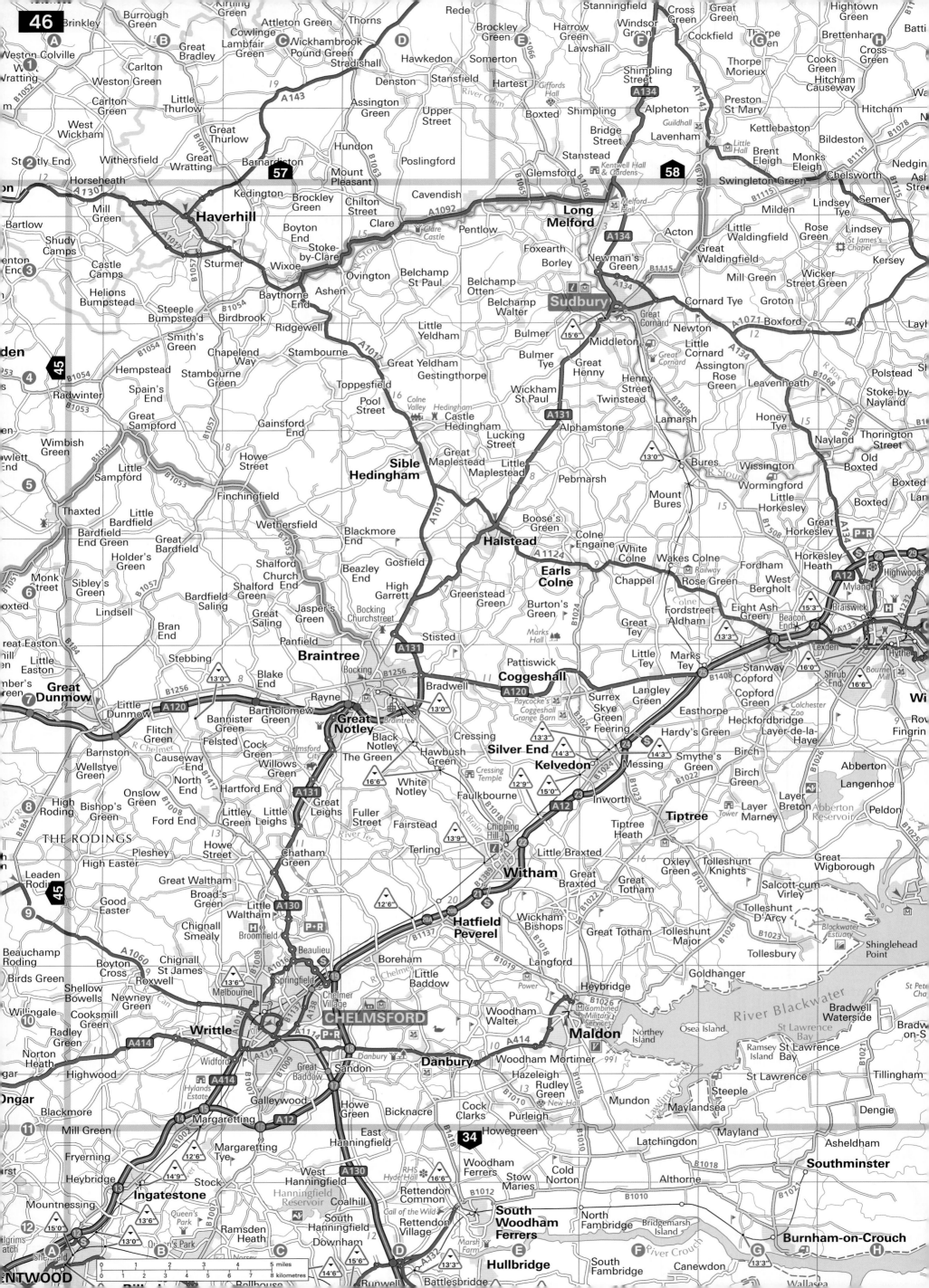

48

A　B　C　D　E　F　G　H

1

2 CARDIGAN

3 BAY

4

5

6

7 Llansantffraid
Llanon

8 Aberarth
Aeron Coast
Aberaeron

New Quay
(Ceinewydd)
Marine
Llanina
Llwyncelyn
A482
Ceredigion Heritage Coast
Maen-y-groes
Gilfachrheda
Llanarth
Oakford
B4339

9 *Cwmtydu*
Cross
Inn
A487
B4342
Dihewyd
Ystr
Aer
Nanternis
Caerwedros
7
Ynys-Lochtyn
Pendinas
Lochtyn
Llwyndafydd
Mydroilyn
Te

Llangrannog
Pontgarreg
Plwmp
B4321
B4338
Cae Hi

Penbryn
B4334
Pentregat
A486
311
Gorsgoch
Cer din
Talgarreg
324

10 *Ceredigion*
Heritage Coast
Mwnt Beach
Sarnau
Brynhoffnant
B4338
Cardigan
Island
Tresaith
B4333
Aberporth
Tan-y-groes
Glynarthen
Rhydlewis
9
Ffostrasol
B4459
Cwrtnewydd
Llanw
Y Ferwig
Blaenannerch
A487
Blaenporth
B4334
A475

Poppit
Sands
Penparc
Tremain
Blaenporth
Bettws
Ifan
Hawen
Penrhiwpal
38
tsian
Llanwenog
Drefac

11 *Pembrokeshire*
Coast Path
Abbey &
Coach House
B4546
B4548
Cardigan
(Aberteifi)
B4570
Beulah
Troedyraur
Maesllyn
Tre-groes
Prengwyn
Rhydowen
Llanybydde
St Dogmaels
Welsh
Wildlife Centre
Ponthirwaun
Brongest
Croes-lan
A486
258

ymael ylgrove
ge Coast
Ceibwr
Bay
Pen-y-
bryn
A484
Teifi
Marshes
Llandygwydd
B4333
Penrhiwllan
Llandysul
Llanfihangel-
ar-arth

Moylegrove
37
Castle
Cilgerran
Afon Teifi
TIVY SIDE
Cenarth Falls
National Coracle
Centre
Cwm-cou
B4571
Llandyfriog
A475
Teifi Valley
Railway
Llandi ul
Llangeler
Pontwelly
B4336

12 **Nevern** A
Felindre
Farchog
B4582
Pengelli
Forest
B Rhosi C
Abercych
Cenarth
Pen-rhiw
Adpar
Newcastle D
Emlyn
(Castell Newydd Emlyn)
E Henllan
Afon Teifi
A484
Drefach
F
Drefach
G
H
A48

0　1　2　3　4　5 miles
0　1　2　3　4　5　6　7　8 kilometres

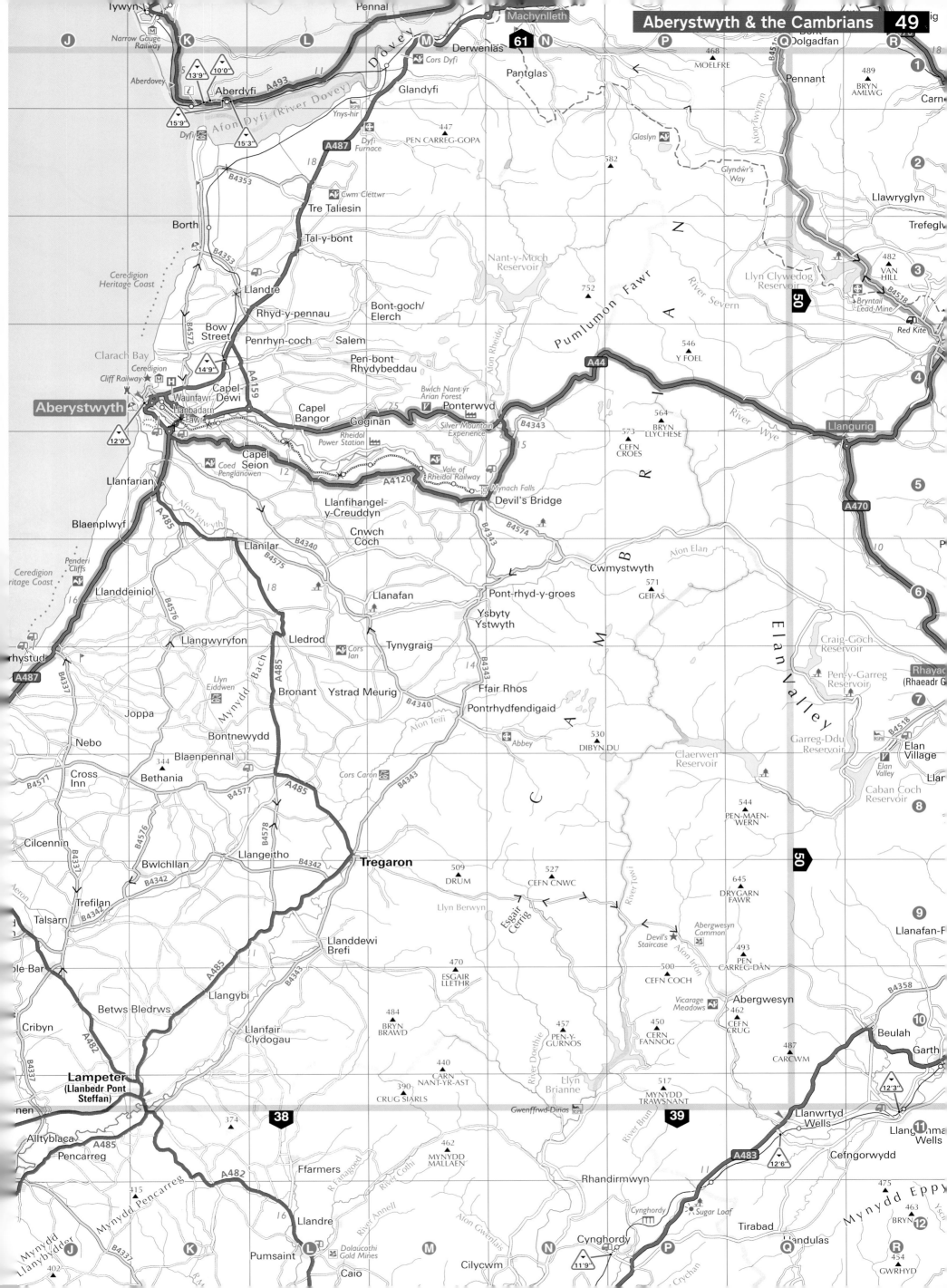

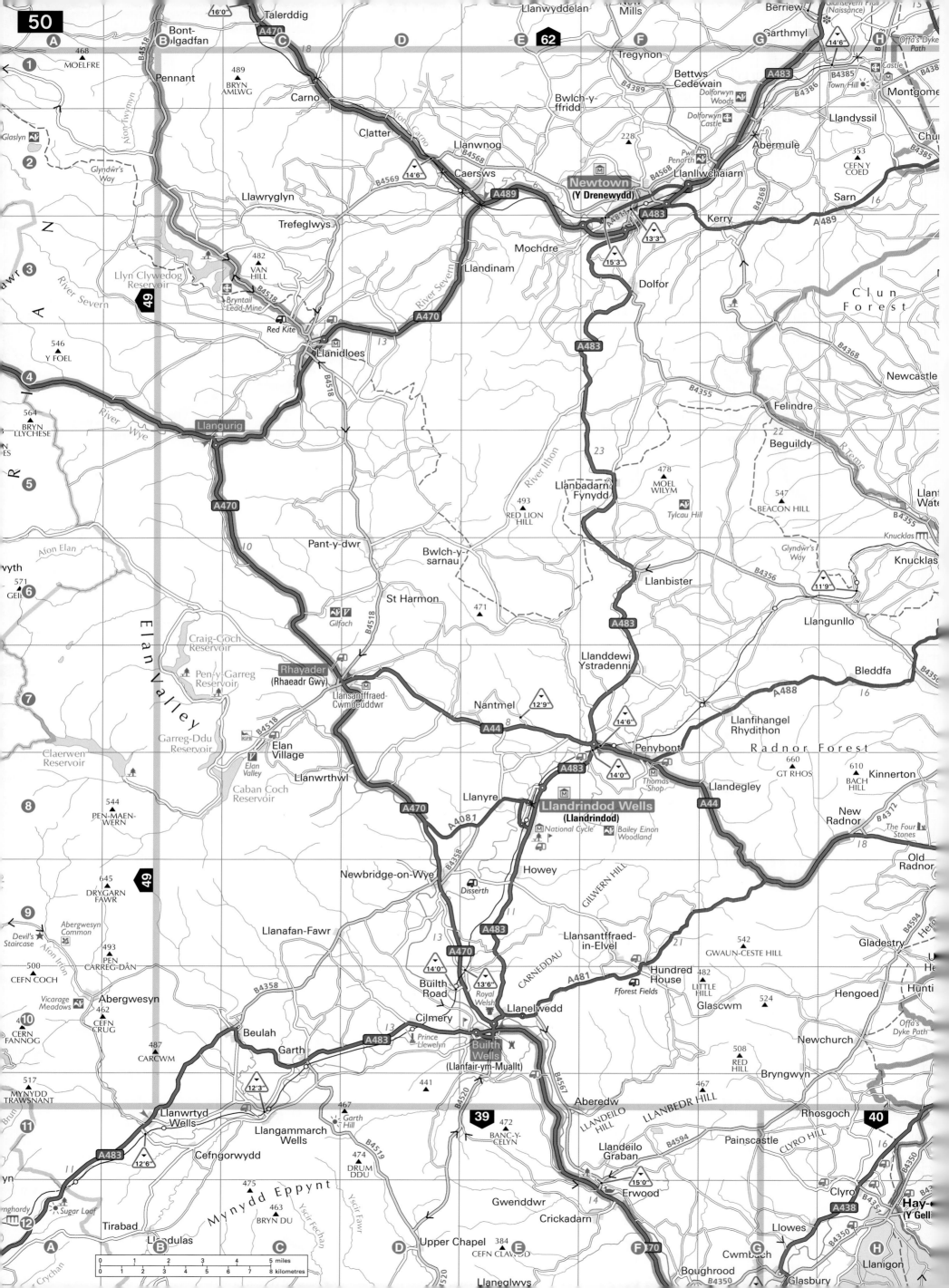

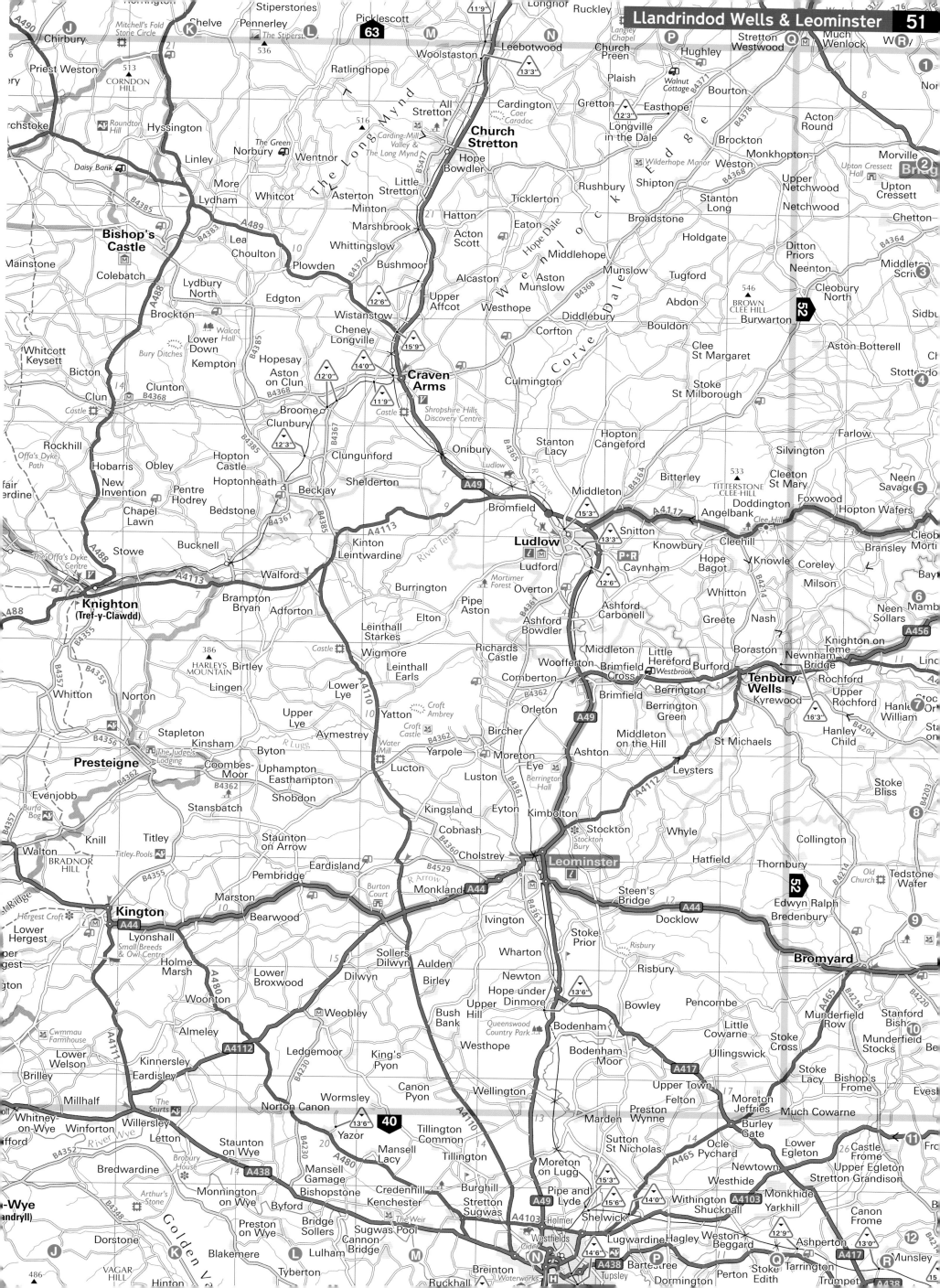

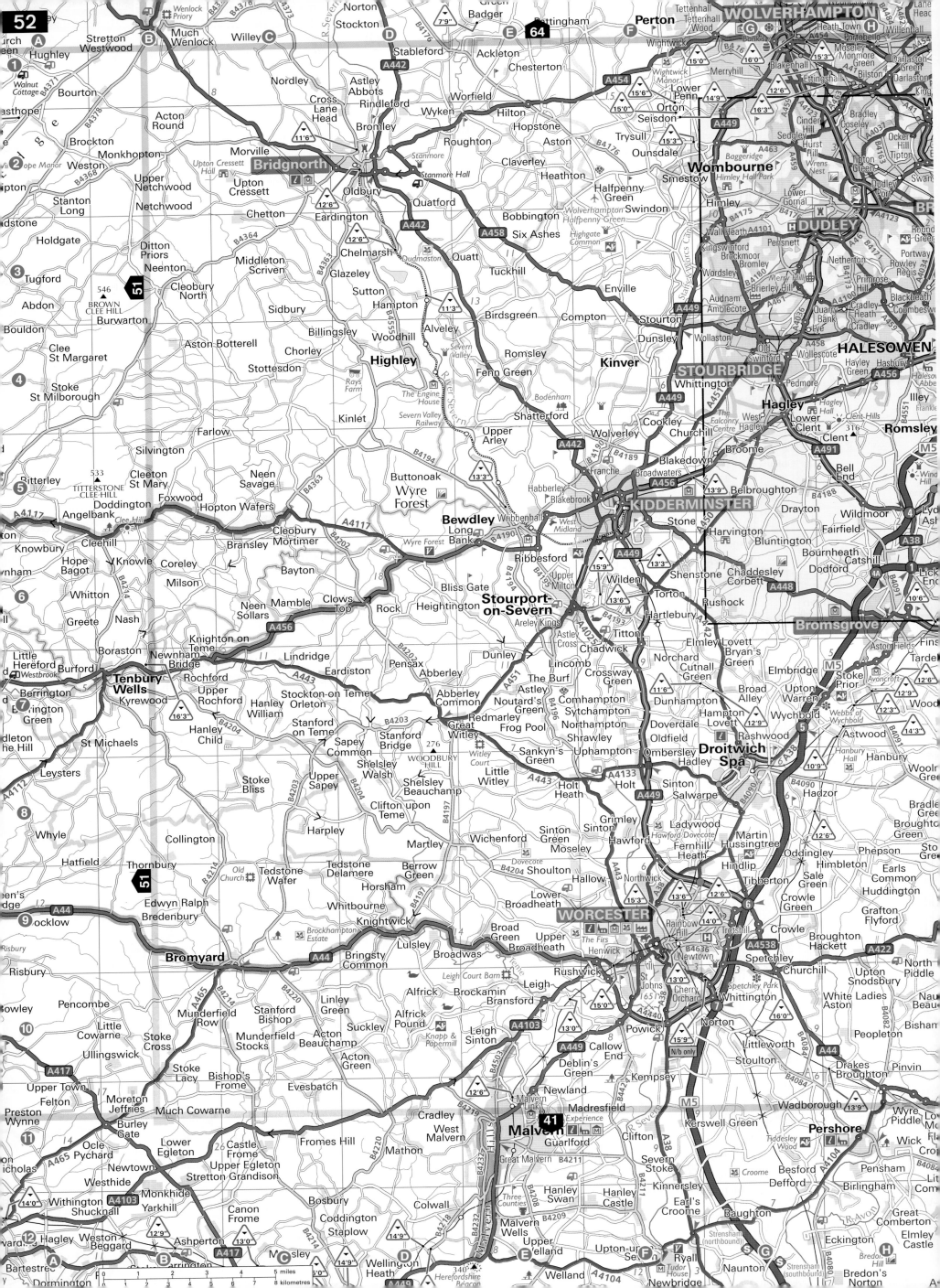

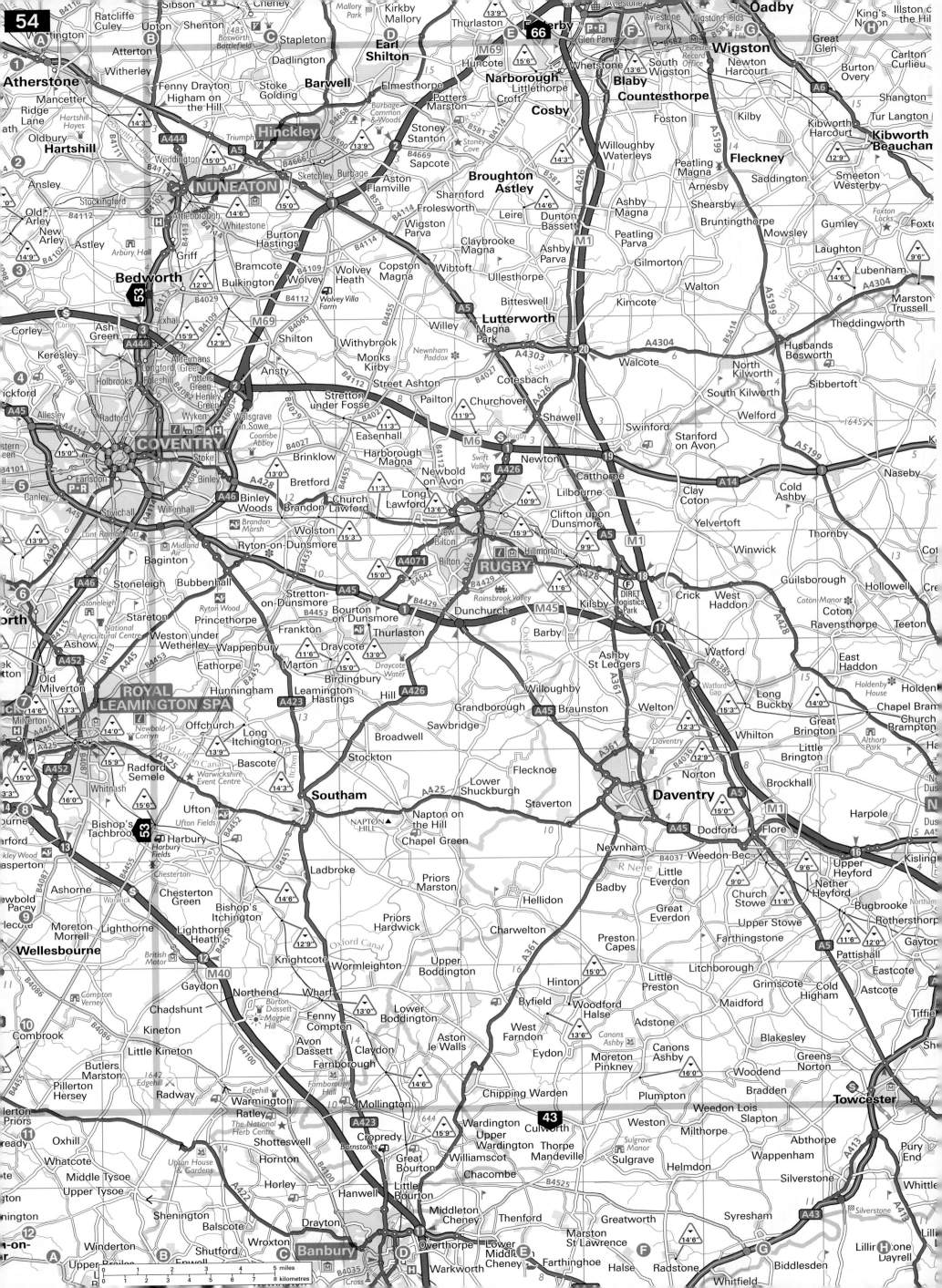

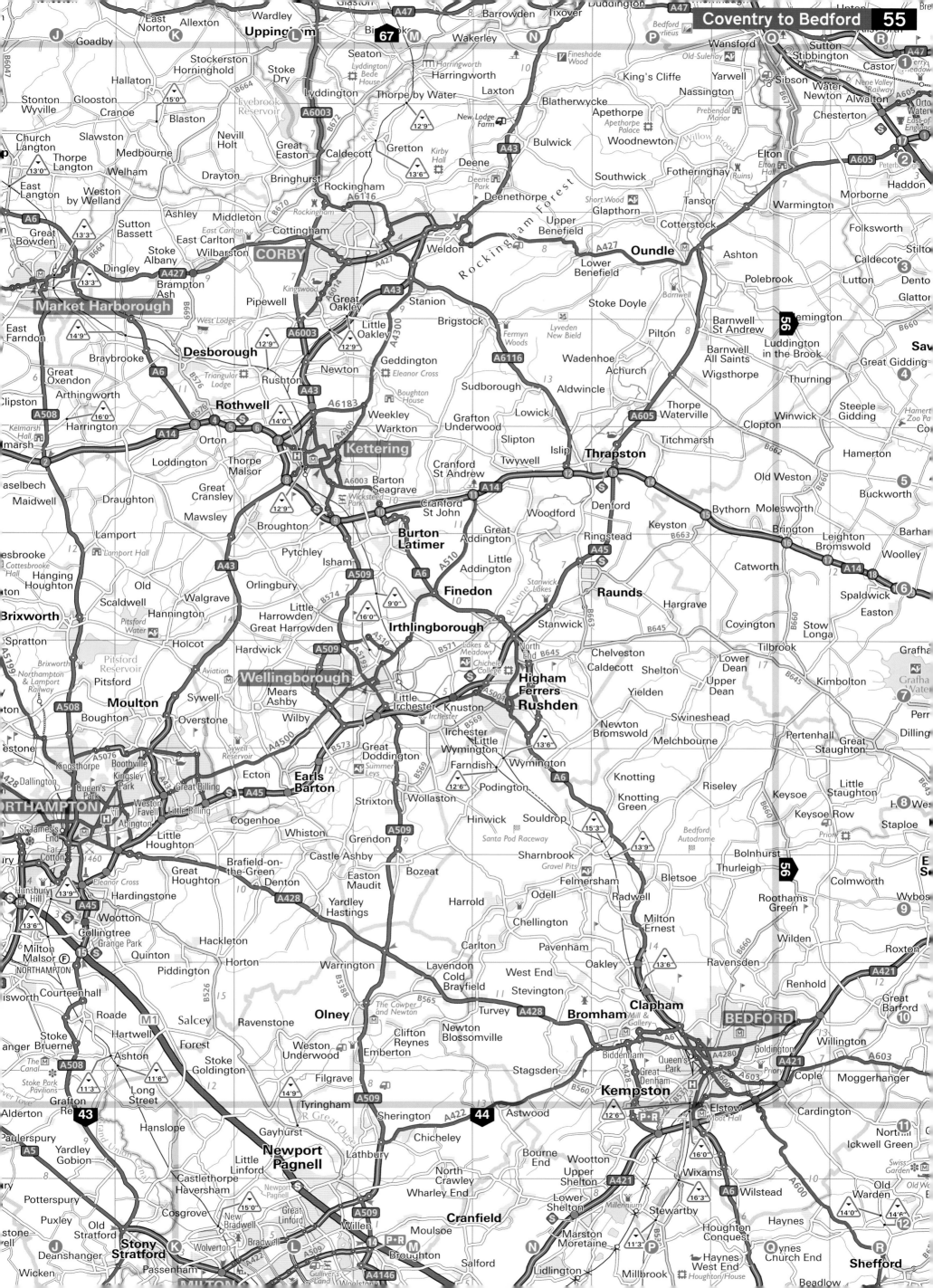

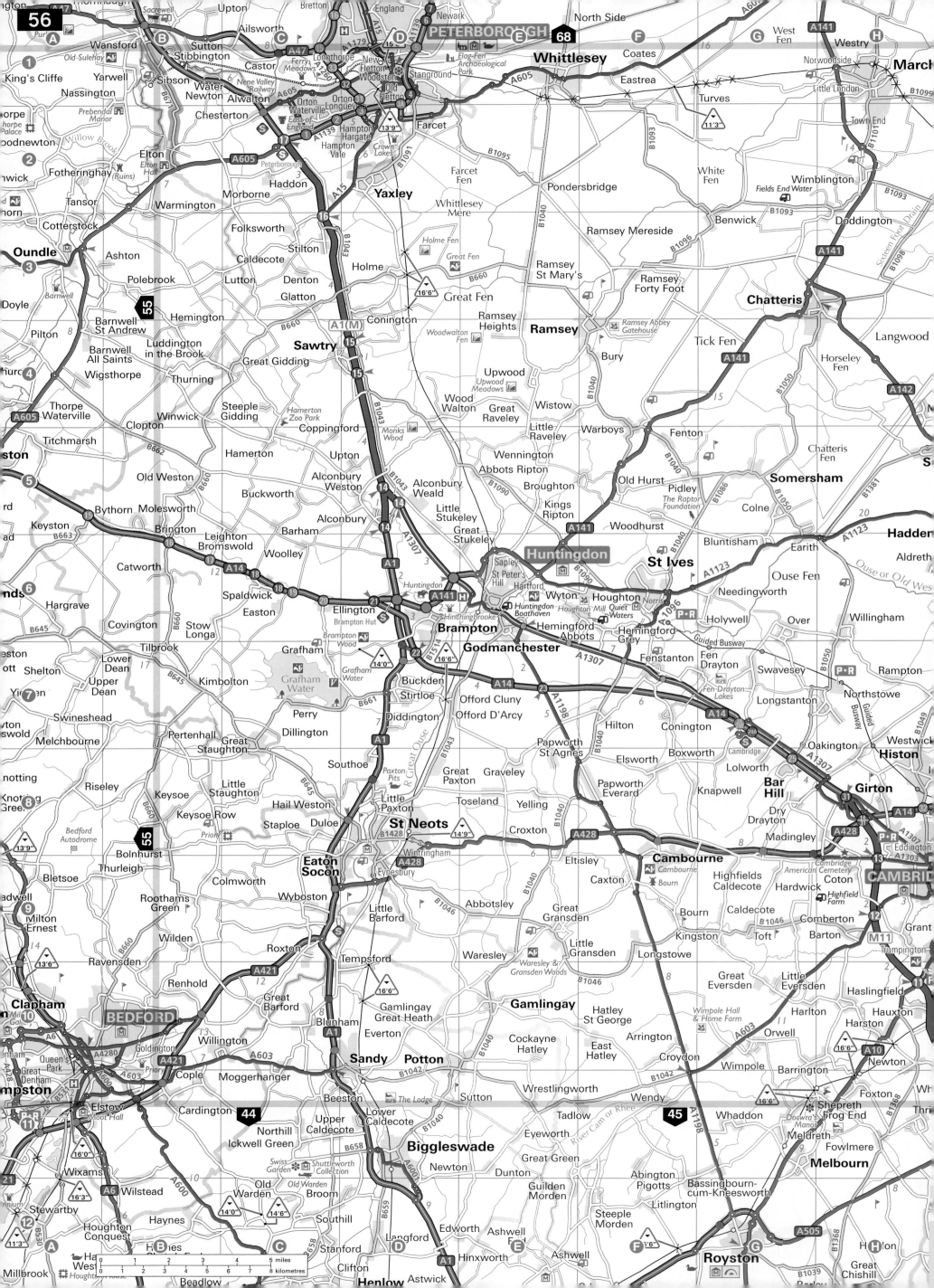

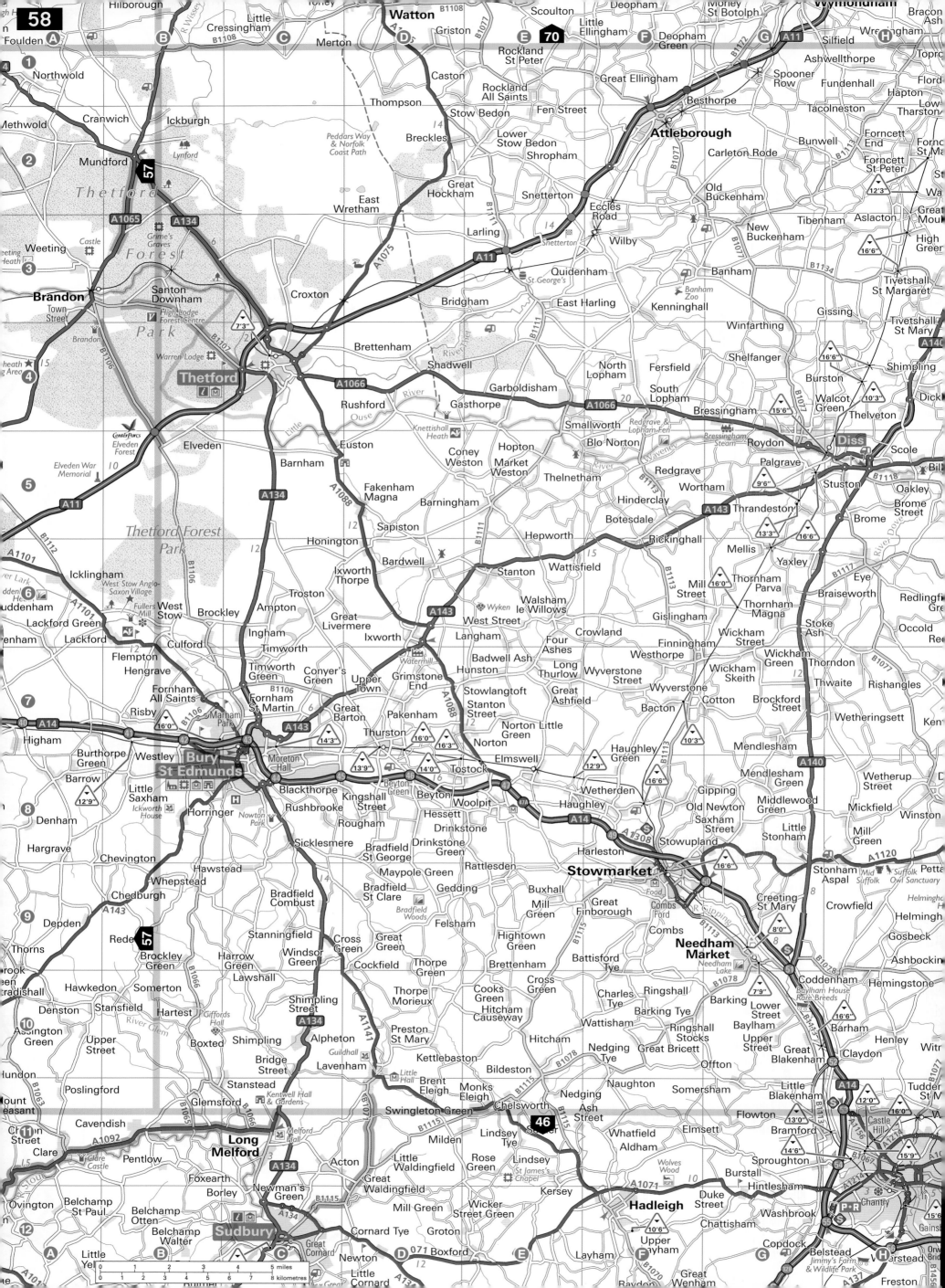

72

C A E R N A R F O N

B A Y

Llandwrog
Groeslon
Parc Glynllifon
Carmel
Inigo Jones Slateworks
Nant Slate L
Penygroes
Pontllyfni
Llanllyfni
Nebo
Talysarn
Nasareth
Clynnog Fawr
Pant Glas
Gaeau-Tan-y-Bwlch
Y GYRN-DDU
Bryncir
Garndol
Dolb
Lleyn Heritage Coast
Trefor
Tre'r Ceiri
Llanaelhaearn
Trwyn y Grolech
YR EIFL
St Cybi's Well
Llangybi
Llithfaen
Carreg Ddu
Porth Nefyn
Pistyll
Y Fôr
Llwyn-Bugeilydd
Pentref
Eisteddfa
Morfa Nefyn
Nefyn
B4354
B4354
Llanystumdwy
Lloyd George
Edern
Boduan
Llannor
Abererch
Penarth Fawr Medieval House
Chwilog
Criccieth
Castle
Porth Ysgaden
L L Y N
Efailnewydd
Hafan y Môr
Tudweiliog
Dinas
Carn Fadrun
Rhyd-y-clafdy
Abererch Sands
Pen-ychain
Trema Ba
Porth Colman
Llaniestyn
Pwllheli
Pen-y-graig
Sarn Mellteyrn
Bryn-mawr
Botwnnog
Penrhos
Pen
Llangwnnadl
Llanbedrog
Porth Oer
Bryncroes
Trwyn Llanbedrog
Rhoshirwaun
Plas yn Rhiw
Llangian
St Tudwal's Road
Rhydolion
Deucoch
Abersoch
Y Rhiw
Llanengan
Beach View
Aberdaron
Llanfaelrhys
Porth Neigwl or Hell's Mouth
Bwlchtocyn
Machroes
St Tudwal's Island East
Bardsey Sound
Aberdaron Bay
Porth Ysgo
Bryn Bach
St Tudwal's Island West
Porth Ceiriad
Lleyn Heritage Coast
St Mary's
Ynys Enlli
BARDSEY ISLAND

P E N I N S U L A
A487
A499
A497
A499
B4413
B4417
B4415
B4411

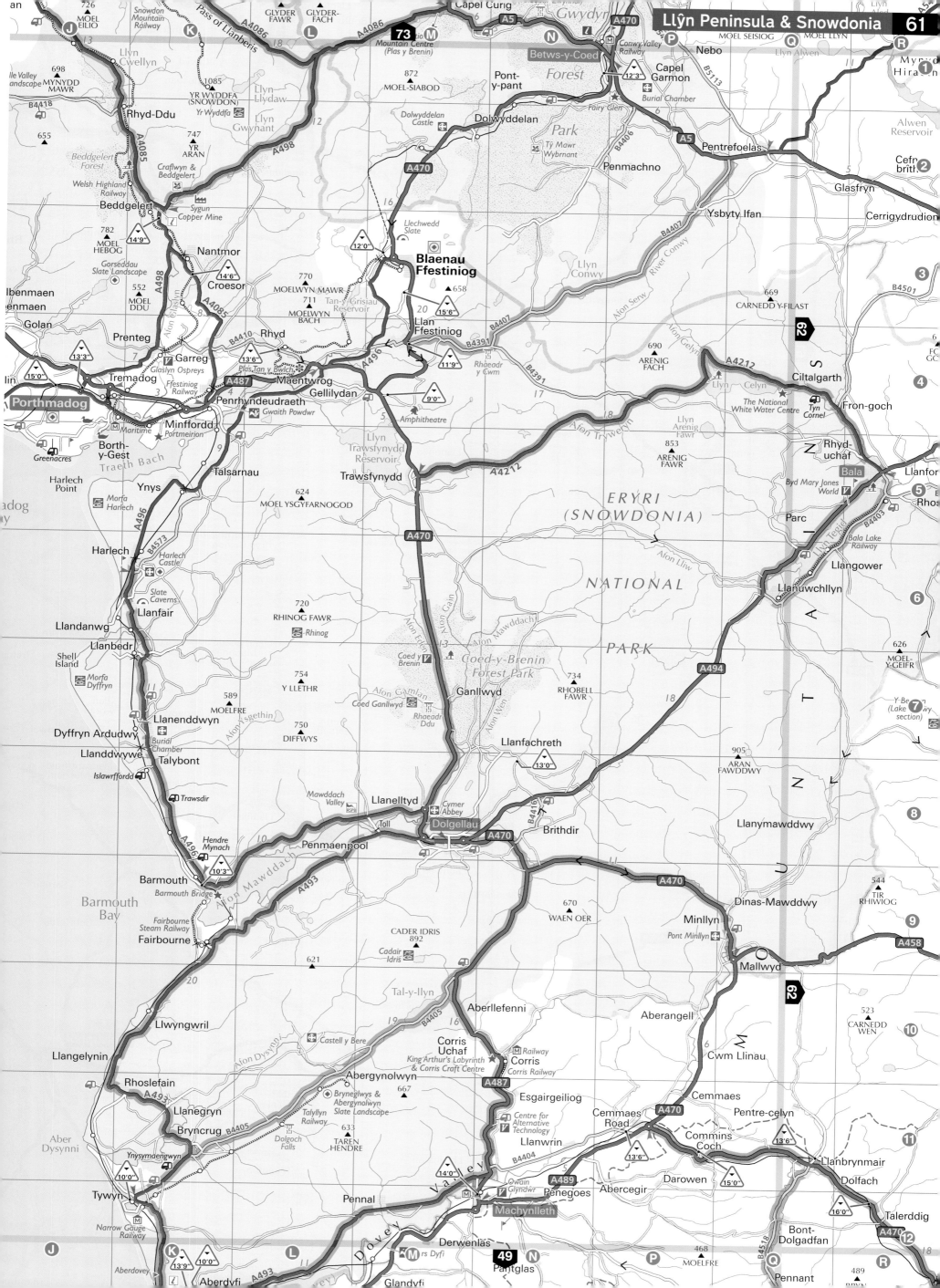

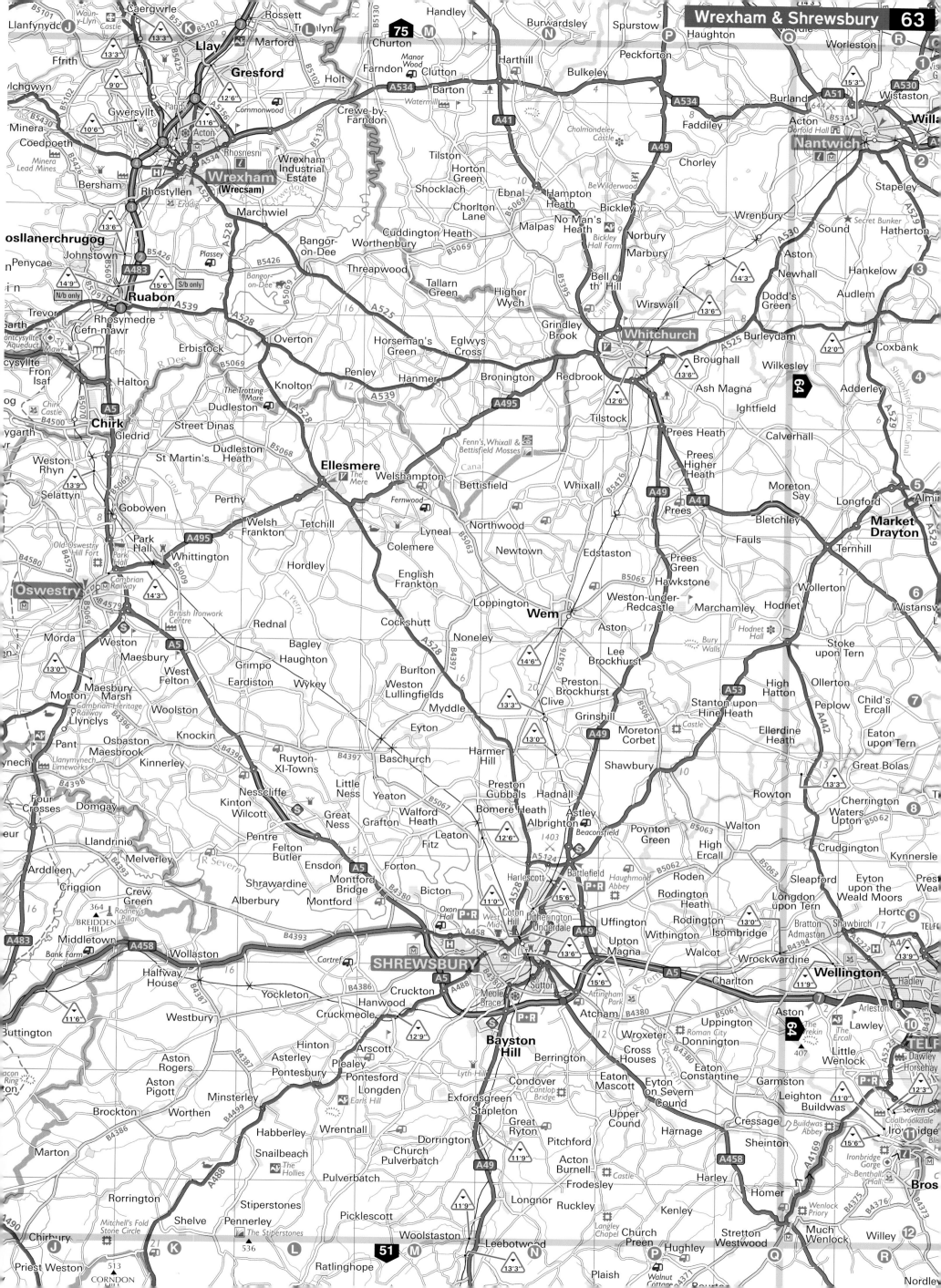

THE WASH

Wainfleet St Mary
skney
Gibraltar Point
Brancaster Bay
Scolt Head Island
Holkham
Peddars Way & Norfolk Coast Path
Titchfield Marsh
Brancaster Staithe
Burnham Deepdale
Burnham Norton
Burnham Overy Staithe
Holme next the Sea
Holme Dunes
Brancaster
Burnham Overy
Burnham Market
Burnham Thorpe
Old Hunstanton
Thornham
Titchwell
Branodunum Roman Fort
Deepdale
Hunstanton
Ringstead
Summerfield
North Creake
Creake Abbey
Searles
Norfolk Lavender
Docking
Stanhoe
South Creake
Heacham
Peddars Way & Norfolk Coast Path
Sedgeford
The Rickels
70
Fring
Bircham Newton
Syderstone
Wicken Green Village
Snettisham
Snettisham Park
Shernborne
Great Bircham
Bircham Tofts
Sculthorpe
Ingoldisthorpe
Anmer
Tattersett
Dunton
Coxford
Shereford
Gedney Drove End
Dersingham
Pinecones
Dersingham Bog
Sandringham
West Newton
Houghton Hall
West Rudham
East Rudham
Tatterford
Wolferton
Flitcham
New Houghton
A148
Helhoughton
West Raynham
East Raynham
South Raynham
Castle Rising
Hillington
Little Massingham
Great Massingham
Harpley
Sutton
Sutton Bridge
Terrington St Clement
North Wootton
Congham
Roydon
Grimston
Weasenham St Peter
Walpole Cross Keys
Castle
South Wootton
Roydon Common
Weasenham All Saints
Rougham
Tydd Gote
Clenchwarton
West Lynn
N/b only
13'6"
16'6"
Gaywood
A149
Bawsey
B1145
Gayton
Well
Four Gotes
Walpole St Andrew
Tilney All Saints
South Lynn
King's Lynn
Fair Green
Gayton Thorpe
A1065
West Walton
Walpole St Peter
Tilney High End
A47
East Winch
Ashwicken
Castle Acre
East Lexham
West Lexham
Walton Highway
Walpole Highway
Tilney St Lawrence
Terrington St John
West Winch
North Runcton
Middleton
Blackborough End
East Walton
West Acre
Priory
South Acre
Newton
Little Dunham
Great Dunham
Wisbech
New Walsoken
Wiggenhall St Germans
16'6"
Setchey
West Bilney
Pentney
Narborough
11'3"
Fransham
Marshland St James
Wiggenhall St Mary the Virgin
Watatunga Wildlife Reserve
Wormegay
River Nar
Sporle
Necton
Emneth
Watlington
Wiggenhall St Mary Magdalen
Tottenhill
Marham
Swaffham
Holme Hale
Emneth Hungate
Elm
Stowbridge
South Runcton
Fincham
Shouldham
Barton Bendish
Beachamwell
North Pickenham
Little Ranch
Friday Bridge
Outwell
Stow Bardolph Fen
Wimbotsham
Stow Bardolph
Stradsett
Shouldham Thorpe
Boughton
Oxborough
Goodsestone Water
Cockley Cley
South Pickenham
Downham Market
Bexwell
Crimplesham
Wereham
Gooderstone
Great Cressingham
Laddus Fen
Upwell
Nordelph
Denver
Fordham
West Dereham
Oxburgh Hall
Hilborough
Euximoor Fen
Upwell Fen
Denver Sluice
Lakeside
16'6"
11'9"
Wretton
Stoke Ferry
Foulden
Whittington
Little Cressingham
Christchurch
Ten Mile Bank
57
Northwold
A134

Holyhead Harbour

Marina
Salt Island
Maritime
Porth-y-Felin
BEACH ROAD
PRINCE OF WALES ROAD
VICTORIA ROAD
A5154
Hertz Car Rental
FERRY TERMINAL
TERMINAL BUILDING
Short stay
HOLYHEAD
HOLYHEAD STATION
Long stay
Stryd
Môrawelon
NEWRY STREET
PLAS ROAD
KINGSLAND ROAD
PORTHDAFARCH
B4545
CELTIR ROAD
A5153
Kingsland
A5 LONDON ROAD
BANGOR
SAC
0   500 m

The Skerries
North Anglesey Heritage Coast
Hen Borth
Cemlyn Bay
Wylfa Head
Cemaes Bay
Porth Wen
Bull Bay
Amlwch
Copper Kingdom
Point Lynas
CARMEL HEAD
Cemaes
A5025
Burwen
Llaneilian
Llanfairynghornwy
Tregele
Swtan Heritage
Llanfechell
Bodewryd
10'0"
Penysarn
Nebo
Llanrhyddlad
17
Carreglefn
Rhosybol
Capel Parc
Tyddyn Isaf
Dulas Bay
Church Bay
Holyhead Bay
13'9"
Llyn Alaw
Ty'n Rhos
Din Lligwy
Llanfaethlu
Llanddeusant
Llynon Mill
Aton Alaw
Llanerchymedd
Home Farm
Dublin
Porth Tywynmawr
Elim
Capel Coch
Brynteg
B5111
B5108
North Stack
Gogarth Bay
10'9"
Holyhead Maritime
Llanfwrog
Llyn Llywenan
Presaddfed
B5112
Cors Erddreiniog
Llanbedrgoch
Dublin (Mar-Oct)
Breakwater
Holyhead (Caergybi)
A N G L E S E Y
Cors Goch
Holyhead Mountain Hut Circles
Llanfachraeth
B5109
21
South Stack
Holyhead Mountain Heritage Coast
Ellins Tower
Penrhos Feliw
Kingsland
Llanynghenedl
B5110
Llanddyfnan
Penrhyn Mawr
Trefignath
A5
Valley
A5025
Bodedern
Rhosmeirch
Talwrn
B5109
Trearddur Bay
B4545
A55
Caergeiliog
Bryngwran
Bodffordd
Gwalchmai
Cefni Reservoir
Oriel Môn
Llangefni
B5420
HOLY ISLAND
Four Mile Bridge
Llanfihangel yn Nhowyn
Valley
A5
Anglesey
18
A55
A5114
Llanfair-yn-Neubwll
9'6"
Penmynedd
Rhoscolyn
Ty Newydd
10
Pencarnisiog
Din Dryfol
Llangristiolus
Llanfairpw
Rhoscolyn Head
A4080
Llanfaelog
Henblas
Pentre Berw
Cymyran Bay
14'3"
Bethel
13'3"
Gaerwen
A4419
Bryn Celli Ddu
Rhosneigr
15'9"
Aton Cefni
A4080
Barclodiad y Gawres
9'9"
Llangadwaladr
Malltraeth
Bodowyr Burial Chamber
Brynsiencyn
Y Felir
Porth Trecastell
Aberffraw
15'0"
21
Llangaffo
Caer Lêb
Anglesey Sea Zoo
A4080
Anglesey Circuit
Castell Bryn Gwyn
A4871
Dwyran
Bet
Aberffraw Bay
Newborough
Foel Farm Park
Bodwyr
A4080
Caernarfon
Caernarfon Castle
Riverside
A4086
Aberffraw Bay Heritage Coast
Llanddwyn Island
Malltraeth Bay
Newborough Warren
Abermenai Point
Gypsy Wood
A4085
Cae at
Ce
Llanddwyn Bay
Foryd Bay
Welsh Highland Railway
Segontium
C A E R N A R F O N
Airworld Aviation
White Tower
Llanwnda
Bontnewydd
A487
B A Y
Dinlle
11'9"
Parc Glynllifon
Llandwrog
Groes on
Inigo Jones Slateworks
Carmel
Rhostry

0   1   2   3   4   5 miles
0 1 2 3 4 5 6 7 8 kilometres

Liverpool Docks

Dangerous goods restriction: Category D

15'9" 15'0"

12'9"

SOUTHPORT
SEATRUCK TERMINAL
BOOTLE
New Brighton
Kirkdale
Anfield
Everton
PIER HEAD FERRY & CRUISE TERMINAL
LIVERPOOL
LIME STREET STATION
12 QUAYS FERRY TERMINAL
BIRKENHEAD
SAC
SPEKE
WIDNES
LODGE LANE

1 km

LIVERPOOL BAY

Dublin
Douglas (Apr–Oc
Belfast

Hoylake
Royal Liverpool
Hilbre Island
Red Rocks Marsh
Middle Eye
Little Eye
West Kirby
Greasby
Thurstaston
River Dee
Heswall
Hes

Point-of-Ayr
Presthaven Sands
Prestatyn
Gronant
Gwespyr
Ffynnongroyw
Rhyl
14'9"
Kinmel Bay
Llanasa
Gwaenysgor
Trelogan
10'0"
Mostyn
Glan-y-don
Abergele Roads
Kinmel Bay
Meliden
Miniature Railway
Basingwerk Abbey
Greenfield

Little Ormes Head
Penrhyn Bay
13'3"
Rhôs-on-Sea
Llandrillo-yn-Rhôs
Colwyn Bay (Bae Colwyn)
Towyn
A547
Dyserth
Cwm
Trelawnyd
Whitford
Greenfield Valley
Gorsedd
Carmel
St Winefride's Well

Welsh
Old Colwyn
Llanddulas
Pensarn
Rhuddlan
Offa's Dyke
Penisar Mynydd
Lloc
Pantasaph
Haulfryn
Holywell (Treffynnon)
andudno Junction
13'3"
Llanelian-yn-Rhôs
Llysfaen
Rhyd-y-foel
Abergele
St George
Bodelwyddan
Rhuallt
Calcoed
Brynford
Bagillt
nsanffraid n Conwy
Bryn-y-Maen
Dolwen
Betws-yn-Rhos
Hunters Hamlet
St Asaph
Tremeirchion
Caerwys
Lixwm
Rhes-y-cae
Dolphin
Flint (Y Fflint)
Halkyn
Clwydian Range

aig
wysbach
Llanfair Talhaiarn
River Elwy
Llannefydd
Trefnant
Bodfari
Afon-wen
Ysceifiog
Pen-y-felin
Nannerch
Northop
Rhosesmor

nrwst
Pentre-tafarn-y-fedw
Llangernyw
Llansannan
Henllan
Denbigh Friary
Bylchau
Nantglyn
Groes
Pentre Llanrhaeadr
Llandyrnog
Llanynys
Gellifor
Moel Famau
Cilcain
Pantymwyn
Gwernaffield
Mold (Yr Wyddgrug)
Gwernymynydd
Nercwy
Lees
Pony

Bodnant
Gwytherin
Denbigh (Dinbych)
Offa's Dyke Path
Llangynhafal
MOEL FAMAU
Loggerheads
Rhewl
Llanferres
Llanarmon-yn-Ial

Pandy Tudur
MOEL SEISIOG
MOEL LLYN
Gors Maen Llwyd
Archaeological Trail
Llyn Brenig Reservoir
Cyffylliog
Ruthin (Rhuthun)
Llanfwrog
Bontuchel
Llanbedr-Dyffryn-Clwyd
Eryrys
Treuddy

Nebo
Capel Garmon
Llyn Aled
Llyn Brenig
Efenechtyd
Dyffryn Clwyd
Llanfai
Pwll
Graigfechan

0 1 2 3 4 5 miles
0 1 2 3 4 5 6 7 8 kilometres

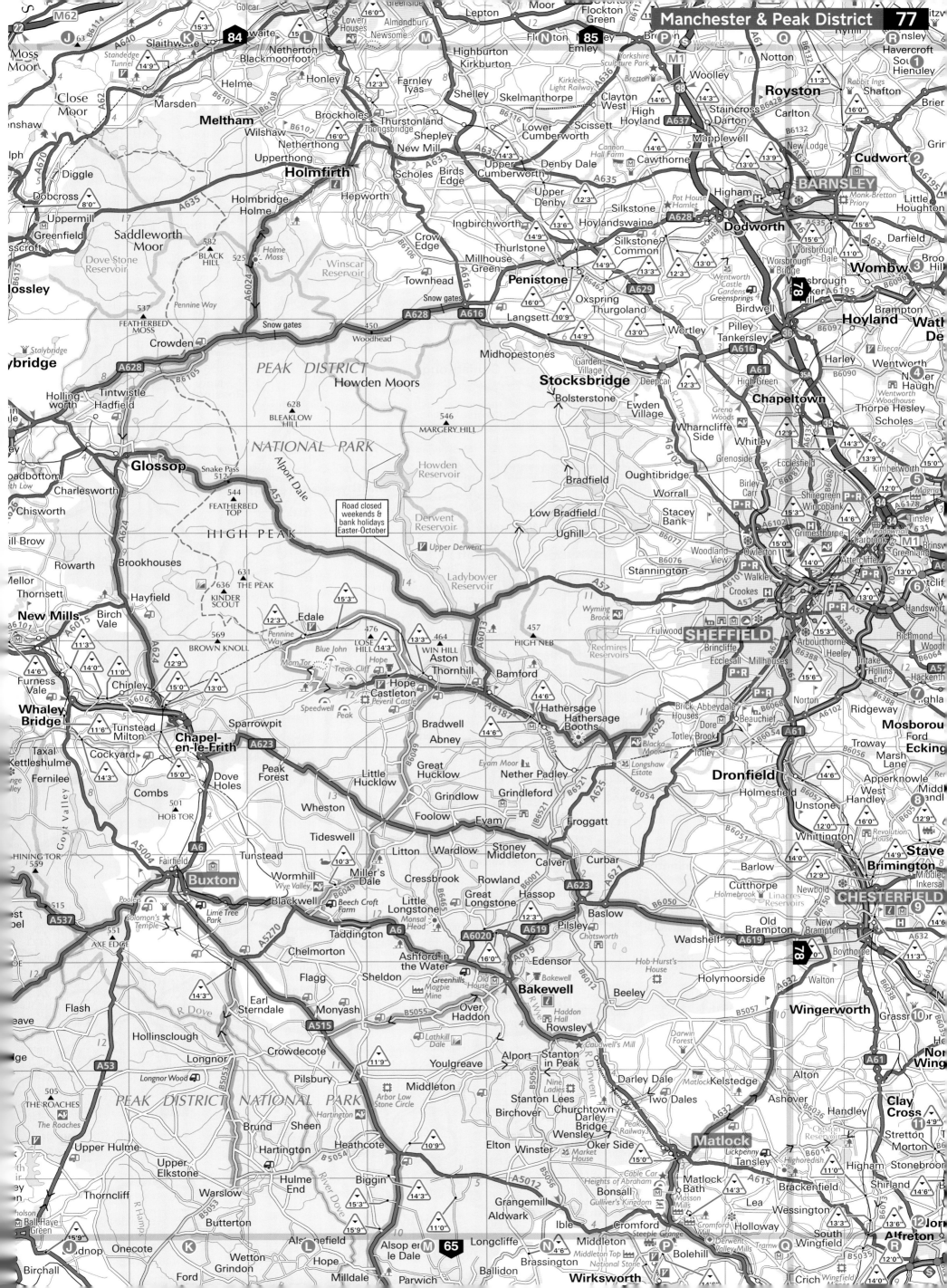

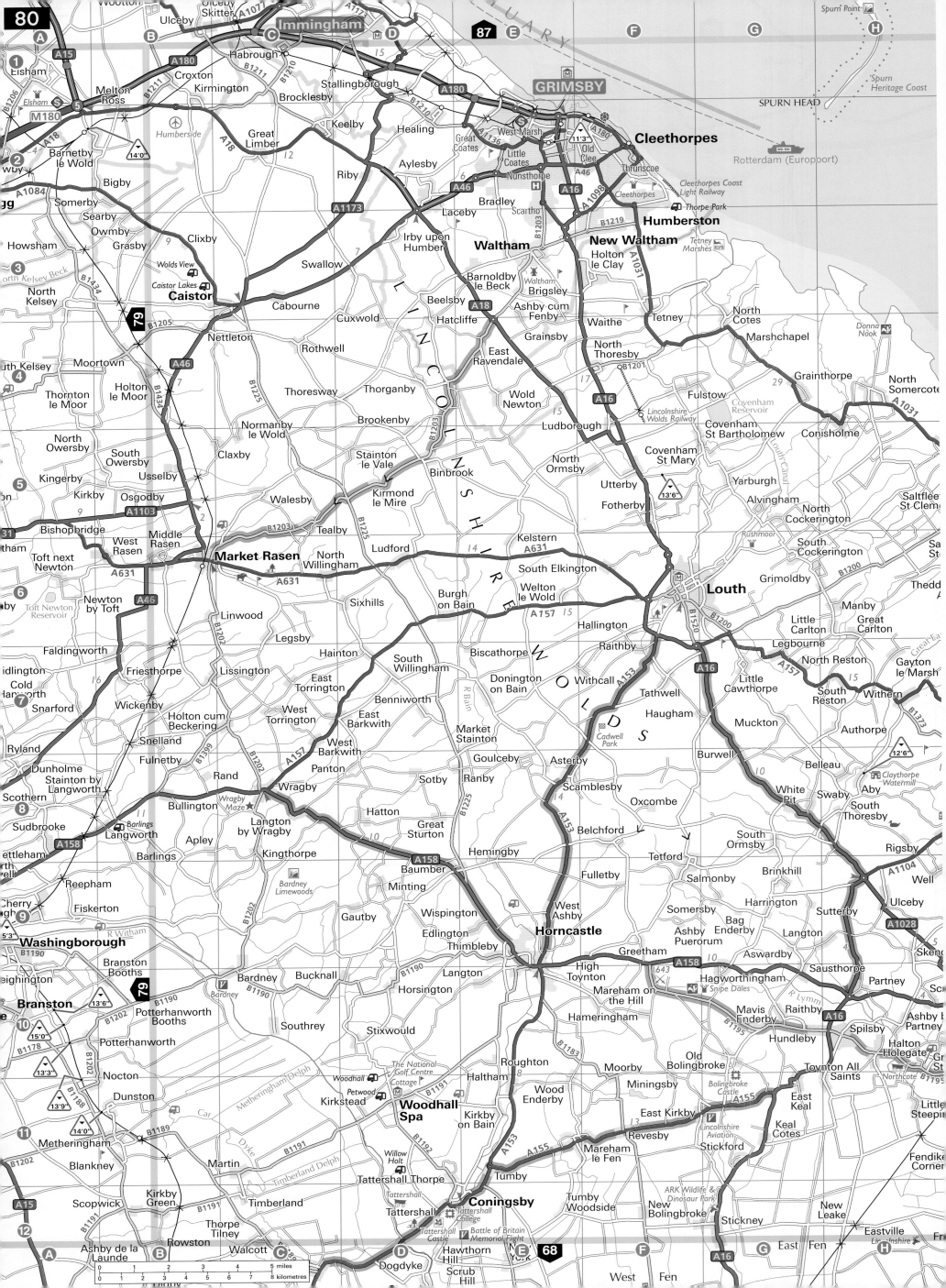

Saltfleet

Saltfleetby -
Theddlethorpe Dunes

Saltfleetby
All Saints

Theddlethorpe
St Helen

Seal Sanctuary &
Wildlife Centre

Golden Sands

Mablethorpe

Kirkstead Trusthorpe

Maltby
le Marsh Sutton on Sea

Sandilands

Beesby
Saleby

Markby King Charles III
England Coast Path

Huttoft

Bilsby
Thurlby

Alford

Anderby

Farlesthorpe

Mumby

Cumberworth Chapel Point

Hogsthorpe **Chapel
St Leonards**

Willoughby

Eastview

Sloothby Chapel Fields

Fantasy Island

Habertoft Addlethorpe

Ingoldmells

Welton
le Marsh

Candlesby Ingoldmells
Point

Orby Lincolnshire Coast
Light Railway

Gunby
Hall

Monksthorpe

Burgh le Marsh

Natureland Seal
Sanctuary

Bratoft

Village Church
Farm

Irby in the Marsh **Skegness**

Firsby Skegness

Croft

Thorpe St Peter

Wainfleet
Haven

Wainfleet
All Saints

Batemans

Wainfleet
St Mary

Gibraltar Point

skney

Heysham Harbour

0   500 m

MORECAMBE

A589

Lower Heysham

LONGLANDS LANE

HEYSHAM

Heysham Sands

Half Moon Bay

MIDDLETON WAY

P   Higher Heysham

HEYSHAM PORT STATION

Freight Terminal

A683

A683

LANCASTER

ISLE OF MAN FERRY TERMINAL   P

A683

MIDDLETON ROAD

Nuclear Power Stations

SAC

BARROW-IN-FURNESS

alton-in-Furness

Scales

Baycliff

Hawc'

Newton

Staintor with Adgarley

6'0"

Furness Abbey

Bow Bridge

Dendron

Watermill

Gleaston

Aldingham

Vickerstown

A590

Barrow Island

A5087

Leece

14'3"

Rampside

ISLE OF WALNEY

Sheep Island

Piel Castle

Foulney Island

Piel Island

South End

Piel Bar

Hilpsford Point

South Walney

Douglas

Fleetwood

Kr

Rossall Point

River Wyre

A587

B5268

A585

Cleveleys

Thornton

A584

B5124

A586

15'6"

Warbreck

North Shore

Hoohill

BLACKPOOL

Model Village

Great Marton

Marton Mere

A58

15'3"

South Shore

B5262

15'9"

B5261

A5

14'0"

B5410

B5261

8

St Anne's

B5

B5261

Royal Lytham & St Annes

Ansdell

Fairhaven

Lytham St Annes

Discover Centr

13'0"

SOUTHPORT

Pleasureland

P+R

British Lawnmower

Birkdale

The Royal Birkdale

Ainsdale

Shi

King Charles III England Coast Path

0   1   2   3   4   5 miles
0   1   2   3   4   5   6   7   8 kilometres

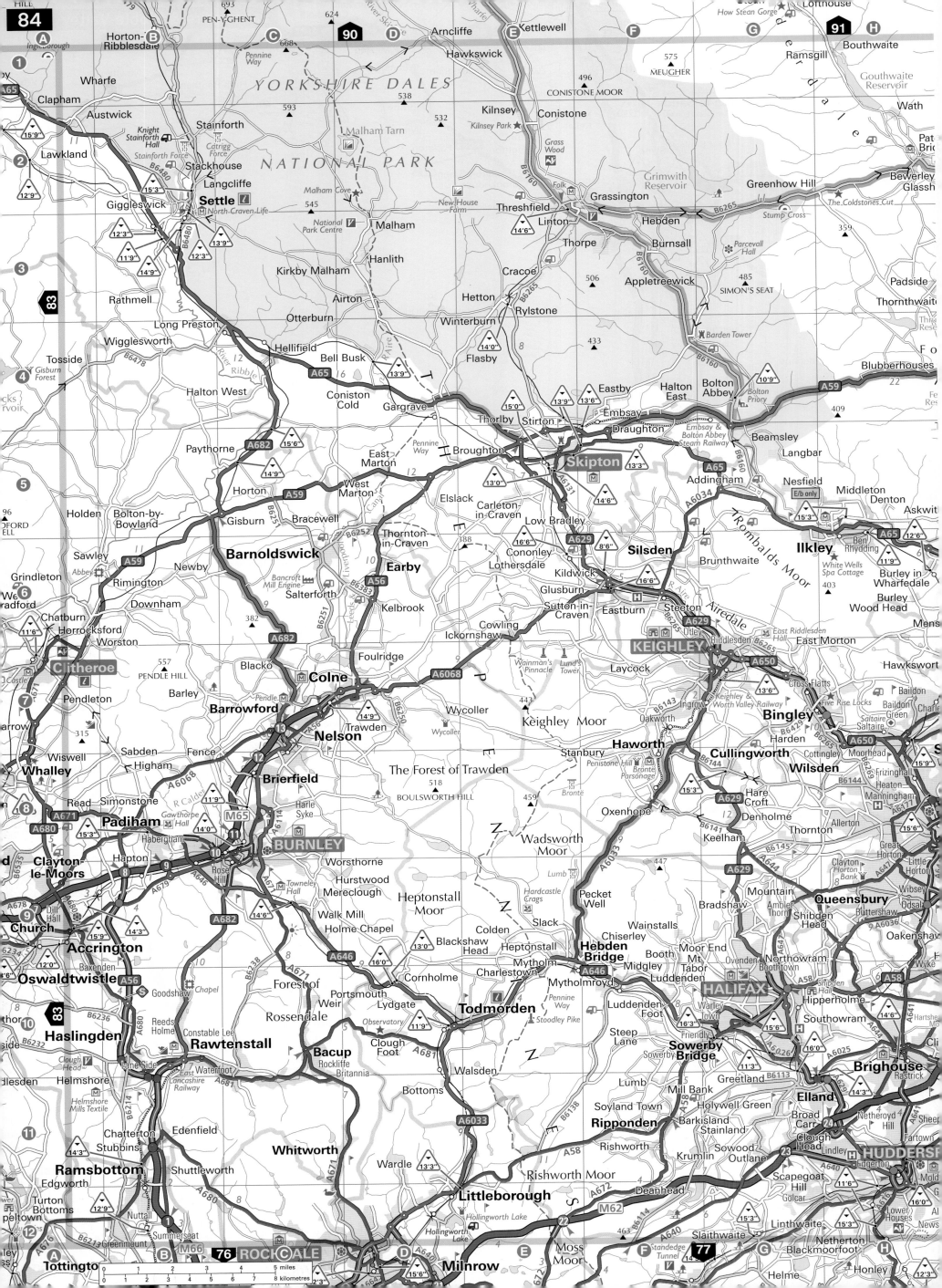

Port of Hull

0   1 km

SAC

BRIDLINGTON BAY

HUMBER ESTUARY

Bridlington

Driffield

Hornsea

Beverley

KINGSTON UPON HULL

Cottingham

Hessle

Hedon

Withernsea

Barton-upon-Humber

Immingham

HOLDERNESS

WOLDS

Foxholes
Newton
Burton Fleming
Buckton
Bempton
Thornwick Bay
North Landing
Flamborough Cliffs
Selwicks Bay
Grindale
Flamborough
FLAMBOROUGH HEAD
Thwing
Fir Tree
Sewerby
Boynton
Bondville Model Village
Thorpe Hall
Rudston
Monolith
Hildenthorpe
Langtoft
Kilham
Bessingby
Carnaby
Haisthorpe
Thornholme
Burton Agnes
World of Rock
Bridlington Animal Park
Fraisthorpe
Ruston Parva
Lowthorpe
Harpham
Garton-on-the-Wolds
Nafferton
Gransmoor
Barmston
Great Kelk
Lissett
Little Driffield
Wansford
Gembling
Ulrome
Skipsea Castle
Skipsea
Kirkburn
Southburn
Skerne
Foston on the Wolds
Beeford
Brigham
Skirlington
Hutton
North Frodingham
Dunnington
Atwick
Hutton Cranswick
Kilnwick
Watton
Bewholme
Beswick
Honeysuckle Farm
Lockington
Tophill Low
Brandesburton
Thorpe
Aike
Dacre Lakeside
Blue Rose
Seaton
Wassand Hall & Gardens
Hornsea Mere
Hornsea Freeport
Scorborough
Arram
Foss Hill
Leven
Catwick
Sigglesthorne
Rolston
Leconfield
Routh
Long Riston
Rise
Goxhill
Mappleton
Mappleton Sands
Great Hatfield
Tickton
Arnold
New Ellerby
Withernwick
Great Cowden
Molescroft
Weel
Skirlaugh
Marton
Aldbrough
Woodmansey
West Newton
Thearne
Dunswell
Old Ellerby
Flinton
Swine
Burton Constable Hall
Kingswood
Bransholme
Coniston
Ganstead
Burton Constable
Sproatley
Humbleton
Hilston
Skidby
Little Weighton
Wawne
Wyton
Bilton
Lelley
Owstwick
Willerby
Sutton-on-Hull
Preston
Elstronwick
Tunstall
Kirk Ella
West Ella
East Ella
Newland
Stoneferry
Sand le Mere
Anlaby
Marfleet
Burton Pidsea
Roos
Rimswell
North Ferriby
International Ferry Terminal
Owthorne
Northfield
South Field
Thorngumbald
Halsham
Winestead
Hollym
Paull
Keyingham
Holmpton
Humber Bridge
Waters' Edge
New Holland
Ottringham
Patrington
Barton Waterside
St Peter's Church
Barrow Haven
Goxhill
Patrington Haven
Welwick
Baysgarth House
Barrow-upon-Humber
East Halton
RAF Holmpton Bunker
South Ferriby
Weeton
Skeffling
Wootton
Thornton Abbey & Gatehouse
Thornton Curtis
North Killingholme
South Killingholme
Immingham Dock
Spurn Heritage Coast
Bonby
Ulceby Skitter
Ulceby
Worlaby
Elsham
Croxton
Kilnsea
Spurn Point
Melton
Kirmington
Spurn Heritage Coast
Stallingborough
GRIMSBY
Worlab

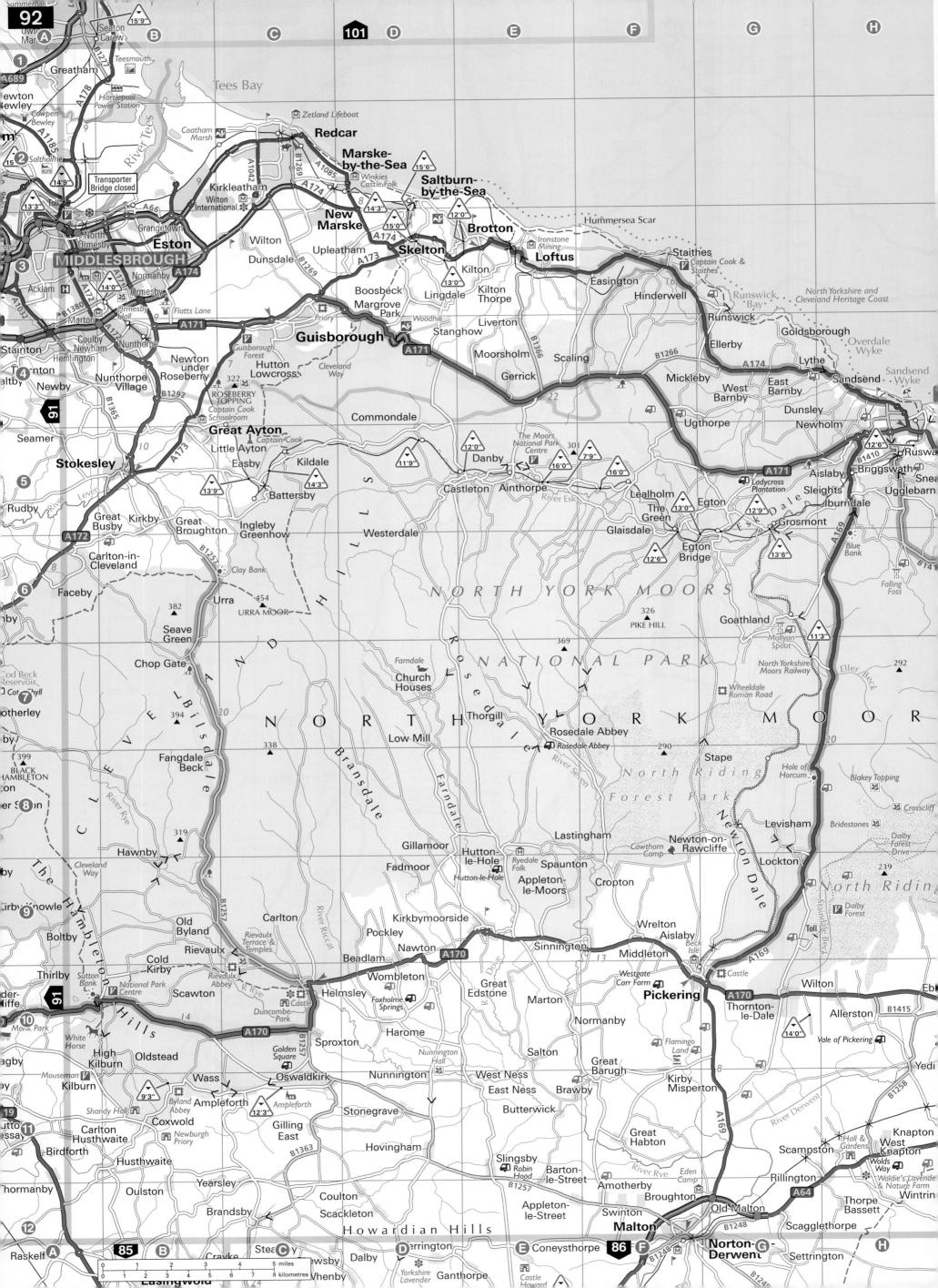

J   K   L   M   N   P   Q   R

Whitby
Abbey   Saltwick Bay
King Charles III
England Coast Path
14'0"
Stainsacre
High Hawsker
Ness Point or
North Cheek
Robin Hood's Bay
Fylingthorpe
Old Coastguard
Robin
Hood's Bay
Old Peak or
South Cheek
A171
Ravenscar
Grouse Hill
20
Staintondale
Harwood
Dale
Hayburn
Wyke
10'9"
Cloughton
Wyke
Bickley   Broxa   Silpho   Cloughton   9'3"
Suffield   Cromer Point
Langdale   Hackness   Burniston   Cleveland Way
End   10'3"   Scalby
Forest Park   Newby   North Bay Railway
River Derwent   Castle
Sea Cut   Falsgrave   Scarborough
A170   Oliver's Mount
Forge Valley   East   P·R
Wood   Ayton   A165   P·R   Cayton
West   Betton   Eastfield   Osgodby   Bay
Sawdon   Ayton   The
St Helens   Flower of May   Wyke
Hutton   Irton   Crossgates   Crows Nest
Ruston   Buscel   Seamer   Cayton   Blue Dolphin
Snainton   Wykeham   Killerby Old Hall   Fair Collection
Brompton-   Lebberston   Filey Brigg
by-Sawdon   Jasmine   Gristhorpe   A1039   Filey Brigg
A64   Bird Garden   Filey
R Hertford   & Animal Park
Folkton   Muston
Willerby   A1039   Orchard Farm
Staxton   Flixton   7   14'6"   Filey Bay
Ganton   Primrose Valley
Sherburn   Yorkshire Wolds Way   Reighton Sands
East Heslerton   Hunmanby   Reighton   Flamborough Head
Potter   13'9"   Heritage Coast
Brompton   Speeton
Jackson's   Fordon   Bempton
Wold   Cliffs   Thornwick
Foxholes   Wold   15'6"   14'3"   Bay
Butterwick   Newton   Buckton   Thornwick   North
Burton   Bempton   Bay   Landing
Fleming   Grindale   A165   Flamborough Cliffs
B1249   Flamborough   Selwick Bay
West Lutton   Thwing   A165   FLAMBOROUGH
Helperthorpe   HEAD
East Lutton   Fir Tree

86   87

1
2
3
4
5
6
7
8
9
10
11
12

A B C D E F G **104** H

1
2
3
4
5
6
7
8
9
10
11
12

Bennane Head

Colmonell

River Stinchar

Ballantrae

Heronsford

Water of Tig

Currarie Port

Belfast

BENERAIRD
437

CARLOCK HILL
321

Larne

ALTIMEG HILL
387

Milleur Point

Glen App

Corsewall Point

Lady Bay

Glenwhilly

Laggang Standing S

Barnhills

Portencalzie

Cairnryan

Penwhirn Reservoir

Glenwhilly

Kirkcolm

Loch Connell

Braid Fell

New Luce

Ervie

Low Barbeth

Low Salchrie

Leswalt

Loch Ryan

Innermessan

Black Loch

Castle Kennedy

Knocknain

Ryan Bay

White Loch

CRAIG FELL
164

Castle of St John

Balgracie

Stranraer

Aird

Castle Kennedy

13'3"

Glenluc

Auchnotteroch

Aird Donald

Chlenry

Dunragit

Glenluc

Portslogan

Broadsea Bay

Lochans

Kildrochet House

Piltanton Burn

13'3" 13'9" A75 10

Glenwhan

Whitecrook

12'9"

Black Head

181
CAIRN PAT 8

B7077

14

B7084

Ringdoo Point

14'3"

Portpatrick

A77

Stoneykirk

North Milmain

18

Luce Sands

Stairhave

Mull of S

Sands of Luce

Sandhead

Cairngarroch

Kirkmadrine Stones

Money Head

12'0"

High Ardwell

Ardwell Bay

Ardwell

Chapel Rossan

Drumbreddon

Balgowan

L U C E

Logan

Port Logan Bay

Port Logan

B7065

A716

Garrochtrie

Clanyard Bay

Kilstay

Laggantalluch Head

Kirkmaiden

Drummore

Cailiness Point

Barncorkrie

High Drummore

Damnaglaur

Maryport

B7041

Cardryne

Cardrain

West Cairngaan

MULL OF GALLOWAY

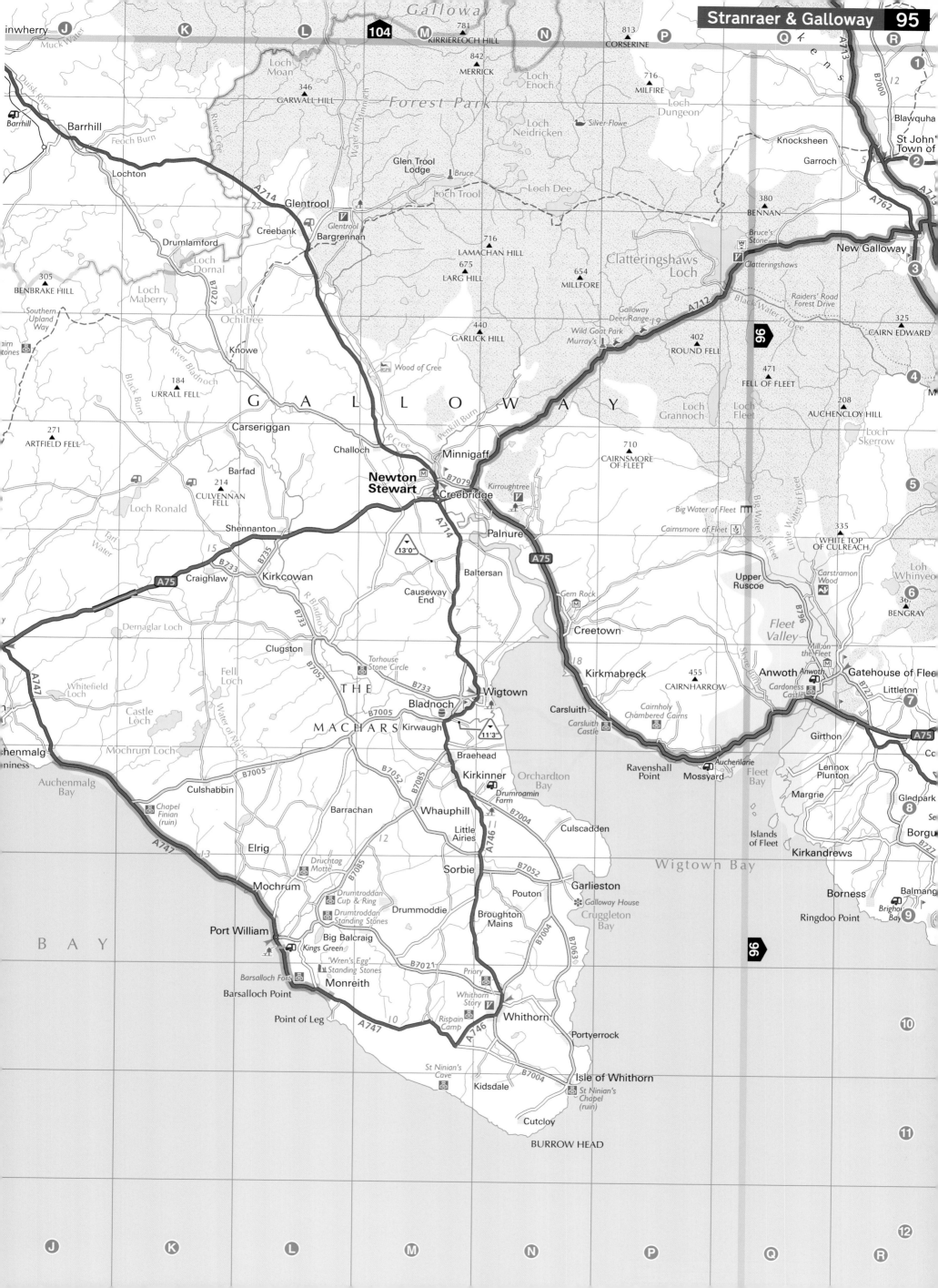

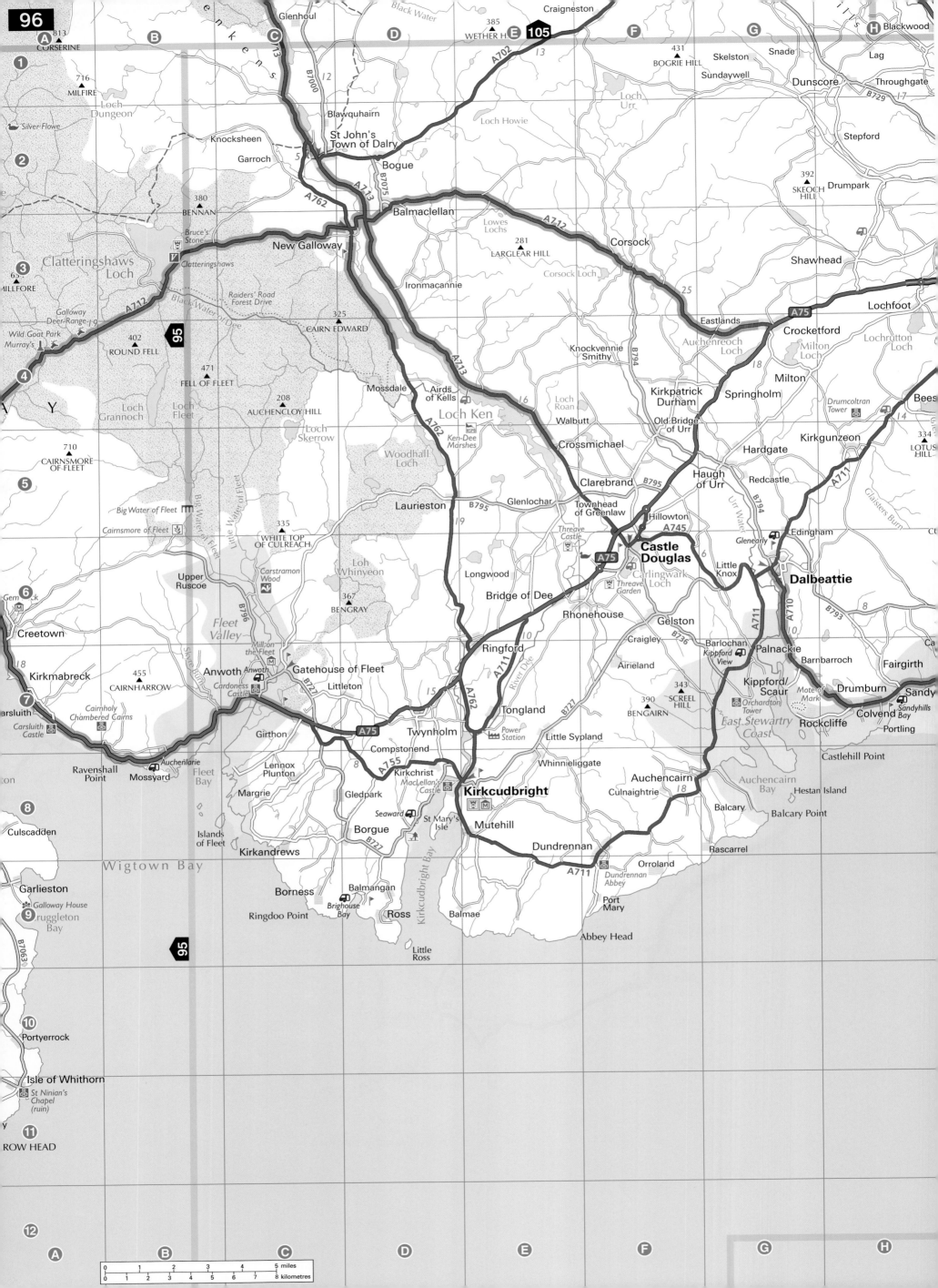

SOLWAY FIRTH

Dumfries
Lochmaben
Locharbriggs
Lockerbie
Annan
Gretna
Gretna Green
Kirkpatrick-Fleming
Eaglesfield
Kirtlebridge
Ecclefechan
Middlebie
Waterbeck
Solwaybank
Chapelknowe
Springfield
Hollee
Rigg
Eastriggs
Dornock
Newbie
Powfoot
Cummertrees
Ruthwell
Clarencefield
Mouswald
Carrutherstown
Brydekirk
Kelhead
Hoddom Mains
Dalton
Kettleholm
Hightae
Greenhill
Torthorwald
Roucan
Collin
Greenlea
Racks
Kelton
Conheath
Glencaple
Bankend
Kirkconnel
New Abbey
Sweetheart Abbey
Bowhouse
Shearington
Caerlaverock Castle
Blackshaw
Caerlaverock Wetland Centre
Nith Estuary
Kirkbean
Carsethorn
Southerness
Southerness Point
Mainsriddle
Loaningfoot
Borron Point
Arbigland
John Paul Jones Cottage
Gill Foot Bay
Criffell
Carse Bay
Loch Kindar
Mabie Forest
Lochober Loch
Kirkconnell Flow
Kingholm Quay
Islesteps
Cargenbridge
Terregles
Newbridge
Holywood
Holywood Village
Twelve Apostles
Lincluden Collegiate Church
Maxwelltown
Lincluden
Kirkton
Amisfield
Tinwald
Heath Hall
Dalswinton
Duncow
Auchencairn
Kirkton
Holywood
Auldgirth
Dalswinton
Parkgate
Nethermill
Jardine Hall
Ae Bridgend
Cumrue
Templand
Shieldhill
Millhousebridge
Marjoribanks
Applegarth Town
Nethercleuch
Corrie
Cauldkinerig
Bankshill
Grange Fell
Bigholms
Collin Hags
Tundergarth
Burnswark Hill
Hoddom Castle
Hoddom Cross
Thomas Carlyle's Birthplace
Creca
Bonshaw Tower
Robgill Tower
Merkland Cross
King Robert the Bruce's Cave
Bruce's Porridge
Devil's Porridge
Galabank
Howes
Savings Banks
Torduff Point
Redkirk Point
Bowness-on-Solway
Port Carlisle
Glasson
Drumburgh
Hadrian's Wall Path
Campfield Marsh
Glasson Moss
Bowness Common
Drumburgh Moss
Cardurnock
Anthorn
Grune Point
Moricambe Bay
Skinburness
Silloth
Hylton
Stanwix
Seaville
Newton Arlosh
Kirkbride
Biglands
Abbeytown
Holm Cultram
Kelsick
Dundraw
Oulton
Lessonhall
Waverbridge
Waverton
Wigton
West Curthwaite
South Solway Mosses
Drumleaning
Little Bampton
Great Orton
Aikton
Wiggonby
Kirkbampton
Burgh by Sands
Thurstonfield
Moorhouse
Monkhill
Finglandrigg Woods
Beckfoot
Newtown
Holme St Cuthbert
Mawbray
Dubmill Point
Langrigg
Westnewton
Allonby
Allonby Bay
Bromfield
Blencogo
Bolton Low Houses
Westward
Rosley
Welton
Crosscanonby
Crosby
Maryport
Dearham
Gilcrux
Plumbland
Bothel
Torpenhow
Ireby
High Ireby
Uldale
Branthwaite
Caldbeck
Hesket Newmarket
Sunderland
Binsey
Blindcrake
Bridekirk
Tallentire
Aspatria
Hayton
Prospect
Allerby
Oughterside
Blennerhasset
Larches
Boltongate
Faulds Brow
Bassenthwaite
Lake District Wildlife Park
Embleton
Papcastle
Cockermouth
Brigham
Greysouthen
Dovenby
Great Broughton
Camerton
Broughton Moor
Standingstone
Flimby
Seaton
Great Clifton
Little Clifton
Stainburn
Workington
Mossbay
Eaglesfield
Mirehouse
Skiddaw
Carrock Fell
Bowscale Fell
Blencathra
Knott
Great Calva
A76
A709
A75
A711
A710
A780
A74(M)
A596
A595
A594
A66
A591
A597
B724
B725
B7020
B723
B7076
B7068
B722
B6357
B6357
B721
B5307
B5302
B5301
B5300
B5299
B5305
B5291

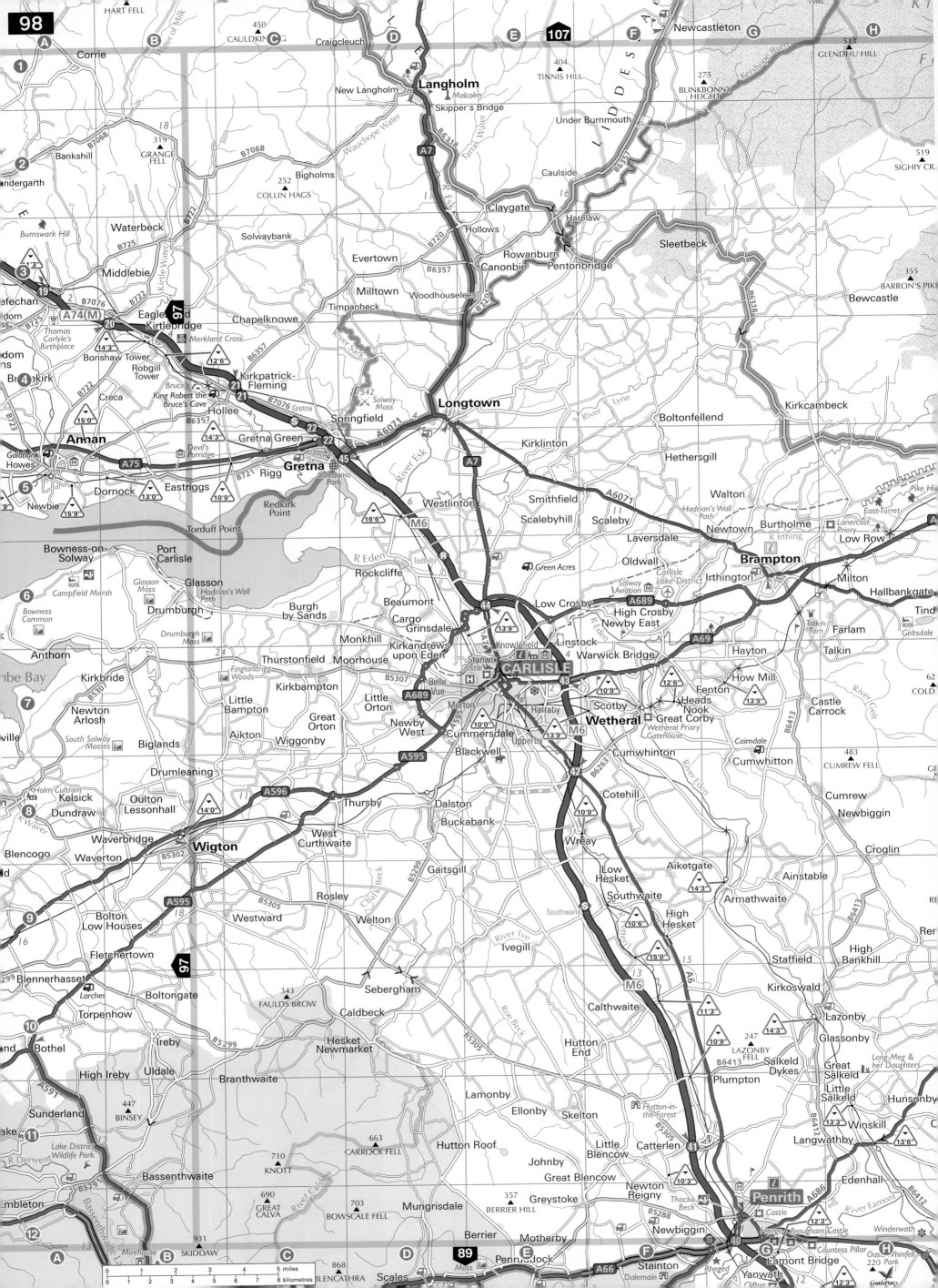

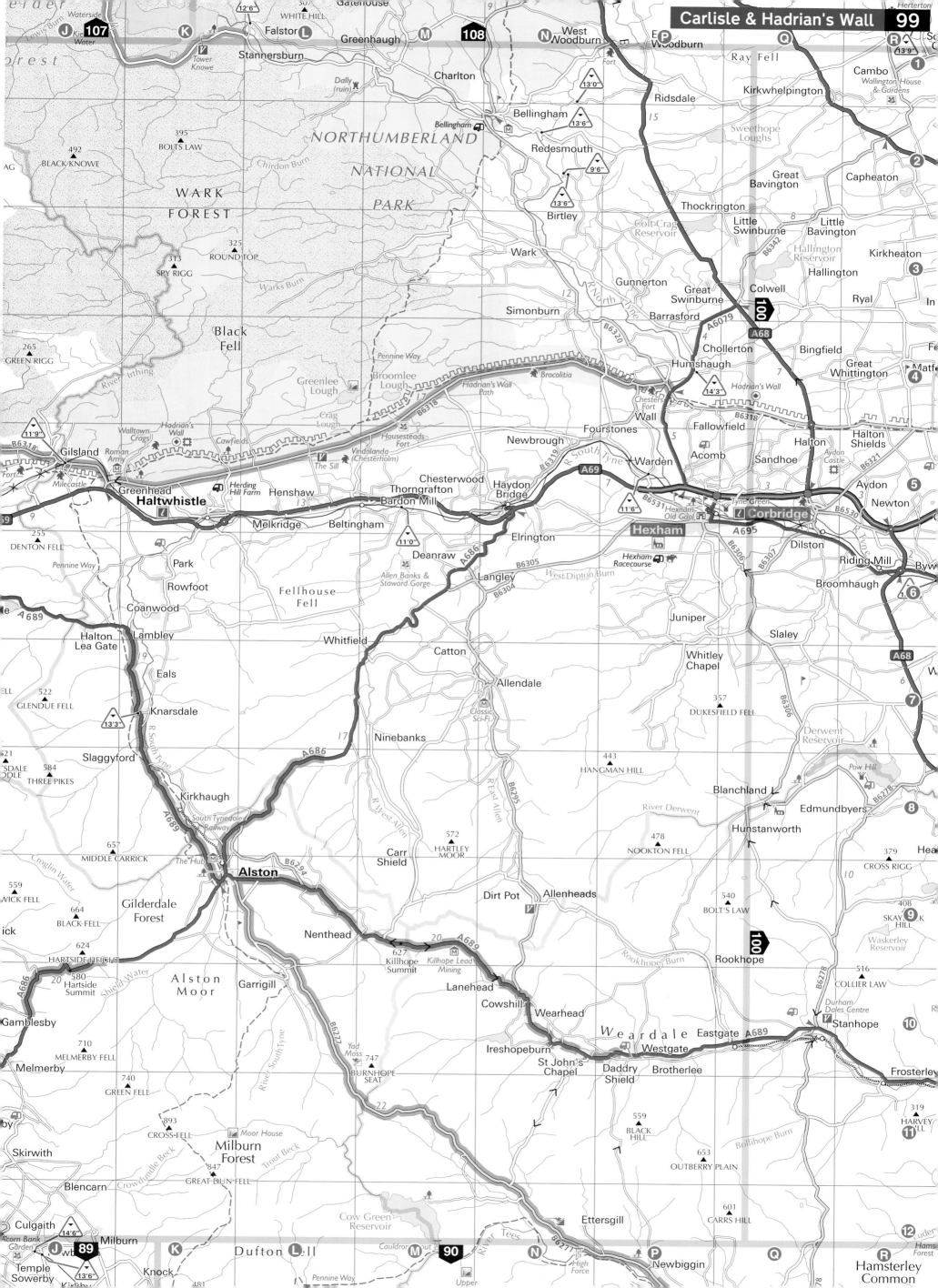

J   K   L   M   N   P   Q   R

1

Grogport
Barmollack
Penrioch
112
P 334
CAISTEAL ABHAIL
Corrie
Pirnmill
North Arran

2
354
CRUACH NAN GABHAR
Whitefarland
715
BEINN BHARRAIN
874
GOATFELL
Loch
Tanna
Merkland Point
6
Brodick Castle, Garden
& Country Park
Brodick
Bay
Muasdale
Imachar
Balliekine
792
BEINN NUIS
Glen Iorsa
Glen Rosa
B842
Carradale
B879
Port Righ
Carradale Village
Bridgend
Dippen
Carradale Bay
Waterfoot
Iorsa Water
104

3
A83
454
BEINN AN TUIRC
Torrisdale
Carradale Point
Carradale
Bay
A R R A N
Strathwhillan
Brodick
Corriegills
319
408
BÒRD MOR
Auchagallon
Stone Circle
Machrie
11
512
A'CHRUACH
A841
4
H
Clauchlands
Point
Margnaheglish
Cleongart
N
Saddell Water
Machrie
Bay
Machrie Moor
Stone Circles
Balmichael
Shiskine
Lamlash
Lamlash
Bay
Bellochantuy
Saddell
Moss Farm Road
Stone Circle
503
BEINN BHREAC
Cordon
Holy Island

4
396
SGREADAN HILL
Saddell Bay
Torbeg
Drumadoon
Point
Blackwaterfoot
Kilpatrick
Kilpatrick Dun
Carn Ban
Glen Scorrodale
Auchencairn
4
Kingscross
Knockenkelly
Lussa
Loch
Ugadale
Drumadoon
Bay
Whiting Bay
Whiting
Bay
Glen Lussa
Peninver
Ardnacross
Bay
Brown Head
Glenashdale
Largymore
Tangy Loch
B842

5
A83
Kilmichael
Corriecravie
Sliddery
Kilmory Water
Dippin
Largybeg
Dippin Head
Torr a' Chaisteal Fort
Campbeltown
Lagg
Torrylin
Cairn
Kilmory
Bennan
Seal Shore
Bennan Head
Kildonan
Pladda

6
B842
Stewarton
Kilkerran
Kildalloig
Campbeltown
Loch
Island Davaar
V
Campbeltown-Ardrossan (May-Sept)
(May-Sept, Sat only)
B843
6
352
BEINN GHUILEAN
Achinhoan
Ballycastle
(Apr-Sept)

7
10
Conie Glen
Glen Kerran
Ru Stafnish

8
B842
Cattadale
Polliwilline Bay
Macharioch
Southend
Dunaverty
skey Bay
ore
Sound of Sanda
Sheep Island
Sanda Island

9
104

Ailsa
Craig
340

10

11

12

J   K   L   M   N   P   Q   R

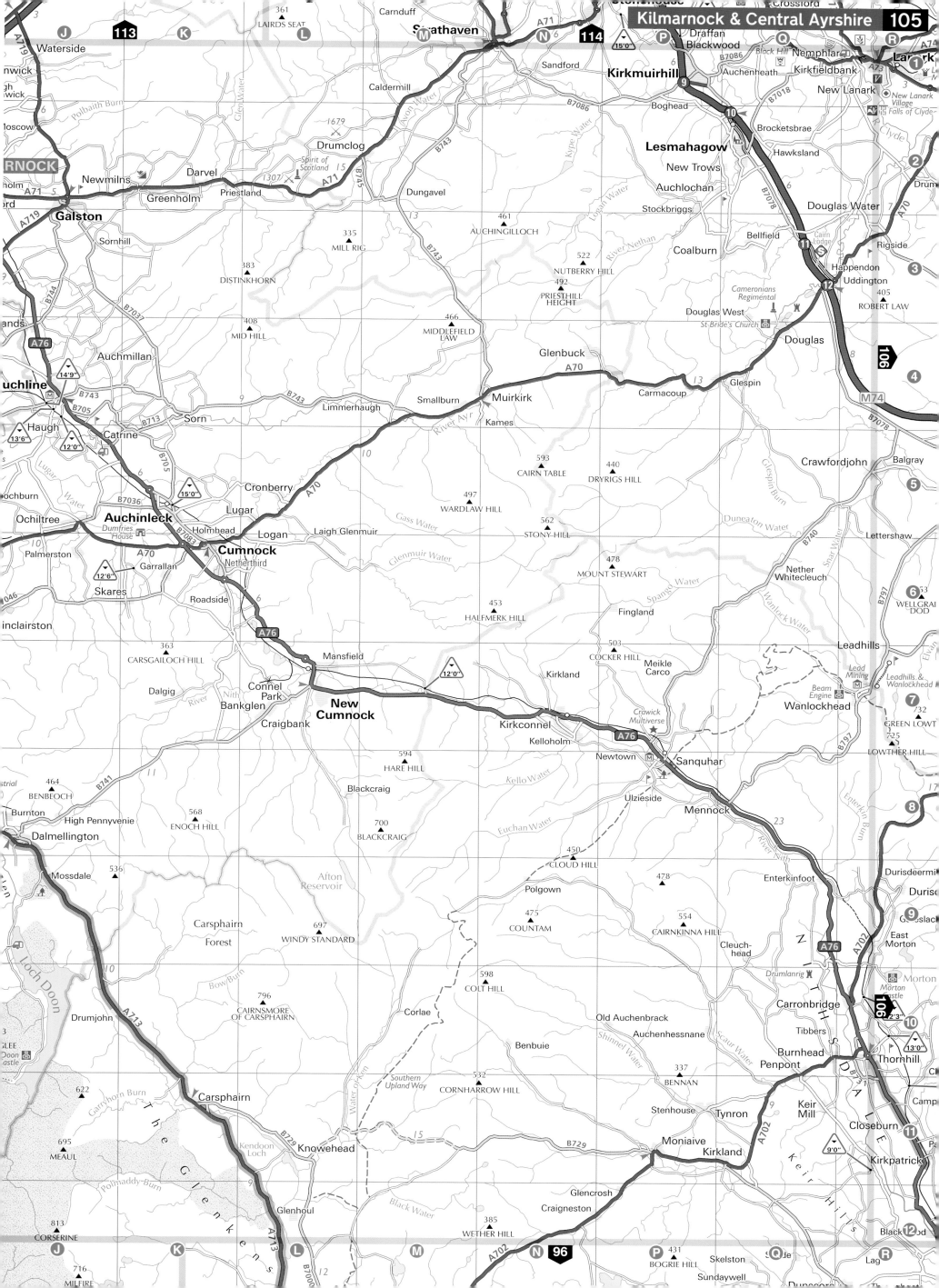

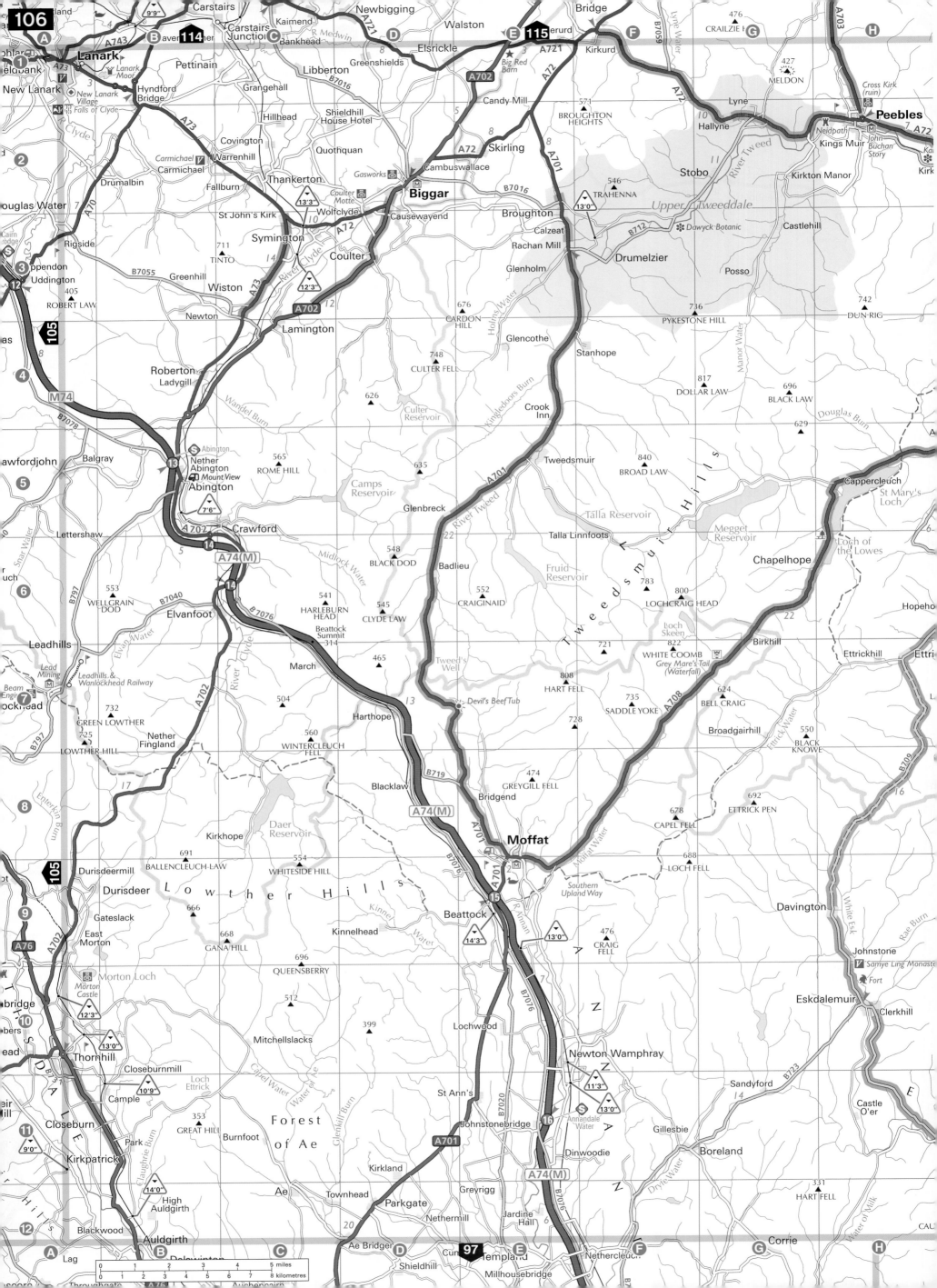

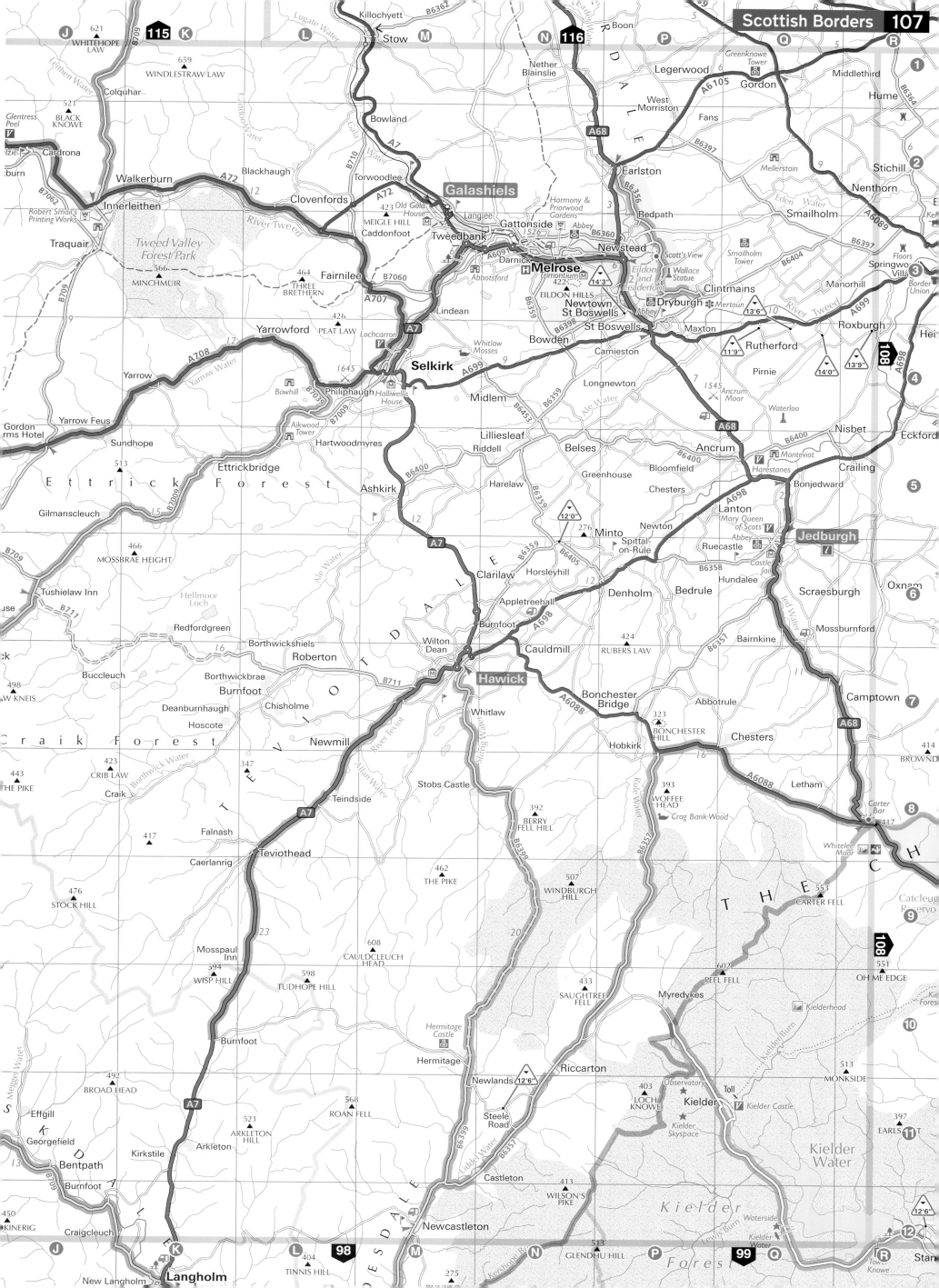

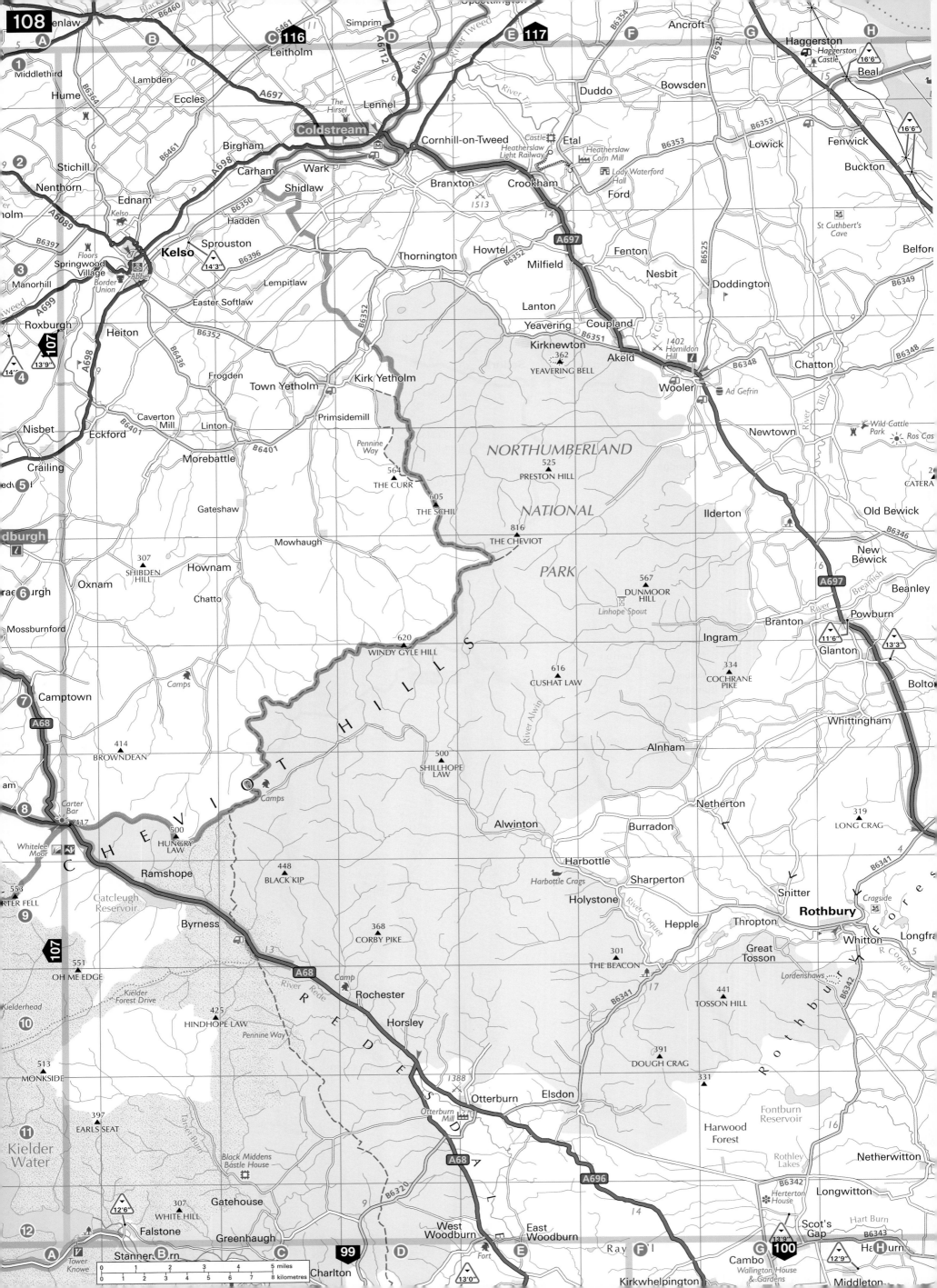

A B C D E F G H

1

2

COLONSAY

Kilchattan

B8086

3

Colonsay

Garvard

Oronsay

Dubh Eilean

ORONSAY

Oronsay

4

5

6

Nave Island

Ardnave Point

Gortantaoid Point

Tòn Mhòr

7

Kilnave

Eilean Mòr

Sanaigmore

Loch Gruinart

Loch Gòrr

Rubha Lamanais

Lecht Gruinart

B8017

Saligo Bay

B8018

B8017

Gruinart

Gleann Mòr

Eir

8

Loch Gorm

A847

Coul Point

B8018

Sunderland

Machir Bay

Kilchoman

Bridgend

Gartacho

Bruichladdich

Loch Indaal

9

Kilchiaran Bay

Bowmore

RHINNS OF ISLAY

15

Islay Life

Port Charlotte

IS

River Laggan

231

BEINN TART A'MHILL

Lossit Bay

Nerabus

Laggan Point

Duich R.

A846

B8016

10

Rubha na Faing

A847

Glenegedale

Islay

Portnahaven

Laggan Bay

Port Wemyss

Orsay

RHINNS POINT

11

Rubha Mòr

Kintra

MAOL BUIDHE

165

12

THE OA

Lo

Killeyan

Risabus

Kinnabus

A B C D E F G H

0 1 2 3 4 5 miles

0 1 2 3 4 5 6 7 8 kilometres

J   K   **119**   L   M   N   **120**   P   Q   **R**

Gulf of Corryvreckan

1

Eilean Dubh

Rubh' a' Geodha

Aird

Craignish Point

Island Macaskin

Slock

Temple Wood Stone Circle

Ri C Pol

Kiloran Bay

143
CARNAN
EOIN

V Oban

Glengarrisdale Bay

295
CRUACH NA
SEILCHEIG

Loch Crinan

Crinan

Kiloran

B8086

Glendebadel Bay

Kilmahumaig

Bellanoch

Scalasaig

364
BEN GARRISDALE

112

3

J U R A

Argyll
Beaver

B8085

Corpach Bay

466
BEINN
BHREAC

Glen Grundale

Knapdale

Carsaig Bay

Tayvallich

Achnamara

4

Rubha
Bàn

Lussa River

Kilmichael of Inv

Eilean
Ghaoideamal

Shian Bay

453
RAINBERG MÒR

Ardlussa

Lussa Point
Lussagiven

Taynish

Leall Burn

Rubh' an t-Sàilein

A846

Keills Chapel

5

Loch
Righ Mòr

Rubha a' Mhàil

Loch Tarbert

Kilbride

Castle
Sween

Lochead

Rubha
Bholsa

363
SGARBH
BREAC

Danna
Island

St Cormac's
Chapel

Achahoisl

6

506
SCRINADLE

Jura Forest

398
BEINN
TARSUINN

Kilmory Knap
Chapel

Kilmory

Ellary

Bunnahabhain

784
BEINN AN OIR

Kilmory
Bay

316
GUIR-
BHEINN

Loch a'
Chnuic Bhric

734

Paps of Jura

Point of Knap

Ormsary

Druimdrishaig

48
DUBH
CHREAG

7

J u r a

24

Knockrome

Ardfernal

Loch-nan
Torran

Port
Askaig

Finlaggan

560
GLAS BHEINN

A846

Cretshengan

Keills

Feolin Ferry

Jura - Tayvallich (Apr-Sept)

Coulaghailtro

8

allygrant

Loch
Ballygrant

Loch
Lossit

529
DUBH
BHEINN

Keils

Small
Isles

Kilberry
Sculptured
Stones

Kilberry

Torinturk

8

A846

266
BEINNE
DUBH

342
BRAT
BHEINN

Craighouse

Rubha na
Caillich

Kilberry Head

Keppoch Point

213
CRUACH AIRDE

Cabrach

Tiretigan

9

san

429
SGÒRR NAM
FAOILEANN

Am-Fraoch
Eilean

Brosdale
Island

Rubha na Tràille

Loch Stornoway

Kilcham

112

471

McArthur's
Head

Ardpatrick

LAY

490
BEINN BHEIGEIR

Port Askaig - Kennacraig

Portachoillan

Clachan

454
BEINN URARAIDH

Loch Uraraidh

Rubha Liath

Ardtalla

Ronachan Point

Ronachan

10

Claggain
Bay

Kinerarach

Loch
Cìaran

R

346
BEINN SHOLUM

Kintour

Kildalton
Cross

Ardmore
Point

Tarbert

Loch
Garasdale

247
CRUACH MHIC
GOUGAIN

11

Eilean
a' Chùirn

GIGHA

Rhunahaorine
Point

CNOC AN T
SAMHLAIDH

Ardbeg

A846

Rubha na
Gainmhich

Port Ellen - Kennacraig

Ardminish

Achamore

Rhunahaorine

Lagavulin

Cara

Tayinloan

12

Laphroaig

Texa

J   K   **102**   L   M   N   P   **103**   Q   R

354

J   K   L   M   N   P   Q   R

1
2
3
4
5
6
7
8
9
10
11
12

Fast Castle Head

196 ▲
BROWN RIG
Coldingham Loch

ST ABB'S HEAD

St Abbs

Coldingham Bay

house

Coldingham

A1107 22

B6438

Houndwood

Heugh Head

Cairncross

Eyemouth

262 ▲
14'0"
HORSELEY HILL

Reston   A1

Ayton

Burnmouth

B6438

12'9"

Auchencrow

11'9"

rygold

16'0"

14'3"

Lamberton

B6437

B6355

Chirnside

Marshall Meadows Bay

B6355

Foulden

North Northumberland
Heritage Coast

Chirnsidebridge

Broadhaugh

Edington

Whiteadder Water

Foulden
Tithe Barn

1333
×

Allanton

Hutton

A6105

Berwick-upon-Tweed

Blackadder

Paxton

Castle

B6437

Town
Ramparts
Tweedmouth

Barracks &
Main Guard

B6461

Whitsome

Hilton

Paxton

Ord House

Spittal

16'3"

nclair's

Huds
Head

B6461

Horndean

Horncliffe

Scremerston

B6437

Ladykirk

Murton

Castle

16'6"

Swinton

Norham

B6470

A698

Thornton

A1

Cheswick

Upsettlington

River Tweed

Causeway
flooded at
high tide

Simprim

B635A

Ancroft

Haggerston

Castle

HOLY ISLAND

Beal

Duddo

Bowsden

126

A B C D E F G H

1

Arnabost

Grishipoll

Clabhach

Loch
Cliad

B8071

Hogh Bay   Ballyhaugh   **Arinagour**

CO

2

Bàgh a' Chaisteil
(Castlebay)

V

(Apr–Oct. Weds only)

Coll

Totronald

Feall
Bay

Ariléod   Acha

Arileod

Crossapol
Bay

Calgary Point   Uig

Loch Breachacha   Rubha
Fàsachd

Gunna   Eilean
Ornsay

3

Rubha Port
Bhiosd

Clachan
Mor   Balephetrish
Bay

Caoles   Rubha Dubh

B8069

Ruaig

Loch
Bhasapoll

B8068

Hough
Bay

Ballevullin   Cornoigmore   Gott
Bay

Kenovay

Tiree

4

Kilkenneth

B8068

Moss   Heylipoll   Scarinish

Middleton   B8065

Barrapoll   **Crossapol**   **TIREE**

Loch a
Phuill   B8067   **Balemartine**   Hynish Bay

Mannal

TRESHNIS
ISLES

5

Rinn
Thorbhais   Hynish   Skerryvore
Lighthouse   Balephuil Bay

V

Bac N

Bac Bea

6

7

8

9   Soa Island

10

11

12

A B C D E F G H

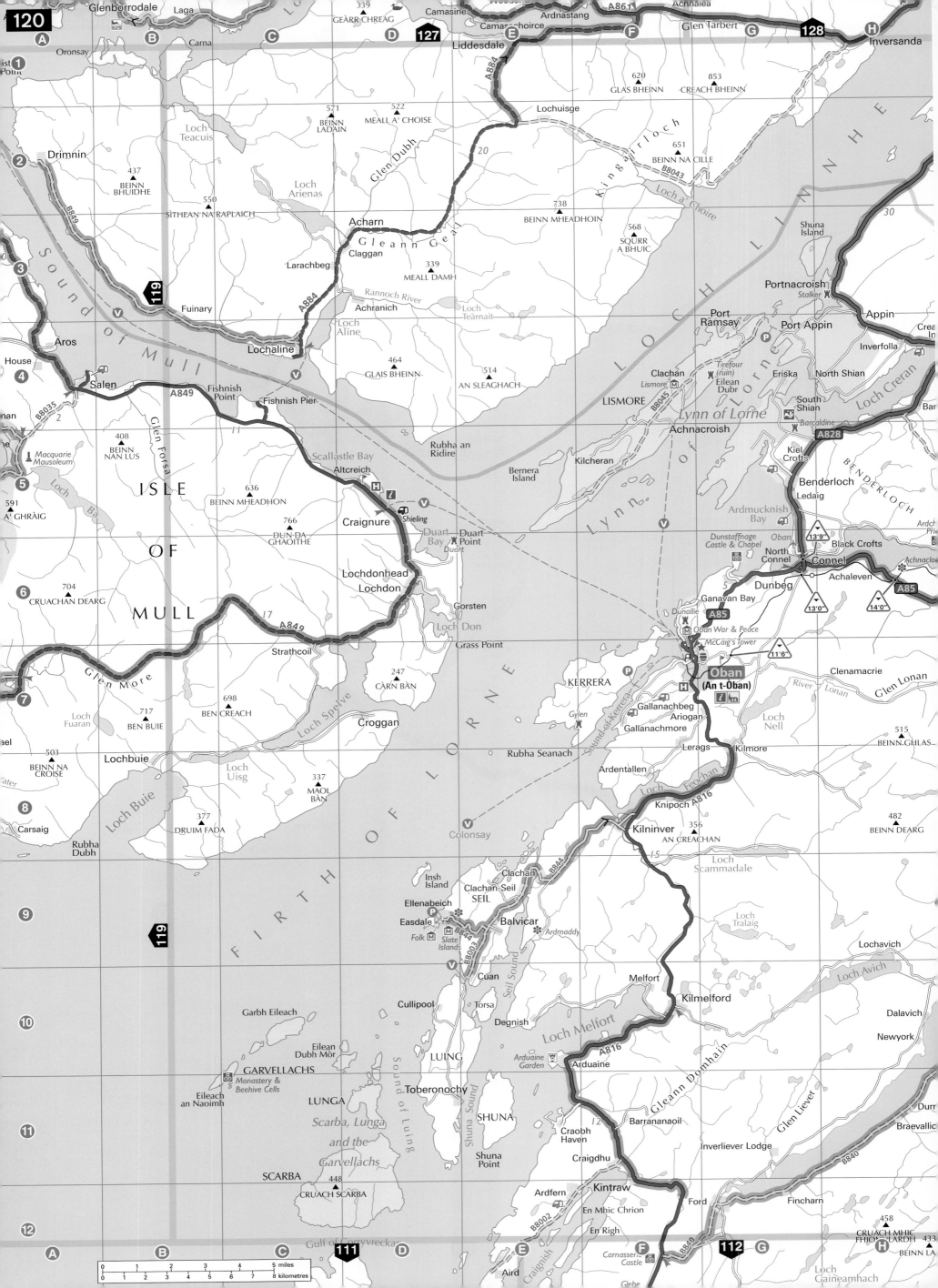

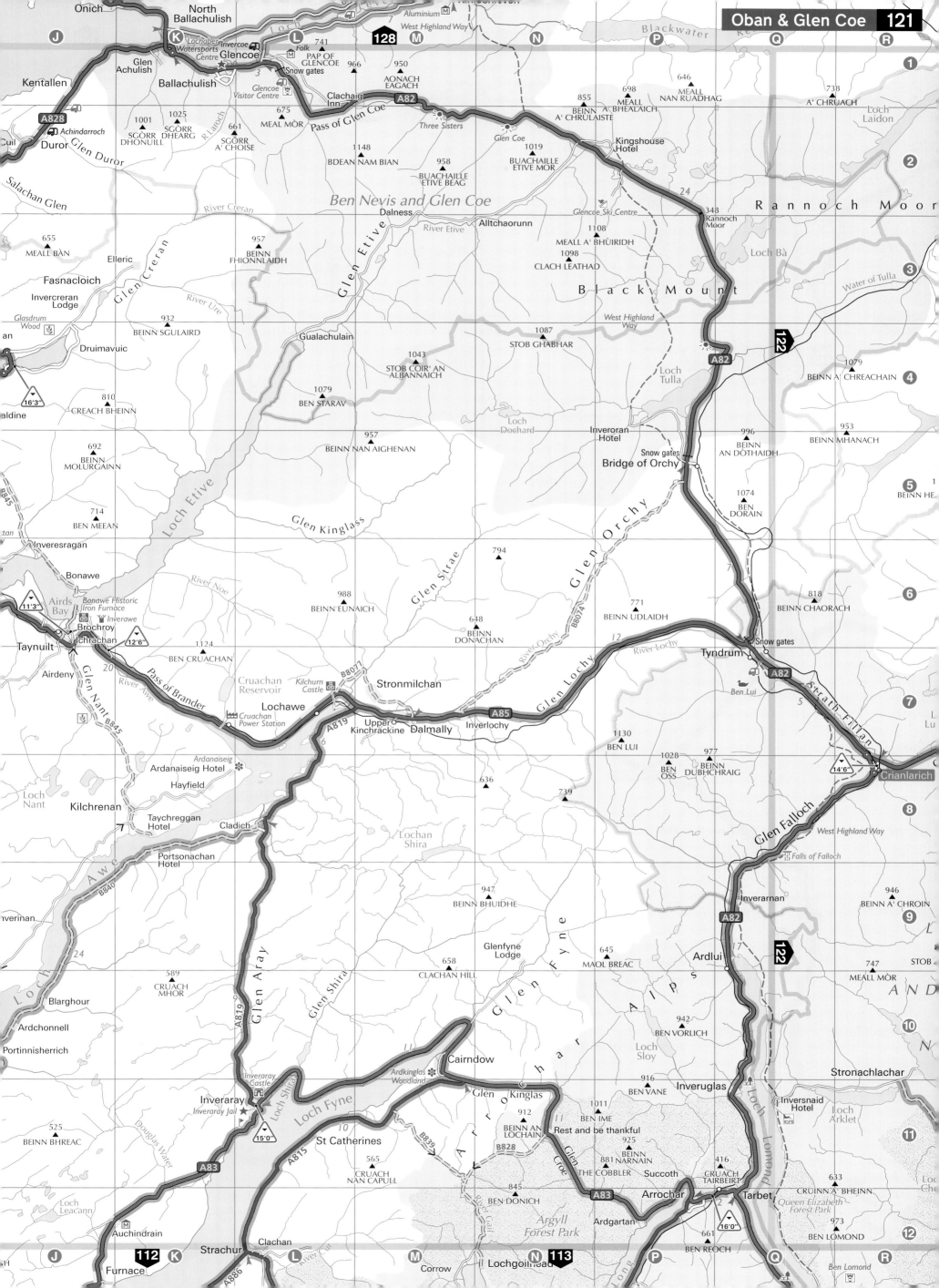

Onich
North Ballachulish
J
Kentallen
Glen Achulish
Ballachulish
A828
Duror
Achindarroch
Glen Duror
Salachan Glen
655
MEALL BÀN
Elleric
Fasnacloich
Invercreran Lodge
Glasdrum Wood
Druimavuic
810
CREACH BHEINN
16'3"
1001
SGORR DHONUILL
1025
SGORR DHEARG
661
SGORR A' CHOISE
675
MEAL MÒR
K
Lochaber Watersports Centre
Glencoe
Invercoe
741
PAP OF GLENCOE
Snow gates
Glencoe Visitor Centre
Clachaig Inn
L
West Highland Way
Aluminium
966
950
AONACH EAGACH
1148
BDEAN NAM BIAN
958
BUACHAILLE ETIVE BEAG
Pass of Glen Coe
Three Sisters
Glen Coe
Ben Nevis and Glen Coe
Dalness
River Etive
Alltchaorunn
128
M
855
BEINN A' CHRULAISTE
1019
BUACHAILLE ETIVE MOR
Kingshouse Hotel
698
MEALL A' BHEALAICH
646
MEALL NAN RUADHAG
N
738
A' CHRUACH
P
Blackwater
Loch Laidon
1
2
Rannoch Moor
Q
R
1
2

957
BEINN FHIONNLAIDH
932
BEINN SGULAIRD
Gualachulain
1043
STOB COIR' AN ALBANNAICH
1079
BEN STARAV
957
BEINN NAN AIGHENAN
Glen Etive
Glencoe Ski Centre
1108
MEALL A' BHÙIRIDH
1098
CLACH LEATHAD
348
Rannoch Moor
24
West Highland Way
1087
STOB GHABHAR
Loch Dochard
Inveroran Hotel
Black Mount
Loch Tulla
A82
122
1079
BEINN A' CHREACHAIN
953
BEINN MHANACH
Water of Tulla
Loch Bà
3
4

Loch Etive
692
BEINN MOLURGAINN
714
BEN MEEAN
Inveresragan
Bonawe
Bonawe Historic Iron Furnace
Inverawe
Brochroy
Airds Bay
11'3"
Taynuilt
Ichrachan
12'6"
Airdeny
20
Glen Nant B845
River Awe
Pass of Brander
1124
BEN CRUACHAN
Cruachan Reservoir
Kilchurn Castle
B8077
Stronmilchan
Lochawe
Cruachan Power Station
A819
Upper Kinchrackine
Dalmally
Inverlochy
A85
Glen Kinglass
Glen Strae
794
988
BEINN EUNAICH
648
BEINN DONACHAN
Glen Orchy
B8074
River Orchy
12
771
BEINN UDLAIDH
Glen Lochy
River Lochy
Tyndrum
Snow gates
A82
Ben Lui
818
BEINN CHAORACH
Snow gates
Bridge of Orchy
996
BEINN AN DÒTHAIDH
1074
BEN DORAIN
7
Strath Fillan
5
5
BEINN HE
6
7

Loch Nant
Kilchrenan
Ardanaiseig Hotel
Hayfield
Taychreggan Hotel
7
Cladich
Portsonachan Hotel
B840
Glen Aray
A819
9
589
CRUACH MHOR
636
739
Ardanaiseig
Lochan Shira
947
BEINN BHUIDHE
Glenfyne Lodge
658
CLACHAN HILL
Glen Shira
Glen Fyne
1130
BEN LUI
1028
BEN OSS
977
BEINN DUBHCHRAIG
14'6"
Crianlarich
Glen Falloch
West Highland Way
Falls of Falloch
645
MAOL BREAC
A82
Inverarnan
122
946
BEINN A' CHROIN
747
MEALL MÒR
STOB
AND
A
N
D
8
9
10

Loch Awe
24
Blarghour
Ardchonnell
Portinnisherrich
Inveraray Castle
Inveraray
Inveraray Jail
525
BEINN BHREAC
A815
St Catherines
565
CRUACH NAN CAPULL
15'0"
Loch Shira
Loch Fyne
10
Douglas Water
A83
Ardkinglas Woodland
Cairndow
Glen Kinglas
11
Arrochar Alps
916
BEN VANE
912
BEINN AN LOCHAIN
Rest and be thankful
925
BEINN NARNAIN
881
THE COBBLER
B828
B839
Glen Croe
845
BEN DONICH
661
BEN REOCH
A83
Ardgartan
Argyll Forest Park
River Goil
Loch Sloy
1011
BEN IME
Succoth
Cruach Tairbeirt
416
Arrochar
Ardlui
Inveruglas
Loch Lomond
Stronachlachar
Inversnaid Hotel
Loch Arklet
973
BEN LOMOND
633
CRUINN A' BHEINN
Tarbet
Queen Elizabeth Forest Park
16'0"
10
11
12

J
112
K
Strachur
Furnace
A886
L
113
M
Corrow
Lochgoilhead
N
P
Q
R
inverinan
 Inverinan
Loch Leacann
Auchindrain
Clachan
River Cur
A815
A83

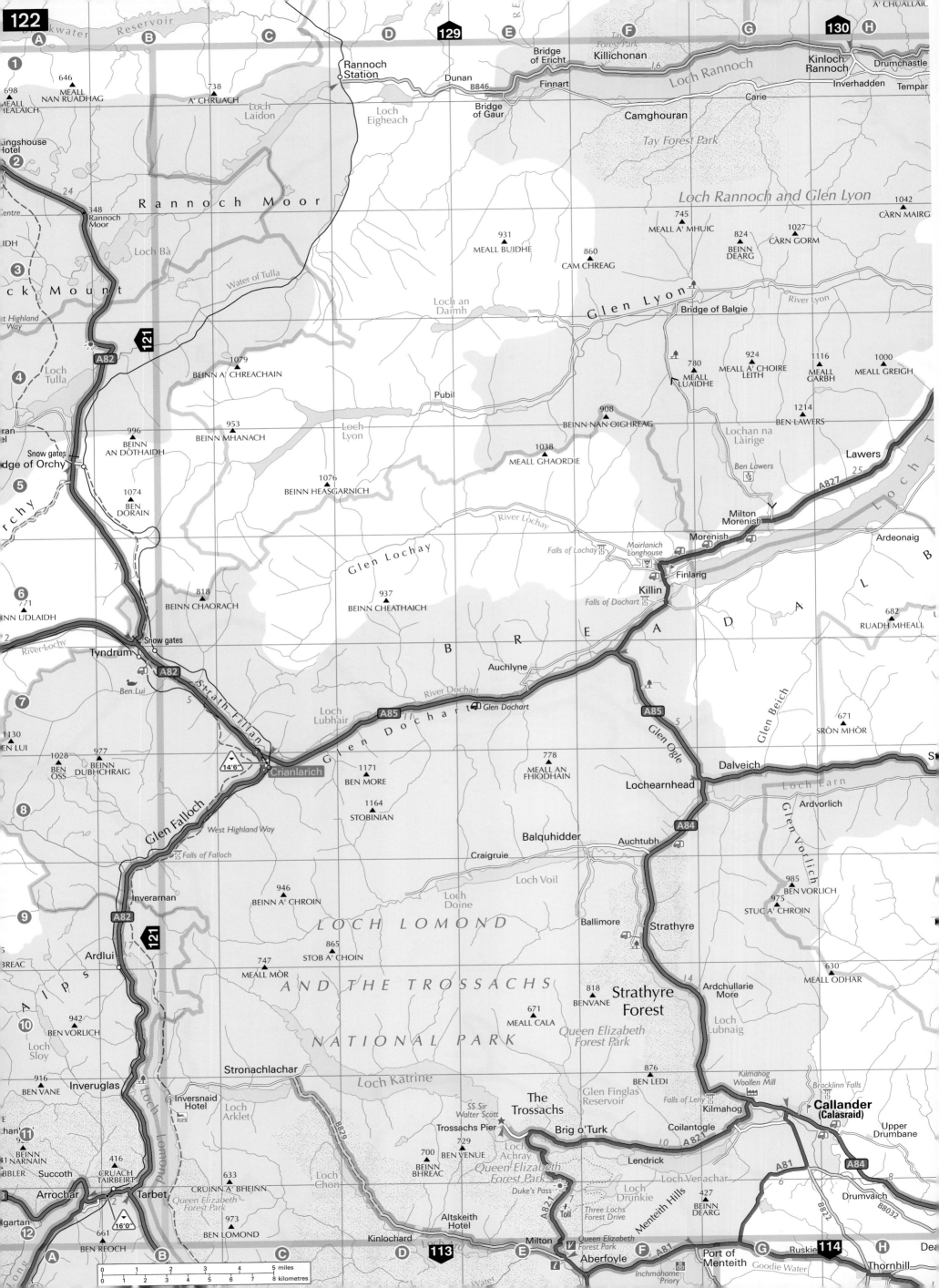

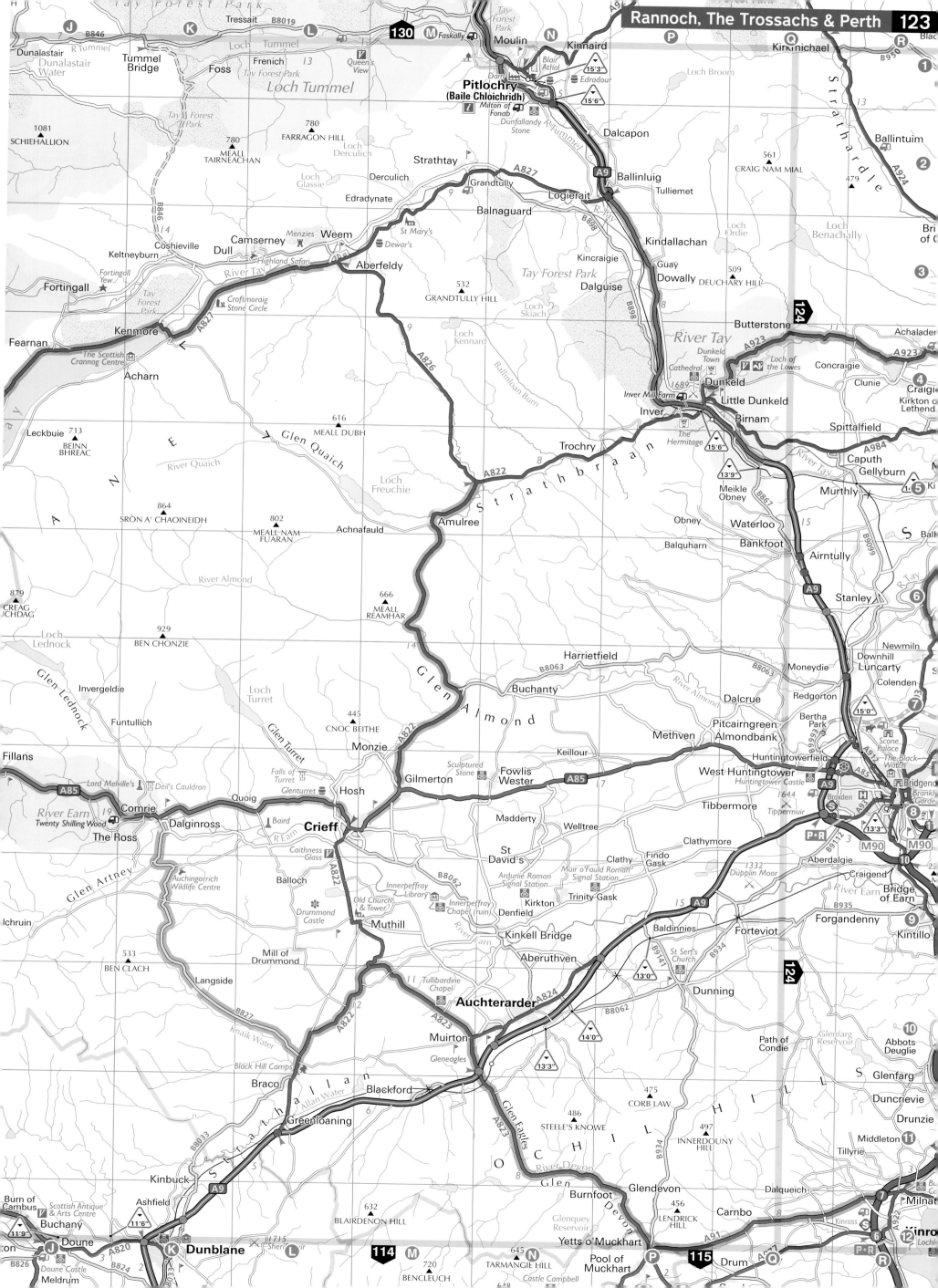

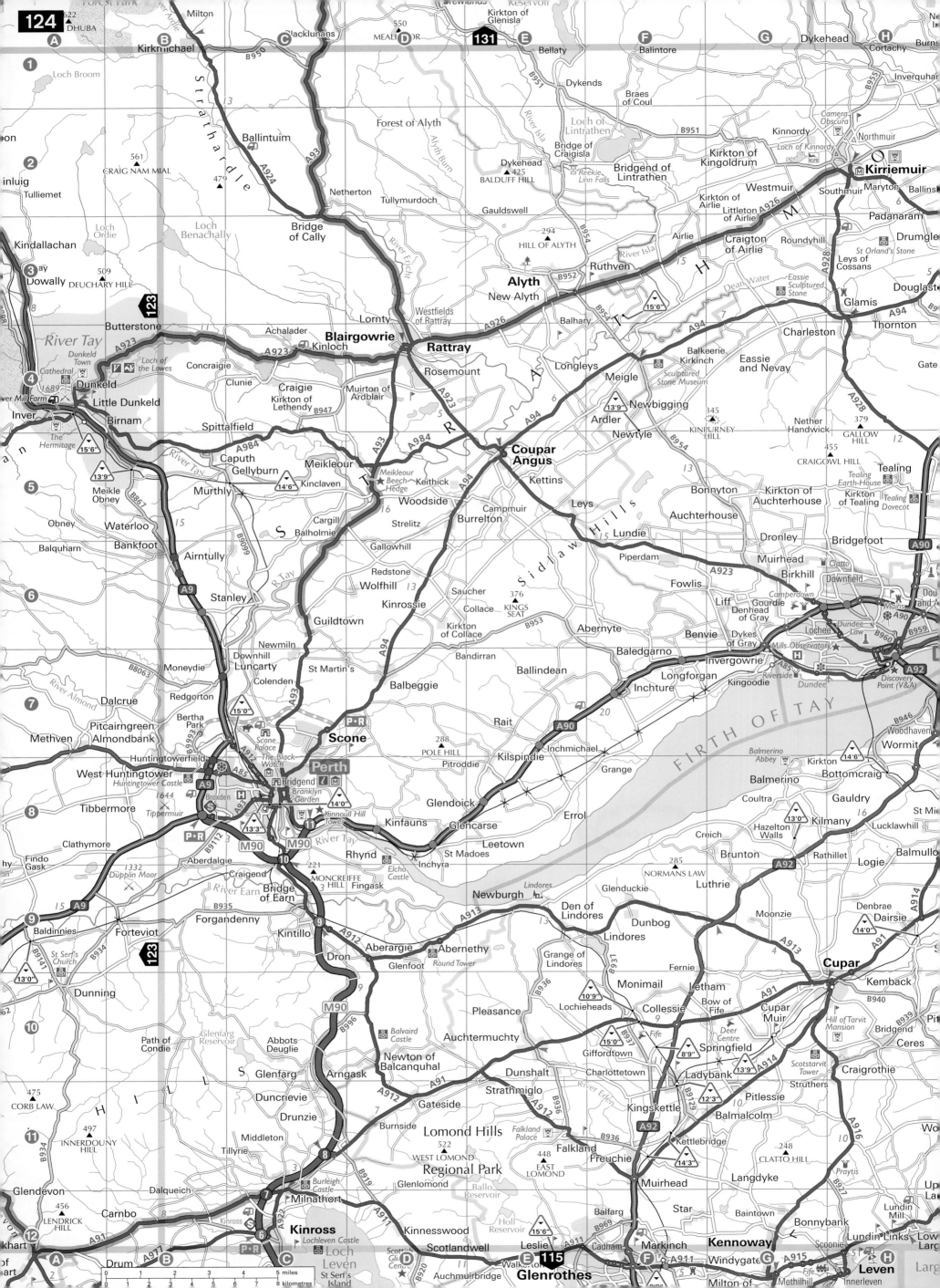

A | B | C | D | E | F | **134** | G | H

1 Rubha an Dùnain

CEANN NA BEINNE

225

GARS BHEINN

Soay Sound

139
BEINN
BHREAC

Mol-chlach

SOAY

2 Loch Baghasdail
(Lochboisdale)

Rubh'
Aonghais

C U I L L I N   S O U N D

3 CANNA

Garrisdale Point

210
CÀRN A' GHAILL

A'Chill

Canna
Harbour

Sanday

Kilmory
Bay

Rubha
Shamhnan
Insir

4

Sound of Canna

302
MULLACH MÒR

Rubha
na Roinne

A' Bhrìdeanach

570
ORVAL

Kinloch

Loch Scresort

5 Oigh-sgeir

RÙM

810
ASKIVAL

All vehicles must have
the relevant island
permit prior to travel
to The Small Isles.
Services are seasonal,
day & weather dependent.

6

Harris
Bay

763
SGÙRR NAN
GILLEAN

The Small Isles

Rubha nam
Meirleach

Sound of Rùm

Bay of
Laig

7

Rubha an
Fhasaidh

Laig

EIGG

393
AN SGÙRR

Sound of Eigg

8

Eilean
nan Each

MUCK

Port Mòr

9

10

Sanna Point

Sanna
Bay

Sanna

Portuairk

Achnah

Ardnamurchan
Point

Achosnich

B8007

11

Eilean Mòr

Rubha
Mòr

Rubha
Sgor-innis

Bàgh a' Chaisteil
(Castlebay)
Loch Baghasdail
(Lochboisdale)
(Oct-Mar)

342
BEINN NA SEILG

Ormsaigmore

Bousd

Sorisdale

Cliad
Bay

B8072

Arnabost

B8071

Grishipoll

Clabach

118

Ardmore
Point

12

A | B | C | **118** | D | E | F | **119** | G | Sorne Point | H

Mull - Oban

Arinagour

0 1 2 3 4 5 miles
0 1 2 3 4 5 6 7 8 kilometres

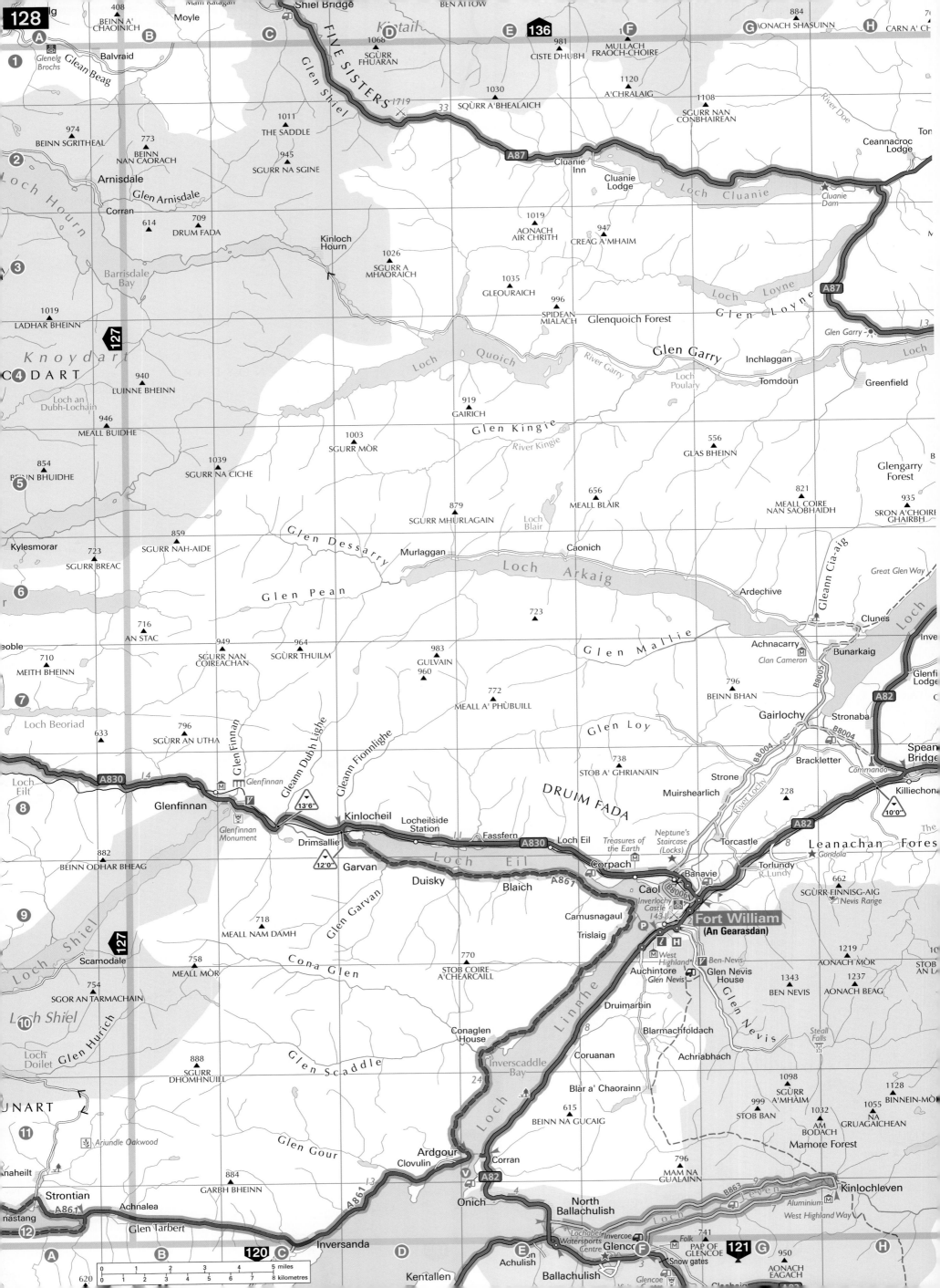

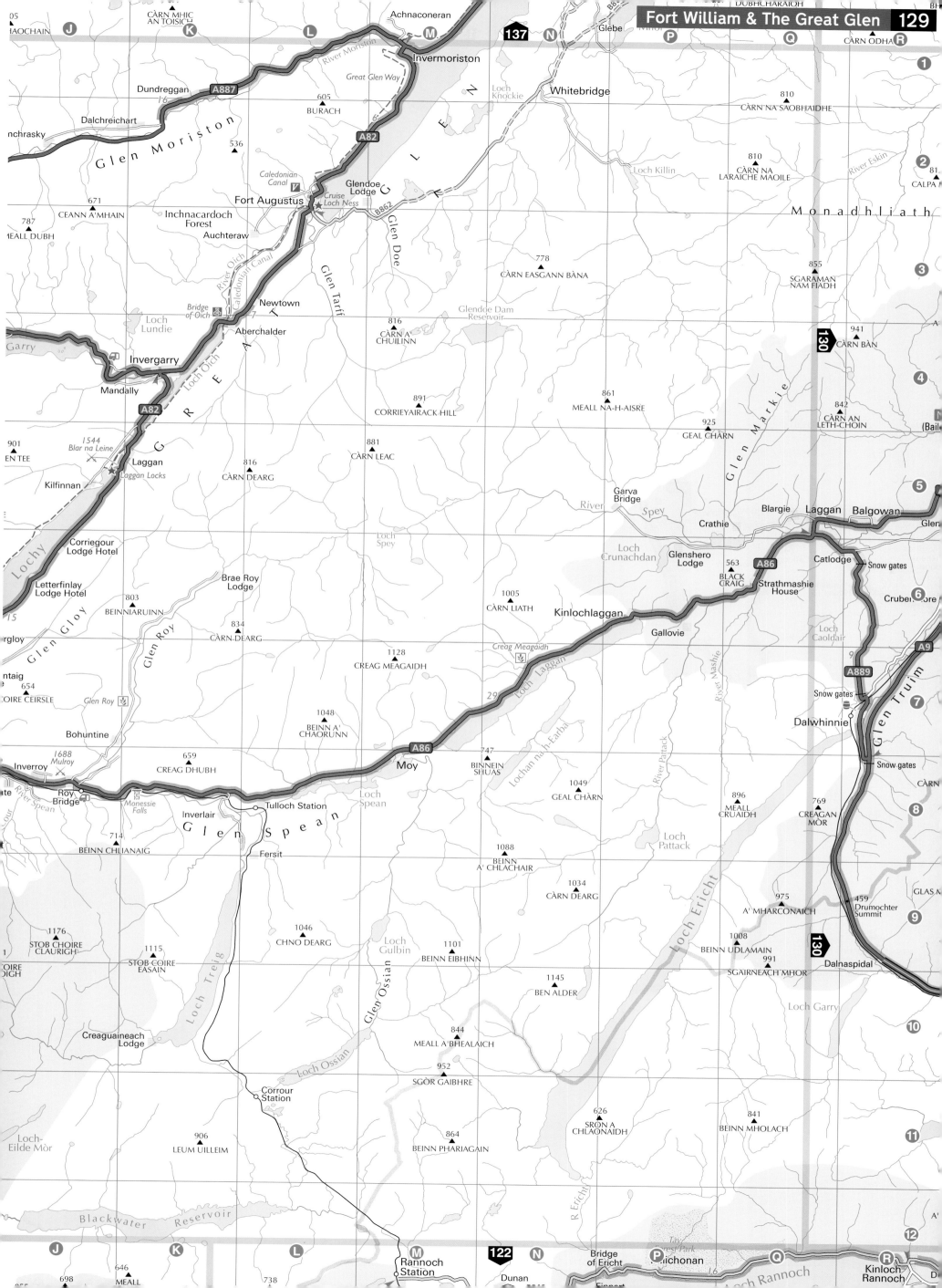

J   K   L   M   137   N   P   Q   R

1

2

3

4

5

6

7

8

9

10

11

12

IAOCHAIN   J

CÀRN MHIC
AN TOISICH
K

Achnaconeran

DUBHCHARAIDH

Glebe

CÀRN ODHA   R

River Moriston

Invermoriston

A887

Dundreggan

Great Glen Way

A82

Whitebridge

Loch
Knockie

810
CÀRN NA SAOBHAIDHE

Dalchreichart

nchrasky

16

605
BURACH

Glen Moriston

810
CÀRN NA
LARAICHE MAOILE

River Eskin

CALPA

2

Glen Moriston

Caledonian
Canal

536

Glendoe
Lodge

Loch Killin

Monadhliath

81

671
CEANN A'MHAIN

Fort Augustus

A82

B862

778
CÀRN EASGANN BÀNA

855
SGARAMAN
NAM FIADH

787
MEALL DUBH

Inchnacardoch
Forest

Cruise
Loch Ness

Glen Doe

Glendoe Dam
Reservoir

3

Auchteraw

Glen Tarff

130

941
CÀRN BÀN

Newtown

816
CÀRN A'
CHUILINN

Bridge
of Oich

Loch
Lundie

Aberchalder

842
CÀRN AN
LETH-CHÒIN

(Baile

Invergarry

891
CORRIEYAIRACK HILL

861
MEALL NA-H-AISRE

925
GEAL CHÀRN

Glen Markie

N

Garry

Mandally

A82

901
EN TEE

1544
Blar na Leine

881
CÀRN LEAC

River

Garva
Bridge

Spey

Blargie

Laggan   Balgowan

Glen

5

Laggan

Loch'Oich

Kilfinnan

Laggan Locks

816
CÀRN DEARG

Loch
Crunachdan

Glenshero
Lodge

Crathie

563
BLACK
CRAIG

A86

Catlodge

Snow gates

Corriegour
Lodge Hotel

Loch
Spey

Strathmashie
House

Cruben More

6

Lochy

Letterfinlay
Lodge Hotel

803
BEINNIARUINN

Brae Roy
Lodge

1005
CÀRN LIATH

Kinlochlaggan

Gallovie

Loch
Caoldair

A9

15

Glen Gloy

Glen Roy

834
CÀRN-DEARG

Creag Meagaidh

River Mashie

A889

A86

7

rgloy

Glen Roy

1128
CREAG MEAGAIDH

29

Loch Laggan

Snow gates

Dalwhinnie

Glen Truim

654
OIRE CEIRSLE

Bohuntine

1048
BEINN A'
CHAORUNN

Moy

747
BINNEIN
SHUAS

Lochan na h-Earba

River Pattack

8

Inverroy

1688
Mulroy

659
CREAG DHUBH

A86

1049
GEAL CHÀRN

896
MEALL
CRUAIDH

769
CREAGAN
MÒR

Snow gates

CÀRN

Roy
Bridge

Monessie
Falls

Inverlair

Tulloch Station

Loch
Spean

Glen Spean

Fersit

1088
BEINN
A' CHLACHAIR

Loch
Pattack

975
A' MHARCONAICH

459
Drumochter
Summit

GLAS M

9

714
BEINN CHLIANAIG

1034
CÀRN DEARG

Loch Ericht

River Spean

1176
STOB CHOIRE
CLAURIGH

1046
CHNO DEARG

Loch
Gulbin

1101
BEINN EIBHINN

1008
BEINN UDLAMAIN

130

Dalnaspidal

OIRE
DIGH

1115
STOB COIRE
EASAIN

Loch Treig

Glen Ossian

1145
BEN ALDER

991
SGAIRNEACH MHOR

Loch Garry

10

Creaguaineach
Lodge

Loch-
Eilde Mòr

844
MEALL A'BHEALAICH

Loch Ossian

626
SRON A
CHLAONAIDH

841
BEINN MHOLACH

11

906
LEUM UILLEIM

Corrour
Station

952
SGÒR GAIBHRE

864
BEINN PHARIAGAIN

R Ericht

Loch
Garry

Blackwater   Reservoir

646
MEALL

698

738

J   K   L   122   M   N   Q   R

Rannoch
Station

Dunan

Bridge
of Ericht

Phichonan

Loch Rannoch

Kinloch
Rannoch

12

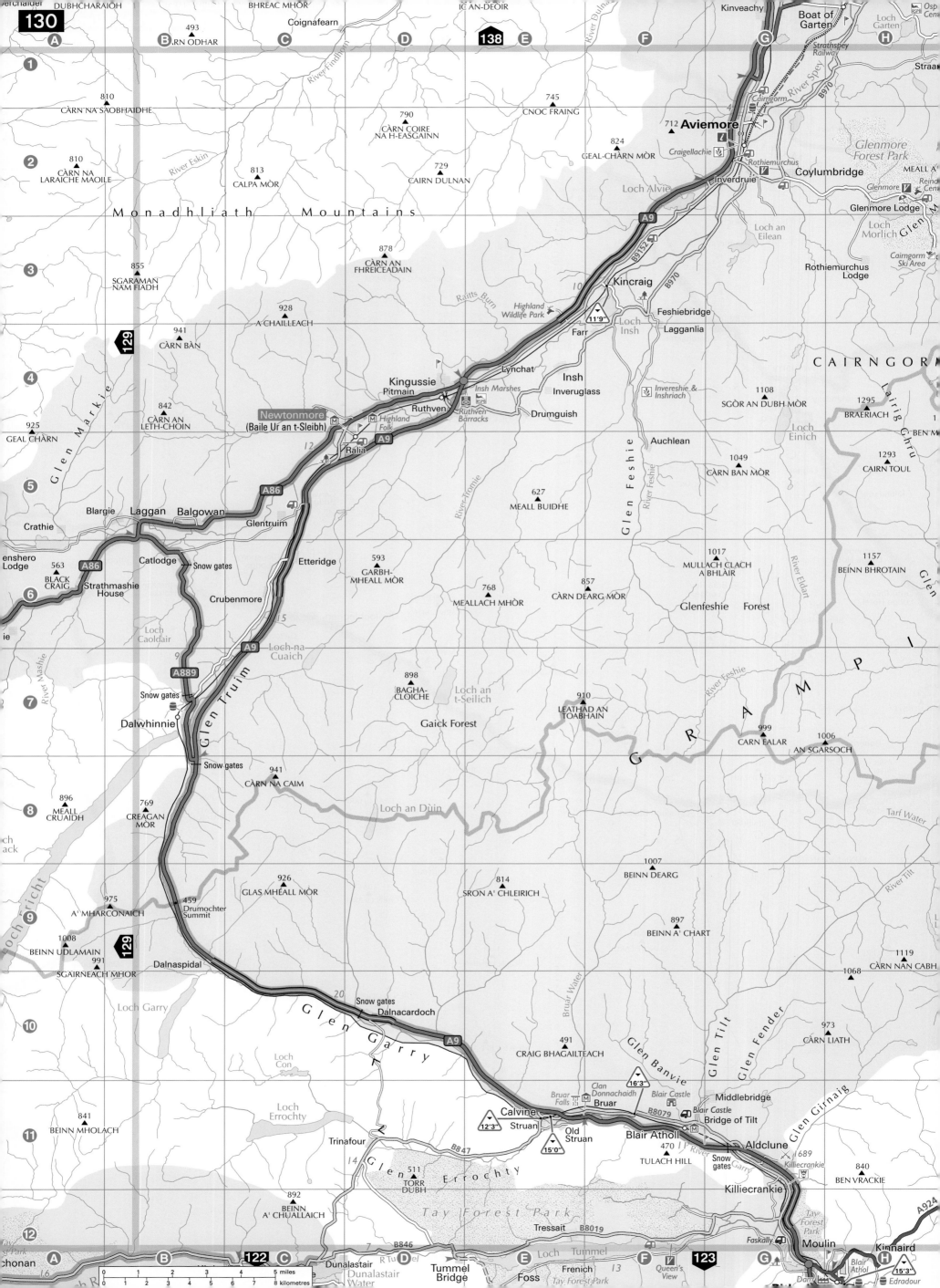

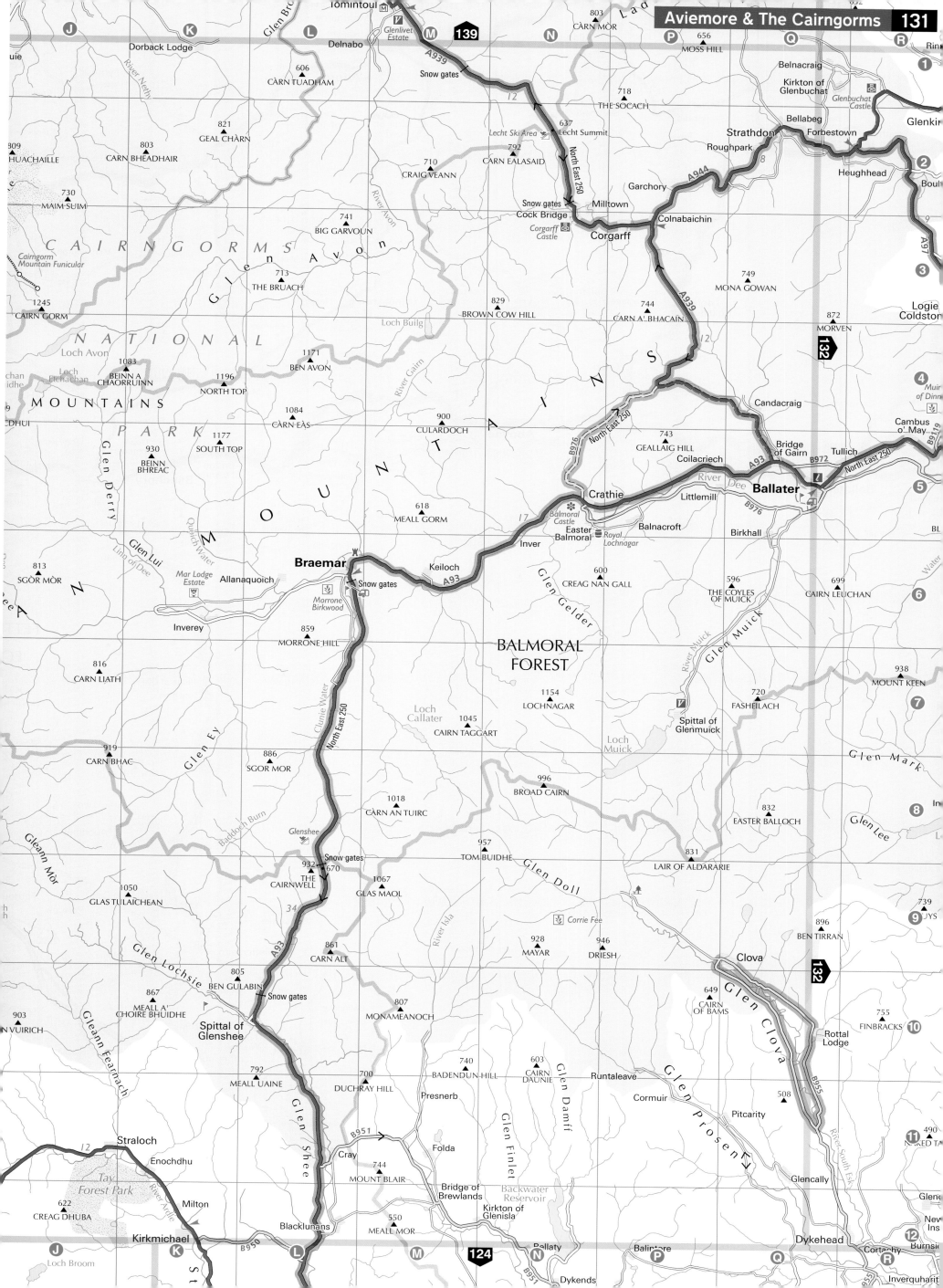

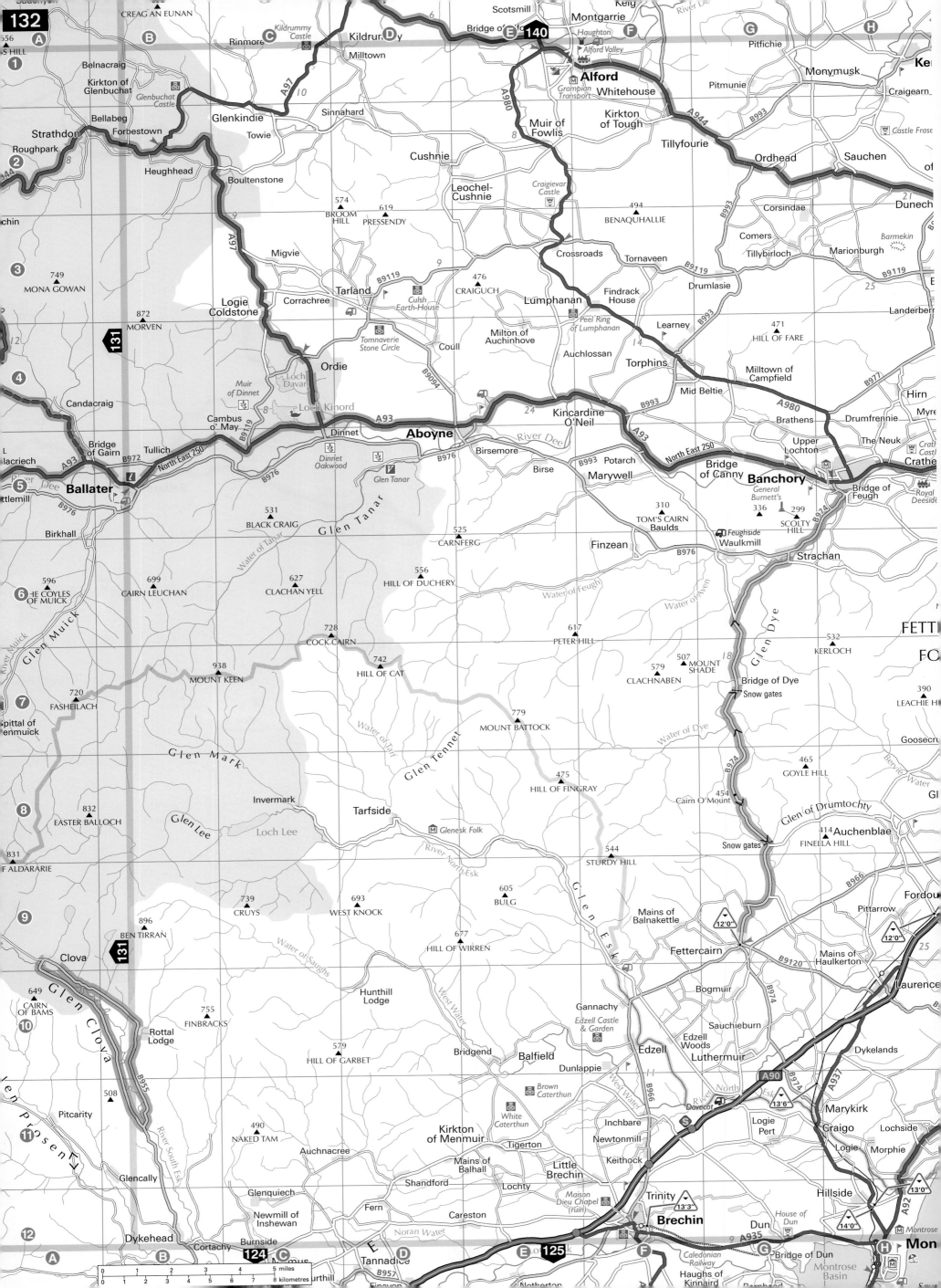

Aberdeen Harbour

ELGIN   PETERHEAD

A96

WESTBURN
ROAD

HUTCHEON
STREET

A944

A96

KING STREET

SKENE STREET A9119

ABERDEEN

UNION STREET

A92

ABERDEEN
STATION

FERRY
TERMINAL

BEACH BOULEVARD

Footdee

North Pier

River Dee

Albert Basin

Victoria Dock

Torry

SINCLAIR   ROAD

WILLOWBANK   ROAD

Ferryhill

15'6"

13'3"

VICTORIA   ROAD

BALNAGASK   ROAD

GIRDLENESS   ROAD

ST   FITTICKS   ROAD

DUNDEE

Low Emission Zone   SAC

0   500 m

Thainstone
Kinkell
Church

J

Hillhead

Kintore

Kingseat

K

Hatton of
Fintray

L

Kinmundy

Whitecairns

B979

M

Belhelvie

141

N

Balmedie

P

Q

R

1

mnay

B994

Cottown

Leylodge

Lyne
of Skene

Skene
House

B9126

Blackburn

Clinterty

A96

B977

A90

Overton

Dyce

Stoneywood

Bankhead

Bucksburn

Potterton

A90

Blackdog

A92

B999

Middleton
Park

Denmore

Bridge of Don

P+R

2

Westhill

Kirkton
of Skene

Garlogie

Kingswells

Kingsford

Elrick

Carnie

A944

A9119

Countesswells

Blacktop

Kittybrewster

Old Aberdeen

H

ABERDEEN

Ruthrieston

Torry

Nigg Bay

3

Easter
Ord

Benthoul

Craigton

14'6"

Peterculter

Kirkton of
Maryculter

Milltimber

Kingcausie

Milton of
Murtle

Bieldside

Cults

Mannofield

Banchory-
Devenick

Charlestown

Kincorth

Nigg

Altens Haven

Cove Bay

13'3"

Loirston

4

Drumoak

Drum
Castle

West
Park

A93

River Dee

Kirkton of
Durris

Denside
of Durris

Woodlands
of Durris

Crossroads

Hillside

Auchlee

Findon

Portlethen

Old Portlethen

Cammachmore
Bay

Downies

5

Durris
Forest

A90

Cammachmore

Cookney

Netherley

Chapelton

Newtonhill

Skateraw

Muchalls

6

ESSO

REST

376
MONGOUR

HILL OF TRUSTA
320

A957

B979

Bridge of
Muchalls

Doonie Point

A92

13'6"

Ury

Garron Point

Stonehaven Bay

7

Elfhill

Tannachie

ives

New Mill

Drumlithie

Temple
of Fiddes

Kirktown of
Fetteresso

11'9"

Stonehaven

Tolbooth

Dunnottar

A90

8

nbervie

Mondynes

12'6"

Fowlsheugh

Crawton

Catterline

9

Redmyre

Arbuthnott

Grassic Gibbon
Centre

B967

Kinneff

Todhead Point

A92

10

Inverbervie

Bervie
Bay

Maritime

Gourdon

11

rk

Redford

Benholm

B9120

12

Bush

Milton Ness

Johnshaven

St Cyrus

J

K

L

M

N

P

Q

R

ose

J K L M N Q R

Eilean Flodigarry

Staffin Island

Staffin
Staffin
Ellishader
Valtos
Rubha nam Brathairean
Garros
Culnaknock
Lealt
Tote
A855

Old Man
of Storr
719
THE
STORR

Loch
Cleathan

Loch
Fada

Penifiler 412
BEN
TIANAVAIG

Torvaig 312

Camastianavaig
Tianavaig
Bay
Ollach
B883
Clachan
Inverarish

The Braes
444
BEN LEE
Peinchorran
Suisnish
Point
Sconser

Eyre
Point

773
GLAMAIG
A87
Loch Ainort
Ard
Dorch
Dunan
Luib
Strollamus

564
GLAS BHEIN
MHOR

Cuillin Hills

927
BLAVEN
708
BEINN NA
CAILLICH
BEINN
DEORG MHOR
Torrin

Loch na
Creitheach

Kirkibost
B8083
Loch
Slapin

Longa
Island

Loch
Gairloch

Gairloch
Charlestown
MEALL AN
DOIREIN

Port
Henderson
B8056
Badachro
Opinan

River Kerry
Loch Bad
an Sgalaig

Victoria Falls 19

South Erradale

Red Point

Talladale

Loch Ghaineamhach

Loch na
h-Oidhche

875
BAOSBHEINN

619
BEINN BHREAC

855
BEI
AN EOIN

Red
Point

Loch Torridon

Rubha
na Fearn

Fearnmore

Lower
Diabaig

985
BEINN
ALLIGIN

914
BEINN DEARG

Ob
Chuaig

Fearnbeg

Arrina

Loch
Diabaig

Inveralligin

136

1024

Cuaig

Kenmore

Alligin Shuas

Torridon
House

Torridon 19

Callakille

Ardheslaig

Loch
Shieldaig
Shieldaig

Upper Loch Torridon

Deer

Countr

Lonbain

492
AN GARBH-
MHEALL

493
CROIC-
BHEINN

A896

Wester Ross

Anna

North Coast 500

Loch
Damph

902
BEINN
DAMPH

Glenshieldaig Forest

Loch Lundie

CHEAN

River Applecross

Applecross

895
BEINN BHAN

Loch
Coultrie

730
SGURR A GHARAIDH

Applecross Bay

Milltown

Applecross

Rassal
Ashwood

RAASAY

626
Pass of the Cattle
774
Bealach na Ba
SGURR A'CHAORACHAIN

Camusteel

Camusterrach

Aird Dhubh

888
Kishorn
A896
Kirkton

Lochcarron

Culduie

Ardarroch

Penifiler 412

444
DUN CAAN

Oskaig

Rubha na' Leac

Achintraid

394
BAD A
CHREAMHA

310
BEINN NA LEAC

Kishorn
Island

Toscaig

River Toscaig

Ardaneaskan
Strome

Slumba

Caolas Mor

Loch Kishorn

Loch Carron

Ardnarff

Eilean
Meadhonach

Eilean
Mor

Stromeferry

A890

CROWLIN
ISLANDS

Plockton

Achmore

SCALPAY

Port-an-Eorna

Braeintra

67
Longay

Duirinish

447
BEINN RAIMH

Moll

396
MULLACH
NA CARN

Drumbuie

Loch Long

Pabay

Badicaul
Balmacara

Conchra

Kyle of Lochalsh
(Caol Loch Aillse)
Skye Bridge

Auchtertyre

136

Caolas Scalpay

27

Reraig

Nostie

Kirkton

Ardelve
Eilean Donan
Dornie

Bunacloich

Carndu

Kyleakin
Lochalsh
Woodland
Garden

A87

Loch Alsh

A87

Keppoch

Corry
Broadford
Bay
Waterloo
Lower
Breakish

Broadford
Harrapool
Skulamus
Breakish

Letterfearn

603
BEINN A'CHUIRN

Loch Duich

732
SGURR NA
COINNICH

Otter
Hide

Kyle Rhea

Bernera
Galltair

A851

Kylerhea

605
BEN ASLAK

(Apr-Oct)
Glenelg
Bay

Glenelg

350
Mam Ratagan

Loch na
Creitheach

300
BEINN
NAN CARN
Heaste

Eilanreach

408
BEINN A'
CHAOINICH

Moyle

Drumfearn

Suisnish

561
BEINN NA
SEAMRAIG

Glenelg
Brochs

Glean Beag

Balvraid

143

127

J K L M N P Q R

1
2
3
4
5
6
7
8
9
10
11
12

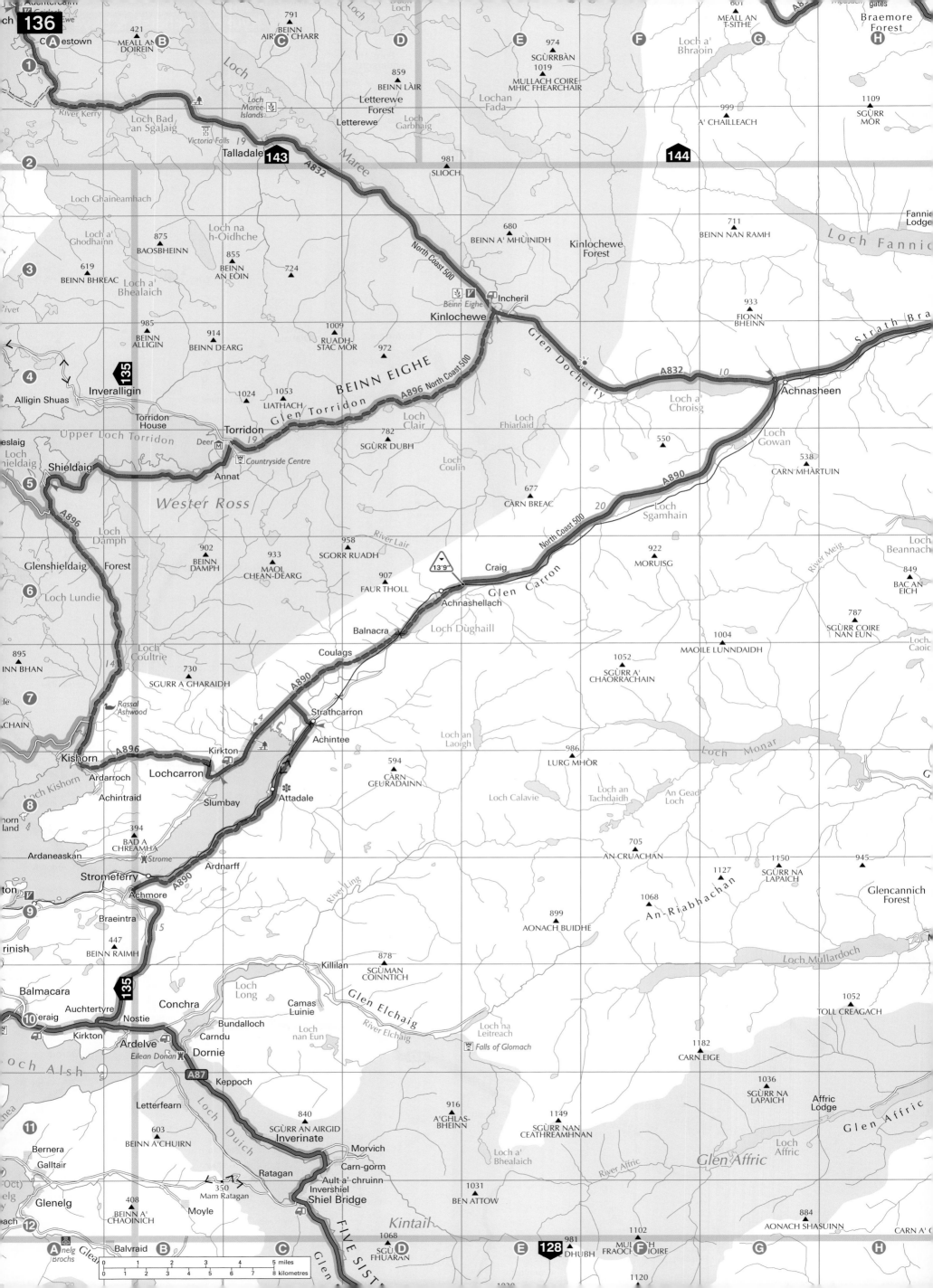

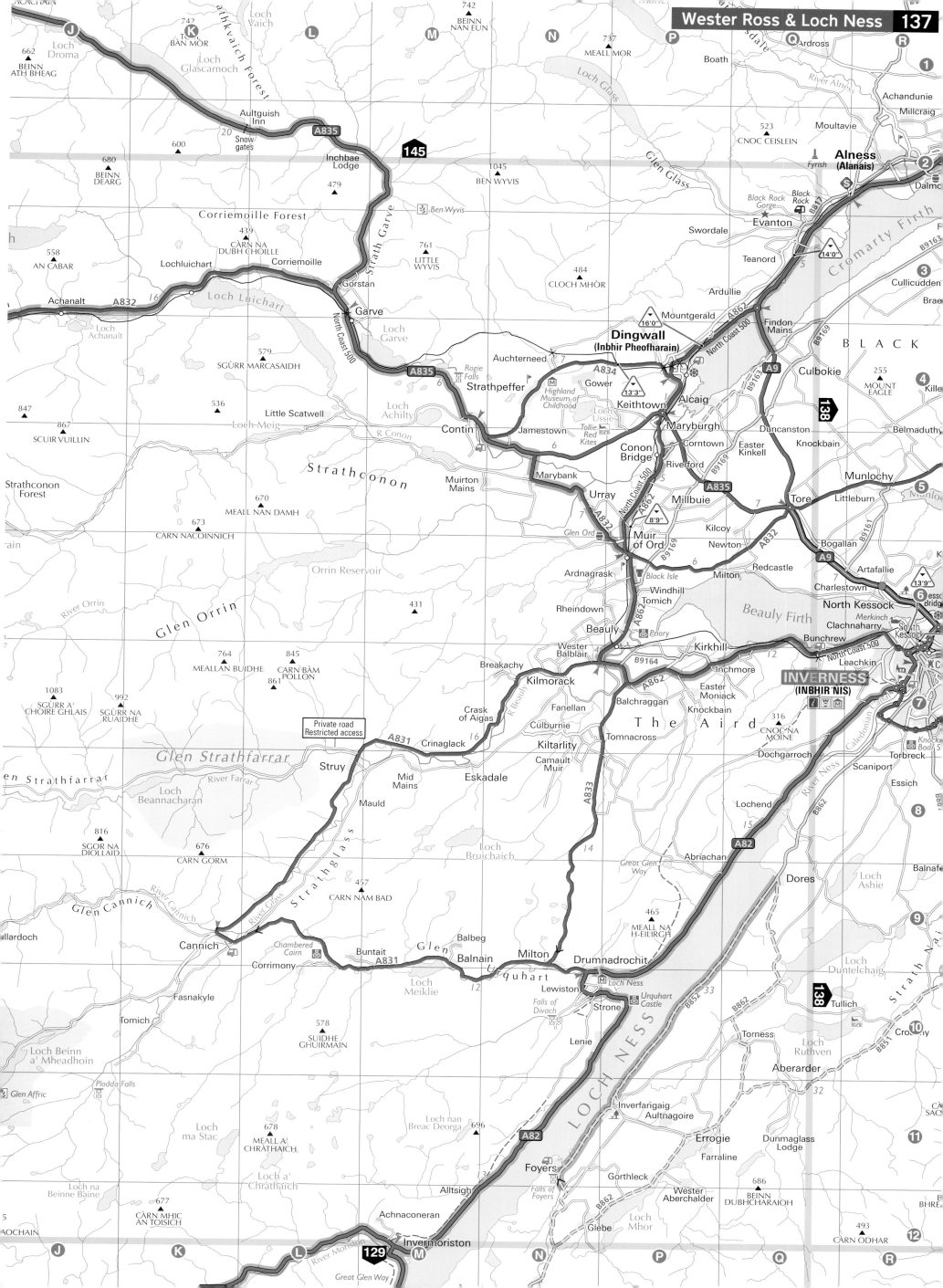

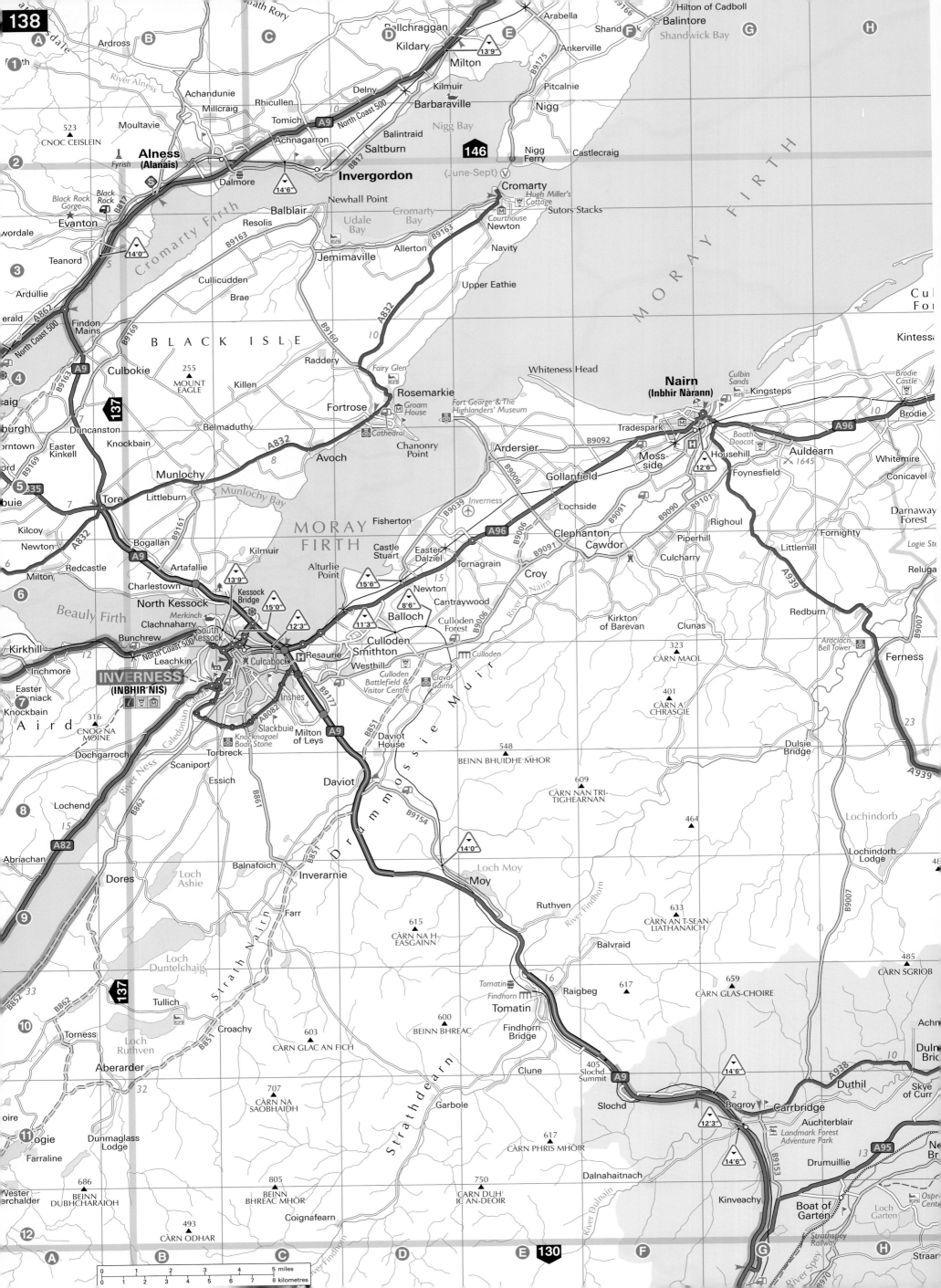

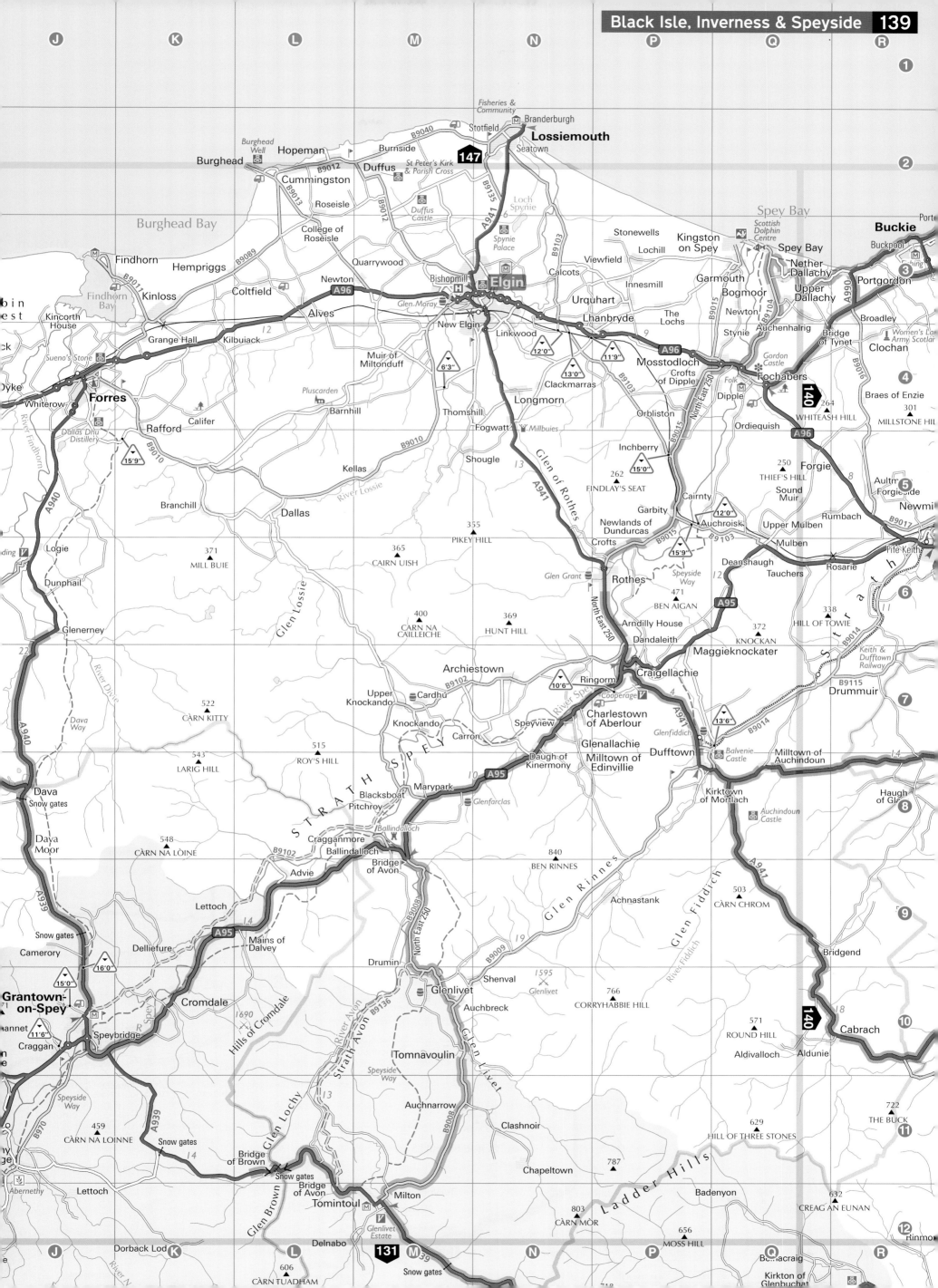

J K L M N P Q R

1
2
3
4
5
6
7
8
9
10
11
12

Fisheries & Community
Branderburgh
Stotfield
Lossiemouth
Seatown
147
B9040
Burnside
Hopeman
Burghead Well
Burghead
Duffus
St Peter's Kirk & Parish Cross
Cummingston
B9012
Roseisle
B9013
Duffus Castle
Spynie Palace
Loch Spynie
Spey Bay
Stonewells
Kingston on Spey
Scottish Dolphin Centre
Buckie
Buckpool
College of Roseisle
Quarrywood
B9012
Bishopmill
Viewfield
Lochill
Calcots
Garmouth
Nether Dallachy
Upper Dallachy
Portgordon
A990
Findhorn
Hempriggs
B9089
Newton
A96
Elgin
Glen Moray
New Elgin
Urquhart
Innesmill
Bogmoor
Newton
Broadley
Clochan
Kinloss
Findhorn Bay
Coltfield
Alves
Grange Hall
Kilbuiack
Linkwood
Lhanbryde
The Lochs
Stynie
Auchenhalrig
Bridge of Tynet
Women's Land Army Scotlar
Kincorth House
Dyke
Sueno's Stone
Forres
Whiterow
Muir of Miltonduff
12'0"
11'9"
Mosstodloch
Crofts of Dipple
Gordon Castle
Fochabers
140
River Findhorn
Dallas Dhu Distillery
Rafford
Califer
6'3"
13'0"
Clackmarras
Longmorn
B9103
Dipple
Folk
264
WHITEASH HILL
A96
Braes of Enzie
301
MILLSTONE HILL
Pluscarden
Barnhill
Thomshill
Orbliston
Ordiequish
15'9"
B9010
Fogwatt
Millbuies
Inchberry
15'0"
B9015
Thief's Hill
250
Forgie
8
Aultm Forgieside
Logie
Branchill
Kellas
Shougle
13
A941
262
FINDLAY'S SEAT
Garbity
Cairnty
Sound Muir
Newmi
Dallas
River Lossie
Newlands of Dundurcas
12'0"
Auchroisk
Upper Mulben
Rumbach
B9017
Glen Lossie
355
PIKEY HILL
371
MILL BUIE
365
CAIRN UISH
Crofts
B9015
15'9"
B9103
Mulben
Fife Keith
Dunphail
Glen Grant
Rothes
Speyside Way
Deanshaugh
Tauchers
Rosarie
Glenerney
400
CÀRN NA CAILLEICHE
369
HUNT HILL
471
BEN AIGAN
A95
338
HILL OF TOWIE
22
Dava Way
522
CÀRN KITTY
Arndilly House
Dandaleith
372
KNOCKAN
B9014
Keith & Dufftown Railway
Strath
Archiestown
B9102
Upper Knockando
Cardhu
Ringorm
10'6"
Craigellachie
Maggieknockater
B9115
Drummuir
7
A940
543
LARIG HILL
515
ROY'S HILL
Knockando
Carron
Speyview
Cooperage
Charlestown of Aberlour
A941
4
13'6"
B9014
Dava
Snow gates
Daugh of Kinermony
A95
Glenallachie
Glenfiddich
Milltown of Edinvillie
Dufftown
Balvenie Castle
Milltown of Auchindoun
14
8
Dava Moor
548
CÀRN NA LÒINE
Blacksboat
Pitchroy
Marypark
Glenfarclas
10
840
BEN RINNES
Kirktown of Mortlach
Auchindoun Castle
Haugh of Gla
A940
B9102
Cragganmore
Ballindalloch
Bridge of Avon
Glen Rinnes
Achnastank
A941
Glen Fiddich
503
CÀRN CHROM
9
Snow gates
Advie
Lettoch
14
B9008
North East 250
B9009
19
Bridgend
A95
Mains of Dalvey
Drumin
Shenval
1595
Glenlivet
766
CORRYHABBIE HILL
571
ROUND HILL
140
18
10
Snow gates
Camerory
16'0"
Delliefure
Glenlivet
Auchbreck
503
CÀRN CHROM
Aldivalloch
Aldunie
Cabrach
15'0"
Grantown-on-Spey
11'6"
Cromdale
1690
Hills of Cromdale
Tomnavoulin
Speyside Way
Strath Avon
B9136
Glen Livet
Auchnarrow
629
THE BUCK
722
Craggan
Speybridge
A939
Clashnoir
571
HILL OF THREE STONES
11
Chapeltown
787
459
CÀRN NA LOINNE
Snow gates
14
Bridge of Brown
Lettoch
Glen Lochy
13
Milton
Bridge of Avon
Badenyon
632
CREAG AN EUNAN
Abernethy
River N
B970
Dorback Lod
Glen Brown
Bridge of Brown
Snow gates
Tomintoul
Glenlivet Estate
131
B9
Delnabo
803
CÀRN MÒR
656
MOSS HILL
Ba   craig
Rin   m
12
CÀRN TUADHAM
606
Snow gates
Kirkton of Glenbuchat

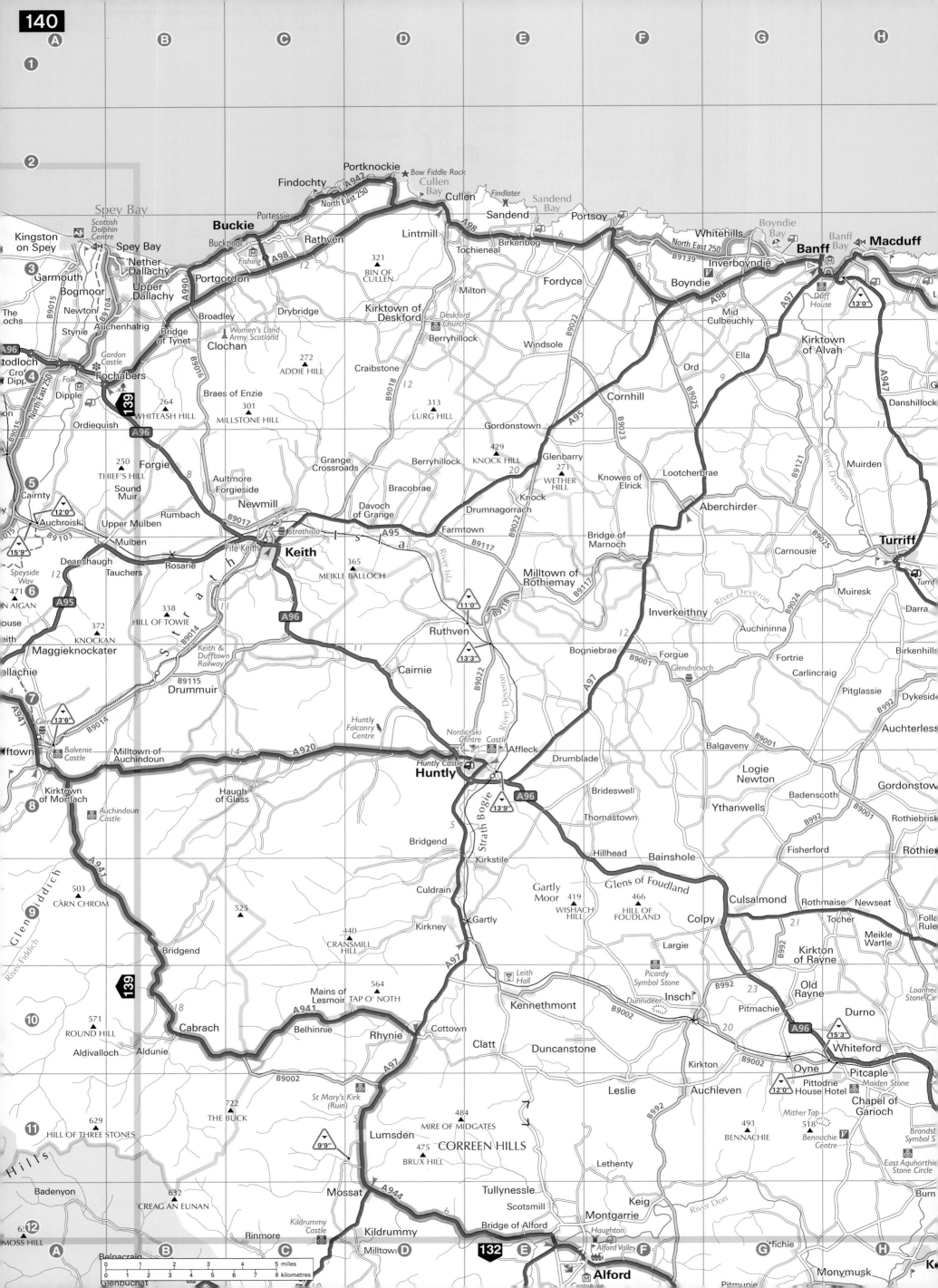

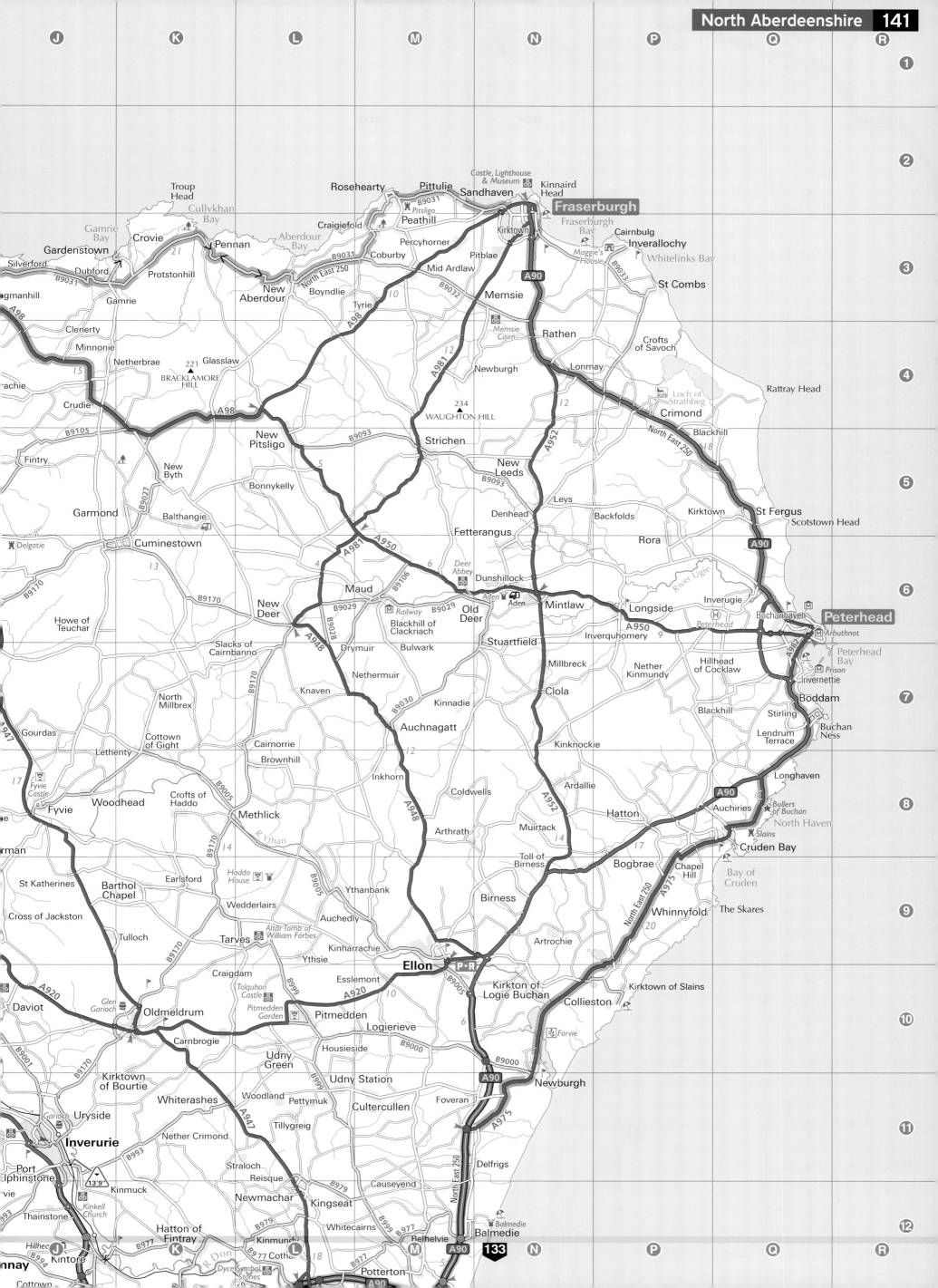

A B C D E F G H

1

Baile Ailein
(Balallan)
Lacasaig
(Laxay)
Cromor
(Cromore)
Loch Erisort

iridh a Bhruaich
(Aribruach)

Gearraidh Bhaird
(Garyvard)

Cearsiadar
(Kershader)

Marbhig
(Marvig)

2

B8060

Grabhair
(Gravir)

Loch Ouirn

401
MÒR
MHONADH

A' Chabag

152

3

PARK

Eishken
(Eisgein)

Leumrabhagh
(Lemreway)

571
BEINN MHOR

Loch
Brollum

Loch Shell

4

Loch Seaforth

Loch Claidh

Reinigeadal
(Rhenigidale)

Loch
Brollum

SOUND OF SHIANT

5

Caolas Scalpaigh
(Kyles Scalpay)

SHIANT
ISLANDS

6

Sgalpaigh
(Scalpay)

SCALPAY

152

T H

7

The   Little   Minch

8

9

Fladda-chùain

Eilean Troidday

10

Rubha Hunish

Duntulm
Kilmaluag

A855

An Tairbeart
(Tarbert)

Lùb Score

Skye Museum
of Island Life

Flodigarry

Eilean Flodigarry

V

Borneskitaig

Kilmuir

Heribusta

542

Poldorais

Staffin
Bay

Staffin Island

11

Bhatairnis

Kilvaxter

Balgown

MEAL NA
SUIREAMACH

Digg

Brogaig

134

135

Stenscholl

Staffin

Staffin

Linicro

464

Kilt Rock

Totscore

BIODA
BUIDHE

Trotternish

Ellishader

Maligar

Idrigill

River Rha

12

Ascrib
Islands

River Conon

Marishader

Valtos

Rubha nam Brathai

283
BEN

Uig Bay

(Uige)

Fairy
Glen

BEINN
EDRA

Garros

Culnaknock

A B C D E F G H

0   1   2   3   4   5 miles
0   1   2   3   4   5   6   7   8 kilometres

148 Q

144

J K L M N P Q R

1
Baddidarrach
Inverkirkaig

2
Enard Bay
Rubha Còigeach
Eilean Mòr
Rubha Mòr
Reiff
Achnahaird

3
Eilean Mullagrach
Altandhu
144
Polbain
Badentarbet
Loch Osgaig
Loch Bad a' Ghaill

SUMMER ISLES
Isle Ristol
Glas-leac Mòr
Achiltibuie
Polglass
Badentarbat Bay
Ben M Coigea

4
Steòrnabhagh (Stornoway)
Tanera Beg
Tanera Mòr
Glas-leac Beag
Horse Island
Horse Sound
Achduart
Culnacraig
BE C

5
Leac Dhonn
Isle Martin
Eilean Dubh
Priest Island

6
Cailleach Head
Scoraig
Annat Bay
Ruigh'riabhach
BEINN GHOBHLACH
635
Little Loch Broom

Greenstone Point
Rubha Beag
Stattic Point
Badluarach
A832
Badrallach
Badcaul
North Coast 500
Ardessie
Camus...gaul
7
Mellon Udrigle
Achgarve
GRUINARD ISLAND
Gruinard Bay
Laide
Gruinard
SAIL MHOR
764
Dundonnell
32

Foura
Rubha nan Sasan
Mellon Charles
Ormiscaig
Aultbea
Loch a' Bhaid-luachraich
Little Gruinard River
Gruinard River
Lochan Gaineamhaich
Rubha Rèidh
Cove
296
AN CUAIDH
CREAG-MHEAL BEAG
347
Loch Fada
AN TEALLACH
1062
8
Melvaig
ISLE OF EWE
Loch Ewe
Loch na Sealga
Strathnasheallag Forest

Aultgrishin
293
CNOC BREAC
Inverasdale
Naast
Inverewe Garden
MEALL NA MEINE
250
BEINN A' CHAISGEIN BEAG
681
Rhidorroch Forest
144
BEINN DEARG MHOR
906
9
North Erradale
B8021
Poolewe
Londubh
Fionn Loch
Wester Ross

Big Sand
Strath
A832
Heritage
Auchtercairn
Gairloch & Loch Ewe
Gairloch
BEINN AIRIDH CHARR
791
Dubh Loch
10
Longa Island
Loch Gairloch
Lonemore
Charlestown
MEALL AN DOIREIN
421
BEINN LAIR
859
Letterewe Forest
Letterewe
SGÙRRBÀN
974
MULLACH COIRE MHIC FHEARCHAIR
1019
Port Henderson
B8056
Eilean Horrisdale
River Kerry
Loch Maree Islands
Loch Maree
Lochan Fada

Badachro
Opinan
South Erradale
Loch Bad an Sgalaig
Victoria Falls 19
Talladale
A832
SLIOCH
981
11
Red Point
135
Loch Ghaineamhach
136
Maree
BEINN A' MHÙINIDH
680
Kinlochewe Forest

Red Point
BAOSBHEINN
875
Loch na h-Oidhche
724
North Coast 500
Incheril
Kinlochewe
12
Rubha na Fearn
Loch Torridon
BEINN BHREAC
619
Loch a' Chealaich
BEINN AN EÒIN
855
Beinn Eighe
985

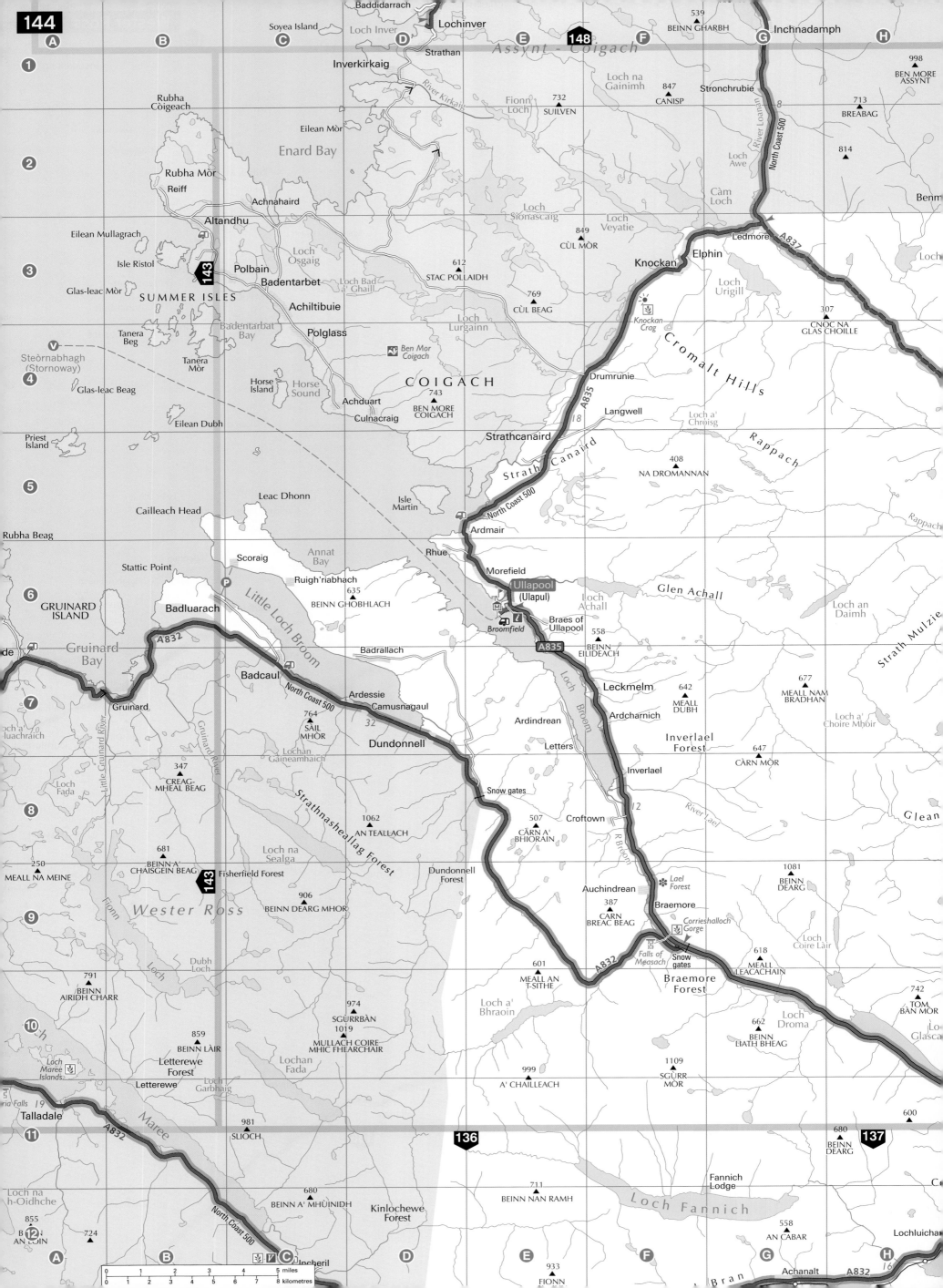

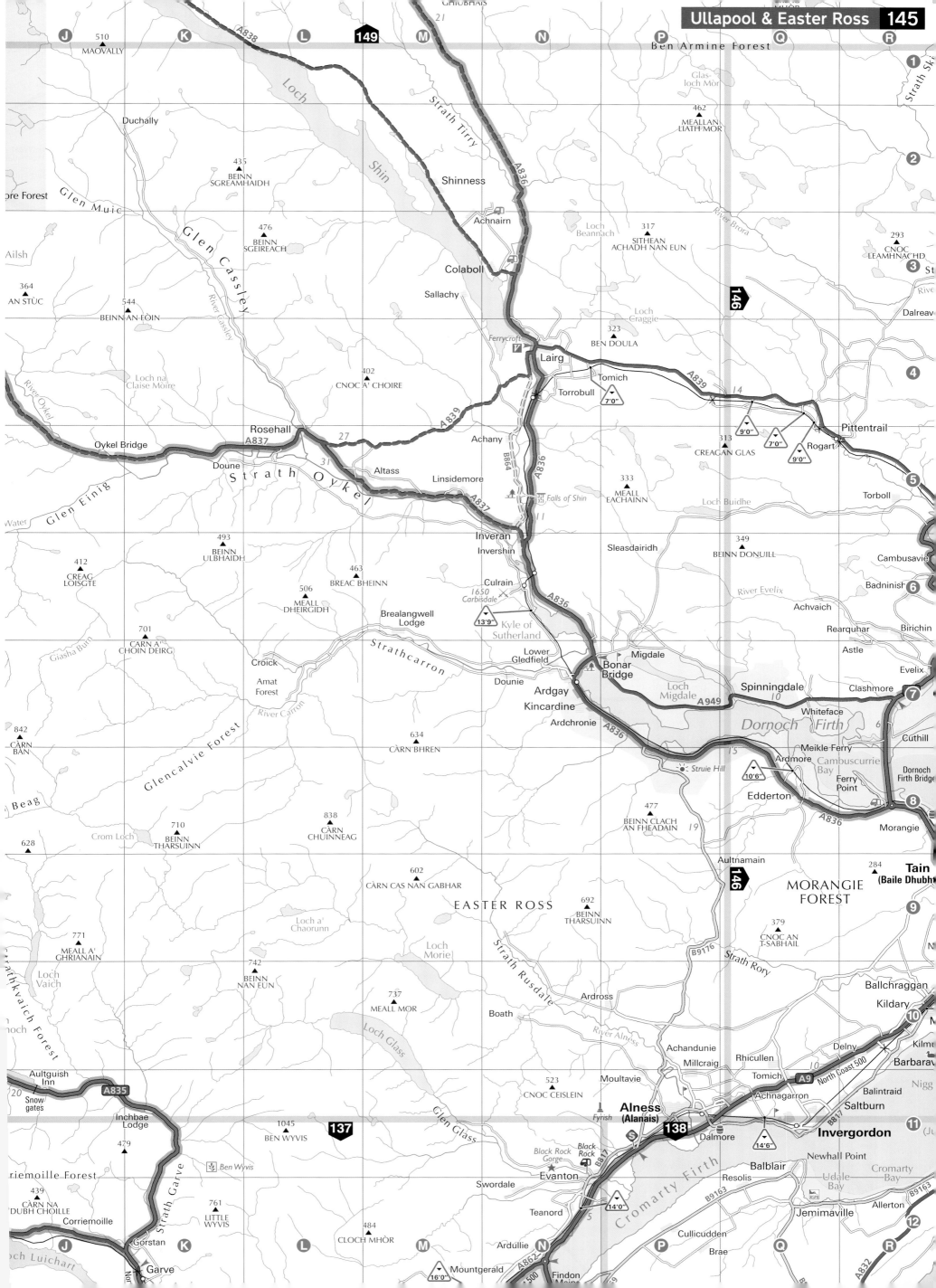

J K L M N P Q R

149

146

Ben Armine Forest

1
510
MAOVALLY

Strath Ski

Loch

Duchally

Strath Tirry

Glas-
loch Mòr

2
435
BEINN
SGREAMHAIDH

Shinness

462
MEALLAN
LIATH MÒR

Shin

Achnairn

A836

River Brora

293
CNOC
LEAMHNACHD

Glen Muic

476
BEINN
SGEIREACH

Loch
Beannach

317
SITHEAN
ACHADH NAN EUN

St

3
Colaboll

Glen Cassley

364
AN STÙC

River Cassley

Sallachy

Loch
Craggie

146

Dalrea

544
BEINN AN-LÒIN

Ferrycroft

323
BEN DOULA

River

402
CNOC A' CHOIRE

Lairg

Tomich

A839

14

4
Loch na
Claise Mòire

Torrobull

7'0"

A837
Rosehall

A839

313
9'0"

7'0"

Pittentrail

Oykel Bridge

27

Achany

CREAGAN GLAS

9'0"

Rogart

5
River Oykel

Doune

31

Altass

B864

A836

333
MEALL
EACHAINN

Torboll

Strath Oykel

Linsidemore

A837

Falls of Shin

Loch Buidhe

Glen Einig

11

349
BEINN DONUILL

Cambusavie

Water

493
BEINN
ULBHAIDH

Inveran

Invershin

Sleasdairidh

River Evelix

Badninish

6
412
CREAG
LOISGTE

463
BREAC BHEINN

Culrain

1650
Carbisdale

Achvaich

Rearquhar

Astle

Birichin

506
MEALL
DHEIRGIDH

Brealangwell
Lodge

13'9"

Kyle of
Sutherland

Evelix

701
CÀRN A'
CHOIN DEIRG

Croick

Strathcarron

Lower
Gledfield

Migdale

Spinningdale

10

Clashmore

7
Giasha Burn

Amat
Forest

Dounie

Bonar
Bridge

Loch
Migdale

A949

Dornoch Firth

Whiteface

Cuthill

842
CÀRN
BAN

River Carron

Ardgay
Kincardine

Meikle Ferry

Ardmore

6

Cambuscurrie
Bay

Dornoch
Firth Bridge

Glencalvie Forest

634
CÀRN BHREN

Ardchronie

A836

15

Struie Hill

10'6"

Ferry
Point

8
Beag

838
CÀRN
CHUINNEAG

477
BEINN CLACH
AN FHEADAIN

19

Edderton

A836

Morangie

Crom Loch

710
BEINN
THARSUINN

146

Aultnamain

284
Tain
(Baile Dhubh

628

602
CÀRN CAS NAN GABHAR

EASTER ROSS

692
BEINN
THARSUINN

MORANGIE
FOREST

9
771
MEALL A'
GHRIANAIN

Loch a'
Chaorunn

379
CNOC AN
T-SABHAIL

Loch
Vaich

742
BEINN
NAN EUN

Loch
Morie

Strath Rory

B9176

Ballchraggan

athkvaich Forest

737
MEALL MÒR

Strath Rusdale

Kildary

10
och Forest

Boath

Ardross

A9

North Coast 500

Delny

Kilm

Barbara

Aultguish
Inn

A835

Achandunie

Millcraig

Rhicullen

Tomich

Balintraid

11
Snow
gates

523
CNOC CEISLEIN

Moultavie

Achnagarron

B817

Saltburn

Inchbae
Lodge

Fyrish

Alness
(Alanais)

138

Dalmore

14'6"

Invergordon

Nigg

479

1045
BEN WYVIS

137

Black Rock
Gorge

Black
Rock

Newhall Point

Balblair

Cromarty
Bay

iemoille Forest

Ben Wyvis

Glen Glass

Evanton

14'0"

Resolis

Udale
Bay

B9163

12
439
CÀRN NA
DUBH CHOILLE

761
LITTLE
WYVIS

Swordale

Cromarty Firth

Jemimaville

B9163

Corriemoille

Strath Garve

484
CLOCH MHÒR

Teanord

Allerton

ch Luichart

Gorstan

Ardullie

A862

Cullicudden

Garve

J K L M N P Q R

Mountgerald

Findon

16'0"

500

Brae

A832

CAPE WRATH

Kearvaig
Bay

Cléit
Dhubh

371
SGRIBHIS-
BHEINN

297
CNOC A'
GHIUBHAIS

300
MAOVALLY

THE PARPH

457
FASHVEN

Loch Àirigh
na Beinne

Sandwood
Bay

Sandwood
Loch

485
CREAG
RIABHACH

467
AN GRIANAN

464
MEALL
NA MÒINE

331
GHLAS-
BHEINN

Rubh' an Fhir Lèithe

Sheigra

521
FARRMHEALL

19

Balchrick

Blairmore

Oldshoremore

355
AN SOCACH

773
BEINN
SPIONNAIDH

801
CRANSTACKIE

Kinlochbervie

Loch Clash

Badcall

North Coast 500

Strath Dionard

River Dionard

Achriesgill

B801

Loch Inchard

Achlyness

Loch na
Claise Càrnaich

Rubha Ruadh

Skerricha

Rhiconich

A838

908
FOINAVEN

Fanagmore

Tarbet

Foindle

Loch Laxford

North-west Sutherland

Loch na Tuadh

HANDA
ISLAND

7

Laxford
Bridge

River Laxford

786
ARKLE

Scourie Bay

Scourie

A894

721
BEN STACK

Loch
Stack

SÀBHAL

Scourie More

Lower
Badcall

Strath Stack

Upper
Badcall

386
BEN
AUSKAIRD

333
BEN
SCREAVIE

800

Badcall
Bay

Loch a'
Mhuilinn

Achfary

A838

Loch More

Rubh a'
Mhucard

North Coast 500

17

419
BEN STROME

Kinloch

Point of Stoer

OLDANY
ISLAND

Eddrachillis
Bay

Locha Chàirn Bhàin

Kylestrome

Loch an
Leathaid Bhuain

Glendhu Forest

Old Man
of Stoer

Culkein
Drumbeg

Kylesku

Loch Glendhu

613
MEALL AN FHEUR

Culkein

Clashnessie
Bay

Oldany

Drumbeg

Unapool

The Rock Stop

525
BEINN AIRD
DA LOCH

Achnacarnin

B869

Nedd

Loch
Glencoul

792
BEINN LEOID

Clashmore

Clashnessie

Loch
Poll

Glen Leirg

776

Loch an
Leothaid

SAIL GHORM

809
QUINAG

Loch na
Gainmhich

Loch-Beag

Stoer

B869

Loch
Beannach

A894

774

Eas-a' Chùal Aluinn

Clachtoll

North Coast 500

GLAS BHEINN

Bay of Clachtoll

Rhicarn

A837

11

Loch Assynt

Achmelvich
Bay

Achmelvich

Baddidarrach

Ardvreck

539
BEINN GHARBH

Inchnadamph

Soyea Island

Loch Inver

Lochinver

Assynt - Coigach

998
BEN MORE
ASSYNT

Inverkirkaig 144

Strathan

Stronchrubie

Loch na
Gainimh

847

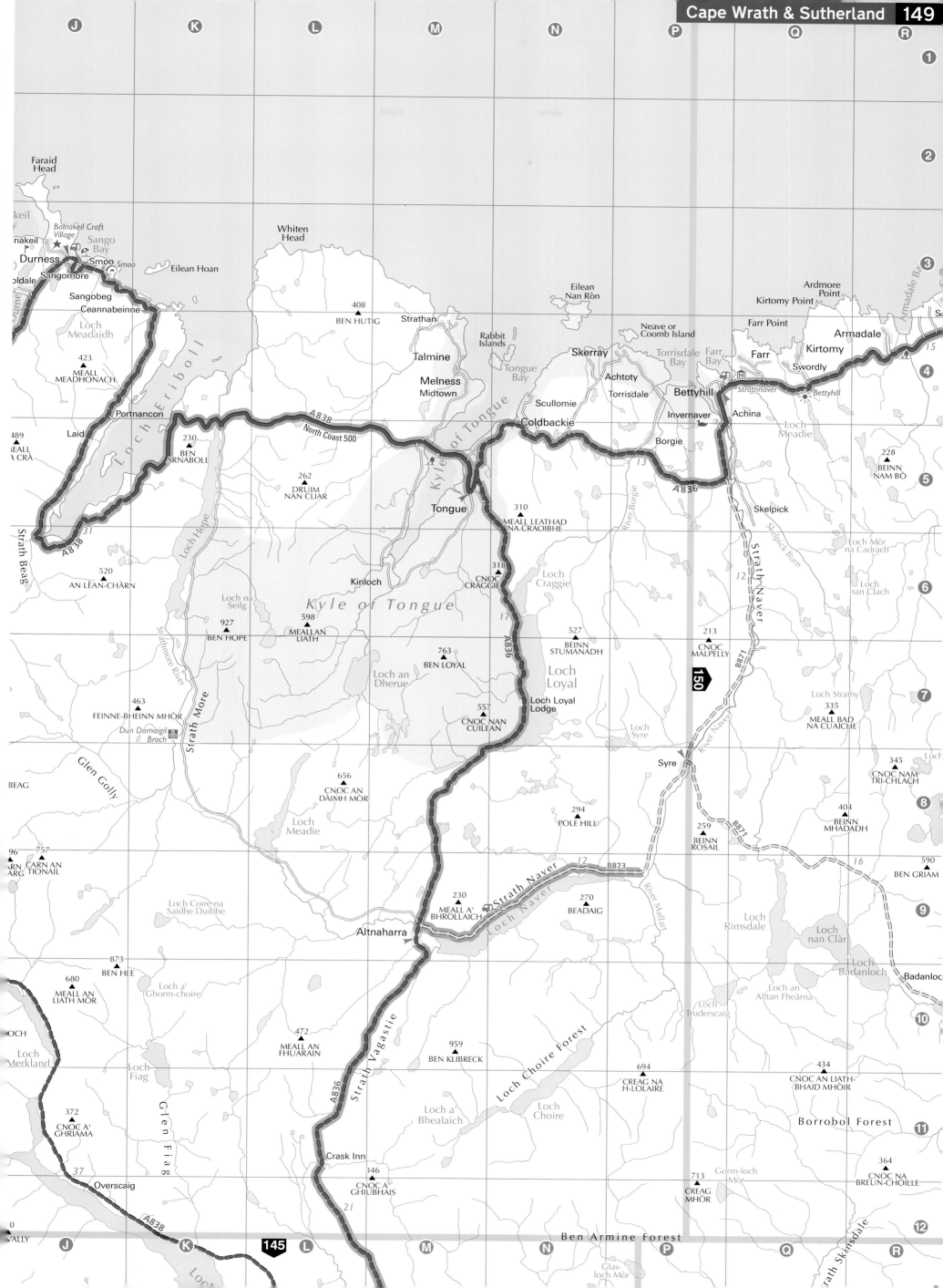

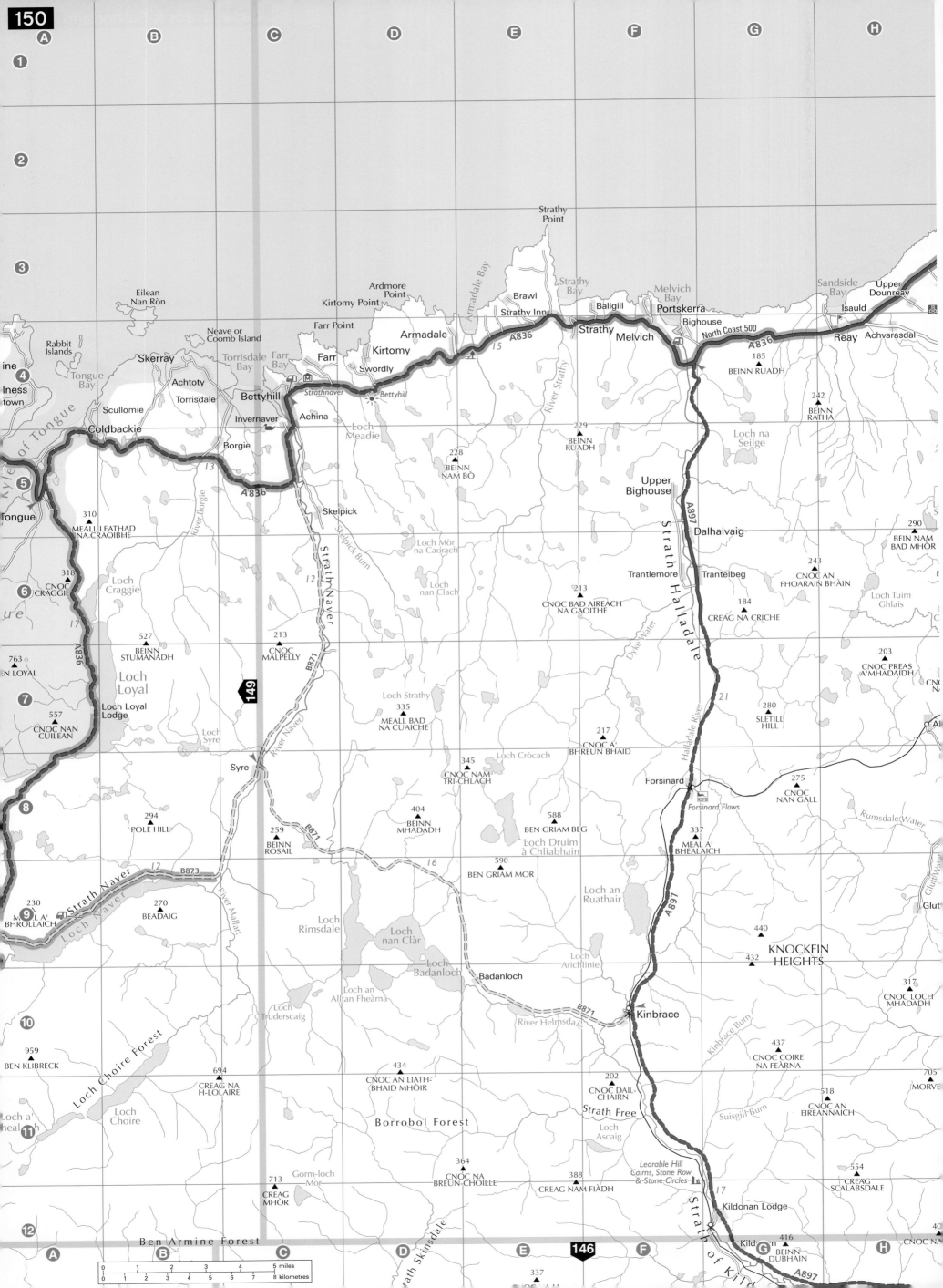

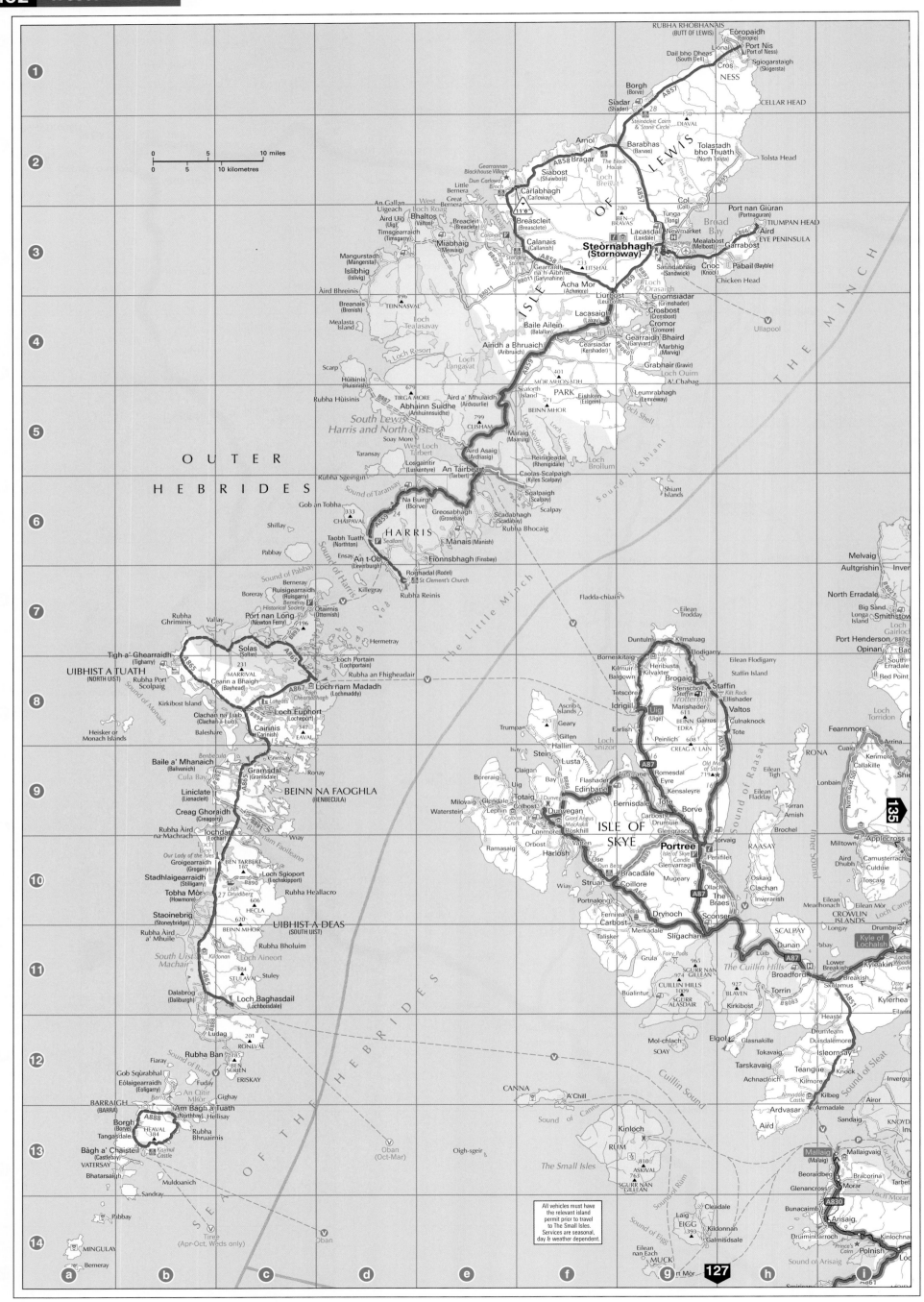

Motorway and primary route junctions which have access or exit restrictions are shown on the map pages thus:

M1 London - Leeds

Junction	Northbound	Southbound
2	Access only from A1 *(northbound)*	Exit only to A1 *(southbound)*
4	Access only from A41 *(northbound)*	Exit only to A41 *(southbound)*
6A	Access only from M25 (no link from A405)	Exit only to M25 (no link from A405)
7	Access only from A414	Exit only to A414
17	Exit only to M45	Access only from M45
19	Exit only to M6 *(northbound)*	Exit only to A14 *(southbound)*
21A	Exit only, no access	Access only, no exit
24A	Access only, no exit	Access only from A50 *(eastbound)*
35A	Exit only, no access	Access only, no exit
43	Exit only to M621	Access only from M621
48	Exit only to A1(M) *(northbound)*	Access only from A1(M) *(southbound)*

M2 Rochester - Faversham

Junction	Westbound	Eastbound
1	No exit to A2 *(eastbound)*	No access from A2 *(westbound)*

M3 Sunbury - Southampton

Junction	Northeastbound	Southwestbound
8	Access only from A303, no exit	Exit only to A303, no access
10	Exit only, no access	Access only, no exit
14	Access from M27 only, no exit	No access to M27 *(westbound)*

M4 London - South Wales

Junction	Westbound	Eastbound
1	Access only from A4 *(westbound)*	Exit only to A4 *(eastbound)*
2	Access only from A4 *(westbound)*	Access only from A4 *(eastbound)*
21	Exit only to M48	Access only from M48
23	Access only from M48	Exit only to M48
25	Exit only, no access	Access only, no exit
25A	Exit only, no access	Access only, no exit
29	Exit only to A48(M)	Access only from A48(M)
38	Exit only, no access	No restriction
39	Access only, no exit	No access or exit
42	Exit only to A483	Access only from A483

M5 Birmingham - Exeter

Junction	Northeastbound	Southwestbound
10	Access only, no exit	Exit only, no access
11A	Access only from A417 *(westbound)*	Exit only to A417 *(eastbound)*
18A	Exit only to M49	Access only from M49
18	Exit only, no access	Access only, no exit

M6 Toll Motorway

Junction	Northwestbound	Southeastbound
T1	Access only, no exit	No access or exit
T2	No access or exit	Exit only, no access
T5	Access only, no exit	Exit only to A5148 *(northbound)*, no access
T7	Exit only, no access	Access only, no exit
T8	Exit only, no access	Access only, no exit

M6 Rugby - Carlisle

Junction	Northbound	Southbound
3A	Exit only to M6 Toll	Access only from M6 Toll
4	Exit only to M42 *(southbound)* & A446	Exit only to A446
4A	Access only from M42 *(southbound)*	Exit only to M42
5	Exit only, no access	Access only, no exit
10A	Exit only to M54	Access only from M54
11A	Access only from M6 Toll	Exit only to M6 Toll
with M56 (jct 20A)	No restriction	Access only from M56 *(eastbound)*
20	Exit only to M56 *(westbound)*	Access only from M56 *(eastbound)*
24	Access only, no exit	Exit only, no access
25	Exit only, no access	Access only, no exit
30	Access only from M61	Exit only to M61
31A	Exit only, no access	Access only, no exit
45	Exit only, no access	Access only, no exit

M8 Edinburgh - Bishopton

Junction	Westbound	Eastbound
6	Exit only, no access	Access only, no exit
6A	Access only, no exit	Exit only, no access
7	Access only, no exit	Exit only, no access
7A	Exit only, no access	Access only from A725 *(northbound)*, no exit
8	No access from M73 *(southbound)* or from A8 *(eastbound)* & A89	No exit to M73 *(northbound)* or to A8 *(westbound)* & A89
9	Access only, no exit	Exit only, no access
13	Access only from M80 *(southbound)*	Exit only to M80 *(northbound)*
14	Access only, no exit	Exit only, no access
16	Exit only to A804	Access only from A879
17	Exit only to A82	No restriction
18	Access only from A82 *(eastbound)*	Exit only to A814
19	No access from A814 *(westbound)*	Exit only to A814 *(westbound)*
20	Exit only, no access	Access only, no exit
21	Access only, no exit	Exit only to A8
22	Exit only to M77 *(southbound)*	Access only from M77 *(northbound)*
23	Exit only to B768	Access only from B768
25	No access or exit from or to A8	No access or exit from or to A8
25A	Exit only, no access	Access only, no exit
28	Exit only, no access	Access only, no exit
28A	Exit only to A737	Access only from A737
29A	Exit only to A8	Access only, no exit

M9 Edinburgh - Dunblane

Junction	Northwestbound	Southeastbound
2	Access only, no exit	Exit only, no access
3	Exit only, no access	Access only, no exit
6	Access only, no exit	Exit only to A905
8	Exit only to M876 *(southwestbound)*	Access only from M876 *(northeastbound)*

M11 London - Cambridge

Junction	Northbound	Southbound
4	Access only from A406 *(eastbound)*	Exit only to A406
5	Exit only, no access	Access only, no exit
8A	Exit only, no access	No direct access, use jct 8
9	Exit only to A11	Access only from A11
13	Exit only, no access	Access only, no exit
14	Exit only, no access	Access only, no exit

M20 Swanley - Folkestone

Junction	Northwestbound	Southeastbound
2	Staggered junction; follow signs - access only	Staggered junction; follow signs - exit only
3	Exit only to M26 *(westbound)*	Access only from M26 *(eastbound)*
5	Access only from A20	For access follow signs - exit only to A20
6	No restriction	For exit follow signs
10	Access only, no exit	Exit only, no access
11A	Access only, no exit	Exit only, no access

M23 Hooley - Crawley

Junction	Northbound	Southbound
7	Exit only to A23 *(northbound)*	Access only from A23 *(southbound)*
10A	Access only, no exit	Exit only, no access

M25 London Orbital

Junction	Clockwise	Anticlockwise
1B	No direct access, use slip road to jct 2 Exit only	Access only, no exit
5	No exit to M26 *(eastbound)*	No access from M26
19	Exit only, no access	Access only, no exit
21	Access only from M1 *(southbound)* Exit only to M1 *(northbound)*	Access only from M1 *(southbound)* Exit only to M1 *(northbound)*
31	No exit (use slip road via jct 30), access only	No access (use slip road via jct 30), exit only

M26 Sevenoaks - Wrotham

Junction	Westbound	Eastbound
with M25 (jct 5)	Exit only to clockwise M25 *(westbound)*	Access only from anticlockwise M25 *(eastbound)*
with M20 (jct 3)	Access only from M20 *(northwestbound)*	Exit only to M20 *(southeastbound)*

M27 Cadnam - Portsmouth

Junction	Westbound	Eastbound
4	Staggered junction; follow signs - access only from M3 *(southbound)*. Exit only to M3 *(northbound)*	Staggered junction; follow signs - access only from M3 *(southbound)*. Exit only to M3 *(northbound)*
10	Exit only, no access	Access only, no exit
12	Staggered junction; follow signs - exit only to M275 *(southbound)*	Staggered junction; follow signs - access only from M275 *(northbound)*

M40 London - Birmingham

Junction	Northwestbound	Southeastbound
3	Exit only, no access	Access only, no exit
7	Exit only, no access	Access only, no exit
8	Exit only to M40/A40	Access only from M40/A40
13	Exit only, no access	Access only, no exit
14	Access only, no exit	Exit only, no access
16	Access only, no exit	Exit only, no access

M42 Bromsgrove - Measham

Junction	Northeastbound	Southwestbound
1	Access only, no exit	Exit only, no access
7	Exit only to M6 *(northwestbound)*	Access only from M6 *(northwestbound)*
7A	Exit only to M6 *(southeastbound)*	No access or exit
8	Access only from M6 *(southeastbound)*	Exit only to M6 *(northwestbound)*

M45 Coventry - M1

Junction	Westbound	Eastbound
Dunchurch (unnumbered)	Access only from A45	Exit only, no access
with M1 (jct 17)	Access only from M1 *(northbound)*	Exit only to M1 *(southbound)*

M48 Chepstow

Junction	Westbound	Eastbound
21	Access only from M4 *(westbound)*	Exit only to M4 *(eastbound)*
23	No exit to M4 *(eastbound)*	No access from M4 *(westbound)*

M53 Mersey Tunnel - Chester

Junction	Northbound	Southbound
11	Access only from M56 *(westbound)* Exit only to M56 *(eastbound)*	Access only from M56 *(westbound)* Exit only to M56 *(eastbound)*

M54 Telford - Birmingham

Junction	Westbound	Eastbound
with M6 (jct 10A)	Access only from M6 *(northbound)*	Exit only to M6 *(southbound)*

M56 Chester - Manchester

Junction	Westbound	Eastbound
1	Access only from M60 *(westbound)*	Exit only to M60 *(eastbound)* & A34 *(northbound)*
2	Exit only, no access	Access only, no exit
3	Access only, no exit	Exit only, no access
4	Exit only, no access	Access only, no exit
7	Exit only, no access	No restriction
8	Access only, no exit	No access or exit
9	No exit to M6 *(southbound)*	No access from M6 *(northbound)*
15	Exit only to M53	Access only from M53
16	No access or exit	No restriction

M57 Liverpool Outer Ring Road

Junction	Northwestbound	Southeastbound
3	Access only, no exit	Exit only, no access
5	Access only from A580 *(westbound)*	Exit only, no access

M60 Manchester Orbital

Junction	Clockwise	Anticlockwise
2	Access only, no exit	Exit only, no access
3	No access from M56	Access only from A34 *(northbound)*
4	Access only from A34 *(northbound)*. Exit only to M56	Access only from M56 *(eastbound)*. Exit only to A34 *(southbound)*
5	Access and exit only from and to A5103 *(northbound)*	Access and exit only from and to A5103 *(southbound)*
7	No direct access, use slip road to jct 8. Exit only to A56	Access only from A56. No exit, use jct 8
14	Access from A580 *(eastbound)*	Exit only to A580 *(westbound)*
16	Access only, no exit	Exit only, no access
20	Exit only, no access	Access only, no exit
22	No restriction	Exit only, no access
25	Exit only, no access	No restriction
26	No restriction	Exit only, no access
27	Access only, no exit	Exit only, no access

M61 Manchester - Preston

Junction	Northwestbound	Southeastbound
3	No access or exit	Exit only, no access
with M6 (jct 30)	Exit only to M6 *(northbound)*	Access only from M6 *(southbound)*

M62 Liverpool - Kingston upon Hull

Junction	Westbound	Eastbound
23	Access only, no exit	Exit only, no access
32A	No access to A1(M) *(southbound)*	No restriction

M65 Preston - Colne

Junction	Northeastbound	Southwestbound
9	Exit only, no access	Access only, no exit
11	Access only, no exit	Exit only, no access

M66 Bury

Junction	Northbound	Southbound
with A56	Exit only to A56 *(northbound)*	Access only from A56 *(southbound)*
1	Exit only, no access	Access only, no exit

M67 Hyde Bypass

Junction	Westbound	Eastbound
1A	Access only, no exit	Exit only, no access
2	Exit only, no access	Access only, no exit

M69 Coventry - Leicester

Junction	Northbound	Southbound
2	Access only, no exit	Exit only, no access

M73 East of Glasgow

Junction	Northbound	Southbound
1	No exit to A74 & A721	No exit to A74 & A721
2	No access from or exit to A89. No access from *(eastbound)*	No access from or exit to A89. No exit to M8 *(westbound)*

M74 Glasgow - Abington

Junction	Northbound	Southbound
3	Exit only, no access	Access only, no exit
3A	Access only, no exit	Exit only, no access
4	No access from A74 & A721	Access only, no exit to A74 & A721
7	Access only, no exit	Exit only, no access
9	No access or exit	Exit only, no access
10	No restriction	Access only, no exit
11	Access only, no exit	Exit only, no access
12	Exit only, no access	Access only, no exit

M77 Glasgow - Kilmarnock

Junction	Northbound	Southbound
with M8 (jct 22)	No exit to M8 *(westbound)*	No access from M8 *(eastbound)*
4	Access only, no exit	Exit only, no access
6	Access only, no exit	Exit only, no access
7	Access only, no exit	No restriction
8	Exit only, no access	Exit only, no access

M80 Glasgow - Stirling

Junction	Northbound	Southbound
4A	Exit only, no access	Access only, no exit
6A	Access only, no exit	Exit only, no access
8	Exit only to M876 *(northeastbound)*	Access only from M876 *(southwestbound)*

M90 Edinburgh - Perth

Junction	Northbound	Southbound
1	No exit, access only	Exit only to A90 *(eastbound)*
2A	Exit only to A92 *(eastbound)*	Access only from A92 *(westbound)*
7	Access only, no exit	Exit only, no access
8	Exit only, no access	Access only, no exit
10	No access from A912. No exit to A912 *(southbound)*	No access from A912 *(northbound)* No exit to A912

M180 Doncaster - Grimsby

Junction	Westbound	Eastbound
1	Access only, no exit	Exit only, no access

M606 Bradford Spur

Junction	Northbound	Southbound
2	Exit only, no access	No restriction

M621 Leeds - M1

Junction	Clockwise	Anticlockwise
2A	Access only, no exit	Exit only, no access
4	No exit or access	No restriction
5	Access only, no exit	Exit only, no access
6	Exit only, no access	Access only, no exit
with M1 (jct 43)	Exit only to M1 *(southbound)*	Access only from M1 *(northbound)*

M876 Bonnybridge - Kincardine Bridge

Junction	Northeastbound	Southwestbound
with M80 (jct 5)	Access only from M80 *(northeastbound)*	Exit only to M80 *(southwestbound)*
with M9 (jct 8)	Exit only to M9 *(eastbound)*	Access only from M9 *(westbound)*

A1(M) South Mimms - Baldock

Junction	Northbound	Southbound
2	Exit only, no access	Access only, no exit
3	No restriction	Exit only, no access
5	Access only, no exit	No access or exit

A1(M) Pontefract - Bedale

Junction	Northbound	Southbound
40	Exit only to A162 (M62), No access	Access only, no exit
41	No access to M62 *(eastbound)*	No restriction
43	Access only from M1 *(northbound)*	Exit only to M1 *(southbound)*

A1(M) Scotch Corner - Newcastle upon Tyne

Junction	Northbound	Southbound
57	Exit only to A66(M) *(eastbound)*	Access only from A66(M) *(westbound)*
65	No access Exit only to A194(M) & A1 *(northbound)*	No exit Access only from A194(M) & A1 *(southbound)*

A3(M) Horndean - Havant

Junction	Northbound	Southbound
1	Access only from A3	Exit only to A3
4	Exit only, no access	Access only, no exit

A38(M) Birmingham, Victoria Road (Park Circus)

Junction	Northbound	Southbound
with B4132	No exit	No access

A48(M) Cardiff Spur

Junction	Westbound	Eastbound
29	Access only from M4 *(westbound)*	Exit only to M4 *(eastbound)*
29A	Exit only to A48 *(westbound)*	Access only from A48 *(eastbound)*

A57(M) Manchester, Brook Street (A34)

Junction	Westbound	Eastbound
with A34	No exit	No access

A58(M) Leeds, Park Lane and Westgate

Junction	Northbound	Southbound
with A58	No restriction	No access

A64(M) Leeds, Clay Pit Lane (A58)

Junction	Westbound	Eastbound
with A58	No exit (to Clay Pit Lane)	No access (from Clay Pit Lane)

A66(M) Darlington Spur

Junction	Westbound	Eastbound
with A1(M) (jct 57)	Exit only to A1(M) *(southbound)*	Access only from A1(M) *(northbound)*

A74(M) Gretna - Abington

Junction	Northbound	Southbound
18	Exit only, no access	Access only, no exit

A194(M) Gateshead

Junction	Northbound	Southbound
with A1(M) (jct 65)	Access only from A1(M) *(northbound)*	Exit only to A1(M) *(southbound)*

A12 M25 - Ipswich

Junction	Northeastbound	Southwestbound
13	Access only, no exit	No restriction
14	Exit only, no access	Access only, no exit
20A	Exit only, no access	Access only, no exit
20B	Access only, no exit	Exit only, no access
21	No restriction	Access only, no exit
23	Exit only, no access	Access only, no exit
24	Access only, no exit	Exit only, no access
27	Exit only, no access	Access only, no exit
Dedham & Stratford St Mary (unnumbered)	Exit only	Access only

A14 M1 - Felixstowe

Junction	Westbound	Eastbound
with M1/M6 (jct19)	Exit only to M6 and M1 *(northbound)*	Access only from M6 and M1 *(southbound)*
4	Exit only, no access	Access only, no exit
21	Access only, no exit	Exit only, no access
22	Exit only, no access	Access only from A1 *(southbound)*
23	Access only, no exit	Exit only, no access
31	No restriction	Access only, no exit
34	Access only, no exit	Exit only, no access
36	Exit only to A11, access only from A1303	Access only from A11
38	Access only from A11	Exit only to A11
39	Exit only, no access	Access only, no exit
61	Access only, no exit	Exit only, no access

A55 Holyhead - Chester

Junction	Westbound	Eastbound
8A	Exit only, no access	Access only, no exit
23A	Access only, no exit	Exit only, no access
24A	Exit only, no access	No access or exit
27A	No restriction	No access or exit
33A	Exit only, no access	No access or exit
33B	Exit only, no access	Access only, no exit
36A	Exit only to A5104	Access only from A5104
39	Access only, no exit	Exit only, no access

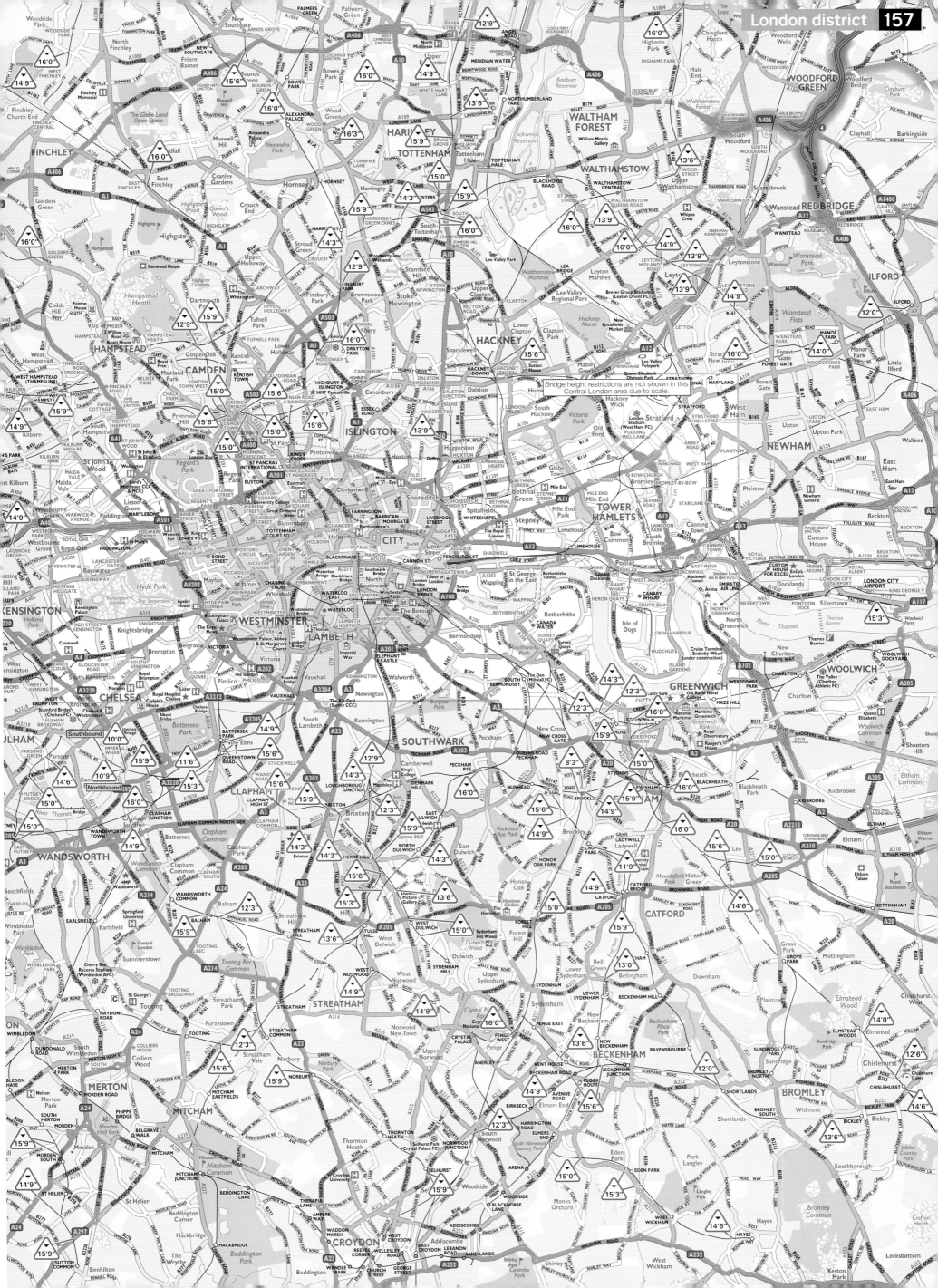

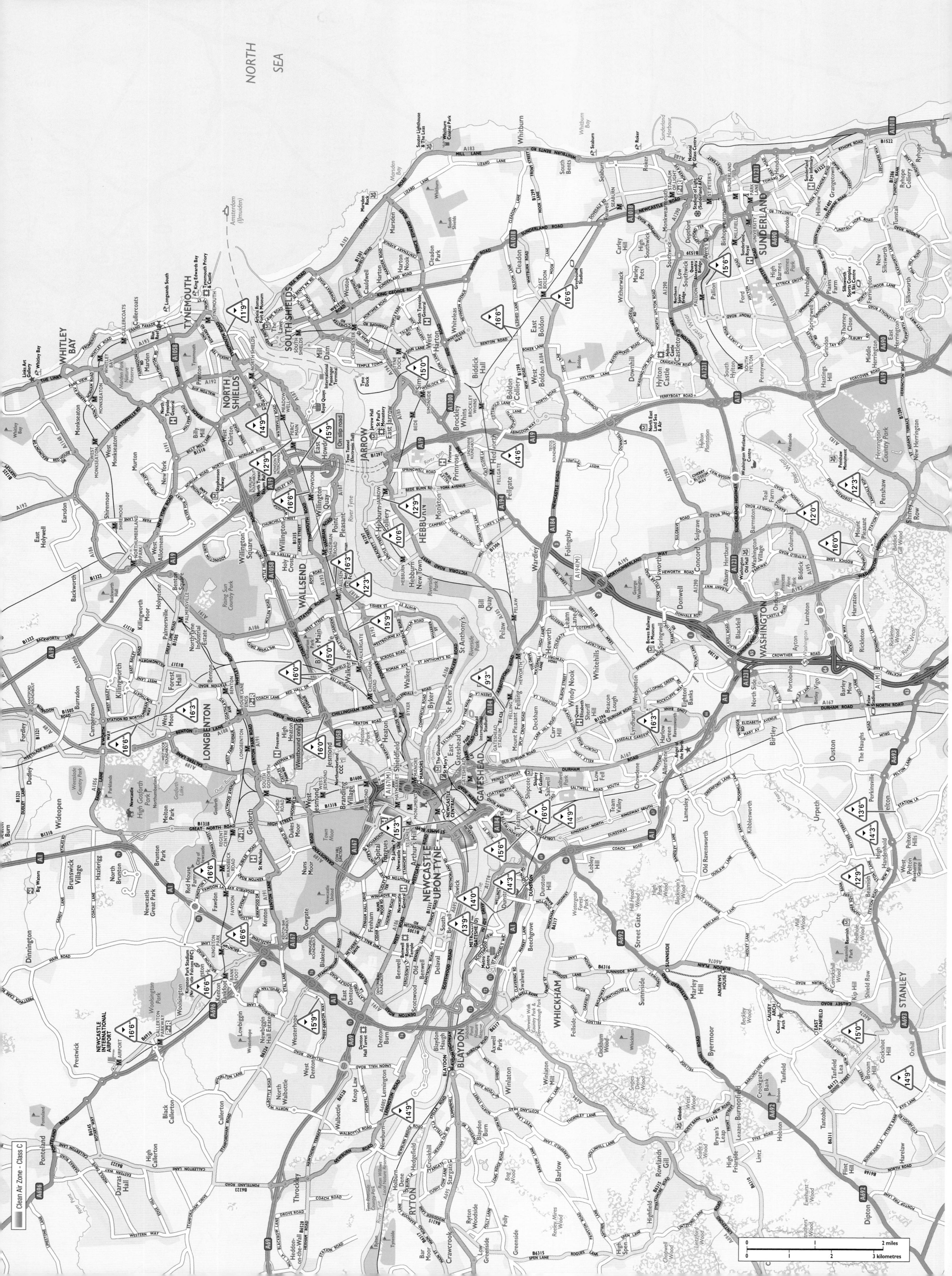

NORTH SEA

WHITLEY BAY

TYNEMOUTH

NORTH SHIELDS

SOUTH SHIELDS

JARROW

HEBBURN

WALLSEND

LONGBENTON

SUNDERLAND

WASHINGTON

NEWCASTLE UPON TYNE

GATESHEAD

WHICKHAM

BLAYDON

RYTON

STANLEY

This index lists places appearing in the main map section of the atlas in alphabetical order. The reference following each name gives the atlas page number and grid reference of the square in which the place appears. The map shows counties, unitary authorities and administrative areas, together with a list of the abbreviated name forms used in the index.

The top 100 places of tourist interest are indexed in **red**, World Heritage sites in **green**, motorway service areas in **blue** and National Parks in green *italic*.

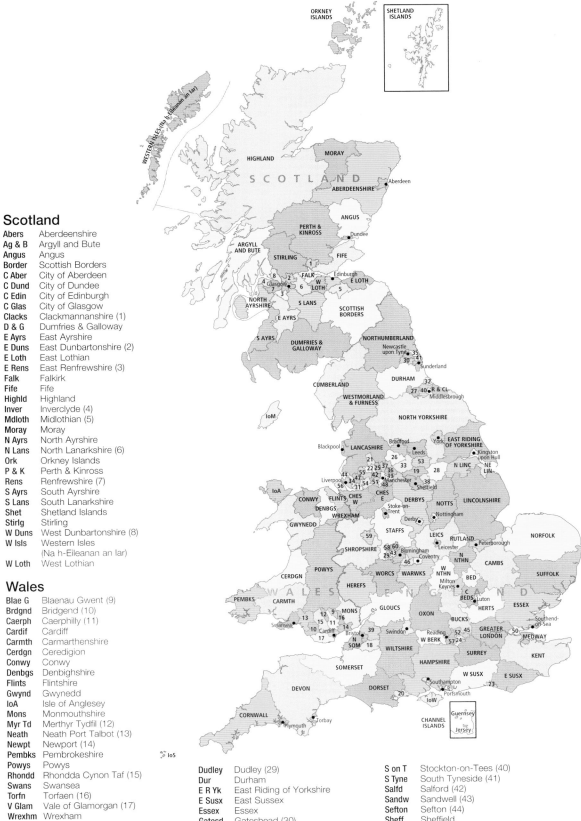

Scotland

Abers Aberdeenshire
Ag & B Argyll and Bute
Angus Angus
Border Scottish Borders
C Aber City of Aberdeen
C Dund City of Dundee
C Edin City of Edinburgh
C Glas City of Glasgow
Clacks Clackmannanshire (1)
D & G Dumfries & Galloway
E Ayrs East Ayrshire
E Duns East Dunbartonshire (2)
E Loth East Lothian
E Rens East Renfrewshire (3)
Falk Falkirk
Fife Fife
Highld Highland
Inver Inverclyde (4)
Mdloth Midlothian (5)
Moray Moray
N Ayrs North Ayrshire
N Lans North Lanarkshire (6)
Ork Orkney Islands
P & K Perth & Kinross
Rens Renfrewshire (7)
S Ayrs South Ayrshire
S Lans South Lanarkshire
Shet Shetland Islands
Stirlg Stirling
W Duns West Dunbartonshire (8)
W Isls Western Isles (Na h-Eileanan an Iar)
W Loth West Lothian

Wales

Blae G Blaenau Gwent (9)
Brdgnd Bridgend (10)
Caerph Caerphilly (11)
Cardif Cardiff
Carmth Carmarthenshire
Cerdgn Ceredigion
Conwy Conwy
Denbgs Denbighshire
Flints Flintshire
Gwynd Gwynedd
IoA Isle of Anglesey
Mons Monmouthshire
Myr Td Merthyr Tydfil (12)
Neath Neath Port Talbot (13)
Newpt Newport (14)
Pembks Pembrokeshire
Powys Powys
Rhondd Rhondda Cynon Taf (15)
Swans Swansea
Torfn Torfaen (16)
V Glam Vale of Glamorgan (17)
Wrexhm Wrexham

England

BaNES Bath & N E Somerset (18)
Barns Barnsley (19)
BCP Bournemouth, Christchurch and Poole (20)
Bed Bedford
Birm Birmingham
Bl w D Blackburn with Darwen (21)
Bolton Bolton (22)
Bpool Blackpool
Br & H Brighton & Hove (23)
Br For Bracknell Forest (24)
Bristl City of Bristol
Bucks Buckinghamshire
Bury Bury (25)
C Beds Central Bedfordshire
C Brad City of Bradford
C Derb City of Derby
C KuH City of Kingston upon Hull
C Leic City of Leicester
C Nott City of Nottingham
C Pete City of Peterborough
C Plym City of Plymouth
C Port City of Portsmouth
C Sotn City of Southampton
C Stke City of Stoke-on-Trent
C York City of York
Calder Calderdale (26)
Cambs Cambridgeshire
Ches E Cheshire East
Ches W Cheshire West and Chester
Cnwll Cornwall
Covtry Coventry
Cumb Cumberland
Darltn Darlington (27)
Derbys Derbyshire
Devon Devon
Donc Doncaster (28)
Dorset Dorset
Dudley Dudley (29)
Dur Durham
E R Yk East Riding of Yorkshire
E Susx East Sussex
Essex Essex
Gatesd Gateshead (30)
Gloucs Gloucestershire
Gt Lon Greater London
Halton Halton (31)
Hants Hampshire
Hartpl Hartlepool (32)
Herefs Herefordshire
Herts Hertfordshire
IoS Isles of Scilly
IoW Isle of Wight
Kent Kent
Kirk Kirklees (33)
Knows Knowsley (34)
Lancs Lancashire
Leeds Leeds
Leics Leicestershire
Lincs Lincolnshire
Lpool Liverpool
Luton Luton
M Keyn Milton Keynes
Manch Manchester
Medway Medway
Middsb Middlesbrough
N Linc North Lincolnshire
N Nthn North Northamptonshire
N Som North Somerset
N Tyne North Tyneside (35)
N u Ty Newcastle upon Tyne
N York North Yorkshire
NE Lin North East Lincolnshire
Norfk Norfolk
Notts Nottinghamshire
Nthumb Northumberland
Oldham Oldham (36)
Oxon Oxfordshire
R & Cl Redcar & Cleveland
Readg Reading
Rochdl Rochdale (37)
Rothm Rotherham (38)
Rutlnd Rutland
S Glos South Gloucestershire (39)
S on T Stockton-on-Tees (40)
S Tyne South Tyneside (41)
Salfd Salford (42)
Sandw Sandwell (43)
Sefton Sefton (44)
Sheff Sheffield
Shrops Shropshire
Slough Slough (45)
Solhll Solihull (46)
Somset Somerset
St Hel St Helens (47)
Staffs Staffordshire
Sthend Southend-on-Sea
Stockp Stockport (48)
Suffk Suffolk
Sundld Sunderland
Surrey Surrey
Swindn Swindon
Tamesd Tameside (49)
Thurr Thurrock (50)
Torbay Torbay
Traffd Trafford (51)
W & F Westmorland & Furness
W & M Windsor & Maidenhead (52)
W Berk West Berkshire
W Nthn West Northamptonshire
W Susx West Sussex
Wakefd Wakefield (53)
Warrtn Warrington (54)
Warwks Warwickshire
Wigan Wigan (55)
Wilts Wiltshire
Wirral Wirral (56)
Wokham Wokingham (57)
Wolves Wolverhampton (58)
Worcs Worcestershire
Wrekin Telford & Wrekin (59)
Wsall Walsall (60)

Channel Islands & Isle of Man

Guern Guernsey
Jersey Jersey
IoM Isle of Man

A

Abbas Combe Somset 22 F9
Abberley Worcs 52 D7
Abberley Common Worcs 52 D7
Abberton Essex 46 H8
Abberton Worcs 53 J10
Abbess Roding Essex 45 Q9
Abbeydale Sheff 77 Q7
Abbey Dore Herefs 40 E5
Abbey Green Staffs 76 H12
Abbey Hulton C Stke 64 G2
Abbey St Bathans Border 116 G9
Abbeystead Lancs 83 M4
Abbeytown Cumb 97 N8
Abbey Village Lancs 83 P10
Abbey Wood Gt Lon 33 N6
Abbotrule Border 107 P7
Abbots Bickington Devon 18 H10
Abbots Bromley Staffs 65 K7
Abbotsbury Dorset 10 E7
Abbots Deuglie P & K 124 C10
Abbotsham Devon 18 H8
Abbotskerswell Devon 5 P3
Abbots Langley Herts 44 F11
Abbots Leigh N Som 28 H7
Abbotsley Cambs 56 E9
Abbots Morton Worcs 53 J9
Abbots Ripton Cambs 56 E5
Abbot's Salford Warwks 53 K10
Abbots Worthy Hants 24 H7
Abbotts Ann Hants 24 E5
Abbott Street Dorset 11 N5
Abdon Shrops 51 P3
Aberaeron Cerdgn 48 G8
Aberaman Rhondd 27 N2
Aberangell Gwynd 61 P10
Aberarder Highld 138 B10
Aberargie P & K 124 D9
Aberarth Cerdgn 48 H8
Aberavon Neath 26 H4
Abercanaid Myr Td 39 P11
Abercarn Caerph 28 B3
Abercastle Pembks 36 G4
Abercegir Powys 61 P11
Aberchalder Highld 129 K4
Aberchirder Abers 140 F5
Abercorn W Loth 115 K5
Abercraf Powys 39 K9
Abercregan Neath 27 K3
Abercwmboi Rhondd 27 N2
Abercych Pembks 37 P2
Abercynon Rhondd 27 P3
Aberdalgie P & K 124 B9
Aberdare Rhondd 39 N11
Aberdaron Gwynd 60 B7
Aberdeen C Aber 133 M3
Aberdour Fife 115 M4
Aberdulais Neath 27 J2
Aberdyfi Gwynd 49 K1
Aberedw Powys 39 P2
Abereiddy Pembks 36 F4
Abererch Gwynd 60 F5
Aberfan Myr Td 27 P2
Aberfeldy P & K 123 L3
Aberffraw IoA 72 F10
Aberford Leeds 85 N8
Aberfoyle Stirlg 113 Q1
Abergavenny Mons 40 D9
Abergele Conwy 74 C8
Abergorlech Carmth 38 E5
Abergwesyn Powys 49 Q10
Abergwili Carmth 38 C7
Abergwynfi Neath 27 L3
Abergwyngregyn Gwynd 73 L9
Abergynolwyn Gwynd 61 L10
Aberkenfig Brdgnd 27 L5
Aberlady E Loth 116 B5
Aberlemno Angus 125 K2
Aberllefenni Gwynd 61 N10
Aberllynfi Powys 40 A4
Aberlour, Charlestown of Moray 139 N7
Abermule Powys 50 G2
Abernant Carmth 37 R6
Abernant Rhondd 39 N11
Abernethy P & K 124 D9
Abernyte P & K 124 E6
Aberporth Cerdgn 48 D10
Abersoch Gwynd 60 E6
Abersychan Torfn 40 C11
Aberthin V Glam 27 N7
Abertillery Blae G 40 B11
Abertridwr Caerph 27 Q4
Abertridwr Powys 62 E8
Aberuthven P & K 123 N9
Aberystwyth Cerdgn 49 K4
Abingdon-on-Thames Oxon 31 K3
Abinger Common Surrey 14 G2
Abinger Hammer Surrey 14 F1
Abington S Lans 106 B5
Abington W Nthn 55 K8
Abington Pigotts Cambs 45 K3
Abington Services S Lans 106 B5
Abingworth W Susx 14 G7
Ab Kettleby Leics 67 J7
Ablington Gloucs 42 C10
Abney Derbys 77 M7
Aboyne Abers 132 E5
Abhainn Suidhe W Isls 152 d5
Abram Wigan 75 Q3
Abriachan Highld 137 P9
Abridge Essex 33 N3
Abronhill N Lans 114 E6
Abson S Glos 29 L7
Abthorpe W Nthn 43 N2
Aby Lincs 80 H8
Acaster Malbis C York 86 A6
Acaster Selby N York 85 R7
Accrington Lancs 84 A9
Acha Ag & B 118 G2
Achahoish Ag & B 112 A6
Achalader P & K 124 C4
Achaleven Ag & B 120 H6
Acha Mor W Isls 152 f3
Achanalt Highld 137 J3
Achandunie Highld 145 P10
Achany Highld 145 N5
Acharacle Highld 127 M10
Acharn Highld 120 D3
Acharn P & K 123 K4
Achavanich Highld 151 M8
Achduart Highld 144 C4
Achfary Highld 148 G8
Achgarve Highld 143 N6
A'Chill Highld 126 E3
Achiltibuie Highld 144 C3
Achina Highld 150 C4
Achinhoan Ag & B 103 K6
Achintee Highld 136 C7
Achintraid Highld 135 Q8
Achlyness Highld 148 F6
Achmelvich Highld 148 C11
Achmore Highld 135 Q9
Achmore W Isls 152 f3
Achnacarnin Highld 148 C10
Achnacarry Highld 128 G7
Achnacloich Highld 127 K3
Achnaconeran Highld 137 M12
Achnacroish Ag & B 120 F4
Achnadrish Ag & B 119 M2
Achnafauld P & K 123 M5
Achnagarron Highld 146 C11
Achnaha Highld 126 H10
Achnahaird Highld 144 C2
Achnahannet Highld 138 H10
Achnairn Highld 145 M3
Achnalea Highld 127 Q12
Achnamara Ag & B 112 A4
Achnasheen Highld 136 G4
Achnashellach Highld 136 D6
Achnastank Moray 139 P9
Achosnich Highld 126 H10
Achranich Highld 120 D3
Achreamie Highld 151 J3
Achriabhach Highld 128 G10
Achriesgill Highld 148 F6
Achtoty Highld 149 P4
Achurch N Nthn 55 P4
Achvaich Highld 146 C6
Achvarasdal Highld 150 H4
Ackergill Highld 151 Q6
Acklam Middsb 91 R3
Acklam N York 86 E3
Ackleton Shrops 52 E1
Acklington Nthumb 109 L9
Ackton Wakefd 85 N10
Ackworth Moor Top Wakefd 85 N12
Acle Norfk 71 M10
Acock's Green Birm 53 L4
Acol Kent 35 P9
Acomb C York 85 R5
Acomb Nthumb 99 P5
Aconbury Herefs 40 G5
Acton Ches E 64 B2
Acton Gt Lon 32 H6
Acton Staffs 64 F4
Acton Suffk 46 F3
Acton Wrexhm 63 K2
Acton Beauchamp Herefs 52 C10
Acton Bridge Ches W 75 Q8
Acton Burnell Shrops 63 P11
Acton Green Herefs 52 C10
Acton Round Shrops 52 B2
Acton Scott Shrops 51 M3
Acton Trussell Staffs 64 H8
Acton Turville S Glos 29 N6
Adbaston Staffs 64 E6
Adber Dorset 22 D9
Adbolton Notts 66 F4
Adderbury Oxon 43 K4
Adderley Shrops 64 C4
Addiewell W Loth 114 H8
Addingham C Brad 84 G5
Addington Bucks 43 Q6
Addington Gt Lon 33 L9
Addington Kent 34 B10
Addiscombe Gt Lon 33 L9
Addlestone Surrey 32 F9
Addlethorpe Lincs 81 K10
Adeyfield Herts 44 F10
Adfa Powys 62 E12
Adforton Herefs 51 L6
Adisham Kent 35 M11
Adlestrop Gloucs 42 F6
Adlingfleet E R Yk 86 F11
Adlington Lancs 75 Q1
Admaston Staffs 65 K7
Admaston Wrekin 64 B9
Adpar Cerdgn 37 Q2
Adsborough Somset 21 L7
Adscombe Somset 21 J6
Adstock Bucks 43 Q6
Adstone W Nthn 54 F10
Adswood Stockp 76 G6
Adversane W Susx 14 F6
Advie Highld 139 L9
Adwick le Street Donc 78 E2
Adwick upon Dearne Donc 78 D3
Ae D & G 106 C12
Ae Bridgend D & G 97 K1
Affleck Abers 140 E8
Affpuddle Dorset 11 K6
Affric Lodge Highld 136 H11
Afon-wen Flints 74 F9
Afton IoW 12 F7
Agglethorpe N York 90 H9
Aigburth Lpool 75 L6
Aike E R Yk 87 K6
Aiketgate W & F 98 F9
Aikton Cumb 98 C7
Ailsworth C Pete 68 C12
Ainderby Quernhow N York 91 N10
Ainderby Steeple N York 91 N8
Aingers Green Essex 47 K7
Ainsdale Sefton 75 K1
Ainstable W & F 98 G9
Ainsworth Bury 76 E2
Ainthorpe N York 92 E5
Aintree Sefton 75 L4
Ainville W Loth 115 K8
Aird Ag & B 111 R1
Aird D & G 94 F6
Aird Highld 127 K4
Aird W Isls 152 h3
Àird a' Mhulaidh W Isls 152 e5
Aird Asaig W Isls 152 e5
Aird Dhubh Highld 135 N8
Airdeny Ag & B 121 J7
Airdrie N Lans 114 D8
Airdriehill N Lans 114 E8
Airds of Kells D & G 96 D4
Àird Uig W Isls 152 d3
Airidh a bhruaich W Isls 152 f4
Airieland D & G 96 F7
Airlie Angus 124 F3
Airmyn E R Yk 86 D10
Airntully P & K 124 C6
Airor Highld 127 N3
Airth Falk 114 G4
Airton N York 84 D3
Aisby Lincs 67 P4
Aisby Lincs 79 L5
Aish Devon 5 L4
Aish Devon 5 P5
Aisholt Somset 21 K6
Aiskew N York 91 M9
Aislaby N York 92 F9
Aislaby N York 92 H5
Aislaby S on T 91 P4
Aisthorpe Lincs 79 N7
Aith Shet 147 i6
Akeld Nthumb 108 F4
Akeley Bucks 43 P4
Albaston Cnwll 7 M10
Alberbury Shrops 63 K9
Albourne W Susx 15 J7
Albrighton Shrops 63 N8
Albrighton Shrops 64 E11
Alburgh Norfk 59 K3
Albury Herts 45 N7
Albury Surrey 14 F1
Albury Heath Surrey 14 F2
Alcaig Highld 137 P4
Alcaston Shrops 51 M3
Alcester Warwks 53 K9
Alciston E Susx 15 P9
Alcombe Somset 20 F4
Alconbury Cambs 56 D5
Alconbury Weald Cambs 56 D5
Alconbury Weston Cambs 56 D5
Aldborough N York 85 N2
Aldborough Norfk 71 J5
Aldbourne Wilts 30 F7
Aldbrough E R Yk 87 N7
Aldbrough St John N York 91 K4
Aldbury Herts 44 D9
Aldcliffe Lancs 83 L3
Aldclune P & K 130 G11
Aldeburgh Suffk 59 P9
Aldeby Norfk 59 N2
Aldenham Herts 32 G3
Alderbury Wilts 24 C8
Alderford Norfk 70 H8
Alderholt Dorset 23 P10
Alderley Gloucs 29 M4
Alderley Edge Ches E 76 F8
Aldermans Green Covtry 54 B4
Aldermaston W Berk 31 M9
Alderminster Warwks 53 N11
Aldershot Hants 25 Q3
Alderton Gloucs 42 B5
Alderton Suffk 47 P3
Alderton W Nthn 43 Q2
Alderton Wilts 29 N6
Aldfield N York 85 K1
Aldford Ches W 75 M11
Aldgate Rutlnd 67 N11
Aldham Essex 46 G6
Aldham Suffk 47 J3
Aldingbourne W Susx 14 C9
Aldingham W & F 82 G1
Aldington Kent 17 J3
Aldington Worcs 42 C3
Aldington Corner Kent 17 J3
Aldivalloch Moray 139 Q10
Aldochlay Ag & B 113 M3
Aldreth Cambs 56 H6
Aldridge Wsall 65 K12
Aldringham Suffk 59 N8
Aldsworth Gloucs 42 D9
Aldunie Moray 139 Q10
Aldwark Derbys 77 N12
Aldwark N York 85 P3
Aldwick W Susx 14 C11
Aldwincle N Nthn 55 P4
Aldworth W Berk 31 L6
Alexandria W Duns 113 M5
Aley Somset 21 J6
Alfington Devon 9 L5
Alfold Surrey 14 E4
Alfold Crossways Surrey 14 E4
Alford Abers 132 F1
Alford Lincs 81 J8
Alford Somset 22 E7
Alfreton Derbys 66 C1
Alfrick Worcs 52 D10
Alfrick Pound Worcs 52 D10
Alfriston E Susx 15 P10
Algarkirk Lincs 68 F5
Alhampton Somset 22 E6
Alkborough N Linc 86 G11
Alkham Kent 17 N2
Alkmonton Derbys 65 M4
Allaleigh Devon 5 N6
Allanaquoich Abers 131 L6
Allanbank N Lans 114 F9
Allanton Border 117 J10
Allanton N Lans 114 F10
Allanton S Lans 114 D10
Allaston Gloucs 41 K10
Allbrook Hants 24 G9
All Cannings Wilts 30 C10
Allendale Nthumb 99 N7
Allen End Warwks 53 M1
Allenheads Nthumb 99 N9
Allen's Green Herts 45 N8
Allensmore Herefs 40 G4
Allenton C Derb 66 B6
Aller Devon 19 P8
Aller Somset 21 N7
Allerby Cumb 97 M10
Allercombe Devon 9 K6
Allerford Somset 20 D4
Allerston N York 92 H10
Allerthorpe E R Yk 86 E6
Allerton C Brad 84 H8
Allerton Highld 138 D3
Allerton Lpool 75 L6
Allerton Bywater Leeds 85 N9
Allerton Mauleverer N York 85 N4
Allesley Covtry 53 P4
Allestree C Derb 65 Q4
Allexton Leics 67 K12
Allgreave Ches E 76 H10
Allhallows Medway 34 E7

Barwick Devon 8 B3
Barwick Somset 22 D10
Barwick in Elmet Leeds 85 N7
Baschurch Shrops 63 M8
Bascote Warwks 54 C8
Bashall Eaves Lancs 83 Q6
Basildon Essex 34 C4
Basingstoke Hants 25 L3
Baslow Derbys 77 N9
Bason Bridge Somset 21 M4
Bassaleg Newpt 28 C5
Bassendean Border 116 E12
Bassenthwaite Cumb 97 P11
Bassett S'oton 24 G10
Bassingbourn-cum-Kneesworth Cambs 45 L3
Bassingham Lincs 79 M11
Bassingthorpe Lincs 67 N6
Bassus Green Herts 45 K6
Baston Lincs 68 C9
Bastwick Norfk 71 N8
Batchworth Herts 32 F3
Batcombe Dorset 10 F4
Batcombe Somset 22 F5
Batford Herts 44 G8
Bath BaNES 29 M9
Bathampton BaNES 29 M9
Bathealton Somset 20 H8
Batheaston BaNES 29 M9
Bathford BaNES 29 M9
Bathgate W Loth 114 H7
Bathley Notts 79 K11
Bathpool Cnwll 7 K9
Bathpool Somset 21 L8
Bath Side Essex 47 N5
Bathville W Loth 114 H8
Bathway Somset 22 D3
Batley Kirk 85 K10
Batsford Gloucs 42 E5
Battersby N York 92 C5
Battersea Gt Lon 33 K7
Battisford Suffk 58 F10
Battle E Susx 16 D7
Battle Powys 39 N5
Battledykes Angus 125 J2
Battlefield Shrops 63 N9
Battlesbridge Essex 34 D3
Battleton Somset 20 E8
Baughton Worcs 41 P3
Baughurst Hants 31 M10
Baulds Abers 132 C5
Baulking Oxon 30 G4
Baumber Lincs 80 D9
Baunton Gloucs 42 B10
Baverstock Wilts 23 M7
Bawburgh Norfk 70 H10
Bawdeswell Norfk 70 F8
Bawdrip Somset 21 M5
Bawdsey Suffk 47 P4
Bawtry Donc 78 G5
Baxenden Lancs 84 B10
Baxterley Warwks 53 P1
Bay Highld 134 E5
Bayble W Isls 152 h3
Baybridge Hants 25 J8
Baycliff W & F 89 J12
Baydon Wilts 30 G7
Bayford Herts 45 K10
Bayford Somset 22 G7
Bayhead W Isls 152 b8
Baylham Suffk 58 G10
Bayston Hill Shrops 63 N10
Baythorne End Essex 46 C3
Bayton Worcs 52 C6
Bayworth Oxon 31 K4
Beachampton Bucks 43 Q4
Beachamwell Norfk 69 N11
Beacon Devon 9 M4
Beacon End Essex 46 G6
Beacon Hill Notts 67 K1
Beacon Hill Surrey 14 C3
Beacon's Bottom Bucks 31 N4
Beaconsfield Bucks 32 D4
Beaconsfield Services Bucks 32 D5
Beadlam N York 92 D10
Beadlow C Beds 44 G4
Beadnell Nthumb 109 L4
Beaford Devon 19 L10
Beal N York 85 Q10
Beal Nthumb 108 H1
Bealsmill Cnwll 7 L4
Beaminster Dorset 10 D4
Beamish Dur 100 B8
Beamish - The Living Museum of the North Dur 100 B8
Beamsley N York 84 G5
Beanacre Wilts 29 N8
Beanley Nthumb 108 H6
Beardon Devon 7 P8
Beare Devon 9 K4
Beare Green Surrey 14 H2
Bearley Warwks 53 M8
Bearpark Dur 100 G9
Bearsden E Duns 113 Q7
Bearsted Kent 34 E11
Bearstone Shrops 64 D4
Bearwood BCP 11 P5
Bearwood Birm 53 J3
Bearwood Herefs 51 L9
Beattock D & G 106 E9
Beauchamp Roding Essex 45 Q9
Beauchief Sheff 77 Q7
Beaufort Blae G 40 A9
Beaulieu Hants 12 F4
Beaulieu (National Motor Museum/Palace House) Hants 12 F4
Beauly Highld 137 P6
Beaumaris IoA 73 K8
Beaumaris Castle IoA 73 K8
Beaumont Cumb 98 D6
Beaumont Essex 47 L7
Beaumont Jersey 3 b2
Beaumont Leys C Leic 66 F10
Beausale Warwks 53 N6
Beauworth Hants 25 K8
Beaworthy Devon 7 N2
Beazley End Essex 46 C6
Bebington Wirral 75 K7
Bebside Nthumb 100 H2
Beccles Suffk 59 N4
Becconsall Lancs 83 K10
Beckbury Shrops 64 E11
Beckenham Gt Lon 33 L8
Beckermet Cumb 88 D5
Beckfoot Cumb 97 M8
Beckford Worcs 41 R4
Beckhampton Wilts 30 C8
Beckingham Lincs 67 L1
Beckingham Notts 79 K6
Beckington Somset 22 H3
Beckjay Shrops 51 L5
Beckley E Susx 16 E6
Beckley Oxon 43 M9
Beck Row Suffk 57 N5
Beck Side W & F 88 H10

Beckton Gt Lon 33 M6
Beckwithshaw N York 85 K4
Becontree Gt Lon 33 M5
Becquet Vincent Jersey 3 b1
Bedale N York 91 M9
Bedchester Dorset 23 J10
Beddau Rhondd 27 P5
Beddgelert Gwynd 61 K3
Beddingham E Susx 15 N9
Beddington Gt Lon 33 K9
Beddington Corner Gt Lon 33 K9
Bedfield Suffk 59 J7
Bedford Bed 55 P10
Bedgrove Bucks 44 B9
Bedhampton Hants 13 M3
Bedingfield Suffk 58 H7
Bedlam N York 85 K7
Bedlington Nthumb 100 H2
Bedlinog Myr Td 39 Q11
Bedminster Bristl 29 J8
Bedminster Down Bristl 29 J8
Bedmond Herts 44 G11
Bednall Staffs 64 H8
Bedrule Border 107 P6
Bedstone Shrops 51 L5
Bedwas Caerph 28 A4
Bedwellty Caerph 27 R2
Bedworth Warwks 54 B3
Beeby Leics 66 H10
Beech Hants 25 M5
Beech Staffs 64 F4
Beech Hill W Berk 31 P9
Beechingstoke Wilts 30 C10
Beedon W Berk 31 K7
Beeford E R Yk 87 L4
Beeley Derbys 77 P10
Beelsby NE Lin 80 D3
Beenham W Berk 31 M8
Beer Devon 9 N7
Beer Somset 22 B7
Beercrocombe Somset 21 M9
Beer Hackett Dorset 10 F2
Beesands Devon 5 N8
Beesby Lincs 81 J7
Beeson Devon 5 N8
Beeston C Beds 56 D11
Beeston Ches W 75 P12
Beeston Leeds 85 L9
Beeston Norfk 70 D9
Beeston Notts 66 E5
Beeston Regis Norfk 70 H4
Beeswing D & G 96 H4
Beetham W & F 89 M11
Beetley Norfk 70 E8
Begbroke Oxon 43 K9
Begelly Pembks 37 M9
Beguildy Powys 50 G5
Beighton Norfk 71 M10
Beighton Sheff 78 D7
Bein Na Faoghla W Isls 152 c9
Beith N Ayrs 113 L10
Bekesbourne Kent 35 M11
Belaugh Norfk 71 K8
Belbroughton Worcs 52 G5
Belchalwell Dorset 11 J3
Belchamp Otten Essex 46 E3
Belchamp St Paul Essex 46 D3
Belchamp Walter Essex 46 E3
Belchford Lincs 80 F8
Belford Nthumb 109 J3
Belgrave C Leic 66 F10
Belhaven E Loth 116 F5
Belhelvie Abers 141 M12
Belhinnie Abers 140 C10
Bellabeg Abers 131 Q2
Belladrum Highld 137 P6
Bellamore Staffs 64 D2
Bellanoch Ag & B 112 B3
Bellaty Angus 124 E1
Bell Busk N York 84 D4
Belleau Lincs 80 H8
Bell End Worcs 52 H5
Bellerby N York 91 J8
Belle Vue Cumb 98 D7
Belle Vue Wakefd 85 M11
Bellfield S Lans 105 Q3
Bellingdon Bucks 44 E10
Bellingham Nthumb 99 N2
Belloch Ag & B 103 J2
Bellochantuy Ag & B 103 J3
Bell o' th' Hill Ches W 63 N2
Bellshill N Lans 114 D9
Bellshill Nthumb 109 J3
Bellside N Lans 114 E9
Bellsquarry W Loth 115 J8
Bells Yew Green E Susx 15 R4
Belluton BaNES 29 J9
Belmaduthy Highld 138 B4
Belmesthorpe Rutlnd 67 Q9
Belmont Bl w D 83 P12
Belmont Gt Lon 33 J10
Belmont S Ayrs 104 F6
Belmont Shet 147 J3
Belnacraig Abers 132 B1
Belper Derbys 66 B2
Belsay Nthumb 100 E2
Belses Border 107 P5
Belsford Devon 5 N7
Belsize Herts 32 E2
Belstead Suffk 47 K3
Belstone Devon 8 E6
Belthorn Bl w D 83 Q10
Beltinge Kent 35 M9
Beltingham Nthumb 99 M5
Beltoft N Linc 79 K2
Belton Leics 66 D8
Belton Lincs 67 M4
Belton N Linc 79 K2
Belton Norfk 71 N11
Belton House Lincs 67 M4
Belton in Rutland Rutlnd 67 K12
Belvedere Gt Lon 33 N6
Belvoir Leics 67 K5
Bembridge IoW 13 L7
Bemerton Wilts 23 P7
Bempton E R Yk 93 P12
Benacre Suffk 59 P4
Benbecula W Isls 152 c9
Benbuie D & G 105 N10
Benderloch Ag & B 120 G5
Benenden Kent 16 E4
Benfieldside Dur 100 C7
Bengate Norfk 71 L7
Bengeo Herts 45 K9
Bengeworth Worcs 42 B3
Benhall Green Suffk 59 M8
Benhall Street Suffk 59 M8
Benholm Abers 133 N10
Beningbrough N York 85 Q4
Benington Herts 45 J7
Benington Lincs 68 H3
Benington Sea End Lincs 68 H3
Benllech IoA 72 H7
Benmore Ag & B 112 H4
Bennan N Ayrs 103 Q5
Benniworth Lincs 80 D7
Benover Kent 16 D2

Ben Rhydding C Brad 84 H6
Benslie N Ayrs 104 F1
Benson Oxon 31 N4
Benthoul C Aber 133 J4
Bentley Donc 78 F3
Bentley E R Yk 87 J8
Bentley Hants 25 N4
Bentley Suffk 47 K4
Bentley Warwks 53 P2
Bentpath D & G 107 J11
Bentwichen Devon 19 P6
Bentworth Hants 25 L5
Benville Dorset 10 D4
Benwick Cambs 56 G3
Beoley Worcs 53 K7
Beoraidbeg Highld 127 M5
Bepton W Susx 25 N6
Berden Essex 45 N6
Bere Alston Devon 4 G3
Bere Ferrers Devon 4 G3
Bere Regis Dorset 11 K6
Bergh Apton Norfk 71 L12
Berinsfield Oxon 31 M3
Berkeley Gloucs 29 K2
Berkhamsted Herts 44 E10
Berkley Somset 22 H3
Berkswell Solhll 53 N5
Bermondsey Gt Lon 33 L7
Bernera Highld 135 P11
Bernisdale Highld 134 G6
Berrick Prior Oxon 31 N3
Berrick Salome Oxon 31 N4
Berriedale Highld 151 K12
Berrier W & F 98 E12
Berriew Powys 62 G12
Berrington Nthumb 108 H2
Berrington Worcs 51 P7
Berrington Green Worcs 51 P7
Berrow Somset 21 M3
Berrow Green Worcs 52 D9
Berryfields Bucks 43 R8
Berryhillock Moray 140 D4
Berryhillock Moray 140 D5
Berrynarbor Devon 19 L4
Berry Pomeroy Devon 5 P4
Bersham Wrexhm 63 J3
Berwick E Susx 15 N9
Berwick Bassett Wilts 30 C7
Berwick Hill Nthumb 100 F3
Berwick St James Wilts 23 N5
Berwick St John Wilts 23 L9
Berwick St Leonard Wilts 23 K7
Berwick-upon-Tweed Nthumb 117 M10
Bescar Lancs 75 L1
Besford Worcs 41 Q3
Bessacarr Donc 78 G4
Bessingby E R Yk 87 M2
Bessingham Norfk 70 H5
Besthorpe Norfk 70 H12
Besthorpe Notts 79 K10
Bestwood Village Notts 66 E4
Beswick E R Yk 87 J5
Betchworth Surrey 33 J12
Bethania Cerdgn 49 K8
Bethel Gwynd 73 J10
Bethel IoA 72 F9
Bethersden Kent 16 G3
Bethesda Gwynd 73 K10
Bethesda Pembks 37 L7
Bethlehem Carmth 38 G6
Bethnal Green Gt Lon 33 L6
Betley Staffs 64 D2
Betsham Kent 33 Q8
Betteshanger Kent 35 P11
Bettiscombe Dorset 10 B5
Bettisfield Wrexhm 63 L4
Betton Shrops 64 D5
Bettws Brdgnd 27 L5
Bettws Newpt 28 C4
Bettws Cedewain Powys 50 F1
Bettws Ifan Cerdgn 48 E11
Bettws-Newydd Mons 40 E10
Bettyhill Highld 150 C4
Betws Bledrws Cerdgn 49 K10
Betws Gwerfil Goch Denbgs 62 E3
Betws-y-Coed Conwy 61 N1
Betws-yn-Rhos Conwy 74 B9
Beulah Cerdgn 48 D11
Beulah Powys 50 C10
Bevercotes Notts 78 H9
Beverley E R Yk 87 J7
Beverston Gloucs 29 P3
Bewaldeth Cumb 98 H3
Bewcastle Cumb 98 H3
Bewdley Worcs 52 E6
Bewerley N York 84 H2
Bewholme E R Yk 87 M5
Bexhill-on-Sea E Susx 16 C9
Bexley Gt Lon 33 P7
Bexleyheath Gt Lon 33 N7
Bexwell Norfk 69 M11
Beyton Suffk 58 D8
Beyton Green Suffk 58 D8
Bhaltos W Isls 152 e3
Bhatarsaigh W Isls 152 b13
Bibury Gloucs 42 D10
Bicester Oxon 43 M7
Bickenhill Solhll 53 M4
Bicker Lincs 68 E5
Bickerstaffe Lancs 75 M3
Bickerton N York 85 P5
Bickford Staffs 64 G9
Bickington Devon 8 E10
Bickington Devon 19 K7
Bickleigh Devon 4 H4
Bickleigh Devon 8 H3
Bickley Ches W 63 P3
Bickley Gt Lon 33 M8
Bickley N York 93 J8
Bicknacre Essex 46 D11
Bicknoller Somset 20 H5
Bickton Hants 24 F10
Bicton Shrops 51 L7
Bicton Shrops 63 M9
Bidborough Kent 15 Q2
Bidden Hants 25 M4
Biddenden Kent 16 E3
Biddenham Bed 55 P11
Biddestone Wilts 29 P7
Biddisham Somset 21 M3
Biddlesden Bucks 43 N4
Biddulph Staffs 76 G12
Biddulph Moor Staffs 76 G12
Bideford Devon 19 J8
Bidford-on-Avon Warwks 53 L10
Bielby E R Yk 86 E6
Bieldside C Aber 133 L4
Bierley IoW 12 H9
Bierton Bucks 44 B8
Big Balcraig D & G 95 M9
Bigbury Devon 5 J8
Bigbury-on-Sea Devon 5 K8

Bigby Lincs 79 Q2
Biggar S Lans 106 D2
Biggin Derbys 77 M11
Biggin Hill Gt Lon 33 N10
Biggleswade C Beds 44 H3
Bigholms D & G 98 C2
Bighouse Highld 150 F4
Bighton Hants 25 K6
Biglands Cumb 97 Q7
Bignall End Staffs 64 E2
Bignor W Susx 14 D8
Bigrigg Cumb 88 D4
Big Sand Highld 143 K9
Bigton Shet 147 i9
Bilborough C Nott 66 E4
Bilbrook Somset 20 G5
Bilbrough N York 85 Q6
Bilbster Highld 151 N6
Bildershaw Dur 91 K2
Bildeston Suffk 58 E10
Billericay Essex 34 B3
Billesdon Leics 67 J11
Billesley Warwks 53 L9
Billingborough Lincs 68 C5
Billinge St Hel 75 N4
Billingford Norfk 70 F8
Billingford Norfk 58 H5
Billingham S on T 91 Q2
Billinghay Lincs 68 C1
Billingley Barns 78 B3
Billingshurst W Susx 14 F6
Billingsley Shrops 52 D4
Billington C Beds 44 D7
Billington Lancs 83 Q8
Billockby Norfk 71 N9
Billy Row Dur 100 F10
Bilsborrow Lancs 83 L7
Bilsby Lincs 81 J8
Bilsham W Susx 14 D10
Bilsington Kent 17 J4
Bilsthorpe Notts 78 G11
Bilston Mdloth 115 P8
Bilston Wolves 52 H1
Bilstone Leics 66 B11
Bilting Kent 17 J2
Bilton E R Yk 87 M8
Bilton N York 85 L4
Bilton Warwks 54 D6
Bilton-in-Ainsty N York 85 P5
Binbrook Lincs 80 D5
Bincombe Dorset 10 G8
Binegar Somset 22 E3
Binfield Br For 32 B8
Binfield Heath Oxon 31 N7
Bingfield Nthumb 100 C4
Bingham Notts 66 H4
Bingley C Brad 84 H7
Binham Norfk 70 E4
Binley Covtry 54 C5
Binley Hants 25 J2
Binniehill Falk 114 F7
Binscombe Surrey 14 D2
Binsted Hants 25 M5
Binsted W Susx 14 D9
Binton Warwks 53 L10
Bintree Norfk 70 F7
Birch Essex 46 H7
Birchall Staffs 65 J1
Bircham Newton Norfk 69 P5
Bircham Tofts Norfk 69 P6
Birchanger Green Essex 45 P7
Birch Cross Staffs 65 L6
Bircher Herefs 51 N7
Birchfield Birm 53 K2
Birch Green Essex 46 H6
Birchgrove Cardif 28 A6
Birchgrove Swans 26 H5
Birchgrove W Susx 15 M5
Birchington Kent 35 N8
Birchley Heath Warwks 53 P2
Birchover Derbys 77 N11
Birch Services Rochdl 76 F2
Birch Vale Derbys 77 J6
Birchwood Lincs 79 M10
Birch Wood Somset 21 J10
Birchwood Warrtn 76 C5
Bircotes Notts 78 G5
Birdbrook Essex 46 C3
Birdforth N York 91 P11
Birdham W Susx 13 P5
Birdingbury Warwks 54 C7
Birdlip Gloucs 41 Q9
Birdsall N York 86 H2
Birds Edge Kirk 77 L4
Birds Green Essex 45 Q10
Birdsgreen Shrops 52 E4
Birdsmoorgate Dorset 10 B4
Birdwell Barns 77 Q4
Birdwood Gloucs 41 N8
Birichin Highld 146 D6
Birkby N York 91 N6
Birkdale Sefton 82 H12
Birkenbog Abers 140 E3
Birkenhead Wirral 75 K6
Birkenhead (Queensway) Tunnel Lpool 75 K6
Birkenhills Abers 140 H7
Birkenshaw N York 85 J9
Birkhall Abers 131 Q5
Birkhill Angus 124 G6
Birkholme Lincs 67 N6
Birkin N York 85 M10
Birley Herefs 51 N10
Birley Carr Sheff 77 Q5
Birling Kent 34 B10
Birlingham Worcs 41 Q3
Birmingham Birm 53 J4
Birnam P & K 123 Q4
Birness Abers 141 N9
Birse Abers 132 E5
Birsemore Abers 132 E5
Birstall Kirk 85 K10
Birstall Leics 66 F11
Birstwith N York 85 K4
Birtley Gatesd 100 H7
Birtley Herefs 51 M9
Birtley Nthumb 99 N4
Birts Street Worcs 41 N4
Bisbrooke Rutlnd 67 M12
Biscathorpe Lincs 80 E7
Bisham W & M 32 B6
Bishampton Worcs 53 J10
Bish Mill Devon 19 P8
Bishop Auckland Dur 91 L1
Bishopbridge Lincs 79 P5
Bishopbriggs E Duns 114 A7
Bishop Burton E R Yk 87 J7
Bishop Middleham Dur 101 J12
Bishopmill Moray 139 M4
Bishop Monkton N York 85 L2
Bishop Norton Lincs 79 N5
Bishop's Cannings Wilts 30 B9
Bishop's Castle Shrops 51 K3

Bishop's Caundle Dorset 22 F10
Bishop's Cleeve Gloucs 41 Q6
Bishop's Frome Herefs 52 C11
Bishop's Green Essex 46 A8
Bishop's Hull Somset 21 K8
Bishop's Itchington Warwks 54 C9
Bishops Lydeard Somset 21 J7
Bishop's Norton Gloucs 41 N7
Bishop's Nympton Devon 19 P8
Bishop's Offley Staffs 64 E6
Bishop's Stortford Herts 45 N7
Bishop's Sutton Hants 25 K7
Bishop's Tachbrook Warwks 53 P8
Bishop's Tawton Devon 19 L7
Bishopsteignton Devon 8 G10
Bishopstoke Hants 24 H9
Bishopston Swans 26 A6
Bishopstone Bucks 44 A9
Bishopstone E Susx 15 N10
Bishopstone Herefs 40 F3
Bishopstone Kent 35 M8
Bishopstone Swindn 30 F5
Bishopstone Wilts 23 N8
Bishopstrow Wilts 22 H5
Bishop Sutton BaNES 29 J10
Bishop's Waltham Hants 25 J10
Bishopswood Somset 21 J10
Bishop's Wood Staffs 64 F10
Bishopsworth Bristl 28 H8
Bishop Thornton N York 85 K3
Bishopthorpe C York 86 B6
Bishopton Darltn 91 N2
Bishopton Rens 113 N7
Bishop Wilton E R Yk 86 E4
Bishton Newpt 28 E5
Bishton Staffs 65 J8
Bisley Gloucs 41 P10
Bisley Surrey 32 D10
Bissoe Cnwll 3 J6
Bisterne Hants 12 B4
Bitchfield Lincs 67 N6
Bittadon Devon 19 K5
Bitterley Shrops 51 P5
Bitterne C Sotn 24 G10
Bitteswell Leics 54 E3
Bitton S Glos 29 K8
Bix Oxon 31 P5
Bixter Shet 147 i6
Blaby Leics 54 F1
Blackadder Border 117 J10
Blackawton Devon 5 N6
Blackborough Devon 9 K4
Blackborough End Norfk 69 M9
Black Bourton Oxon 42 G10
Blackboys E Susx 15 P6
Blackbrook Derbys 65 Q3
Blackbrook St Hel 75 P4
Blackbrook Staffs 64 E4
Blackburn Abers 133 K4
Blackburn Bl w D 83 P9
Blackburn W Loth 115 J8
Blackburn with Darwen Services Bl w D 83 Q10
Blackcraig E Ayrs 105 L8
Black Crofts Ag & B 120 H6
Blackdog Abers 133 M1
Black Dog Devon 8 G3
Blackdown Dorset 10 B4
Blacker Hill Barns 78 B3
Blackfen Gt Lon 33 N7
Blackfield Hants 12 G4
Blackford P & K 123 M11
Blackford Somset 21 N4
Blackford Somset 22 G8
Blackfordby Leics 65 Q8
Blackhall C Edin 115 M6
Blackhall Colliery Dur 101 L10
Blackhall Mill Gatesd 100 E7
Blackhaugh Border 107 N3
Blackheath Gt Lon 33 M7
Blackheath Sandw 52 H3
Blackheath Surrey 14 F2
Blackheath Suffk 59 P5
Blackhill Abers 141 P5
Blackhill Abers 141 Q6
Blackhill of Clackriach Abers 141 M6
Blacklaw D & G 106 D8
Blackley Manch 76 F3
Blacklunans P & K 131 L12
Blackmarstone Herefs 40 G4
Blackmill Brdgnd 27 M5
Blackmoor Hants 25 M6
Blackmoor N Som 28 G10
Blackmoorfoot Kirk 77 L1
Blackmore Essex 45 R11
Blackmore End Essex 46 D5
Blackness Falk 115 J5
Blacknest Hants 25 M5
Black Notley Essex 46 D7
Blacko Lancs 84 C7
Black Pill Swans 26 E9
Blackpool Bpool 82 H8
Blackpool Devon 5 P7
Blackpool Zoo Bpool 82 H8
Blackridge W Loth 114 G8
Blackrod Bolton 75 Q2
Blacksboat Moray 139 M8
Blackshaw D & G 97 L5
Blackshaw Head Calder 84 C9
Blackstone W Susx 15 J7
Black Street Suffk 59 P3
Blackthorn Oxon 43 M8
Blackthorpe Suffk 58 D8
Blacktoft E R Yk 86 F9
Blacktop C Aber 133 L4
Black Torrington Devon 7 N2
Blackwall Derbys 65 N3
Blackwall Tunnel Gt Lon 33 M6
Blackwater Cnwll 3 J5
Blackwater Hants 32 C10
Blackwater IoW 12 H7
Blackwater Somset 21 J10
Blackwaterfoot N Ayrs 103 N4
Blackwell Cumb 98 E7
Blackwell Darltn 91 N5
Blackwell Derbys 78 C11
Blackwell Derbys 77 J9
Blackwell Warwks 53 L10
Blackwell Worcs 52 H6
Blackwood Caerph 28 A3
Blackwood D & G 106 B12
Blackwood S Lans 105 P1
Blacon Ches W 75 L10
Bladnoch D & G 95 M7
Bladon Oxon 43 K8
Blaenannerch Cerdgn 48 D11
Blaenau Ffestiniog Gwynd 61 M3

Blaenavon Torfn 40 C10
Blaenavon Industrial Landscape Torfn 40 C10
Blaencwm Rhondd 27 L3
Blaenffos Pembks 37 N3
Blaengarw Brdgnd 27 L4
Blaengwrach Neath 39 K10
Blaengwynfi Neath 27 L3
Blaenpennal Cerdgn 49 K8
Blaenplwyf Cerdgn 49 K5
Blaenporth Cerdgn 48 D11
Blaenrhondda Rhondd 27 M2
Blaenwaun Carmth 37 N5
Blaen-y-coed Carmth 37 N5
Blagdon N Som 28 G10
Blagdon Somset 21 K9
Blagdon Torbay 5 P4
Blagdon Hill Somset 21 K10
Blaich Highld 128 F8
Blain Highld 127 M10
Blaina Blae G 40 B10
Blair Atholl P & K 130 D11
Blair Drummond Stirlg 114 D2
Blairgowrie P & K 124 D4
Blairhall Fife 114 H4
Blairingone P & K 114 H2
Blairlogie Stirlg 114 D1
Blairmore Ag & B 113 J4
Blairmore Highld 148 D5
Blair's Ferry Ag & B 112 H7
Blaisdon Gloucs 41 M8
Blakebrook Worcs 52 F5
Blakedown Worcs 52 G5
Blake End Essex 46 C7
Blakemere Ches W 75 P9
Blakemere Herefs 40 E3
Blakenall Heath Wsall 65 J11
Blakeney Gloucs 41 K10
Blakeney Norfk 70 F3
Blakenhall Ches E 64 D3
Blakenhall Wolves 52 G1
Blakesley Nhants 54 G10
Blanchland Nthumb 100 B8
Blandford Forum Dorset 11 L3
Blandford St Mary Dorset 11 L3
Blanefield Stirlg 113 Q5
Blankney Lincs 79 Q12
Blantyre S Lans 114 C9
Blàr a' Chaorainn Highld 128 F10
Blarghour Ag & B 121 J10
Blargie Highld 129 Q5
Blarmachfoldach Highld 128 F10
Blaston Leics 55 K2
Blatherwycke N Nthn 55 N2
Blawith W & F 89 J9
Blawquhairn D & G 96 C2
Blaxhall Suffk 59 M9
Blaxton Donc 78 H4
Blaydon Gatesd 100 F5
Bleadney Somset 22 B4
Bleadon N Som 28 D11
Bleak Street Somset 22 G6
Bleasby Lincs 80 D7
Bleasby Notts 66 H2
Bleasdale Lancs 83 M6
Blebocraigs Fife 124 H10
Bleddfa Powys 50 F7
Bledington Gloucs 42 F7
Bledlow Bucks 43 Q11
Bledlow Ridge Bucks 31 R3
Blegbie E Loth 116 C9
Blencarn W & F 99 J12
Blencogo Cumb 97 P8
Blendworth Hants 25 M10
Blenheim Palace Oxon 43 J8
Blennerhasset Cumb 97 P9
Bletchingdon Oxon 43 L8
Bletchingley Surrey 33 L12
Bletchley M Keyn 44 B5
Bletchley Shrops 64 B5
Bletchley Park Museum M Keyn 44 B5
Bletherston Pembks 37 L6
Bletsoe Bed 55 P9
Blewbury Oxon 31 L5
Blickling Norfk 70 H6
Blidworth Notts 66 F1
Blidworth Bottoms Notts 66 F1
Blindcrake Cumb 97 N11
Blindley Heath Surrey 15 L2
Blindwells E Loth 115 R6
Blisland Cnwll 6 H6
Blissford Hants 24 B10
Bliss Gate Worcs 52 D6
Blisworth Nhants 55 J10
Blithbury Staffs 65 K8
Blockley Gloucs 42 E5
Blofield Norfk 71 L10
Blofield Heath Norfk 71 L10
Blo Norton Norfk 58 F5
Bloomfield Border 107 P5
Blore Staffs 65 L3
Bloxham Oxon 43 J4
Bloxholm Lincs 67 Q1
Bloxwich Wsall 65 J11
Bloxworth Dorset 11 L6
Blubberhouses N York 85 J4
Blue Anchor Somset 20 G4
Blue Bell Hill Kent 34 D10
Blue John Cavern Derbys 77 L7
Blundellsands Sefton 75 J4
Blundeston Suffk 59 Q1
Blunham C Beds 56 C10
Blunsdon St Andrew Swindn 30 C4
Bluntington Worcs 52 G6
Bluntisham Cambs 56 G6
Blurton C Stke 64 G4
Blyborough Lincs 79 N5
Blyford Suffk 59 N5
Blymhill Staffs 64 F9
Blyth Notts 78 G6
Blyth Nthumb 101 J2
Blyth Bridge Border 115 L12
Blythburgh Suffk 59 N5
Blyth Services Notts 78 G6
Blythe Border 116 D11
Blythe Bridge Staffs 64 H4
Blyton Lincs 79 L5
Boarhills Fife 125 L10
Boarhunt Hants 13 K3
Boarstall Bucks 43 N9
Boath Highld 145 N10
Boat of Garten Highld 138 H12
Bobbing Kent 34 F9
Bobbington Staffs 52 F2
Bocking Essex 46 D7
Bocking Churchstreet Essex 46 D7
Boddam Abers 141 Q6
Boddam Shet 147 i10
Boddington Gloucs 41 P6
Bodedern IoA 72 E7
Bodelwyddan Denbgs 74 D9
Bodenham Herefs 51 P10
Bodenham Wilts 24 C8

Bodenham Moor Herefs 51 P10
Bodewryd IoA 72 F5
Bodfari Denbgs 74 F9
Bodffordd IoA 72 G8
Bodham Norfk 70 H4
Bodiam E Susx 16 D6
Bodicote Oxon 43 K4
Bodinnick Cnwll 3 R4
Bodle Street Green E Susx 16 B8
Bodmin Cnwll 6 F11
Bodsham Kent 17 K2
Boduan Gwynd 60 E4
Bodymoor Heath Warwks 53 M1
Bogallan Highld 138 B5
Bogbrae Abers 141 P8
Bogend S Ayrs 104 G3
Boggs Holdings E Loth 116 B7
Boghall Mdloth 115 M8
Boghall W Loth 114 H7
Boghead S Lans 114 D11
Bogmoor Moray 139 Q3
Bogmuir Abers 132 G10
Bogniebrae Abers 140 F7
Bognor Regis W Susx 14 C10
Bogroy Highld 138 G11
Bogue D & G 96 D3
Bohetherick Cnwll 4 G4
Bohortha Cnwll 3 L8
Bohuntine Highld 129 J7
Bolam Dur 91 K2
Bolberry Devon 5 K9
Boldmere Birm 53 L2
Boldre Hants 12 F5
Boldron Dur 90 G4
Bole Notts 79 K6
Bolehill Derbys 65 P1
Bolenowe Cnwll 2 E10
Bolham Devon 20 E10
Bolham Water Devon 21 J11
Bolingey Cnwll 3 J4
Bollington Ches E 76 H8
Bolney W Susx 15 J6
Bolnhurst Bed 56 B8
Bolnore W Susx 15 L6
Bolshan Angus 125 M3
Bolsover Derbys 78 C9
Bolsterstone Sheff 77 P4
Boltby N York 91 R9
Bolton Bolton 76 D2
Bolton E R Yk 86 E5
Bolton E R Yk 86 E5
Bolton Nthumb 109 J6
Bolton W & F 89 Q2
Bolton Abbey N York 84 G5
Bolton-by-Bowland Lancs 84 B5
Boltonfellend Cumb 98 F6
Boltongate Cumb 97 P10
Bolton-le-Sands Lancs 83 L2
Bolton Low Houses Cumb 97 P9
Bolton-on-Swale N York 91 L7
Bolton Percy N York 85 Q7
Bolton upon Dearne Barns 78 B3
Bomere Heath Shrops 63 M8
Bonar Bridge Highld 145 Q6
Bonawe Ag & B 121 J6
Bonby N Linc 87 J12
Boncath Pembks 37 N3
Bonchester Bridge Border 107 L6
Bondleigh Devon 8 G4
Bonds Lancs 83 L6
Bo'ness Falk 114 H5
Boney Hay Staffs 65 K10
Bonhill W Duns 113 M6
Boningale Shrops 64 F11
Bonjedward Border 107 P5
Bonkle N Lans 114 F10
Bonnington Angus 125 J5
Bonnington Kent 17 J3
Bonnybank Fife 124 G12
Bonnybridge Falk 114 E6
Bonnykelly Abers 141 L5
Bonnyrigg Mdloth 115 P8
Bonnyton Angus 124 G6
Bonsall Derbys 77 P12
Bonshaw Tower D & G 97 P4
Bont-Dolgadfan Powys 62 B12
Bont-goch Cerdgn 49 L3
Bontnewydd Cerdgn 49 L8
Bontnewydd Gwynd 72 H12
Bontuchel Denbgs 74 F12
Bonvilston V Glam 27 P7
Boode Devon 19 J5
Booker Bucks 32 B4
Boon Border 116 D12
Boosbeck R & Cl 92 D3
Boose's Green Essex 46 F4
Boot Cumb 88 H7
Booth Calder 84 D9
Boothby Graffoe Lincs 79 N11
Boothby Pagnell Lincs 67 N5
Boothferry E R Yk 86 E9
Boothstown Salfd 76 D3
Boothtown Calder 84 G8
Boothville N Nthn 55 J8
Bootle Sefton 75 J5
Bootle W & F 88 G9
Boraston Shrops 51 Q6
Bordeaux Guern 3 c1
Borden Kent 34 F9
Bordon Hants 25 N6
Boreham Essex 46 C9
Boreham Wilts 22 H5
Borehamwood Herts 32 H3
Boreland D & G 106 F10
Boreraig Highld 134 C5
Borgh W Isls 152 b13
Borgh W Isls 152 g1
Borgie Highld 149 N5
Borgue D & G 96 C8
Borgue Highld 151 L11
Borley Essex 46 E3
Borneskitaig Highld 142 G11
Borness D & G 96 C8
Boroughbridge N York 85 M2
Borough Green Kent 33 R11
Borrowash Derbys 66 C5
Borrowby N York 91 P9
Borrowstoun Falk 114 H5
Borstal Medway 34 C9
Borth Cerdgn 49 L2
Borthwick Mdloth 115 Q9
Borthwickbrae Border 107 M7
Borthwickshiels Border 107 L6
Borth-y-Gest Gwynd 61 J4
Borve Highld 134 H6
Borve W Isls 152 b13
Borve W Isls 152 e3
Borve W Isls 152 g1
Borwick Lancs 89 N12
Bosbury Herefs 41 L3
Boscastle Cnwll 6 F5
Boscombe BCP 11 Q6
Boscombe Wilts 24 C5
Bosham W Susx 13 P4

Bosherston Pembks 37 J11
Bosley Ches E 76 G10
Bossall N York 86 D3
Bossiney Cnwll 6 F7
Bossingham Kent 17 L1
Bossington Somset 20 D4
Bostock Green Ches W 76 C10
Boston Lincs 68 F3
Boston Spa Leeds 85 N6
Boswinger Cnwll 3 N6
Botallack Cnwll 2 B8
Botany Bay Gt Lon 33 K3
Botesdale Suffk 58 F5
Bothal Nthumb 100 G1
Bothamsall Notts 78 H9
Bothel Cumb 97 N10
Bothenhampton Dorset 10 D6
Bothwell S Lans 114 C9
Bothwell Services (southbound) S Lans 114 C9
Botley Bucks 44 D11
Botley Hants 24 H10
Botley Oxon 43 K10
Botolph Claydon Bucks 43 Q7
Botolphs W Susx 14 H9
Bottesford Leics 67 K4
Bottesford N Linc 79 M2
Bottisham Cambs 57 K8
Bottomcraig Fife 124 G8
Bottoms Calder 84 D11
Botusfleming Cnwll 4 F4
Botwnnog Gwynd 60 D6
Bough Beech Kent 15 P1
Boughrood Powys 39 Q4
Boughspring Gloucs 28 G4
Boughton Nhants 55 J7
Boughton Norfk 69 N11
Boughton Notts 78 H10
Boughton Aluph Kent 17 J1
Boughton Green Kent 34 D12
Boughton Lees Kent 17 J1
Boughton Monchelsea Kent 34 D12
Boughton Street Kent 35 J10
Bouldon Shrops 51 P4
Boulmer Nthumb 109 L6
Boultenstone Abers 132 C2
Boultham Lincs 79 N10
Bourn Cambs 56 F9
Bournbrook Birm 53 K4
Bourne Lincs 68 B8
Bournebridge Essex 33 P3
Bourne End Bucks 32 C5
Bourne End C Beds 44 D3
Bourne End Herts 44 E11
Bournemouth BCP 11 Q6
Bournes Green Sthend 34 H5
Bournheath Worcs 52 H6
Bournmoor Dur 100 H8
Bournville Birm 53 K4
Bourton Bucks 43 Q6
Bourton Dorset 22 G6
Bourton Oxon 30 F5
Bourton Shrops 51 Q3
Bourton Wilts 30 B9
Bourton on Dunsmore Warwks 54 D6
Bourton-on-the-Hill Gloucs 42 E5
Bourton-on-the-Water Gloucs 42 D7
Bousd Ag & B 126 G11
Bouth W & F 89 J9
Bouthwaite N York 84 H1
Boveridge Dorset 23 N10
Bovey Tracey Devon 8 F9
Bovingdon Herts 44 E11
Bovinger Essex 44 E11
Bovington Dorset 11 J8
Bow Devon 8 G4
Bow Gt Lon 33 L6
Bow Ork 147 c6
Bow Brickhill M Keyn 44 C5
Bowbridge Gloucs 41 P10
Bowburn Dur 100 H10
Bowcombe IoW 12 H7
Bowd Devon 9 N6
Bowden Border 107 N4
Bowden Hill Wilts 29 R8
Bowdon Traffd 76 E6
Bower Highld 151 N4
Bowerchalke Wilts 23 M8
Bowermadden Highld 151 N4
Bowers Staffs 64 F5
Bowers Gifford Essex 34 D4
Bowershall Fife 115 J3
Bower's Row Leeds 85 M9
Bowes Dur 90 G4
Bowgreave Lancs 83 L6
Bowhouse D & G 97 L5
Bowland Border 107 M2
Bowley Herefs 51 P10
Bowlhead Green Surrey 14 C3
Bowling C Brad 85 J8
Bowling W Duns 113 N6
Bowmanstead W & F 89 J7
Bowmore Ag & B 110 C8
Bowness-on-Solway Cumb 97 P6
Bowness-on-Windermere W & F 89 L7
Bow of Fife Fife 124 G10
Bowriefauld Angus 125 K3
Bowscale Cumb 98 C11
Bowsden Nthumb 108 G3
Bow Street Cerdgn 49 K4
Bowthorpe Norfk 70 H10
Box Gloucs 29 P2
Box Wilts 29 N8
Boxford Suffk 46 G3
Boxford W Berk 31 J8
Boxgrove W Susx 14 C9
Boxley Kent 34 D10
Boxmoor Herts 44 F10
Boxted Essex 46 H5
Boxted Suffk 58 B10
Boxted Cross Essex 46 H5
Boxworth Cambs 56 G8
Boyden Gate Kent 35 M9
Boylestone Derbys 65 M5
Boyndie Abers 140 G3
Boyndlie Abers 141 L3
Boynton E R Yk 87 L2
Boysack Angus 125 M3
Boythorpe Derbys 78 B10
Boyton Cnwll 7 L6
Boyton Suffk 47 Q2
Boyton Wilts 23 J5
Boyton Cross Essex 46 B10
Boyton End Suffk 46 D3
Bozeat N Nthn 55 M9
Braaid IoM 80 d6
Brabourne Kent 17 J2
Brabourne Lees Kent 17 J2
Brabstermire Highld 151 P3
Bracadale Highld 134 F8
Braceborough Lincs 67 Q9
Bracebridge Heath Lincs 79 N10
Bracebridge Low Fields Lincs 79 N10
Braceby Lincs 67 P5
Bracewell Lancs 84 C5
Brackenfield Derbys 78 B12
Brackenhirst N Lans 114 E8

Calverton M Keyn 43 R4
Calverton Notts 66 G2
Calvine P & K 130 E11
Calzeat Border 106 E3
Cam Gloucs 29 M2
Camasachoirce Highld 127 P12
Camasine Highld 127 N12
Camas Luinie Highld 136 C10
Camastianavaig Highld 135 J8
Camault Muir Highld 137 N8
Camber E Susx 16 H7
Camberley Surrey 32 C10
Camberwell Gt Lon 33 L7
Camblesforth N York 86 C10
Cambo Nthumb 100 C1
Camborne Cnwll 2 G6
Camborne & Redruth
Mining District
Cnwll 2 G6
Cambourne Cambs 56 F8
Cambridge Cambs 57 J9
Cambridge Gloucs 41 M11
Cambrose Cnwll 2 H5
Cambus Clacks 114 F2
Cambusavie Highld 146 D6
Cambusbarron Stirlg 114 E3
Cambuskenneth Stirlg 114 B9
Cambuslang S Lans 114 B9
Cambus o' May Abers 132 C5
Cambuswallace S Lans 106 D2
Camden Town Gt Lon 33 K5
Cameley BaNES 29 J11
Camelford Cnwll 6 G8
Camelon Falk 114 F5
Camerory Highld 139 J7
Camerton BaNES 29 K11
Camerton Cumb 97 L12
Camghouran P & K 122 F2
Camieston Border 107 P4
Cammachmore Abers 133 L5
Cammeringham Lincs 79 N7
Camore Highld 146 D7
Campbeltown Ag & B 103 K6
Cample D & G 106 B11
Campmuir P & K 124 E5
Camps W Loth 115 K7
Campsall Donc 78 E1
Campsea Ash Suffk 59 L9
Campton C Beds 44 G4
Camptown Border 107 N7
Camrose Pembks 36 H6
Camserney P & K 123 L3
Camusnagaul Highld 128 F9
Camusnagaul Highld 144 D7
Camusteel Highld 135 M7
Camusterrach Highld 135 M7
Canada Hants 24 D7
Candacraig Abers 131 Q4
Candlesby Lincs 81 J10
Candy Mill Border 106 E1
Cane End Oxon 31 P6
Canewdon Essex 34 F3
Canford Cliffs BCP 11 P7
Canford Heath BCP 11 P6
Canisbay Highld 151 Q2
Canley Covtry 53 P9
Cann Dorset 23 J9
Canna Highld 126 D3
Cann Common Dorset 23 K9
Cannich Highld 137 N9
Cannington Somset 21 L5
Canning Town Gt Lon 33 M6
Cannock Staffs 64 H10
Cannon Bridge Herefs 40 F3
Canonbie D & G 98 E3
Canon Frome Herefs 41 K3
Canon Pyon Herefs 51 M11
Canons Ashby W Nthn 54 F10
Canonstown Cnwll 2 E7
Canterbury Kent 35 L10
Canterbury Cathedral
Kent 35 L10
Cantley Norfk 71 M11
Canton Cardif 27 R7
Cantraywood Highld 138 E6
Cantsfield Lancs 89 Q12
Canvey Island Essex 34 D6
Canwick Lincs 79 P9
Canworthy Water Cnwll 7 J6
Caol Highld 128 F9
Caolas Scalpaigh
W Isls 152 H4
Caoles Ag & B 118 E3
Caonich Highld 128 E6
Capel Kent 16 B2
Capel Surrey 14 H3
Capel Bangor Cerdgn 49 L4
Capel Coch IoA 72 G7
Capel Curig Conwy 73 M12
Capel Dewi Carmth 38 C7
Capel Dewi Cerdgn 38 C3
Capel-Dewi Cerdgn 49 K4
Capel Garmon Conwy 61 P1
Capel Hendre Carmth 38 F9
Capel Iwan Carmth 37 Q3
Capel-le-Ferne Kent 17 L3
Capelles Guern 12 c2
Capel Parc IoA 72 G6
Capel St Andrew Suffk 59 M11
Capel St Mary Suffk 47 K4
Capel Seion Cerdgn 49 L5
Capelulo Conwy 73 N8
Capenhurst Ches W 75 L9
Capheaton Nthumb 100 D2
Caplaw E Rens 113 N9
Cappercleuch Border 106 H5
Capton Devon 5 P6
Caputh P & K 124 B5
Caradon Mining District
Cnwll 7 K10
Carbeth Stirlg 113 Q5
Carbis Bay Cnwll 2 E7
Carbost Highld 134 G6
Carbost Highld 134 G11
Carbrook Sheff 78 C6
Carbrooke Norfk 70 D11
Car Colston Notts 67 J4
Carcroft Donc 78 E2
Cardenden Fife 115 M2
Cardhu Moray 139 M7
Cardiff Cardif 28 A7
Cardiff Gate Services
Cardif 28 B6
Cardiff West Services
Cardif 27 P6
Cardigan Cerdgn 48 B11
Cardington Bed 56 B11
Cardington Shrops 51 N2
Cardinham Cnwll 6 G11
Cardrain D & G 94 G12
Cardrona Border 107 J2
Cardross Ag & B 113 L6
Cardryne D & G 94 G12
Cardurnock Cumb 97 N6
Careby Lincs 67 P9
Careston Angus 132 G12
Carew Pembks 37 K9
Carew Cheriton Pembks 37 K9
Carew Newton Pembks 37 K9
Carey Herefs 40 H5

Carfin N Lans 114 E9
Carfraemill Border 116 C10
Cargate Green Norfk 71 M9
Cargenbridge D & G 97 J3
Cargill P & K 124 C5
Cargo Cumb 98 D6
Cargreen Cnwll 4 F4
Carham Nthumb 108 C2
Carhampton Somset 20 F5
Carharrack Cnwll 3 J6
Carie P & K 122 G1
Carinish W Isls 152 c8
Carisbrooke IoW 12 H7
Cark Cumb 89 K11
Carkeel Cnwll 4 F4
Càrlabhagh W Isls 152 e2
Carlbury Darltn 91 L4
Carlby Lincs 67 P9
Carleen Cnwll 2 F9
Carleton Forehoe Norfk 70 G11
Carleton-in-Craven
N York 84 E5
Carleton Rode Norfk 58 G2
Carleton St Peter
Norfk 71 L11
Carlincraig Abers 140 G7
Carlingcott BaNES 29 L10
Carlisle Cumb 98 E7
Carloway W Isls 152 e2
Carlops Border 115 L10
Carlton Barns 78 B2
Carlton Bed 55 N9
Carlton Cambs 57 M10
Carlton Leeds 85 M9
Carlton Leics 66 C11
Carlton N York 86 D10
Carlton N York 90 H10
Carlton N York 92 C9
Carlton Notts 66 G4
Carlton S on T 91 P2
Carlton Suffk 59 M8
Carlton Colville Suffk 59 P3
Carlton Curlieu Leics 54 H1
Carlton Green Cambs 57 M10
Carlton Husthwaite
N York 92 A11
Carlton-in-Cleveland
N York 92 A6
Carlton in Lindrick
Notts 78 F7
Carlton-le-Moorland
Lincs 79 M12
Carlton Miniott N York 91 P10
Carlton-on-Trent Notts 79 K11
Carlton Scroop Lincs 67 N3
Carluke S Lans 114 F11
Carmacoup S Lans 105 P4
Carmarthen Carmth 38 B7
Carmel Carmth 38 E8
Carmel Flints 74 G8
Carmel Gwynd 60 H1
Carmichael S Lans 106 B2
Carmunnock C Glas 114 A9
Carmyle C Glas 114 B9
Carmyllie Angus 125 L4
Carnaby E R Yk 87 L2
Carnbee Fife 125 K11
Carnbo P & K 123 Q12
Carn Brea Cnwll 2 H6
Carnbrogie Abers 141 K10
Carnduff S Lans 114 B12
Carnell E Ayrs 105 J3
Carnforth Lancs 83 L11
Carn-gorm Highld 136 C11
Carnhell Green Cnwll 2 F7
Carnie Abers 133 K3
Carnkie Cnwll 2 H6
Carnkie Cnwll 2 H5
Carno Powys 50 C1
Carnock Fife 115 J3
Carnon Downs Cnwll 3 K6
Carnousie Abers 140 G6
Carnoustie Angus 125 L6
Carnwath S Lans 114 H12
Carol Green Solhll 53 N5
Carperby N York 90 H9
Carradale Ag & B 103 L2
Carradale Village
Ag & B 103 L2
Carrbridge Highld 138 G11
Carrefour Jersey 13 b1
Carreglefn IoA 72 F6
Carr Gate Wakefd 85 L10
Carrhouse N Linc 79 K2
Carrick Ag & B 112 A12
Carriden Falk 115 J5
Carrington Mdloth 115 P9
Carrington Traffd 76 D5
Carrog Denbgs 62 F3
Carron Falk 114 F5
Carron Moray 139 N7
Carronbridge D & G 105 R10
Carron Bridge Stirlg 114 D4
Carronshore Falk 114 G5
Carr Shield Nthumb 99 M8
Carruthersdown D & G 97 M4
Carruth House Inver 113 M8
Carrville Dur 100 H9
Carsaig Ag & B 119 P8
Carseriggan D & G 95 K5
Carsethorn D & G 97 K6
Carshalton Gt Lon 33 K9
Carsington Derbys 65 N2
Carskey Ag & B 103 J8
Carsluith D & G 95 N7
Carsphairn D & G 105 K11
Carstairs S Lans 114 G12
Carstairs Junction
S Lans 114 H12
Carterton Oxon 42 G10
Carthew Cnwll 3 N3
Carthorpe N York 91 M10
Cartland S Lans 114 F12
Cartmel Cumb 89 K11
Carway Carmth 38 C10
Cashe's Green Gloucs 41 N10
Cassington Oxon 43 K9
Cassop Dur 101 J10
Castel Guern 12 c2
Casterton W & F 89 Q11
Castle Acre Norfk 70 B9
Castle Ashby W Nthn 55 L8
Castlebay W Isls 152 b13
Castle Bolton N York 90 H7
Castle Bromwich Solhll 53 L3
Castle Bytham Lincs 67 N8
Castlebythe Pembks 37 K5
Castle Caereinion
Powys 62 G11
Castle Camps Cambs 46 A3
Castle Carrock Cumb 98 G7
Castlecary N Lans 114 E5
Castle Cary Somset 22 C7
Castle Combe Wilts 29 M7
Castlecraig Highld 146 E11
Castle Donington Leics 66 D7
Castle Douglas D & G 96 F6
Castle Eaton Swindn 30 C5

Castle Eden Dur 101 K10
Castleford Wakefd 85 N10
Castle Frome Herefs 41 K3
Castle Gresley Derbys 65 P8
Castle Hedingham
Essex 46 D4
Castlehill Border 106 G3
Castlehill Highld 151 M3
Castle Hill Suffk 47 L2
Castlehill W Duns 113 M6
Castle Howard N York 86 D1
Castle Kennedy D & G 94 G6
Castle Lachlan Ag & B 112 E2
Castlemartin Pembks 36 H11
Castlemilk C Glas 114 A9
Castlemorton Worcs 41 M4
Castlemorton
Common Worcs 41 M4
Castle O'er D & G 106 H11
Castle Rising Norfk 69 M7
Castleside Dur 100 D8
Castlethorpe M Keyn 44 A3
Castleton Ag & B 112 C4
Castleton Border 107 N11
Castleton Derbys 77 M7
Castleton N York 92 E5
Castleton Newpt 28 C6
Castleton Rochdl 76 G2
Castletown Highld 151 M3
Castletown IoM 102 c7
Castletown Sundld 101 J6
Castley N York 85 K6
Caston Norfk 58 E1
Castor C Pete 56 C1
Catacol N Ayrs 112 D11
Catcliffe Rothm 78 C6
Catcomb Wilts 30 C6
Catcott Somset 21 N5
Caterham Surrey 33 L11
Catfield Norfk 71 M8
Catford Gt Lon 33 L8
Catforth Lancs 83 L8
Cathcart C Glas 113 R9
Cathedine Powys 39 Q6
Catherington Hants 25 M10
Catherston
Leweston Dorset 10 B6
Catisfield Hants 13 J3
Catlodge Highld 130 B6
Catmere End Essex 45 P4
Catmore W Berk 31 K6
Caton Lancs 83 M2
Caton Green Lancs 83 M2
Catrine E Ayrs 105 K5
Catsfield E Susx 16 C8
Catsgore Somset 22 C8
Catshill Worcs 52 H6
Cattadale Ag & B 103 J7
Cattal N York 85 N4
Cattawade Suffk 47 K5
Catterall Lancs 83 L6
Catterick N York 91 L7
Catterick Bridge N York 91 L7
Catterick Garrison
N York 91 K7
Catterlen W & F 98 F11
Catterline Abers 133 L8
Catterton N York 85 Q6
Catteshall Surrey 14 D2
Catthorpe Leics 54 F5
Cattistock Dorset 10 G5
Catton N York 91 N11
Catton Nthumb 99 M7
Catwick E R Yk 87 L6
Catworth Cambs 56 B6
Caudle Green Gloucs 41 Q9
Caulcott Oxon 43 L7
Cauldcots Angus 125 L4
Cauldhame Stirlg 114 B2
Cauldmill Border 107 N6
Cauldon Staffs 65 K3
Cauldwell Derbys 65 N9
Caulkerbush D & G 97 J7
Caulside D & G 98 F2
Caundle Marsh Dorset 22 F10
Caunton Notts 79 J11
Causeway End D & G 95 M6
Causeway End Essex 46 B8
Causewayend S Lans 106 D2
Causewayhead Stirlg 114 E2
Causeyend Abers 141 M12
Causey Park Bridge
Nthumb 109 K10
Cavendish Suffk 46 E2
Cavenham Suffk 57 P6
Caversfield Oxon 43 M6
Caversham Readg 31 P7
Caverswall Staffs 64 H4
Caverton Mill Border 108 B5
Cawdor Highld 138 F6
Cawood N York 86 A8
Cawsand Cnwll 4 F6
Cawston Norfk 70 H7
Cawthorne Barns 77 P2
Caxton Cambs 56 F9
Caynham Shrops 51 P6
Caythorpe Lincs 67 M2
Caythorpe Notts 66 H3
Cayton N York 93 L10
Ceannabeinne Highld 149 K3
Ceann a Bhaigh W Isls 152 b8
Ceannacroc Lodge
Highld 128 H2
Cearsiadar W Isls 152 f4
Cefn Newpt 28 C5
Cefn-brith Conwy 62 C2
Cefn-bryn-brain
Carmth 38 H9
Cefn-coed-y-cymmer
Myr Td 39 N10
Cefn Cribwr Brdgnd 27 K6
Cefneithin Carmth 38 E9
Cefngorwydd Powys 39 L3
Cefn-mawr Wrexhm 63 J4
Cefn-y-pant Carmth 37 N5
Cellardyke Fife 125 L11
Cellarhead Staffs 64 H3
Cemaes IoA 72 F5
Cemmaes Powys 61 N11
Cemmaes Road Powys 61 N11
Cenarth Cerdgn 37 P2
Ceres Fife 124 H10
Cerne Abbas Dorset 10 G4
Cerney Wick Gloucs 30 C3
Cerrigceinwen IoA 72 F7
Cerrigydrudion Conwy 62 C2
Ceunant Gwynd 73 J11
Chaceley Gloucs 41 P5
Chacewater Cnwll 3 J5
Chackmore Bucks 43 N4
Chacombe W Nthn 43 M3
Chadbury Worcs 42 B3
Chadderton Oldham 76 G3
Chaddesden Derby 66 B4
Chaddesley Corbett
Worcs 52 F6
Chaddlehanger Devon 7 M7
Chaddleworth W Berk 31 K7
Chadlington Oxon 42 G7
Chadshunt Warwks 53 Q10

Chadwell Leics 67 K7
Chadwell Heath Gt Lon 33 N5
Chadwell St Mary Thurr 34 B6
Chadwick Worcs 52 F7
Chadwick End Solhll 53 N6
Chaffcombe Somset 9 Q3
Chafford Hundred Thurr 33 R6
Chagford Devon 8 D7
Chailey E Susx 15 M7
Chainhurst Kent 16 C1
Chaldon Surrey 33 K11
Chaldon Herring Dorset 11 J8
Chale IoW 12 H9
Chale Green IoW 12 H9
Chalfont Common
Bucks 32 E4
Chalfont St Giles Bucks 32 E4
Chalfont St Peter Bucks 32 E4
Chalford Gloucs 41 P11
Chalgrove Oxon 31 N3
Chalk Kent 34 B8
Chalkwell Kent 34 F9
Challacombe Devon 19 N5
Challoch D & G 95 M5
Challock Kent 34 H11
Chalton C Beds 44 E6
Chalton Hants 25 M10
Chalvey Slough 32 D6
Chalvington E Susx 15 Q9
Chandler's Cross Herts 32 F3
Chandler's Ford Hants 24 G9
Channel Tunnel Terminal
Kent 17 L3
Chantry Somset 22 G4
Chantry Suffk 47 L3
Chapel Fife 115 N3
Chapel Allerton Leeds 85 L8
Chapel Allerton Somset 21 N3
Chapel Amble Cnwll 6 E9
Chapel Brampton
W Nthn 54 H7
Chapel Chorlton Staffs 64 E5
Chapelend Way Essex 46 C4
Chapel-en-le-Frith
Derbys 77 K7
Chapel Green Warwks 54 D8
Chapel Haddlesey
N York 86 A10
Chapelhall N Lans 114 E9
Chapel Hill Abers 141 P9
Chapel Hill Lincs 68 D1
Chapel Hill N York 85 M6
Chapelhope D & G 106 F6
Chapelknowe D & G 98 C4
Chapel Lawn Shrops 51 L5
Chapel-le-Dale N York 90 B11
Chapel Leigh Somset 20 H7
Chapel of Garioch
Abers 140 H11
Chapel Rossan D & G 94 G9
Chapel Row W Berk 31 M8
Chapel St Leonards
Lincs 81 L9
Chapel Stile W & F 89 J6
Chapelton Abers 133 L6
Chapelton Angus 125 M3
Chapelton Devon 19 L8
Chapelton S Lans 114 C11
Chapeltown Bl w D 83 Q12
Chapeltown Moray 139 N11
Chapeltown Sheff 78 B5
Chapmanslade Wilts 23 J4
Chapmans Well Devon 7 L5
Chapmore End Herts 45 L8
Chappel Essex 46 F6
Chard Somset 9 Q3
Chard Junction Somset 9 Q4
Chardleigh Green
Devon 8 G3
Chardstock Devon 9 Q4
Charfield S Glos 29 J8
Charing Kent 16 G1
Charingworth Gloucs 42 E4
Charlbury Oxon 42 H7
Charlcombe BaNES 29 M9
Charlcutt Wilts 30 A7
Charlecote Warwks 53 P9
Charlemont Sandw 53 J2
Charles Devon 19 N7
Charleston Angus 124 H4
Charlestown C Aber 133 M4
Charlestown C Brad 84 H7
Charlestown Calder 84 E10
Charlestown Cnwll 3 P4
Charlestown Fife 115 J4
Charlestown Highld 138 B6
Charlestown Highld 143 L10
Charlestown Salfd 76 E4
Charlestown of Aberlour
Moray 139 N7
Charles Tye Suffk 58 F10
Charlesworth Derbys 77 J5
Charlinch Somset 21 K6
Charlottetown Fife 124 H8
Charlton Gt Lon 33 M7
Charlton Nthumb 99 M5
Charlton Somset 21 L8
Charlton Somset 22 F3
Charlton Somset 22 C4
Charlton W Nthn 43 L4
Charlton Oxon 31 K5
Charlton Surrey 23 K9
Charlton W Susx 14 C9
Charlton Wilts 42 B3
Charlton Wrekin 63 Q10
Charlton Abbots Gloucs 42 B7
Charlton Adam Somset 22 C7
Charlton All Saints
Wilts 24 B8
Charlton Down Dorset 10 G5
Charlton Horethorne
Somset 22 F8
Charlton Kings Gloucs 41 Q7
Charlton Mackrell
Somset 22 C7
Charlton Marshall
Dorset 11 L4
Charlton Musgrove
Somset 22 F8
Charlton-on-Otmoor
Oxon 43 M8
Charlton on the Hill
Dorset 11 L4
Charlton St Peter Wilts 30 D11
Charlwood Hants 25 M7
Charlwood Surrey 15 J2
Charminster Dorset 10 G6
Charmouth Dorset 10 B6
Charndon Bucks 43 P7
Charney Bassett Oxon 30 H3
Charnock Richard
Lancs 83 M12
Charnock Richard Services
Lancs 83 M12
Charsfield Suffk 59 L9
Charter Alley Hants 31 M10
Charterhouse Somset 21 P2
Chartham Somset 22 C2
Chartershall Stirlg 114 E3

Chartham Kent 35 K11
Chartham Hatch Kent 35 K11
Chartridge Bucks 44 D11
Chart Sutton Kent 16 E1
Charvil Wokham 31 Q7
Charwelton W Nthn 54 E9
Chase Cross Gt Lon 33 P4
Chase Terrace Staffs 65 J10
Chasetown Staffs 65 K10
Chastleton Oxon 42 F6
Chasty Devon 7 L4
Chatburn Lancs 84 A6
Chatcull Staffs 64 E5
Chatham Medway 34 D9
Chatham Green Essex 46 C8
Chathill Nthumb 109 K4
Chatsworth Derbys 77 N9
Chattenden Medway 34 D8
Chatteris Cambs 56 H3
Chatterton Lancs 84 B11
Chattisham Suffk 47 K3
Chatto Border 108 C6
Chatton Nthumb 108 H4
Chawleigh Devon 19 N11
Chawton Hants 25 M6
Cheadle Staffs 65 J3
Cheadle Stockp 76 F6
Cheadle Heath Stockp 76 G6
Cheadle Hulme Stockp 76 G6
Cheam Gt Lon 33 J9
Chearsley Bucks 43 P9
Chebsey Staffs 64 F6
Checkendon Oxon 31 N6
Checkley Ches E 64 D3
Checkley Staffs 65 J5
Chedburgh Suffk 57 Q9
Cheddar Somset 21 P3
Cheddington Bucks 44 C8
Cheddleton Staffs 64 H2
Cheddon Fitzpaine
Somset 21 K8
Chedgrave Norfk 71 M12
Chedington Dorset 10 D4
Chediston Suffk 59 M5
Chedworth Gloucs 42 B9
Chedzoy Somset 21 M6
Cheetham Hill Manch 76 F3
Cheldon Devon 19 P10
Chelford Ches E 76 F9
Chellaston C Derb 66 B6
Chellington Bed 55 N9
Chelmarsh Shrops 52 D3
Chelmer Village Essex 46 C10
Chelmondiston Suffk 47 M4
Chelmorton Derbys 77 L9
Chelmsford Essex 46 C10
Chelmsley Wood Solhll 53 M3
Chelsea Gt Lon 33 K7
Chelsfield Gt Lon 33 N9
Chelsworth Suffk 58 E11
Cheltenham Gloucs 41 Q7
Chelveston W Nthn 55 N7
Chelvey N Som 28 G8
Chelwood BaNES 29 K10
Chelwood Gate E Susx 15 M5
Cheney Longville
Shrops 51 M4
Chenies Bucks 32 E3
Chepstow Mons 28 H4
Cherhill Wilts 30 B8
Cherington Gloucs 29 P3
Cherington Warwks 42 G4
Cheriton Hants 25 K7
Cheriton Kent 17 M3
Cheriton Pembks 37 J11
Cheriton Swans 26 B9
Cheriton Bishop Devon 8 E6
Cheriton Fitzpaine
Devon 8 G3
Cherrington Wrekin 64 D8
Cherry Burton E R Yk 87 J7
Cherry Hinton Cambs 57 J9
Cherry Orchard Worcs 52 F10
Cherry Willingham
Lincs 79 P9
Chertsey Surrey 32 E9
Cherwell Valley Services
Oxon 43 L6
Cheselbourne Dorset 11 J5
Chesham Bucks 44 D11
Chesham Bury 76 E1
Chesham Bois Bucks 32 D3
Cheshunt Herts 45 L11
Cheslyn Hay Staffs 64 H9
Chessetts Wood
Warwks 53 M6
Chessington Gt Lon 32 H9
Chessington World
of Adventures Gt Lon 32 H10
Chester Ches W 75 M8
Chesterblade Somset 22 E4
Chesterfield Derbys 78 C9
Chesterfield Staffs 65 L11
Chester-le-Street Dur 100 H8
Chester Moor Dur 100 H8
Chesters Border 107 P5
Chesters Border 107 P6
Chester Services
Ches W 75 M8
Chesterton Cambs 56 C2
Chesterton Cambs 57 J8
Chesterton Gloucs 30 B2
Chesterton Oxon 43 M7
Chesterton Shrops 52 E1
Chesterton Green
Warwks 54 B9
Chester Zoo Ches W 75 M8
Chestfield Kent 35 K9
Cheston Devon 5 N8
Cheswardine Shrops 64 D6
Cheswick Nthumb 117 M12
Chetnole Dorset 10 F4
Chettiscombe Devon 20 C10
Chettisham Cambs 57 J4
Chettle Dorset 23 L10
Chetton Shrops 52 C3
Chetwynd Wrekin 64 D8
Chetwynd Aston Wrekin 64 E9
Cheveley Cambs 57 N8
Chevening Kent 33 N10
Chevington Suffk 57 Q8
Cheverton IoW 12 F10
Chevithorne Devon 20 C10
Chew Magna BaNES 29 J9
Chew Stoke BaNES 28 H10
Chewton Keynsham
BaNES 29 K9
Chewton Mendip
Somset 22 C3
Chicheley M Keyn 44 C2
Chichester W Susx 14 B10
Chickerell Dorset 10 G8
Chicklade Wilts 23 K6
Chidden Hants 25 L10
Chiddingfold Surrey 14 D4
Chiddingly E Susx 15 P8
Chiddingstone Kent 15 P2
Chiddingstone
Causeway Kent 15 P1

Chideock Dorset 10 C6
Chidham W Susx 13 N4
Chidswell Kirk 85 K10
Chieveley W Berk 31 K7
Chieveley Services
W Berk 31 K8
Chignall St James
Essex 46 B9
Chignall Smealy Essex 46 B9
Chigwell Essex 33 N3
Chigwell Row Essex 33 N4
Chilbolton Hants 24 F5
Chilcomb Hants 24 H7
Chilcombe Dorset 10 E6
Chilcompton Somset 22 E3
Chilcote Leics 65 P10
Childer Thornton
Ches W 75 L8
Child Okeford Dorset 23 J10
Childrey Oxon 30 H5
Child's Ercall Shrops 64 C7
Childswickham Worcs 42 C4
Childwall Lpool 75 L6
Childwick Green
Herts 44 G9
Chilfrome Dorset 10 F5
Chilgrove W Susx 25 P10
Chilham Kent 35 J11
Chillaton Devon 7 N8
Chillenden Kent 35 N11
Chillerton IoW 12 H8
Chillesford Suffk 59 N10
Chillingham Nthumb 108 H5
Chillington Devon 5 N8
Chillington Somset 10 B3
Chilmark Wilts 23 L7
Chilmington Green
Kent 16 H3
Chilson Oxon 42 G8
Chilsworthy Cnwll 7 M10
Chilsworthy Devon 7 L3
Chilthorne Domer
Somset 22 C9
Chilton Bucks 43 P9
Chilton Dur 100 H12
Chilton Oxon 31 K5
Chilton Candover Hants 25 J5
Chilton Cantelo Somset 22 D9
Chilton Foliat Wilts 30 G8
Chilton Polden Somset 21 N5
Chilton Street Suffk 57 P11
Chilton Trinity Somset 21 L5
Chilwell Notts 66 E5
Chilworth Hants 24 G9
Chilworth Surrey 14 G1
Chimney Oxon 30 H2
Chineham Hants 25 L2
Chingford Gt Lon 33 M3
Chinley Derbys 77 K7
Chinnor Oxon 31 Q2
Chipnall Shrops 64 D6
Chippenham Cambs 57 M6
Chippenham Wilts 29 Q7
Chipperfield Herts 44 F11
Chipping Herts 45 L5
Chipping Lancs 83 N6
Chipping Campden
Gloucs 42 D4
Chipping Hill Essex 46 E8
Chipping Norton Oxon 42 G6
Chipping Ongar Essex 45 Q11
Chipping Sodbury
S Glos 29 L6
Chipping Warden
W Nthn 54 E11
Chipstable Somset 20 G8
Chipstead Kent 33 P11
Chipstead Surrey 33 K11
Chirbury Shrops 51 J2
Chirk Wrexhm 63 J5
Chirnside Border 117 J10
Chirnsidebridge
Border 117 J10
Chirton Wilts 30 C11
Chisbury Wilts 30 F9
Chiselborough Somset 21 P10
Chiseldon Swindn 30 D6
Chiselhampton Oxon 31 M2
Chiserley Calder 84 F9
Chisholme Border 107 J7
Chislehurst Gt Lon 33 N8
Chislet Kent 35 M9
Chiswell Green Herts 44 H10
Chiswick Gt Lon 33 J7
Chisworth Derbys 77 J5
Chithurst W Susx 25 P8
Chittering Cambs 57 K7
Chitterne Wilts 23 L3
Chittlehamholt Devon 19 M9
Chittlehampton Devon 19 M8
Chittoe Wilts 29 Q9
Chivelstone Devon 5 N9
Chivenor Devon 19 K6
Chlenry D & G 94 G6
Chobham Surrey 32 D10
Cholderton Wilts 24 C4
Cholesbury Bucks 44 D10
Chollerton Nthumb 99 P4
Cholsey Oxon 31 M5
Cholstrey Herefs 51 M9
Chop Gate N York 92 B7
Choppington Nthumb 100 E6
Chopwell Gatesd 100 E6
Chorley Ches E 63 P2
Chorley Lancs 83 N11
Chorley Shrops 52 C4
Chorleywood Herts 32 E3
Chorleywood West
Herts 32 E3
Chorlton Ches E 64 D2
Chorlton-cum-Hardy
Manch 76 F4
Chorlton Lane Ches W 63 M3
Choulton Shrops 51 L4
Chowley Ches W 75 M12
Chrishall Essex 45 N4
Chrisswell Inver 113 J6
Christchurch BCP 11 Q6
Christchurch Cambs 57 J1
Christchurch Newpt 28 D6
Christian Malford
Wilts 29 Q6
Christon N Som 28 E11
Christon Bank Nthumb 109 K5
Christow Devon 8 F8
Chudleigh Devon 8 G9
Chudleigh Knighton
Devon 8 F9
Chulmleigh Devon 19 N10
Church Lancs 84 B9
Churcham Gloucs 41 M8
Church Aston Wrekin 64 D8
Church Brampton
W Nthn 55 J8
Church Broughton
Derbys 65 M5
Church Cove Cnwll 2 H12
Church Crookham
Hants 25 P3
Church End Essex 46 C6

Church End Gt Lon 33 J4
Church Enstone Oxon 42 H6
Church Fenton N York 85 Q8
Churchfield Sandw 53 J2
Churchgate Street
Essex 45 N9
Church Green Devon 9 M5
Church Hanborough
Oxon 43 J9
Church Houses N York 92 D7
Churchill Devon 9 P4
Churchill Devon 19 N4
Churchill N Som 28 F10
Churchill Oxon 42 G7
Churchill Worcs 52 G3
Churchill Worcs 52 G5
Churchinford Somset 21 K11
Church Knowle Dorset 11 M8
Church Langton Leics 55 J2
Church Lawford
Warwks 54 D5
Church Leigh Staffs 65 J5
Church Lench Worcs 53 J10
Church Mayfield Staffs 65 M3
Church Minshull Ches E 76 C11
Church Norton W Susx 14 B11
Churchover Warwks 54 E4
Church Preen Shrops 51 P3
Church Pulverbatch
Shrops 63 M11
Churchstanton Somset 21 K10
Churchstoke Powys 51 J2
Churchstow Devon 5 N8
Church Stowe W Nthn 54 G9
Church Street Kent 34 C7
Church Stretton Shrops 51 M2
Churchtown Cnwll 6 G9
Churchtown Derbys 77 P11
Churchtown IoM 102 f3
Churchtown Lancs 83 L6
Church Village Rhondd 27 P5
Church Warsop Notts 78 D9
Churt Surrey 25 Q6
Churton Ches W 75 M12
Churwell Leeds 85 K9
Chute Somset 30 F11
Chwilog Gwynd 60 G4
Chyandour Cnwll 2 D8
Cilcain Flints 74 G10
Cilcennin Cerdgn 49 J8
Cilfrew Neath 27 L2
Cilfynydd Rhondd 27 N2
Cilgerran Pembks 37 N2
Cilmaengwyn Neath 38 H10
Cilmery Powys 50 D10
Cilsan Carmth 38 F7
Ciltalgarth Gwynd 62 B4
Cilycwm Carmth 38 H4
Cimla Neath 27 J3
Cinderford Gloucs 41 K9
Cinder Hill Wolves 52 H2
Cippenham Slough 32 D6
Cirencester Gloucs 30 B2
City Gt Lon 33 L6
Clabhach Ag & B 118 G3
Clachaig Ag & B 112 G5
Clachan Ag & B 111 Q10
Clachan Ag & B 112 G1
Clachan Ag & B 120 F4
Clachan Ag & B 120 F4
Clachan Highld 135 J8
Clachan-a-Luib W Isls 152 d8
Clachan Mor Ag & B 118 D3
Clachan na Luib W Isls 152 c8
Clachan of Campsie
E Duns 114 A5
Clachan-Seil Ag & B 120 E9
Clachnaharry Highld 138 B6
Clachtoll Highld 148 C11
Clacket Lane Services
Surrey 33 M11
Clackmannan Clacks 114 G3
Clackmannanshire
Bridge Fife 114 G4
Clackmarras Moray 139 N4
Clacton-on-Sea Essex 47 L8
Cladich Ag & B 121 L8
Cladswell Worcs 53 K9
Claggan Highld 120 D3
Claigan Highld 134 D5
Clandown BaNES 25 M10
Clanfield Hants 25 M10
Clanfield Oxon 42 G11
Clanville Hants 24 E4
Clanville Somset 22 E7
Claonaig Ag & B 112 C10
Clapgate Herts 45 N7
Clapham Bed 55 N9
Clapham Gt Lon 33 K7
Clapham N York 83 R1
Clapham W Susx 14 F9
Clapton Somset 10 C3
Clapton Somset 22 E3
Clapton-in-Gordano
N Som 28 G7
Clapton-on-the-Hill
Gloucs 42 D8
Claravale Gatesd 100 E5
Clarbeston Pembks 37 K6
Clarbeston Road
Pembks 37 K6
Clarborough Notts 79 J7
Clare Suffk 46 D3
Clarebrand D & G 96 F5
Clarencefield D & G 97 M4
Clarilaw Border 107 N6
Clarkston E Rens 113 Q9
Clashmore Highld 146 E7
Clashmore Highld 148 B10
Clashnessie Highld 148 B10
Clashnoir Moray 139 N11
Clathy P & K 123 P3
Clathymore P & K 123 P8
Clatt Abers 140 E11
Clatter Powys 50 D2
Clatworthy Somset 20 G7
Claughton Lancs 83 M2
Claughton Lancs 83 M7
Claughton Wirral 75 J6
Claverdon Warwks 53 M8
Claverham N Som 28 G9
Clavering Essex 45 N5
Claverley Shrops 52 E2
Claverton BaNES 29 M9
Clawdd-coch V Glam 27 P7
Clawdd-newydd
Denbgs 62 E1
Clawton Devon 7 L5
Claxby Lincs 79 P6
Claxton N York 86 C3
Claxton Norfk 71 M11
Claybrooke Magna
Leics 54 E3
Clay Coton W Nthn 54 F5
Clay Cross Derbys 78 C10
Claydon Oxon 54 D10
Claydon Suffk 47 K2
Claygate D & G 98 F4
Claygate Kent 16 C2
Claygate Surrey 32 H9
Claygate Cross Kent 34 B11
Clayhall Gt Lon 33 N4

Clayhanger Devon 20 G9
Clayhidon Devon 21 J10
Clayhill E Susx 16 E6
Claypits Gloucs 41 M10
Claypole Lincs 67 L2
Clayton C Brad 84 H9
Clayton Donc 78 D2
Clayton W Susx 15 K8
Clayton-le-Moors
Lancs 83 R9
Clayton-le-Woods
Lancs 83 M10
Clayton West Kirk 77 N2
Clayworth Notts 79 J6
Cleadale Highld 126 H6
Cleadon S Tyne 101 K5
Clearbrook Devon 4 H4
Clearwell Gloucs 40 H10
Cleasby N York 91 L4
Cleat Ork 147 c6
Cleatlam Dur 91 J3
Cleator Cumb 88 D4
Cleator Moor Cumb 88 D4
Cleckheaton Kirk 85 J10
Cleehill Shrops 51 Q5
Cleekhimin N Lans 114 E9
Clee St Margaret
Shrops 51 P4
Cleethorpes NE Lin 80 F2
Cleeton St Mary Shrops 51 Q5
Cleeve N Som 28 F9
Cleeve Oxon 31 M6
Cleeve Hill Gloucs 41 R6
Cleeve Prior Worcs 53 K10
Cleghornie E Loth 116 D5
Clehonger Herefs 40 F4
Cleish P & K 115 K2
Cleland N Lans 114 E9
Clenamacrie Ag & B 120 H7
Clenchwarton Norfk 69 L8
Clenerty Abers 141 J4
Clent Worcs 52 H5
Cleobury Mortimer
Shrops 52 C5
Cleobury North Shrops 52 B3
Cleongart Ag & B 103 J3
Clephanton Highld 138 E6
Clerkhill D & G 106 H10
Cleuch-head D & G 105 Q9
Clevancy Wilts 30 B7
Clevedon N Som 28 F8
Cleveleys Lancs 82 H6
Cleverton Wilts 29 R5
Clewer Somset 21 P3
Cley next the Sea Norfk 70 F3
Cliburn W & F 89 P2
Cliddesden Hants 25 L3
Cliff Warwks 53 M1
Cliffe Medway 34 C7
Cliffe N York 86 C9
Cliff End E Susx 16 F8
Cliffe Woods Medway 34 C7
Clifford Herefs 40 C3
Clifford Leeds 85 N6
Clifford Chambers
Warwks 53 M10
Clifford's Mesne Gloucs 41 L7
Cliffsend Kent 35 N10
Clifton Bristl 28 H7
Clifton C Beds 44 H4
Clifton Ches W 75 M9
Clifton C Nott 66 B5
Clifton Calder 84 H10
Clifton Derbys 65 M3
Clifton Devon 19 L4
Clifton Donc 78 E4
Clifton Lancs 83 L9
Clifton N York 85 J5
Clifton Oxon 43 K5
Clifton W & F 89 N1
Clifton Worcs 41 N2
Clifton Campville Staffs 65 N10
Clifton Hampden Oxon 31 L3
Clifton Reynes M Keyn 55 N10
Clifton upon Dunsmore
Warwks 54 E5
Clifton upon Teme
Worcs 52 D8
Cliftonville Kent 35 Q8
Climping W Susx 14 E10
Clink Somset 22 G4
Clint N York 85 K3
Clinterty C Aber 133 L2
Clint Green Norfk 70 F10
Clintmains Border 107 P3
Clippesby Norfk 71 N9
Clipsham Rutlnd 67 N9
Clipston N Nthn 54 H4
Clipston Notts 66 G6
Clipstone C Beds 44 D6
Clipstone Notts 78 F11
Clitheroe Lancs 83 R7
Clive Shrops 63 N7
Cliveden Bucks 32 C5
Clixby Lincs 80 B3
Cloatley Wilts 29 R4
Clocaenog Denbgs 62 E1
Clochan Moray 140 D3
Clodock Herefs 40 D6
Clola Abers 141 N7
Clophill C Beds 44 F4
Clopton N Nthn 55 N5
Clopton Suffk 59 J10
Clopton Corner Suffk 59 J10
Clos du Valle Guern 12 d1
Closeburn D & G 106 B11
Closeburnmill D & G 106 B10
Closworth Somset 10 E3
Clothall Herts 45 K5
Clothall Common Herts 45 K5
Clotton Ches W 75 N11
Clough Foot Calder 84 D10
Clough Head Calder 84 G11
Cloughton N York 93 K8
Clousta Shet 147 h6
Clova Angus 131 Q9
Clovelly Devon 18 F8
Clovenfords Border 107 L2
Clovulin Highld 128 D11
Clowne Derbys 78 D9
Clows Top Worcs 52 D6
Cluanie Inn Highld 128 F2
Cluanie Lodge Highld 128 F2
Clugston D & G 95 L7
Clunas Highld 138 F6
Clunbury Shrops 51 L4
Clun Shrops 51 J4
Clunderwen Carmth 37 M6
Clune Highld 138 D10
Clunes Highld 128 H6
Clungunford Shrops 51 L5
Clunie P & K 124 C4
Clunton Shrops 51 J4
Cluny Fife 115 K2
Clutton BaNES 29 K10
Clutton Ches W 63 M1
Clutton Hill BaNES 29 K10
Clydach Mons 40 B9
Clydach Swans 26 G2
Clydach Vale Rhondd 27 M3